New Directions in Crime and Deviancy

Criminology is at a crossroads. In the last two decades it has largely failed to produce the kind of new intellectual frameworks and empirical data that might help us explain the high levels of crime and interpersonal violence that beset inner city areas and corrode community life. Similarly, it has failed to adequately explain forms of antisocial behaviour that are just as much a part of life in corporate boardrooms as they are in the ghettos of North America and the sink estates of Britain. Criminology needs to rethink the problem of crime and re-engage its audience with strident theoretical analysis and powerful empirical data.

In *New Directions in Crime and Deviancy* some of the world's most talented and polemical critical criminologists come together to offer new ideas and new avenues for analysis. The book contains chapters that address a broad range of issues central to twenty-first century critical criminology: ecological issues and the new green criminology; the broad impact of neoliberalism upon our cultural and economic life; recent signs of political resistance and opposition; systemic and interpersonal forms of violence; growing fear and enmity in cities; the backlash against the women's movement; the subjective pathology of the serial killer; computer hacking and so on.

Based on key papers presented at the historic York Deviancy Conference, this cutting-edge volume also contains important critical essays that address criminological research methods and the production of criminological knowledge. It is key reading material for those with an academic interest in critical, cultural and theoretical criminology, and crime and deviance more generally.

Simon Winlow is Professor of Criminology at Teesside University, UK.

Rowland Atkinson is Reader in Urban Studies and Criminology at the University of York, UK.

New Directions in Crime and Deviancy

Edited by
Simon Winlow and Rowland Atkinson

Routledge
Taylor & Francis Group

LONDON AND NEW YORK

First published 2013
by Routledge
2 Park Square, Milton Park, Abingdon, Oxon, OX14 4RN

Simultaneously published in the USA and Canada
by Routledge
711 Third Avenue, New York, NY 10017

Routledge is an imprint of the Taylor & Francis Group, an informa business

British Library Cataloguing in Publication Data
A catalogue record for this book is available from the British Library

Library of Congress Cataloging-in-Publication Data
New directions in crime and deviancy / edited by Simon
Winlow and Rowland Atkinson.
p. cm.
Includes bibliographical references.
1. Criminology. 2. Deviant behavior. I. Winlow, Simon. II. Atkinson,
Rowland.
HV6025.N493293 2012
364--dc23
2012021436

ISBN: 978-0-415-62648-4 (hbk)
ISBN: 978-0-415-62649-1 (pbk)
ISBN: 978-0-203-10265-7 (ebk)

Typeset in Times New Roman
by Taylor & Francis Books

MIX
Paper from
responsible sources
FSC
www.fsc.org   FSC® C004839

Printed and bound in Great Britain by the MPG Books Group

Contents

PART 3
Researching crime and deviance   111

PART 4
Issues in contemporary crime and deviance   189

Notes on contributors

Craig Ancrum has been a Senior Lecturer at Teesside University since 2005. He has teaching interests in drug use, criminal markets, criminal culture, the media and criminological theory. Craig is involved in ongoing ethnographic research into criminal markets, drug-related violence and consumerism in the north-east of England, and has published in this area. He is also currently conducting participant observation studies with a splinter group of the English Defence League. Other research projects include the growth in British cannabis cultivation and the normalisation of cocaine use.

Rowland Atkinson is Reader in Urban Studies and Criminology at the University of York. Since finishing his PhD on gentrification and displacement in London he has worked largely as an academic contract researcher conducting work on housing and urban policy, as well as questions of urban social exclusion and area effects. With colleagues he pioneered the first study of gated communities in the UK in the early 2000s and has increasingly sought to connect the lives and impacts of the wealthy upon those with few resources. Much of his research has sought to advance understandings of the links between wealth and poverty in urban contexts and the ways in which apparently benign, high-income lives can exert a disordering and violent impact on city life more broadly. Working in this vein his most recent work (*Domestic Fortress: Fear and the New Home Front*, with Sarah Blandy of Sheffield University) considers the way that housing tenure has come to be one of the primary means of understanding questions of social fear and anxiety, neoliberal governance and the rise of an aggressive form of 'defensive homeownership' that seeks to obliterate any threat to household wealth and intrusions upon life in the private home.

Daniel Briggs is Reader in Criminology and Criminal Justice at the University of East London. He works with a range of social groups – from the most vulnerable to the most dangerous to the most misunderstood. His work takes him inside prisons, crack houses, mental health institutions, asylum seeker institutions, hostels, care homes and hospices, and homeless services. His research interests include social exclusion, culture, deviance, and postmodern identities. He has recently undertaken work in Spain on gypsies, youth risk behaviours while on holiday and on the English riots of 2011. He is the author of *Crack Cocaine Users* (Routledge, 2011).

Avi Brisman is an assistant professor in the School of Justice Studies at Eastern Kentucky University in Richmond, KY (USA). Dr Brisman's research interests include the anthropology of law, critical criminology, cultural criminology, and green criminology, and his writing has appeared in *Contemporary Justice Review, Crime, Law and Social Change, Crime Media Culture, Critical Criminology, Journal of Contemporary Criminal Justice, Race and Justice, Theoretical Criminology*, and *Western Criminology Review*, among other journals. He is co-editor, with Nigel South, of *The Routledge International Handbook of Green Criminology* (2012), and co-author, with Nigel South, of *Green Cultural Criminology* (Routledge, 2013).

Walter S. DeKeseredy is Professor of Criminology at the University of Ontario Institute of Technology (UOIT). In 2008, the Institute on Violence, Abuse and Trauma gave him the Linda Saltzman Memorial Intimate Partner Violence Researcher Award. He also jointly received the 2004 Distinguished Scholar Award from the American Society of Criminology's (ASC) Division on Women and Crime and the 2007 inaugural UOIT Research Excellence Award. In 1995, he received the Critical Criminologist of the Year Award from the ASC's Division on Critical Criminology (DCC) and in 2008 the DCC gave him the Lifetime Achievement Award.

Joseph F. Donnermeyer is a Professor of Rural Sociology in the School of Environment and Natural Resources at the Ohio State University (OSU). He has published over 100 peer-reviewed journal articles, book chapters on rural crime and other sociological dimensions of rural society. As well, he is the author or editor of eight monographs and textbooks. He is the recipient of the 2004 OSU Alumni Association Distinguished Teaching Award and served for five years as chair of the Executive Council for the OSU Academy of Teaching. Recently, Dr Donnermeyer founded a new online journal through the OSU Libraries – *The International Journal of Rural Criminology* – the first peer-reviewed journal of its kind devoted to both empirical and theoretical work on rural crime in societies around the world.

Molly Dragiewicz is Associate Professor in the Faculty of Social Science and Humanities at the University of Ontario Institute of Technology. Dr Dragiewicz's work focuses on violence and gender and the backlash against the battered women's movement. She is author of *Equality with a Vengeance* (2011) and co-editor of *The Routledge Handbook of Critical Criminology* (2012). Dr Dragiewicz received the New Scholar Award from the American Society of Criminology Division on Women and Crime in 2009.

Steve Hall is Professor of Criminology at Teesside University. He is the co-author of *Violent Night* (2006), and his recent co-authored book *Criminal Identities and Consumer Culture* (Willan/Routledge, 2008) has been described as 'an important landmark in criminology'. He is also the author of

Theorizing Crime and Deviance: A New Perspective (2012) and co-editor of *New Directions in Criminological Theory* (Routledge, 2012).

Audra Mitchell is Lecturer in International Relations at the University of York. She is author of *Lost in Transformation: Violent Peace and Peaceful Conflict in Northern Ireland* (2011), co-editor (with Oliver P. Richmond) of *Hybrid Forms of Peace: From the Everyday to Post-liberalism* (2011) and author of articles in the *British Journal of Politics and International Relations, Review of International Studies, Millennium, Alternatives, International Peacekeeping* and other journals.

Ioannis Papageorgiou is Doctoral Researcher in Criminology at the University of Edinburgh. He works on the historical development of the prison system under the prism of State Theory and Political Philosophy and in connection with the class struggle. He holds an MSc in Criminology and Criminal Justice (University of Edinburgh), LLB (University of Athens) and is a qualified lawyer (Athens Bar Association) with experience in company and criminal law.

Georgios Papanicolaou is Senior Lecturer in Criminology at Teesside University, UK. He works from a materialist theoretical perspective on the history, organisation and role of the police apparatus. His current research interests include the politics of transnational policing and the policing of national and transnational illegal markets. His book *Transnational Policing and Sex Trafficking in Southeast Europe: Policing the Imperialist Chain* was published in 2011.

Nathan W. Pino is Professor of Sociology at Texas State University in San Marcos, where he conducts research on sexual and other forms of extreme violence as well as policing and police reform in an international context. In addition to numerous academic journal articles, he is co-editor of *Democratic Policing in Transitional and Developing Countries* (2006); and co-author of *Globalization, Police Reform and Development* (2012).

Robert Shanafelt is an anthropologist in the Department of Sociology and Anthropology, Georgia Southern University. His interest in extreme human violence developed initially from general reading about the Holocaust, the Soviet Gulag system, and apartheid South Africa. Research relevant to alternative perspectives on crime and deviance include: 'Crime, power, and policing in South Africa: Beyond Privileged Protection and Protected Privilege,' in Pino and Wiatrowski (eds) *Democratic Policing in Transitional and Developing Countries* (2006); and 'Human rights, political violence, and struggles for power in Lesotho', in Cohen, Hyden and Nagen (eds) *Human Rights in Africa* (1993).

Oliver Smith is Lecturer in Criminology at Plymouth University. His research interests utilise cultural and critical criminological perspectives in relation to infantilisation, narcissism and gratification in the night-time economy and the long history, and central role, of alcohol to the economic and cultural life of the city. His most recent empirical work focuses on the changing relationship between ageing and 'youthful' consumption practices in urban spaces.

Nigel South is Professor in the Department of Sociology, a member of the Human Rights Centre and currently Pro-Vice-Chancellor for the Faculty of Law and Management, at the University of Essex, Colchester. He has published on green criminology; drug use, health and crime; inequalities and citizenship; and theoretical and comparative criminology. He serves on the editorial boards of *Critical Criminology* and *Deviant Behavior*. With Avi Brisman, he is co-editor of the *Routledge International Handbook of Green Criminology* (2013).

Craig Webber is Senior Lecturer in Criminology at the University of Southampton. He is author of *Psychology and Crime* (2010). He has also published in the areas of culture, media and criminological theory, including 'Revaluating relative deprivation theory' (2007) in *Theoretical Criminology*, 11 (1), 'Background, foreground, foresight: the third dimension of cultural criminology?' (2007) in *Crime Media Culture* 3 (2), and with Jeff Vass, 'Crime, film and the cybernetic imagination' in Y. Jewkes and M. Yar (eds) *Handbook of Internet Crime*. He is currently researching hacking and hacktivists. He is also on the steering committee of the Web Science Doctoral Training Centre at Southampton.

Colin Webster is Professor of Criminology at Leeds Metropolitan University. His previous publications include *Poor Transitions* (2004) and *Understanding Race and Crime* (2007). He is co-author of *Poverty and Insecurity* (2012) and is currently co-authoring *Youth on Religion* (Routledge, 2012) and co-editing *New Directions, New Generations: Ethnicity, Crime and Justice* (Routledge, 2013).

Rob White is Professor of Criminology at the University of Tasmania. He is the author of *Law, Capitalism and the Right to Work* (1986), *No Space of Their Own: Young People and Social Control in Australia* (1990) and *Transnational Environmental Crime* (Routledge, 2011). He is also the editor of *Global Environmental Harm* (2010) and *Environmental Crime: A Reader* (2009).

Jörg Wiegratz researches matters of political economy, moral economy, neoliberalism, economic fraud, development politics and African development, among others. To date, he has taught at the universities of Bath, Sheffield and Makerere. For several years, he has worked as a researcher and consultant in Uganda. He was trained at the universities of Sheffield (PhD, Politics), Warwick (MA, International Political Economy), Cologne (MA, Economics), Münster and Bloomington.

Simon Winlow is Professor of Criminology at Teesside University. He is the author of *Badfellas* (2001), and co-author of *Bouncers* (2003), *Violent Night*

(2006) and *Criminal Identities and Consumer Culture* (2008). He is also the co-editor of *New Directions in Criminological Theory* (Routledge, 2012), and author of the forthcoming *Rethinking Social Exclusion* (2013).

Michael Yip is a PhD student at the Web Science Doctoral Training Centre, University of Southampton. His research is on the study of online criminal social networks using social network analysis and criminology. He is working in collaboration with the Serious Organised Crime Agency (SOCA) from the United Kingdom.

Acknowledgements

The editors would like first of all to thank all of those who have contributed to this volume. In an age in which collections such as this are considered marginal to research assessment exercises and the careful and seemingly interminable construction of impressive publishing records and CVs, our contributors have given up their time and put aside instrumental career-building to write a range of polemical, theoretical and empirical papers that are right at the cutting-edge of our discipline. Their desire to push critical criminology into a new stage of its development and to produce the ideas necessary to address the huge problems faced by twenty-first century Western societies is a clear indication that we might yet discard the restrictive empiricism and prescriptive theoretical frameworks of a dour academic criminology imprisoned at the end of history.

We would also like to thank all of those who helped us to organise and administer the 2011 Deviancy conference, on which this collection is based. Josine Opmeer's hard work over many months was invaluable and helped to secure the success of the conference. Kate Burdis, Sara Stephenson, Mark Horsley, Will Paterson and Jack Denham also assisted us in various ways and we are very grateful for their support. Oliver Smith helped with planning and contributed to the original concept for the meeting, and his detailed knowledge of York's night-time economy helped to lubricate the cultural side of the conference. We must also thank our plenary speakers. Their intellectual reputations generated the academic interest that made the conference a resounding success.

We are particularly grateful to Stan Cohen, who travelled to York from London despite ill-health, for his involvement and encouragement. Roy Bailey, a key figure at the early conferences and now a professional musician, also made a crucial contribution to our opening plenary session. Jock Young provided a spirited denunciation of administrative criminology and Francis Heidensohn, perhaps the most important figure in the development of feminist criminology, offered a fascinating insight into the early conferences and also provided a stirring closing plenary address to a packed house. Rob White subjected himself to a round-the-world trip, all the way from Tasmania, and was an active member of the conference. His fascinating and deeply personal analysis of the boundaries of the criminological project is included in this volume. Jeff Ferrell travelled from Texas to deliver a bravura performance outlining his new theory of drift. Keith Hayward's plenary presentation encouraged us to look away from the foreground of criminality and towards harms of consumer culture and the problems of identity construction and 'life-stage dissolution' in a rapidly changing world. Steve Hall gave a character-istically brilliant realist analysis of liberal criminology's obsession with defending criminals from labelling processes and its squeamish reluctance to consider the huge harms of crime and violence in low-income areas. Alex Callinicos, one of the most notable Marxist political theorists working today, provided some much-needed context with his analysis of the current global financial crisis. Pat Carlen, current editor of the *British Journal of Criminology* and recent recipient of the British Society of Criminology's lifetime achievement award, offered a detailed analysis of the problems associated with occupying the two distinct spaces of the critical criminologist and the political activist, and Tony Jefferson, the author of so many crucial works in critical criminology, also contributed to a star-studded opening session.

We were also lucky enough to be joined by some of the most important criminologists working today: Elliott Currie offered one of the best presentations of the conference, and his analysis of 'failed societies' won much support. John Lea, certainly one of the most consistently reliable and insightful critical criminologists of the recent period, together with Simon Hallsworth, offered an outstanding assessment of criminological analyses of the state. Robert Reiner, Kevin Stenson, Joe Sim, Katja Franko Aas, Walter DeKeseredy, Reece Walters, Nigel South, Vincenzo Ruggiero and many other notable names also attended and made a full contribution to the success of the conference, despite the fact that our budget for plenary speakers was exhausted and we couldn't afford to cover their attendance. Beyond this stellar cast, a great deal of the conference's intellectual energy was provided by younger criminologists and postgraduate students – it is they who will decide the future of a critical criminology, and their enthusiasm for the event seems to bode well.

SW and RA, York, UK
24 May 2012

Introduction

Simon Winlow and Rowland Atkinson

I Crime and deviance in the End Times

This volume stands in the intellectual shadow of a number of texts generated by earlier York Deviancy conferences. Rejecting naturalism and political conservatism, the academics and practitioners who were to meet in York sought to critique the dominant state-based statistical analysis of modern criminology and to inject the intellectual and political energy of those times into deliberations about crime, deviance and disorder. Taking inspiration from Foucault and the critical approaches of US writers like Matza and Chambliss, the group generated significant theoretical impetus and empirical redirection. They stressed the need for progressive change and an understanding of the deep social–political location and the meaning of deviant action. A series of volumes (Cohen 1971; Taylor and Taylor 1973; Taylor *et al.* 1975) focused attention on a range of new topics, some of which now appear slightly outdated and others that became the bedrock of post-1968 criminological inquiry. It is important to remember the economic, political, cultural and intellectual context of the times and that these were significant advances that addressed the problem of crime and its control in new ways.

What then was new about this 'new criminology'? In closing their volume dealing with a social theory of deviance, Taylor, Walton and Young (1973) suggested that the hallmarks of their proposed approach lay in a political economy of criminal action and an explicitly politically located and psychologically informed understanding of the dynamics of action and reaction. In essence the new criminology sought to understand the social contexts of action and reactions that, together, could be thought of as a kind of deviant assemblage, of conditions, influences and labels attached to processes seen to be broadly deviant or overtly criminal. This was not to cut away relevant contexts, forces and drives but rather to move away from classical and positivist notions of criminality that essentialised crime as something that bad people simply enacted. Thus there was a move to psychologise as well as to socialise models of harmful human action, both by referring to conditions of various kinds, and adding to this a sense of the way that social actors operated within contexts that were themselves unequal, demeaning, potentially violent, insecure and so on

(Cohen 1971). Given these concerns deviance was to be seen as a social construction; something contingent upon complex social processes and reactions
that involved actors in contexts that might well vary temporally and spatially.

With the injection of a greater momentum around politicisation and radical
idealism the critical criminology movement expanded, and Cohen (1988)
notes the increasingly sociological concerns of textbooks emerging more generally
in the 1970s. With another notable collection, *Critical Criminology,* appearing
in 1975 (Taylor *et al.*), the development of a clearly definable movement
seemed assured. In addition the almost contemporaneous release of papers
from the York meetings (Cohen 1971; Taylor and Taylor 1973) by Pelican, an
offshoot of Penguin publishing, also highlight the popular appeal and currency
of these ideas at this time. Over at least 14 symposia in York these ideas were
developed, contested and redeveloped. Membership of the National Deviancy
Conference (NDC) cost a mere £1 a year for self-described radicals! The year
1974 saw the launch of the European Group for the Study of Deviance and
Social Control, and the expansion of a European space within which the
development of sociological approaches to crime could be further developed.

A criminology at the End Times

If the new criminology had an intellectual pedigree and sense of innovation,
can we say the same for criminology today? What are the key influences and
texts? Is critical criminology essentially the same beast today as it was in the
early 1970s? Perhaps the first point to make here is that, as Cohen (1988: 86)
notes, one of the most remarkable features of the new deviancy paradigm was
its persistence despite 'schisms, defections, recriminations, collective boredom,
chronic illnesses, and premature burials, the organization survived'. In other
words this 'paradigm' was several, even in its earliest formation. Characteristic
of the political left more generally, the sense of factionalism and argumentation
is profound and a tendency to a self-defeating form of internal debate was
perhaps narrowly avoided. Cohen also notes the move away from ethnography
and close analysis to more macro-sociological perspectives, concerns with
structure, politics and the state. Perhaps a clear maturation of this perspective
has never fully arrived. What assessment would we then make of critical and
realist criminologies today?

Critical criminology, debates about the real cost and impact of crime and
critical socio-political assessments of the roots of crime, and the means to
deal with this, have modulated over the past forty years. A trend towards the
post-structuralist thought that folded much social action into a messy recipe
of phenomenology, indecipherable meaning and theoretical abstraction had
run its course by the mid-1990s. Since then neoliberalism, as the infusion of civic,
political and economic space with the logic of the market and privileging of
wealthy elites, also colonised academia and critical formulations more broadly.
The end of the Cold War and crude conflations of communism with state-based
centralism and violence generated a kind of stasis for those wishing to advance

a critique of the state, penal institutions and the criminal justice system more broadly.

As Elliott Currie (1985) compellingly argued in *Confronting Crime,* a great deal of sympathy was lost for a critical criminological project that appeared to become overly liberal and that tended to ignore the harms of working-class crime and denied criminal responsibility. Violent crime was rising and had profound consequences for vulnerable groups, and idealist critical criminology failed to fully deal with this and failed to win out against populist and neo-biological/racialised explanations of crime that arose in the USA in the 1970s and 1980s. For Currie and writers like Lea and Young (1984) there was an urgent need to recognise both the socio-structural rootedness of crime while having something that communicated and tackled major social problems that publics identified as being of concern, even if such concerns were distorted by media apparatuses that skewed concern with crime to one of violence that itself overstated the incidence of such problems.

Today the position of social science more broadly is part of a broader malaise in which social and economic crisis has not been met by a turn, of politicians and the media, toward social scientists. Some of this has to do with the fact that much sociology has turned toward self-critique and a tendency to tackle ephemeral and indeed trivial issues, but it also has to do with a diminution of the position of social researchers whose voice has been submerged by the paradigmatic dominance of economic forms of thought and an expansion of economics, alongside neoliberalism itself, as a way of framing and tackling a much broader range of social issues.

How can we contextualise criminology today and understand its continuities and breaks from its earlier formations? The tensions of the times that produced the NDC and the European Group are, in several ways, mirrored by our own. Significant social, economic, cultural and technological changes have driven a sense of social anxiety. Taking a global perspective through news media reveals aggressive state actions in distant theatres of conflict, and panic about criminal underclasses, street disorder and immigration. Like the 1970s, a sense of economic crisis is very much with us and the sense of an overlapping of economic malaise and social injustice is strongly apparent. The crash of 2008 has not only appeared to confirm the tendency of capitalism to generate significant social stress, a feature many criminologists are keen to position as central to explanations of much criminal action and causation. In the background to this particular crisis is the additional factor of a more explicitly terminal decline of natural resources, habitats and human fortunes related to our dependence upon fossil fuel and the reckless and short-sighted exploitation of the natural environment. On the back of these shifts we have seen a widening consciousness that seeks to understand how the ebb and flow of markets and fortunes are implicated in the production of these broader crises – economic paradigms of various heritages have become essential in comprehending the nature of the crisis and its interconnections with a range of social harms that are increasingly brought within the terrain of a critical

Herein lies something of the reality and object of study for a revitalised project of a critical criminology since it highlights the importance of a macro-social/political and economic overview in order that human harm might be more adequately captured. More pertinently it is also very clear that such accounts will not be produced by compliant state broadcasters or those whose interests remain tied to the neoliberal project. Instead criminology will need to continue to work hard within an academy that is to be largely privatised, for a public that is either critical or dismissive of social critique and in relation to a media architecture that continues to celebrate rational and economistic accounts of social life and motivation.

II Today

We write these words in the fourth year of the most severe economic downturn in living memory. News broadcasts keep us up to date on a sovereign debt crisis besetting nation-states around the globe. The United States has had its credit rating reduced for the first time in its history. The European Central Bank has had to bail out a series of states in order to shore up the euro, and governments across the West have shed the last vestiges of Keynesian demand management and embarked upon a journey of severe and prolonged spending cuts, in some cases accompanied by significant tax rises for working populations. The impact of these measures has quickly become clear. Many industrialised states have attempted to force down the value of their currency and, despite interest rates being held at record lows, creeping inflation and salary reductions and freezes are reducing the lifestyles of many millions of people across the West. Fuel costs remain incredibly high, and will inevitably rise further. In Britain, public sector pensions are coming under sustained political pressure, and the entire idea of welfare and public sector work is being challenged and reformulated in line with a new political era of neoliberal negative solidarity. Unemployment is already a huge problem in many developed countries, despite the normalisation of low-paid casual work, and things look set to get significantly worse as the new austerity measures kick in. It is in this bleak context that this collection emerges and to which it seeks to respond. Our initial goal is to encourage criminologists and criminology students to position the study of crime and deviance in direct relation to the economic, social and political changes that are driving new forms of social harm, new social antagonisms and growing forms of enmity, distrust and aggressive individualism.

As one might expect, profound economic turmoil has not prevented the rich from aggressively pursuing their class interests. Political debate about the crisis appears to be largely restricted to regressive tax and spending measures. The dominant political message that emerges from within the established ideological space of acceptable discourse about the crisis is that we are inevitably reliant upon a small but incredibly talented group of 'wealth creators' at the top of our class system, and that this group must be spared the debilitating pressure and inconvenience of taxation if they are to be encouraged to inno-vate and invest and, in doing so, drive the national economy back to growth. The economic well-being of the entire nation depends upon their dynamic creativity and entrepreneurial spirit. If we increase taxes on wealth and income, this super-class will simply take its talents to a competitor state that taxes the rich less. For this group, high taxes are supposed to act as a disin-centive for enterprise. So, even though we now face a huge structural deficit, a flat-lining economy and significant cuts to government spending, we are pre-sented with an ideological narrative that suggests to working men and women that they should acquiesce to policies that further advantage the super-rich in order to boost economic growth. This super-stratum may be complicit in the creation of this crisis, but we seem unable to conjure up an ideological and political alternative to the widely held belief that it is only the super-rich who can get us out of it. The rich increased their wealth enormously during the boom years that led to the crash, and political responses to the crash itself have not abated or reversed this trend.

For the ideologues of neoliberalism the recent pattern of creative destruction has enabled the 'fittest' and most talented to absorb devalued assets of their less-talented adversaries at knock-down prices. What is perverse about this movement of postmodern capital is that these gods of high finance have been proven, on the whole, to be abject failures. This is not a Darwinian reallocation of resources from capitalism's failures to its winners, and consequently a process that guarantees future efficiencies in the global marketplace. Our recent history now indicates quite clearly that financiers are often extravagantly rewarded for failure. It is everyday taxpayers and workers in the *real economy* who are the disavowed superheroes of high finance. It is increasingly their money upon which the financial institutions are forced to rely. Pure neoliberal economic theory has been abandoned, and it is the oppressive interventionist state – with its supposed intrusive and restrictive laws, regulations and taxes – that has ridden to the rescue of the gods that failed. In some cases not simply have the gamblers of high finance lost and walked away from their debts; the state has figuratively given them another stack of chips and told them to double-down. For the moment at least, the answer to the question posed by the global failure of neoliberalism can be nothing other than neoliberalism itself.

Gradually, incrementally, faith in our future economic well-being has come to mean an unfailing commitment to abstraction. The real economy of working men and women appears unlikely to deliver the growth to which we have become accustomed, and so we must reinvest in a system we know to be inherently flawed. A suffocating ideological narrative develops that validates the Randian selfishness of the elite, claiming it to be the only fuel available to rejuvenate markets and drive our economy back to growth. Our politicians attempt to convince us that they are now serious about regulation and that they will take a firm hand with speculators and profiteers, while at the same time cutting tax for high income earners and corporations. Beneath the populist soundbites about a new and more socially responsible capitalism, postmodernism's elites work frantically to restart neoliberalism's stalled economic juggernaut.

None of this is hidden from everyday working people in the West. One can't help but get a sense that the cynical voting public know about the corruption of the liberal democratic ideal. We know about many of the grotesque inequalities that result from the normal functioning of global capitalism. We know that a super-rich class of investors and speculators has essentially transcended the social and floated free from its figurations, interdependencies, and its moral and ethical codes. We know all this, but we appear to lack the belief that might enable us to create a new politics that has at its core a progressive model for justice, fairness, equality and sustainability. Beyond the framework of formal politics new political movements are attempting to register their distaste for contemporary global capitalism, but, for the moment at least, there seems little possibility of convincing the cynical and incorporated ex-working classes, who have the numbers to effect real change, that a world beyond capitalism is both desirable and achievable. We now appear to find ourselves in a post-political period that places a restrictive ideological framework on what is practical and achievable in relation to politics, governance and economic practice, and the refusal to even countenance a political and economic alternative ensures we remain marooned in the neoliberal here and now. One of the hidden outcomes of neoliberalism is the denial of political subjectivity. The individualism of the postmodern period tends to work against the establishment of political solidarities and aggressively erodes the forms of universality that are capable of animating a progressive political agenda. Instead, cynicism reigns. Only a return to politics can establish a progressive path away from the wreckage of neoliberalism.

Structural sociopathy

While the accumulation of wealth continues apace at the top of capitalism's obscene pseudo-meritocracy, those scrambling for safe ground in the middle are seeing incomes, pensions and welfare entitlements significantly reduced or scrapped. Those locked in the West's areas of permanent recession continue to be labelled as feckless spongers by an increasingly unsympathetic popular and political order keen to justify further reductions to welfare. Youth unemployment is a huge social problem in a number of European states, and there is little indication that secure and relatively rewarding jobs can once again return to the de-industrialised West and reconnect disaffected young people to the social mainstream.

It is now clear that Britain's renunciation of social democracy during the 1980s and its rapid adoption of neoclassical economic theory have profoundly affected the social fabric of the country. Similar processes occurred throughout the Global North as neoliberalism became the economic architecture of postmodern globalisation. Academics from diverse political backgrounds have long recognised that the relative calm and rising prosperity that typified the middle third of the twentieth century in Britain – with its low crime rates, low rates of imprisonment and stable community life – represented something of a 'golden era' built upon a historic class compromise between the elites of twentieth-century capitalism and the industrial working classes (Hobsbawm 1995; Bauman 2000; Hall 2012). In Britain the radicalism of the late nineteenth century and the early decades of the twentieth century began to dissipate as working-class populations were incorporated into a post-war social democratic project that ensured rising standards of living and a general faith in progress across generations. Now, in the midst of a global twenty-first century economic downturn, this sepia image of social inclusion and faith in progress seems rather quaint, attractive in its innocence and totally divorced from the raw, brutalising economic reality appraised by Britain's new demoralised and depoliticised precariat (Standing 2011; Southwood 2011).

The liberalisation of Britain's economy from the 1980s onwards, despite a few hiccups here and there, appeared to increase the size of our national wealth and, before the crash, produced consistent growth in our nation's gross domestic product. The problematic nature of much of this growth has now been revealed (see for example Callinicos 2010; Harvey 2011). The debt bubble has now burst, and there is a range of compelling reasons to believe that the rapid growth we witnessed before the crash, and the sustained growth seen in post-war Western economies more generally, may never return (Heinberg 2011). We should also remind ourselves that before the crash, despite what in neoliberal economies appeared to be considerable increases in national wealth, many workers in the real economy saw their wages fall or stagnate in real terms (Harvey 2011; Wolff 2010). For the most part productivity and profits continued to grow significantly during the 1980s, 1990s and early years of the twenty-first century, but for many workers this did not translate into higher wages. The actual reduction in wages was disguised by rising house prices and a huge growth of consumer and household debt. Despite what appeared to be a general neoliberal Western affluence, signified by the growing dominance and ubiquity of consumerism (Smart 2010), this strategy disguised a huge movement of capital from the lower classes to the super-rich (Wolff 2010), a process that is one of the most important features of neoliberal governance.

Of course, if capital is not reinvested it returns to its original state and becomes once again merely money (Marx 2008). Before the crash the huge amounts of surplus capital sloshing around the global economy looking for a profitable investment opportunity led to immoral loans to developing countries (Graeber 2011). The sheer scale of this huge pool of surplus capital also prompted a super-class of financial experts to develop a new range of abstract investment schemes. The 'reality' of these postmodern investment mechanisms, and the failure of political elites adequately to regulate them, combined with the evolution of executive remuneration packages and a general trend towards short-term investment to form the greater part of the fundamental causes of the economic crisis we now all face. In many ways the boom before the bust was a smokescreen that masked the reallocation of wealth from working populations to the very richest 1 per cent, a trend that continues apace in our times of austerity.

The class compromise of social democracy is now a dim and distant memory. Ours is an atonal world of shallow freedoms tied to the interests of a capitalist system that blindly follows its own interests, totally ignorant of the human or ecological costs of its activity. For some years, scholars have argued that Eurocentric global markets can be 'humanised' by the process of globalisation itself. The ravenous appetites of 'Western capitalism' will be tamed by enforced adaptation to the cultural climate of Asia and other 'new world economies'; or at least the regional capitalism that develops in these places and begins to challenge American and European economic hegemony will be more considerate and less thoughtlessly instrumental than the dominant 'Western capitalism'. Accounts offered by capital's apologists usually fail to appreciate that contemporary capitalism is now thoroughly deterritorialised. Contemporary capitalism is not rooted in a specific culture, or some mythical 'Western tradition'.

It makes little sense to talk of Western capitalism, as opposed to, say, Eastern capitalism, as if the fundamental nature of capitalist markets is radically different in different parts of the world (Žižek 2008). The difference, inasmuch as one exists, lies in regulation and political responses to markets. Capital, in its raw form, can have no social conscience, no commitment to justice, no commitment to the continuity of our species on this planet, indeed nothing beyond the continuation of profit and investment. It can instrumentally assume the cultural characteristics of any regional, cultural or ethnic identity in order to continue to reproduce itself and extend its interests. In this way, the personification of capitalism is properly sociopathic; it can adopt a pro-social bearing, even give huge amounts of money to charity, but it does so to secure and advance its economic interests.

Do we not gain some insight into the 'true' nature of contemporary global capitalism from corporate commentators who argue that the rapidly developing producer economies of China, India and Brazil can drag the West out of its deficit problem and once again return the global free market to growth? Should we look to these developing economies in the hope that they will be more considerate of the global poor, that they are more attuned to imminent environmental crises or that they are more inclusive, fairer or more 'democratic' than the contemporary West? To do so would be to fundamentally misunderstand the reality of contemporary global capitalism. The ongoing debate about the decline of American economic power and the rise of the new Eastern economies gives us a useful insight into the future as capitalism reaches the natural limits of its growth (Harvey 2011; Heinberg 2011). We in the West often assume that capitalism is dependent upon free and open parliamentary democracy, but it is worth briefly speculating on the ways in which capital might transform the social and political field in order to move on to a yet more efficient system of capital accumulation. Are we not seeing an increased tendency towards exceptionalism and the suspension of civic freedoms in order to ensure the free movement of capital (Agamben 2005)? Has there not been a growing interest in those discourses that advocate the suspension of legal freedoms in order to ensure 'security', and therefore 'freedom' itself (Agamben 2005; Žižek 2008, 2010)?

We should view capital as an *amorphous thing that insists* rather than a framework developed and managed by the rich in order to reproduce their own class privilege (Žižek 2008). History suggests that the ultimate drive of capitalism is simply to continue, to postpone its own end point. In this way the barbarism of nineteenth-century free market accumulation is tempered by the arrival of the social democratic regulated market in order to prevent the rise of a transformative leftist project capable of attracting the support of the massed industrial working classes. Similarly, the austere, pin-striped and steeply hierarchical capitalism of the 1950s and 1960s gives way to a more relaxed and less formal hippy capitalism – typified by Richard Branson or Bill Gates – that eschews the hierarchies and structures of modernity and the absurd Kafka-esque bureaucracies of the state in order to embrace a more charitable and inclusive free market ethic (see Boltanski and Chiapello 2007). Here, the antagonistic discourses of liberal and leftist political movements are co-opted by 'the system' in order to produce a capitalism that seems more open and equal, more democratic, more concerned with the environment, less concerned with oppressive social categorisation – perfectly happy to exploit all equally.

We can now see quite clearly that the personal and civic freedoms that are so important to the image of the contemporary Western social and political order can be suspended in exceptional circumstances (Agamben 2005). Is it absurd to even think that a new post-crash Western capitalism might secure its interests not by the continued expansion of freedoms, but rather by the withdrawal of already established legal entitlements? If, as we are often told, China represents the future of global capitalism, is it too pessimistic to consider a Western free market capitalism supported not by democracy, but by an increasingly authoritarian state apparatus?

Global capitalism is too often seen as a system that creates civilisation, that spreads freedom, that encourages progressive community life, that improves lifestyles. When these aspects of civilised sociality are absent, we assume that something has gone wrong, that contingent events have prevented development or that self-interested individuals have corrupted the system and therefore prevented the huge benefits of progressive capitalism illuminating the lives of those on the margins. In this way, the horrors of Somalia and the Congo reflect uneven economic development, which of course suggests that as soon as these areas become more fully integrated into the project of global capitalism, barbarism will dissipate and these nations will become part of the community of member states engaged in global trade networks for the mutual benefit of all. Similarly, the huge problems of post-industrial American cities, the French *banlieues* or Britain's areas of permanent recession appear to suggest that something is going wrong with Western capitalism, that the system is failing to function effectively and that this is evidenced by rising inequality and increasingly embedded social problems. In the current context, it makes far more sense to make the opposite argument. The horrors of Somalia and the Congo, and the exclusion of Western populations from the legitimate economy, represent not an impediment to capitalist development or a breakdown in the smooth operation of the market. Rather, these things represent the *true reality* of contemporary global capitalism: a capitalism that has no material interest in populations that do not facilitate the expansion of capitalist markets; a capitalism that is happy to let slaughter continue if intervention provides no material benefit.

Ponzi capitalism

As we have suggested, the reality of contemporary capitalism takes on an additional layer of complexity with the speculative trading of futures, credit default swaps or collateralised debt obligations. These financial mechanisms truly reflect postmodern capitalism's new reality as the market transcends the mere buying and selling of material goods. Even things that don't exist can be traded, loaned, swapped or sold for profit. Of course, what the current economic downturn shows us is that these creative abstractions become real in their effects. It is not that the everyday working lives of ordinary men and women together create the abstract world of contemporary capitalism, but rather that the abstract world of the contemporary global marketplace is pulling the strings, carelessly subjecting the lives of ordinary men and women to its flows and eddies (Žižek 2010). This new abstract capitalism has risen alongside new forms of ideological control that we will investigate more fully in the pages that follow.

Making the effort to drag oneself clear of the ideological framework that shapes and gives colour to our experience of everyday life enables us to see a certain strangeness in the media coverage of this our current crisis. A kind of frenetic inertia is at work that seems to reaffirm the growing recognition that the present is a time out of joint, that a barely perceptible falsehood is at work in both the mediation of things and our 'real' experience of popular culture, politics and everyday social life. To be sure, this is more than the mere absence of reasonably intelligent critical commentary on economic policy or even a brief consideration of economic and organisational alternatives to the present zombie neoliberalism that stumbles onwards, despite being mortally wounded. Perhaps the most unusual aspect of this media coverage is the current obsession with fluctuations in the market. Politicians now appear to structure policy in relation to how it will be received by 'the market', as if the market spoke with one voice and is magically free from the 'animal spirits' (Keynes 2008) that can produce frenzied and destructive waves of speculative market activity.

Politicians have sought to justify bank bailouts and new austerity measures to the electorate by denying their ideological character and instead positioning these policies as a pragmatic and concerted attempt to assuage the anxieties of a jittery global marketplace, the fluctuations of which could plunge us into much deeper financial trouble or rapidly propel us to something that takes on the appearance of economic safety. In Britain, George Osborne, the current Chancellor of the Exchequer, finds affirmation for his government's austerity policies in the fact that Britain has managed to maintain its AAA credit rating and can continue to borrow at low rates of interest. In his conversation with the British people, Osborne has suggested that the market's response to the nation's fiscal crisis is effectively an accurate and impartial barometer that gauges the adequacy of policy. He suggests that his concerted efforts to cut public spending are winning the approval of 'the markets' and this approval is a clear indication that the government's approach to dealing with its structural deficit is the right one. In this approach and despite his proclamations to the contrary the Chancellor is acknowledging that government policy is structured not in relation to a real economy built on the labour of real people, but in relation to an ideological abstraction. He is less concerned with the production and sale of tangible commodities in the real economy than he is with satisfying the unpredictable desires of the financial markets. At root, the ideology of Osborne's approach lies in his drive to find satisfaction in creating the economic and social policies that the market itself desires.

Seemingly impartial factual news broadcasting also often contains within it a significant quotient of ideological manipulation that reaffirms the dominant culture of conscious cynicism. Television news reports now often attempt to position the audience as cheer-leaders for the Wall Street Masters of the Universe in their wild speculation and manipulation of financial markets. The audience is encouraged to cheer for the growth of share values, which by implication will mean a better pension, a more stable economic outlook and possibly better employment prospects for the economically active viewer sitting at home. Morning news broadcasts encourage us to be happy if retail sales have risen this month, or despondent and concerned if not enough money has been spent at the tills of our corporate High Street behemoths. Isn't this the perverse 'real abstraction' of contemporary postmodern capitalism, in which everyday people are forced to fanatically support the endeavours of the financial elite who carry on with total disregard for the worker-consumers whose lives are subject to the capricious whims of the market? The real problem here is not one of simple ideological mystification in which everyday people are compelled to warmly welcome the continuation and elaboration of global liberal capitalism. The absurd fluctuations of the market are real in their impact and a sudden return to growth would indeed have an important impact upon the lifestyles of working populations across the world. The problem is that we are forced to live our lives in the shadow of this all-powerful 'real abstraction'. As the initial wave of economic crisis hit, many everyday workers found themselves in the perverse position of advocating bank and corporate bailouts in the hope of calming the economic tsunami that threatened to engulf the real economy in which they found their daily employment.

In a postmodern inversion, deeply indicative of our times, the exploited ride to the rescue of the exploiter as the tax revenues of ordinary workers are used to bail out banks and corporate elites in the hope of allowing the economic system as it is to continue. Is this not yet another indication of the ability of capital to act as its own opposite, and a clear reflection of the ideological stasis of our times?

What's left? Criminology in the End Times

In criminology we are often encouraged to engage in the similar process of cutting through the bullshit of abstract theorisation so that we might get right to the heart of the matter, but theoretical abstraction is not necessarily the cause of our discipline's historical and intellectual stasis. Criminology's general intellectual standstill might just as easily be a reflection of the huge growth in empirical criminology that appears to treat theory as either entirely redundant or as a mere addendum that plays no structuring role in the overall analysis. In both the formal economy and in academic criminology, ideology lies in the attempt to deny abstraction and stick doggedly to the empirical analysis of real people and their real lives. Just as an analysis of capitalism that focuses purely on workers, employers and tradable commodities misses out the funda-mental truth of a self-sustaining global capitalist system that has a reality beyond the material, so criminological work that seeks to jettison abstract analysis and get back to the hard work of empirical research misses out on a fundamental truth of crime causation. In both cases, ideology resides in the attempt to cover up the 'real abstraction' with a faux-reality of good old straightforward empirical analysis.

Perhaps the biggest indictment of contemporary left-wing politics is that we have totally failed to offer a popular and compelling alternative to the dominant right-wing narrative of the current economic crisis. Not only does this mean that, in the absence of a reasonable alternative, the dominant narrative loses its political and ideological hue and takes on the appearance of 'common sense', but also that the true enemy of the piece is fundamentally misidentified.

In the current political situation, 'the left' no longer exists as such. The traditional left, with a future egalitarianism at the heart of its discourse, appeared to implode during the 1980s as liberalism polluted its self-image and its political and economic aspirations. It is almost as if the hammer blows of neoliberalism were so crippling that a strident critique of capital, and the drive to create something different, were abandoned in favour of defending narrow interest groups from oppression and the attempt to advance the legal freedoms of the individual. These days, much of the new left's politics appears to demand nothing more than the amelioration of the harmful effects of global capitalism, a strange hybrid that connects welfarist social democracy with an imprecise liberal push to protect and advance individual freedoms. The left's discourse is now, and has been for some time, predominantly oriented to little more than sticking up for the little guy – a noble calling, but one that tends to treat global capitalism and hollowed-out democratic politics as a fait accompli. Shouldn't a renewed, post-crash leftist politics re-install universality and a deep commitment to egalitarianism at the very heart of its discourse? Is it too naive to once again talk of 'class struggle'?

The entire spectrum of British politics appears to extend only from the social liberalism that seeks to defend the vulnerable from 'power' to the neo-liberalism that seeks to defend the rights of economic elites to benefit from their own creativity and enterprise. This staged performance of 'politics' is no politics at all. It is a strangely domesticated version of real political engagement. Neoliberalism is now a veteran economic power, and the history of its governance and democratic systems reveals quite clearly that, no matter what the electorate decide, the end result is the same. In Britain, the difference between the major political parties is negligible, and what difference there is exists mostly at the level of representation. To be sure, there may be one or two policy differences, but the fundamentals are already in place and must not be tampered with. The implicit mantra of contemporary liberal democratic politics is that we have found the formula – parliamentary democracy and free market economics is the least worst of all systems. Sure, it has its problems. Sure, we have seen democracy polluted by the interests of elites and the corruption of politicians. Sure, capitalism is unstable, ecologically destructive and produces staggering inequalities – *but what could be better than capitalism?* All politics now takes place on this field. All utopian politics, and the Occupy movement is a case in point, suffers the ignominious death generated by 'not being taken seriously'. We have moved from strident politics of the twentieth century to a banal, pragmatic and deeply cynical 'politics of the possible' that refuses to countenance fundamental changes to the system as it currently exists.

Can't we all just get along?

Some of the most outspoken critics of abstract financial speculation have been religious figures who have addressed the rampant greed of bankers and the 'ethically problematic' nature of contemporary global financial markets. In many ways these figures have stepped into the space vacated by the old political left. Others have redirected the righteous indignation of the population back at a consuming public who in the years before the crash bought beyond their means or were too foolish to recognise that property prices can go down as well as up. Others still have looked at the pre-crash media and its obsessions with lifestyle, property and home decoration shows that encouraged consumers to see their houses as a fundamental reflection of identity and achievement and to see the property market as a one-way bet. While there are fragments of truth in all of these responses, they miss the fundamental truth, the truth that should've been central to leftist responses to the crisis: *the roots of the crisis lie not in individual behaviours but in the logic of capitalism itself.*

Marx (1973, 2008) long ago identified the tendency of the profit rate to fall. He also recognised that capital's incessant desire to drive down wages in order

References

Agamben, G. (2005) *State of Exception*, Chicago, IL: University of Chicago Press
Bauman, Z. (2000) *The Individualized Society*, Oxford: Polity
Boltanski, L. and Chiapello, E. (2007) *The New Spirit of Capitalism*, London: Verso
Callinicos, A. (2010) *Bonfire of Illusions*, Oxford: Polity
Cohen, S. (ed.) (1971) *Images of Deviance*, Harmondsworth: Pelican
——(1988) *Against Criminology*, New Brunswick, NJ: Transaction Publishers
Currie, E. (1985) *Confronting Crime: An American Challenge*, New York: Pantheon
Graeber, D. (2011) *Debt*, London: Melville House
Hall, S. (2012) *Theorizing Crime and Deviance*, London: Sage
Harvey, D. (2011) *The Enigma of Capital*, London: Profile
Heinberg, D. (2011) *The End of Growth*, London: Clairview
Hobsbawm, E. (1995) *Age of Extremes*, London: Abacus
Keynes, J. M. (2008) *The General Theory of Employment, Interest and Money*, London: BN Publishing
Lea, J. (2002) *Crime and Modernity: Continuities in Left Realist Criminology*, London: Sage
Lea, J. and Young, J. (1984) *What is to be Done About Law and Order? Crisis in the Eighties*, Harmondsworth: Penguin
Marx, K. (1973) *Grundrisse*, London: Pelican
——(2008) *Capital*, Oxford: Oxford Paperbacks
Presdee, M. (2000) *Cultural Criminology and the Carnival of Crime*, London: Routledge
Smart, B. (2010) *Consumer Society*, London: Sage
Southwood, I. (2011) *Non-Stop Inertia*, London: Zero
Standing, G. (2011) *The Precariat: The New Dangerous Class*, London: Bloomsbury
Taylor, I. and Taylor, L. (eds.) (1973) *Politics and Deviance: Papers from the National Deviancy Conference*, Harmondsworth: Pelican
Taylor, I., Walton, P. and Young, J. (1973) *The New Criminology*, London: Routledge and Kegan Paul
Taylor, I., Walton, P. and Young, J. (eds) (1975) *Critical Criminology*, London: Routledge and Kegan Paul
Wolff, R. (2010) *Capitalism Hits the Fan*, New York: Interlink
Žižek, S. (2008) *Violence*, London: Verso
——(2010) *Living in the End Times*, London: Verso

Part 1
Theorising postmodern capital

1 Is it OK to talk about capitalism again?

Or, why criminology must take a *leap of faith*

Simon Winlow

'All collectivist politics leads to the Gulag.'

Prior to the economic crash of 2008, grand political causes and macro-level critical analysis appeared to have been expunged from mainstream political and academic life. The logic of postmodern capitalism had worked its way into every nook and cranny of the academy, compelling many talented academic criminologists to fix upon boundless diversity as the defining characteristic of twenty-first century social experience. As the UK moved through a period of resounding growth in its gross domestic product and the rapid expansion of consumer lifestyles – a period that seemed to confirm the social benefits of neoliberalism's obsessive concern with economic freedom – it no longer seemed hip to position the economy as the bedrock of everyday life or to engage in a critique of the socially corrosive nature of capitalist markets. The subject's ability to float free from 'repressive' modernist social structures and to make active decisions about its identity and biography seemed to be confirmed by the fluidity and pluralism of the postmodern experience.

Postmodernism's historic attack upon the certainties of the traditional symbolic order was accompanied by a parallel attempt to vanquish the metanarrative on university campuses across the West. Slowly, gradually, incontrovertibly, a dark cloud of cynicism engulfed the social sciences. For liberal postmodernists, 'truth' would always be out of reach; all we could do was creatively deconstruct accounts of it, while committing to an interminable cycle of research grant applications geared towards testing the usefulness of public policy or charting the latest fluctuations in observable empirical reality. During this heady period of rising national wealth and perpetual social flux, a new cultural and intellectual injunction was issued that transformed the nature of social and criminological theory: above all else, the social scientist must avoid the crimes of *generalisation* and *reductionism*.

These words were hurled at critical theorists with abandon during this period, and the dominance of this narrative in textbooks continues to structure the intellectual approach adopted by many of those entering the discipline of criminology for the first time. On the surface of things, accusing a theorist of reductionism seemed to indicate a genuine intellectual engagement and a rational, sceptical and considered response to theories that attempted to generalise meaning. Accusations of this sort contained within them an entirely reasonable call for specificity and a grounded analysis that accounted for a broader range of variables and acknowledged the diversity of social experience and social engagement even in what appeared to be relatively contained sub-sections of society. However, one might be forgiven for thinking that, in some instances at least, this kind of critique functioned as an attempt to cover up an unwillingness to engage in deep thinking about the nature of social reality, replacing it instead with a prefabricated response that appeared to indicate serious intellectual engagement. Many in the social sciences appeared to have reached the conclusion that, in a period of such clear cultural fluidity, nothing could be universalised.

In this intellectual context the symbolic life of the subject was unique and idiosyncratic, and our shared cultural life a mere amalgamation of an apparently infinite assortment of transmutable particularities. Many criminologists took Lyotard's totemic depiction of postmodernism seriously, but often in an indirect or unconscious manner. In the build up to the current crisis – as capital once again reconfigured itself, transforming labour markets, blithely ignoring the degradation of our natural environment and ushering in a new era of 'me first' individualism – we remained resolutely incredulous towards metanarratives. Any attempt to impose a theoretical order upon the messy business of twenty-first century life appeared flawed from the outset, 'reductionist', divorced from social reality and ignorant of the magical ability of the postmodern subject to make the active choices that would shape its social being. These metanarratives merely articulated the ideological prejudices of the author, and could not capture 'reality' as such. Didn't those authors who continued to persevere with 'generalised' accounts of the economy, culture or subjectivity understand that their work would immediately be considered anachronistic by their peers? Didn't they grasp the basic fact that the postmodern twenty-first century was ineluctably diverse and scintillating in its complexity and hybridity? Attempts to universalise meaning were merely a hold-over from an earlier and more naive time. And for those on the left, didn't they understand that 'the postmodern' period was also post-ideological? What good did it do to continue onwards with critical accounts of capitalist markets, and in so doing deny the agency of workers and consumers, when capitalist globalisation was revealing itself as the very vehicle that could advance the lifestyles of Western workforces and counter the leaden bureaucracies of traditional nation-states?

It is also worth considering the claim that a kind of anti-intellectualism began to creep into criminology during this period. The broad current of our shared culture was towards the base populism of neoliberalism and away from a high-minded social democratic idealism that involved public education and social understanding. Intellectualism was dismissed from public culture, a process that appeared to be mirrored in the academy with creeping deprofessionalisation and the transformation of the new professoriate from confirmed intellectuals, able to talk intelligently on a broad range of topics, to technical specialists, unwilling to comment on anything that lay outside their narrow academic area of expertise. In criminology, high theory, abstract theory, theory that did not deal directly with an expansive data set, was increasingly positioned as pompous and elitist. For many of the new breed of postmodern empirical criminologists, they didn't need Marx, Hegel, Freud, Adorno, Lacan or Bourdieu to tell them which way the wind was blowing – theory was viewed as pointless pirouetting in front of one's peers, mere self-aggrandisement that did not illuminate our understanding of the causes of crime one iota. Slowly but surely our theoretical ambitions were stifled and our discipline drifted perilously close to the jagged rocks of 'abstract empiricism' (Mills 2000). There could be no 'truth', in the abstract philosophical sense. All we could do was gather evidence from the 'real world'. Let the ideologues of the old left talk themselves into abstraction while the worldly empiricists of the new order set about the difficult and important task of appraising new innovations in crime control.

At the risk of annoying criminology's liberal empiricists, it is perhaps worth considering the suggestion that the development of this marked distrust of theoretical critique and the rush to declare all meta-theory 'deterministic', suggested a collective form of fetishistic disavowal (Žižek 2002; Winlow and Hall 2012a; Hall *et al.* 2008). This involves the attempt to choose to forget, or to refuse to countenance what the subject knows to be true. Of course, in the dismissal of 'ideological' criminological theorisation, or theories that were themselves built upon an already-in-place commitment to a truth project, the critic was refusing to acknowledge their own latent ideological affiliations. The common suggestion that the world is infinitely diverse and that social experience and social reality cannot be truly captured and used in the creation of macro-level theory is in itself thoroughly ideological. The '*essentialism, determinism, reductionism*' trifecta inevitably took the appearance of a universal injunction. A new mainstream criminology, with its incredulity to metanarratives, imposed its own metanarrative that demanded adherence: the world is infinitely complex; any account of 'truth' is corrupted by ideology; the route forwards must involve a focus on objective empirical 'reality'.

One can see how and why this liberal–relativist discourse gathered pace in criminology from the 1990s onwards. It is certainly true that Western societies were becoming increasingly diverse. At least on the surface of things. In many ways, this apparent diversity and change masked the continuation and reinforcement of the basic foundations of our economic life. A cultural world in which fashions and new cultural identities appeared to emerge magically on a daily basis, and in which we were increasingly surrounded by different religions, ethnicities, languages and accents, appeared to suggest a new era of advanced pluralism and progressive multicultural change. The old political certainties were now extinguished and democratic governments could be taken to task for their failure to satisfy the will of the people at election time. A new century of expansive freedoms seemed to beckon. My first claim is that much of this change existed *so that nothing had to change* (see Žižek 2002). What appeared to be the constant expansion of permissions and entitlements largely failed to translate into our experience of everyday social reality. Rather than feeling free, we increasingly appeared to experience our lives in relation to a palpable lack of freedom, a process that seems to suggest that, at some stage in our recent past, these 'freedoms' had flipped inwards and backwards, and that something vital for progressive social renewal was now inaccessible, or was being actively removed from our civic, political and subjective life. The appearance of change covered up our inability to *truly change* our world in the grand historic sense – what was freedom if not the freedom to vote, to shop, to choose one's own God, to pursue one's individual economic interests or to dedicate one's life to the accumulation of hedonistic experiences?

If we connect the postmodern denial of universality to transformations taking place in the economic realm, we can also see that this push to historicise and contextualise *everything*, to demand that all unique local and cultural specificities are identified and accounted for, also contains an element of falsehood that reflects the 'real abstraction' (Marx 1970; Žižek 2009a; see also Virno 2007; Toscano 2008) of today's capital: capitalism can no longer be considered 'Eurocentric', or rooted in any particular social experience. Postmodern capitalism, as it approaches the limits of the growth upon which it depends, is now thoroughly 'deterritorialised' and can adapt to, or make itself anew in, any cultural or geographic setting (Žižek 2008). It simply continues onwards, blindly following its own self-interest, without any consideration of the human or ecological costs of its activities. In this way, our immediate subjective experience is not in itself separate or abstracted from the logic of capital, as capital *is itself* the very substance of that abstraction. The 'postmodern' world may encourage us to experience contemporary social reality as a fundamentally unknowable and constantly-in-motion diversity, but we are also encouraged to pay scant attention to the postmodern world's disinclination to return to history.

In the years before the crash, capitalism had become so ubiquitous, so unchallengeable, that we ceased any attempt to imagine a world beyond it. Even now, as we witness the market economy's orgy of abstract, speculative investment unravel on our news broadcasts, we appear incapable of articulating a genuinely alternative economic, political and governmental system. Our rootedness in a historical era defined by liberal capitalism and its preferred system of governance means that what we experience as constant change and diversity reflects our historic inability to actually enact the change that might completely transform the contours of our world.

My second claim is that theoretical examination and re-examination of diversity and pluralism before the crash reflects the total dominance of liberal ideology, both in politics and in the academy (Žižek 2008). The logic of neoliberalism is built upon the dissolution of publics and the adoption of the crude ontological frameworks of classical and neoclassical economics. The liberal fear of all forms of collectivism, especially working-class collectivism, is the hidden ideological supplement of much affirmative postmodernism. After all, doesn't all collectivism lead to totalitarianism and therefore the Killing Fields and the Gulag (see Žižek 2001)? Wouldn't a genuine 'working class' political intervention necessarily threaten existing ethnic or cultural particularities? Because of the fundamental threat collectivist politics poses, shouldn't we oppose – by fair means or foul – *all* theoretical or political accounts of universality, and in so doing ensure that we remain frozen at the end of history, in an era defined by 'parliamentary capitalism' (Badiou 2009)?

The true ethical substance of leftist critique these days lies in the search for a new dialectic of universality, a universality that is not, as many sociologists maintain, simply a dull, monotonous homogeneity, but derives from a *universal singularity*: something that is reflective of a contemporary social reality as it is experienced but also something that opens up the space for a truly progressive politics that might return us to history. In the current conjuncture universality is the substance of progressive politics. It is only when we renounce postmodernism's possessive individualism that true progressive politics can really begin. In order for there to be progressive historic motion we need to be able to see and appreciate those things that bind us together, those issues that affect not simply the subject, but the subject and its community. If the left continues to believe in an egalitarian future it must popularise an account of the objective causes of those individual frustrations and dissatisfactions that are effects of contemporary capitalist realism. This account must encourage the subject to see its interests advanced in line with the interests of others: our shared fate on this planet, our collective experience of the harms of global capitalism, our collective dissatisfaction with the polity, our growing recognition that things cannot go on as they are, and our demand to create a fairer, sustainable and more just world. All of these things begin with renouncing solipsism and individualism and identifying the shared interests of the multitude.

What is problematic for the discipline of criminology is that this intellectual acceptance of boundless pluralism appears to have lost its obvious ideological character and has become, to all intents and purposes, 'naturalised', invisible, common sense; a rational and empirically provable assessment of the liberalised, Westernised, diversified and multicultural world in which we live. We have, for the most part, failed to think critically about pluralism, about where it comes from and what it means, and of course about alternative assessments that might be made about the reality of our social, cultural and political life. Are we to believe that our rather desperate scramble to differentiate ourselves from our peers is entirely 'natural', and has no relation to the dominant ideology? Doesn't our subjective desire to 'be different' immediately suggest a structuring universality? Are we to focus solely on religious, ethnic, cultural and sexual diversity and ignore our universal experiences as worker-consumers? Doesn't the fact that postmodernism compels us to understand collective identities as restrictive, to mock our own history, to treat our subjective background as something to escape from on a mythical journey of self-creation, tell us something about contemporary ideology and our current historical inertia, trapped as we are within this deadening period of capitalist realism (Fisher 2009)? Who might fear the return of universality, and why?

The 'objectivity' fetish

In these straitened times, in which we have once again been forced to acknowledge the perpetual boom and bust cycle of capitalist political economy, it is important to remember accurately the boom years of neoliberalism, the years before the crash. The significant growth in gross domestic product of course failed to ensure rising standards of living for all, and indeed served to concentrate wealth in the hands of the few. But it is nonetheless instructive to recall the hubris of the times. Our politicians believed that they had conquered boom and bust. House-buyers believed that house prices would continue to rise. The cultural and political atmosphere seemed to indicate that we believed we had surgically removed the malignant excesses of twentieth-century politics and hit upon a system that, while not perfect, was as good as could ever be expected. Mentioning Marx at an academic conference, or any other major figure from the history of critical theory, was to cling to the past at the expense of the new; it was (although affirmative postmodernists would never admit it) to focus on substance rather than image; and it was to commit the cardinal sin of 'postmodern' consumer culture – the sin of being, well, boring. Why bother to rethink capital accumulation in a rapidly changing age when people appeared to be transforming their lives and moulding their own identities by dipping critically in and out of consumer culture? Why bother to return to Marx when culture itself was now in constant motion and appeared to necessitate not dour political economy but an appreciative analysis of individual creativity, diversity and innovation? Hadn't we heard all there was to say about capitalism in the twentieth century? Couldn't we now move on and analyse all the remarkable things that were now taking place on the field of culture?

Many new criminologists finding their way into academic posts during this period were inculcated with this naturalised ideology. For them, and many more established liberal criminologists, it seemed entirely reasonable that one should withhold unequivocal truth claims and accept non-hierarchical intellectual and cultural heterogeneity. On the surface of things, there appeared to be a vigorous theoretical cut and thrust in criminology, but beneath this surface was a general acceptance that one must avoid expansive truth claims. Instead, if claims were to be made, they should be small, address a specific context or population, and the theorist must always reserve the right to adapt their thesis when more data were gathered. One shouldn't be wedded to any theoretical approach, and must be prepared to radically change direction upon the arrival of new data or in the face of weak liberal criticism. Every intellectual position had its own incontrovertible problems and omissions, and so it was better to avoid full theoretical commitment and focus on one's data. This process reduces theory to a mere addendum, an afterthought with no structuring role in the project or the analysis of its data – a couple of ideas thrown in at the end of the article, none of which the author is fully committed to.

This failure to fully commit to a theoretical and intellectual approach contributes to the historical attempt to prevent forward motion in criminology's stalled disciplinary dialectic. It is only when we argue passionately, when we encounter an alternative ideology and engage in intense debate, and when we are forced to reappraise and refine our own intellectual position, that we gain the traction that might propel us forward in a productive intellectual direction. This is not to say that all productive intellectual debate must be between political opposites. Indeed, there is a sense that critical criminology's ongoing debate with right realist criminology has itself become non-dialectical, with key protagonists on both sides preaching to the converted using established ecclesiastical tropes. As Adorno (1997) has pointed out, the true anti-thesis always emanates from within the thesis itself. It is this point that critical criminology must fix upon. Rather than slavishly revisiting ideas from our shared past, we must, when justified, submit those ideas to withering critique in the hope that we might advance from our current position and produce the ideas that truly reflect the painful realities of the unfolding twenty-first century. In my view, this is how critical criminology advances, not with the interminable rediscovery and reapplication of ideas from the 1960s and 1970s, but by doggedly offering a theoretical and empirical account of the now. Contemporary critical criminologists should therefore consider engaging in a vigorous internal critique of our own discourse as a means of driving our own intellectual renewal; rather than waiting for the painfully predictable blandness of the mainstream to articulate a considered response to critical criminology's account of the real world, critical criminology might attempt to drag itself clear of the historical inertia that engulfs criminology in order to occupy a new space of genuine intellectual innovation and excitement.

There are associated issues that relate closely to the gradual marketisation of higher education in the West. Why bother to challenge received wisdom or risk alienating journal reviewers with commitment to a theoretical truth when it is easier to get published by simply parroting ideas already in circulation? It is certainly far easier to publish an article that endorses established ideas, or suggests minor contextual adjustments, than it is to propose an entirely new idea. If we are to cultivate our research profiles to a degree that merits promotion, it is best to position ourselves as a careful and entirely 'objective' data analyst rather than theoretical maverick. The push towards empiricism and our obsessive concern with adopting the methods and objectivity of the hard sciences has also contributed to criminology's theoretical immobility. There are numerous theorists and empirical researchers attempting to produce new ideas and approaches and drive the discipline out of the darkness and towards the light, but they represent only a small minority of what is increasingly an empirical discipline with limited intellectual ambition. The correct bearing for the archetypal criminologist now is to be entirely without belief or theoretical commitment. We are supposed to abstract ourselves from the world we inhabit in an attempt to ensure our data are not polluted by ideology or theoretical factionalism. We should 'let the facts speak for themselves', a theme I will return to later.

The dominant cultural atmosphere of deep cynicism ensures that virtually all truth claims these days are derided as mere stories covering up instrumental agendas: ideological politicians are judged vulgar and unworldly individuals obsessed with power, using ideology to manipulate the weak; ideological criminologists are positioned as intellectually naive charlatans or shallow self-publicists driven by a base desire for academic recognition. In an era in which we are immediately compelled to be distrustful of everything that appears 'ideological', any theory must first provide voluminous empirical data in order to receive a hearing. Instead of engaging in 'pointless' theoretical abstraction or imagining utopias, we content ourselves with rational and pragmatic analysis, and focus on what is achievable. For example, instead of taking criminal motivations seriously, we cover up our unwillingness to think by regurgitating the postmodern narrative of boundless pluralism. What can we know about criminal motivations when everyone is different and the world is changing so rapidly? Surely any attempt to uncover a universal 'truth' in this field is an entirely pointless undertaking? Instead, we should focus on what we can *know for sure*, and how this knowledge can be used to practically benefit our discipline and the community at large, or how this knowledge might 'humanise' political governance, criminal justice agencies and systems of punishment. As I have already suggested, in the academy this culture of pronounced cynicism appears to manifest itself as a return to the enlightenment principles of scepticism and rationality, principles that demand that each and every new idea is subject to thorough-going critique. But the deep fear of 'strong thought' has prevented us asking searching questions about historical processes, about the changing nature of global capitalism and parliamentary politics. Theories now vie for attention in an apparently open debate in which everyone is entitled to an opinion but no firm conclusions are to be reached.

Negation of the negation

My third claim is that postmodernism's distaste for meta-critique and its cynical, mocking dismissal of ideology is deeply indicative of contemporary capitalist realism – an era in which there ceased to be any sense of progressive historical movement, and in which liberal capitalism has positioned itself as the only viable form of economic and political governance (Žižek 2008, 2009b). The careful surgical removal of universality from politics and the valorisation of possessive individualism in economy and culture are reflective of a historic and precipitous decline in the symbolic efficiency of modernist truths. The twentieth century was an age of passionate political and intellectual engagement because, during that century, it was still possible to be *a true subject of belief*. In the contemporary period we content ourselves that we have overcome these simplistic and rather vulgar passions and position our-selves as calculating, dispassionate *subjects of rationality*. We no longer appear to have faith in anything that cannot be confirmed by the immediacy of our senses (Winlow and Hall 2012a). Even those people in the West who are still willing to acknowledge religious 'belief' tend to instrumentalise and spiritualise that belief in some way, attempting to make their religious belief 'work for them', rather than submitting to ecclesiastical dogma. Faith – in religion, in political ideology and so on – no longer appears to be a part of postmodern subjectivity or the cultural life of twenty-first century Western liberalism.

Yet belief has not disappeared entirely. Despite the postmodern claim that we now occupy a post-ideological era, ideology is around us all the time. Our political opponents on the neoliberal right chastise the radical left for our boundless utopianism and our refusal to deal with the harsh realities of our world. However, theirs is the true unworldly utopianism; it is they who refuse to deal with harsh realities. What could be more utopian than the fetishistic political assumption that what we have can continue indefinitely? Isn't their slavish commitment to a global free market economy the quintessence of fidelity to an ideological truth? Isn't it they who refuse to look at the painful realities of rising inequalities, ecological degradation and impending energy, food and water crises and the massive agglomeration of human harms asso-ciated with these processes? In culture generally, the people too remain true subjects of belief. The crucial issue at stake here is to acknowledge that our beliefs these days are no longer fully conscious. Our belief in subjective rationality covers up our fidelity to the basic coordinates of our current ideological constellation. In the same way as postmodernism's refutation of the metanarrative itself becomes a dominant metanarrative, so our deep commitment to subjective rationality reflects our resolute attachment to blind faith. Our *belief* lies in our firm conviction that we are grounded pragmatists with a firm hold upon rationality.

As Žižek (2008, 2009b, 2011) has recognised, the structure of ideology changes with postmodernism. During the modern era ideology functioned much as Marx originally suggested and took the form of *that which we don't know, but we do*. The models of ideological control constructed by Gramsci and Althusser continue this theme, and encourage us to think of ideology as a problem of knowledge. Modern capitalism secures its interests by ensuring that the multitude is denied access to the truth of their servitude. Postmodern ideology involves a marked shift in emphasis. These days, we know very well the horrors of global capitalism. We know about exploitation and environ-mental degradation; we know that capitalism is plagued by destructive cycles of boom and bust; we know that staggering inequalities and horrific injustices are the necessary outcome of capitalist markets; we know that democratic politics is polluted by the interests of elites. All of these things are now out in the open, and we now know the truth of our servitude (Fisher 2009; Winlow and Hall 2012a).

Postmodern capitalism no longer secures its interests by denying the multitude access to the pain of reality. Rather, capitalism now stages its own critique, encouraging us to laugh at it and to be critical of embedded privilege and the depredations of bankers and corporate elites. The drive is towards *interpassivity*. We are relieved of any personal responsibility we may feel to protest and petition for social renewal (ibid.). We can withdraw from the foreground of struggle, safe in the knowledge that struggle continues without our direct involvement. Our frustrations and dissatisfaction with our world are enacted for us by post-political capitalist realism itself. Even Hollywood blockbusters these days have moved on from identifying the pathological narcissist as the ultimate 'bad guy'. Now, when the curtain is pulled back and the villain is revealed, the asocial institution of 'the corporation' stands before us, and it is the profit motive itself that is pathologised by America's own culture industry.

Lethargic cynicism and even strident critique are everywhere in our culture, yet cynical realism and cultural interpassivity prevent the construction of a genuine oppositional politics that might return us to history. Interpassivity encourages us to rest easy, safe in the knowledge that a critique of the present is being waged daily on our behalf. In this way contemporary capitalism's self-critique has a soporific effect and functions to prevent genuine political opposition. There is no need to make the personal sacrifices necessary to drive social renewal: look! The system is being held to account, and is subject to constant gradualist democratic rehabilitation. The problem is of course that the system is being held to account by its own institutions and cultures, and that this image of constant political critique and dialogue exists in order to ensure that the current order continues.

The calculated and thoughtful construction of prefabricated forms of resistance and dissatisfaction effectively commodify dissent and encourage the controlled and relatively harmless cathartic release of built-up frustrations and dissatisfactions at the obscene spectacle of capitalist realism (Hall and Winlow 2007; Fisher 2009). For the moment at least, anti-war marches, demonstrations against austerity cuts, union campaigns against the erosion of established workplace entitlements and so on, are first greeted with cynicism and are then used to paradoxically reassert the core message of the current order that they oppose: democracy welcomes all viewpoints. Everyone is entitled to protest. If you are dissatisfied with the government, you can make your views known with petitions and peaceful campaigning while waiting for the next election, when you can vote to change things. Look how lucky you are to live in a vibrant democracy! Thank God you don't live in a dictatorship, where protest would be met with an immediate repressive response!

Postmodern capitalism secures its interests by ensuring that the emancipatory potential of ultimate realisation is lost as the subject is encouraged to adopt the world-weary cynicism that is the defining cultural characteristic of postmodernism. This culture increasingly positions us as Nietzschian 'last men': fearful of an excess of life, desperate to keep things as they are, immediately dismissive of all alternatives, puncturing the dull mediocrity of the constant present with shallow bursts of hedonism, with no abiding passions except to prolong life and to accumulate pleasurable sensations:

> "We have discovered happiness" say the last men, and they blink ...
>
> A little poison now and then: that makes for pleasant dreams ...
>
> Who wants to rule? Who wants to obey? Both are too burdensome.
>
> No shepherd, and only one herd! Everyone wants the same; everyone is the same: he who feels differently goes voluntarily to the madhouse.
>
> "Formerly, all the world was insane," says the subtlest of them. And they blink.
>
> They have their little pleasures for the day, and their little pleasures for the night, but they have a regard for health.
>
> "We have discovered happiness," – say the Last Men, and they blink.
>
> (Nietzsche, from *Thus Spoke Zarathustra*)

The scales of modernist ideology have fallen from our eyes. We now believe that we see the truth, the Emperor is naked before us, but we lack the conscious belief that might once have allowed us to intervene and change things. In the wake of the global crisis, watching the debacle as our political leaders try to restart neoliberalism's economic juggernaut, we stand immobilised, disgusted, dissatisfied, but unable to fully commit to an alternative. What the current ideological order is attempting to do is create and maintain a gap between awareness and social action. With postmodern ideology, *we know very well the reality of capitalism, but we are incapable of acting*. In this way, capitalism is perfectly happy to have the multitude mock its vulgar spectacle of excessive consumerism, as long as they continue to buy consumer products. Capitalism is happy for consumers to know about the harms enacted upon workers in the developing world, as long as we continue to obsessively seek out bargains. Capitalism is sanguine about the rapidly approaching energy crisis, about the ecological and social harms that are fundamental to its operation, about impending food and water crises, as long as our cynical bearing holds firm and we continue to believe that there exists no viable alternative to the current order.

As long as we continue to fulfil our role as worker-consumer, our attitude towards the edifice of global capital matters little. Subjectively, we believe our world-weary cynicism and knowledge of reality separates us from ideological manipulation and the obvious excesses of capital. We see the reality and so can continue onwards, safe in the knowledge that while we are subject to the wild fluctuations of the market, we are not truly 'of' capitalism and not subject to its seductions and compulsions. Similarly, we may believe liberal democratic elections to be an empty spectacle, a mere periodic validation of the right of the elite to rule, but as long as we continue to vote, the dominant ideology is untroubled. In the postmodern era, the gap created between our belief and our social action by the prevailing culture of cynicism is the key to ideological domination. We are subjugated by our 'painful awareness', by the impossibility to consciously believe in and fully commit to a radical otherness, and by our deep fidelity to cynical realism. It is our failure to act, our profound and historic immobility that guarantees the continuation of what already exists.

Of course, our shared political life is also tainted by the dank air of post-modern cynicism. Even the ideologues of liberal capitalism no longer attempt to convince the people that capitalism is fundamentally of The Good. Instead, the tactic appears to be to convince the people that it is the *least worst* of all politico-economic systems (Badiou 2002). Capitalism may be hideously exploitative, we are told, but at least it's not totalitarian. Results at election time may not represent the will of the people, but at least the people are given the right to vote. It is now impossible for the defenders of capitalism to deny that the global economy regularly succumbs to destructive convulsions. Instead, they say that the free market still represents the best available means of organising the global economy. Their job in assuring dissenters that – despite significant structural problems – global capitalism is the *least worst* of all systems is made significantly easier by the cultural outcomes of capitalism's recent history in the West. The free market is the economic foundation upon which our deep commitment to consumerism is built. So, capitalism as an economic system contains problems of huge magnitude, but who these days is willing to give up the trinkets of postmodern consumerism in order to move on to an economic system that must involve a net reduction in that which we have been told represents individualism, freedom, the postmodern 'good life'? Is it not easier to push truth from consciousness, and adopt the position of the cynical critic of capitalism, while at the same time hoping that capital itself can continue? And for those on the left, is the absolute limit of our ambition to somehow magically 'humanise' capitalism, or to return to a modernist social democratic governance that contains and harnesses the brutality of the profit motive (Winlow and Hall 2012b)?

Our apparent fetishistic desire to turn away from that which we know to be true prevents us from taking the steps necessary to prevent catastrophe. Capitalism is now reaching the objective limits to its growth (Heinberg 2011; Harvey 2010). *We cannot go on as we are.* This is not simply a matter of liberal economics and financial abstraction. The coming energy crisis and a broad assortment of historic problems that lie just along the road are unpalatable truths that, were we able to truly appraise them with honesty, must necessitate hard thinking and immediate concerted action. Our inability to make hard choices is exacerbated by our refusal to deal with reality with honesty and the deep cynicism we show to all those who dare to suggest an alternative path that threatens our lifestyles. Badiou (2002, 2009), one of the most insightful critics of contemporary politics and culture, maintains that the only pro-gressive route forwards is to re-energise a dialectic of universality and to identify and fully commit to an account of The Good. The *least worst* option is no good to us if we are serious about tackling the problems that lie before us. In the Badiouian schema, we await a Truth Event, the passage through which will redefine the coordinates of our belief and allow us the possibility to look back at the hubris of our recent past as we begin the process of reaffirming our fidelity to a Truth Project.

Anti-politics

For many critical continental theorists we have entered a period of *post-politics* (for example Badiou 2009; Ranciere 2010; Žižek 2008). Here we are exposed to the image of constant political activity and change. If citizens are dissatisfied with the direction of the government, they have the opportunity to vote to change things in free and open elections. But change does not extend beyond the image. Again, the image of change exists in order that nothing has to change. In most Western democracies the policy differences between the major political parties are negligible. In Britain, Labour and Conservative party policy is almost indistinguishable. All talk of utopian political projects has been discarded. All politicians assume that we have discovered the magic formula for the best possible society – liberal democracy coupled with free market capitalism. They immediately admit that there are a few niggles to be worked out, but basically we have the formula. The dominant field of pragmatic reason states clearly that the best that we can hope for is a return to neoliberal economic growth and rising prosperity, perhaps supplemented with some improvements to individual 'rights' and a cultural push towards tolerating difference. Even a genuine political event, like the election of Barack Obama, appears unable to truly transcend the repressive logic of liberal democracy in action.

Twentieth-century politics was full of deeply held affiliations and passionate intensity. Even in Britain, a country whose social democratic class compromise produced a post-war period of relative political and economic stability (Winlow and Hall 2006; Reiner 2007), our politicians expressed deeply held beliefs about the economy, justice, fairness and progress. Many politicians held utopian visions of the future and articulated clear policy agendas that could carry the country to the Promised Land. Of course, Thatcher was Britain's last truly ideological politician. She entered government with a clear agenda to change things in line with her ideological beliefs. Her free market utopianism may be unpalatable to the readers of this book, but she occupied an easily identifiable ideological space. She was a true *subject of belief,* and she was happy to share those beliefs with the electorate and allow those beliefs to inform policy decisions. By the end of her spell in office, and in line with parallel neoliberal administrations around the world, she had banished Britain's prevailing social democratic orthodoxy and established a new orthodoxy in its place with a shallow and regressive interpretation of 'freedom' and an economic model built upon the 'efficiencies' of small government and the global free market. All governments since have treated the global free market as a fait accompli. The few politicians who still dare to discuss an alternative to this model are immediately dismissed as unelectable and dangerous mavericks or unworldly ideologues who have failed to change with the times.

All mainstream politicians these days rush to assure us that they are 'not ideological'. Instead, they position themselves as rational pragmatists who will manage the various instruments of government slightly better than their political opponents. They work on the assumption that the electorate don't really want change. Instead, politicians assume that the electorate simply want more of what is already available. In this way, the politician who can come up with the most convincing account suggesting an increase in purchasing power for the majority is likely to win the day. For these politicians, policy is not structured in relation to embedded ideological belief relating to fairness, justice and progress. Rather, policy is the product of rational calculation, the province of spin doctors, opinion polls and focus groups. In this way, politics becomes pure representation. Politicians go about the business of acting like politicians, while teams of PR people attempt to stage-manage exposure to the strange world of 24-hour news broadcasting in an attempt to encourage voters to see their candidate as 'statesmanlike', and 'someone they can relate to'.

As there is very little to separate the major British parties in terms of actual policy, the stereotypical alienated young voter who believes our politicians to be 'all the bloody same' is unerringly correct. But the most depressing aspect of today's bland, homogenised and stage-managed political scene is the deep commitment all mainstream politicians have to the global free market and the 'transparency' and 'fairness' of democratic elections. Up to the crisis in 2008, the very suggestion that capitalism's global financial system should be subject to comprehensive regulation seemed sufficiently unworldly to attract popular derision. Even now, in the fourth year of the economic crisis, with the Eurozone straining to postpone its implosion and mass unemployment once more casting its shadow, our politicians stick resolutely to neoliberal dogma.

What could be more indicative of the dawning of a post-political age than the 2010 general election in Britain? Here, voters appeared to be aggrieved at Labour's mismanagement of the economy and its inability to rein in the destructive greed of the banking industry. They also appeared to look on with disgust at the MPs expenses scandal, in which elected officials had systematically attempted to enrich themselves by submitting the most frivolous expenses claims. Here, politics follows the logic of transcendent negation (Adorno 1997). The election results were less a positive endorsement of the manifestos of Liberal Democrat and Conservative parties and more a rejection of the sitting Labour administration. In essence, what the electorate voted for was change itself, but what they got was yet another administration geared toward lubricating the movement of capital and facilitating market-led economic growth, in a political era in which the entire project of free market capitalism had been shown to be fundamentally flawed. The true perversity of the situation is revealed when we acknowledge that, in order to register a protest vote against excesses of free market capitalism, one had to vote for a Conservative party that had struggled free from traditional one-nation Toryism to become a political party entirely dedicated to liberal capitalism from root to tip. Disgusted by the greed and impropriety of our political and economic leaders, we elected a new Conservative–Liberal coalition who would ensure that morally bankrupt free market capitalism continued to be the foundation of everyday life.

One might have expected the voter turnout at the election to be way down. But the total absence of real politics didn't seem to dissuade voters. Turnout figures in the election were a surprisingly healthy 65 per cent. For what or for whom were we really voting? Voters appeared keen to endorse something that was entirely absent from the ballot papers placed before them. Mass dissatisfaction with the inequities and injustices of liberal capitalism could only manifest itself in a paradoxical and perverse endorsement of liberal capitalism itself. In the same way, as the British electorate are again forced to countenance these same injustices under the current Conservative–Liberal Democratic coalition, they can always look forward to the next election when they have the opportunity to vote for the neoliberal Labour party. After that coming election, capitalism's apologists can once again announce that the people have spoken. The purity of the liberal–democratic vision, in which the will of the people is reflected in election results and political practice, is now indelibly tarnished by the base pragmatism and cynicism that accompanies democracy in action.

It is not challenging to see that, in the field of democratic politics, we are increasingly compelled to privilege image over substance. Embedded in a post-political era of spin and media manipulation, true political substance appears to remain perennially hidden from view. But our desire to get behind the image and discover what is real in the party leaders Miliband or Cameron misses the point. The 'substance' of their 'true belief' is just as artificial as the surface image. They do not truly exist as political entities in the traditional sense. They have no roots in ideology. They themselves 'do not believe'. They are ciphers, mere surface images representing the public face of a seemingly immovable and unchallengeable ideologico-political system. Rather than being politicians committed to an ideological truth, they are representatives of an unstated ideology that is so omnipresent that we can no longer discern its ideological content. They nobly, and I believe entirely truthfully, commit themselves to the efficient administration of the parliamentary machine in the vague hope that this benefits and is the will of 'the people'. For them, their real ideology is pragmatism. What sense does it make to submit to hazy dreams of a utopian future and interminable quarrels about the abstractions of justice, freedom and progress? Theirs is a profoundly serious job in which there is no time for the luxury of abstraction. In their fealty to 'the people', they will work tirelessly to ensure that representative democracy continues, that GDP moves back to growth, and that individual rights are enshrined in and defended by law. This, I claim, is the reality of contemporary politics, a reality that enforces a horizon upon what is politically achievable these days. All politicians, as a condition of being recognised as such, must accept that politics takes place within the parameters of liberal capitalism and liberal democracy. Politicians must restrict their activities and policies to the dull and dispiriting theatre of 'pragmatic' politics. Everything that exists beyond this horizon can be built upon nothing other than *blind faith.*

But don't ongoing political upheavals in Spain and Greece suggest that a return to real politics is imminent? Don't the Occupy movements and the new wave of student protests clearly indicate that it is a profound mistake to assume that young people are deadened apolitical consumers? Aren't trade unions beginning to stir once again? All these developments and much else besides harbour the potential to develop into real politics, but we should attempt to ensure that our desire to see real politics return does not prompt us to misidentify political dissatisfaction with the current order as the dawning of a new political age. To be sure, the Occupy movement seems to be a progressive intervention that appears to express a quite widely felt dissatisfaction with capitalism's inequalities and injustices, but their message shows no signs of traversing the huge cultural chasm that exists between them and the vast body of the ex-working class who possesses the numbers to actually enact progressive political change. Further, the Occupy group in London seemed to harbour a fundamental belief in the democratic process, fighting an eviction notice through the courts and expecting the liberal–capitalist state to grant them leave to protest indefinitely outside St Paul's cathedral. What they want is for the current political establishment to recognise their voice and to adapt their policies accordingly. They are politely asking the political and corporate elite to change, to be more considerate of the poor, and to face head-on the problems associated with ecological degradation.

The Occupy movement, and other protest movements across Europe, tend to position themselves *against* the worst excesses of the current system, but they are not fundamentally *for* something different that can be easily named and identified by the general public. Some protest groups purport to be of neither the left nor the right, but are rather driven by a post-political desire to see fairness and justice installed at the heart of our politics and economy. Again, the thrust is to rehabilitate what already exists, but we must acknowledge that capitalism has historically shown remarkable resilience and an ability to reconfigure itself in order to incorporate even the most robust political criticism without changing its basic form or direction (Boltanski and Chiapello 2007); it changes only so that it may continue. Further, and as I have tried to indicate above, it is wrong to assume that everyday people in the West are keen to fundamentally transform what already exists, even though it is in their interests to do so. The left must not kid themselves that there exists some fundamental human drive towards equality and justice, and that, if a genuine ideological political candidate of the left were to arise, they would win popular support. It is worth considering if democracy itself must be the vehicle through which we create historic social change. But the current ideological constellation makes it almost impossible to advocate anything other than liberal democracy. No one these days openly endorses a shift to another form of political and economic organisation. How can one be against free and open elections today, even when they deliver no real change? Elections appear to us as fundamental civic entitlements and freedoms that must be retained and expanded. Any attempt to change 'democracy' or challenge the dominance of markets cannot, for the moment, be countenanced.

Wouldn't a return to real politics involve an attempt to topple the current edifice of concentrated ideological and politico-economic power and replace it with something else? As I have said, much political opposition these days involves a drive to rehabilitate what currently exists, and one might reasonably argue that a new humane and ecologically aware capitalism – with rigorous governmental controls on finance and investment, a positive taxation system and a comprehensive welfare system – would indeed be a truly progressive political move symbolising a genuine return to history. I do not contest this point, but I would maintain that it seems impossible, at the moment, to submit global capitalism to this kind of serious, interventionist social democratic reform. The challenge for the politically aware vanguard of Occupy and other such movements is to actually have a plausible programme and present it in such a way that it is immediately understandable to everyday people, and to encourage those people to see their own interests advanced as part of that programme, thus channelling the blind frustration and dissatisfaction so common throughout contemporary culture in a progressive political direction (Winlow and Hall 2012b). To underestimate the difficulty of the times in which we live, or the unpalatable truth-telling and hard thinking required to reactivate politics in the context we have inherited, is to guarantee long-term political failure.

Truth and universality

My main point here is that, after years of liberal pluralism, in which the left was pushed to abandon the 'essentialism' of the class struggle and instead settle for defending the particularities of marginalised communities and identities, it is once again becoming possible to identify *capitalism itself* as the fundamental problem we face today. The crisis of neoliberalism and the growing public distaste for aggressive accumulation – manifest in movements like Occupy – indicate that it is once again possible to create a new and progressive leftist narrative of universality. We can only do this if we are willing to countenance the dark reality of post-political capitalist realism, and accept the hard work and self-sacrifice needed to challenge embedded cultural cynicism and channel blind dissatisfaction in a productive political direction.

In recent years, criminology has created for itself a similar structure to the deadening political conjuncture I have attempted to summarise above. Virtually all ideological commitment and meta-critique have been discarded from mainstream criminology. All who offer a genuine ideological account of the now are immediately dismissed as oddballs who should be tolerated but never taken seriously. Instead, we should dedicate ourselves to small adjustments to the established field of pragmatic reason. A cloud of bland mediocrity descends, and we find ourselves moving closer to the archetypal model of the instrumental careerist: happy to work within the structure as it exists, happy to secure what recognition we can, happy to perennially reassert the received wisdom. And we blink.

Let's be honest with ourselves: even most intellectual radicals these days tend to accept the established horizon of pragmatic reason. The vast majority of the intellectual superheroes and the workaday empirical researchers in criminology treat capitalism and liberal democracy as a fait accompli, and as a result contemporary criminology is bereft of the concepts and analytical frameworks that can deal with the current situation. The righteous indignation of our theoretical radicals paradoxically reasserts the established field of liberal capitalism. The limit of their ambition is to reform what currently exists. Many liberal radicals argue passionately for tolerance and position many of our problems today in relation to our inability to truly tolerate difference. Why are these radicals no longer inclined to position these problems in relation to inequality, injustice and exploitation? One would hope that the ongoing global economic crisis might allow us to think about the harsh realities of contemporary capitalism and its preferred forms of governance, and in so doing reignite the intellectual engine that might drive us forward and into a new period of intellectual vigour and innovation.

In politics the dominant ideology now establishes and enforces a horizon of acceptable political, economic and governmental knowledge. All politics must now take place on the field of liberal democracy and liberal capitalism. This field is supposedly non-ideological, and is instead structured in relation to pragmatism and what is realistically achievable. Criminology has succumbed to a similar fate. Despite some genuine signs of life at the margins, ideological commitment and macro-level theory have been effectively expunged from its corpus. Instead, a horizon is placed upon acceptable knowledge and we focus on what is realistically achievable. Beyond the horizons established by conventional politics and mainstream criminology lies nothing that is pragmatic or realistic. Beyond those horizons lies nothing but *blind faith*.

If we are to truly rejuvenate politics and criminological inquiry, we must be willing to abandon pragmatism and risk *a leap of faith* into this alternative space. We must be willing to imagine a world beyond liberal capitalism and liberal democracy and have the bravery at least to attempt to make our vision of a better world a reality. In my view, the starting point for genuine political renewal is to rediscover universality. In criminology we must be willing to construct new models of crime causation, models that respect the achievements of the past but are resolutely committed to revealing and explaining the true reality of contemporary capitalist realism. Rather than responding to social and governmental anxieties, we should be investigating the social with a view to providing our audience with yet more things to be anxious about, or encouraging them to be anxious about the perennial concerns in new ways. We must embrace our ideological affiliations and use them to push past pragmatic accounts of what is achievable, and in so doing renew our disciplinary dialectic. We must recognise our objectivity fetish for what it is, and challenge all of criminology's naturalised ideological injunctions. This is how we make our discipline and our discourse anew: with unreserved ideological commitment and the willingness to risk a *leap of faith.*

References

Adorno, T. (1997) *Negative Dialectics*, London: Continuum
Badiou, A. (2002) *Ethics*, London: Verso
——(2009) *The Meaning of Sarkovy*, London: Verso
Boltanski, L. and Chiapello, E. (2007) *The New Spirit of Capitalism*, London: Verso
Fisher, M. (2009) *Capitalist Realism*, London: Zero
Hall, S. and Winlow, S. (2007) 'Cultural criminology and primitive accumulation: a formal introduction for two strangers who should really become more intimate', *Crime, Media, Culture*, Vol. 3, No. 1: 82–90
Hall, S., Winlow, S. and Ancrum, C. (2008) *Criminal Identities and Consumer Culture: Crime, Exclusion and the New Culture of Narcissism*, Cullompton: Willan
Harvey, D. (2010) *The Enigma of Capital*, Oxford: Oxford University Press
Heinberg, R. (2011) *The End of Growth*, London: Clairview
Marx, K. (1970) *A Contribution to the Critique of Political Economy*, New York: International Publishers
Mills, C.W. (2000) *The Sociological Imagination*, Oxford: Oxford University Press
Ranciere, J. (2010) *Chronicle of Consensual Times*, London: Continuum
Reiner, R. (2007) *Law and Order*, Oxford: Polity
Toscano, A. (2008) 'The open secret of real abstraction', *Historical Materialism*, 20 (2): 273–87
Virno, P. (2007) 'General intellect', *Historical Materialism*, 15 (3): 3–8
Winlow, S. and Hall, S. (2006) *Violent Night: Urban Leisure and Contemporary Culture*, Oxford: Berg
——(2012a) 'What is an "ethics committee"? Academic governance in an epoch of belief and incredulity', *British Journal of Criminology*, 52 (2): 400–16
——(2012b) 'A predictably obedient riot: post-politics, consumer culture and the English riots of 2011', *Cultural Politics,* in press
Žižek, S. (2001) *Did Somebody Say Totalitarianism?* London: Verso
——(2002) *Welcome to the Desert of the Real*, London: Verso
——(2008) *Violence*, London: Profile Books
——(2009a) *The Sublime Object of Ideology*, London: Zero
——(2009b) *First as Farce, then as Tragedy*, London: Verso
——(2011) *Living in the End Times*, London: Verso

2 Living it down in Havana

Organized crime and the pseudo-pacification process

Steve Hall

The pseudo-pacification process is a psychosocial energy generator that has been essential to capitalist development from the beginning of the project. It is similar to Marcuse's *repressive desublimation* in the sense that desire is rendered submissive to the commodity market, but unlike it in the sense that the liberation of the sensual body is the route to freedom; our bodily sensuousness is far too flexible and prone to cultural manipulation for that to be a way out. In fact the transcendental materialist position on which my work is based posits the body, with it its neurological system and proto-symbolic sensibilities, as the receptacle for congealed ideology (see Hall 2012; Johnston 2008). The concept of pseudo-pacification moves us beyond repressive desublimation, and is also intended to replace both the 'civilising process' (see Elias 1994) and the 'pacifying process' (see Mucchielli 2010), because these concepts furnish us with neither a basic aetiological explanation of temporal conditions nor any discernible reasons for their emergence at particular points in European history, other than some suppositious teleological drive towards a pacified life. There is, however, no convincing evidence – in fact there is more evidence to the contrary – that the individuals who wielded cultural and political influence in the Dark Ages desired peace and wished to dispense with their entitlement to rule by violence, or that the subjugated classes wished for a peaceful transition to an alternative future (Ward-Perkins 2005; Žižek 2010; Hall 2012). There is, on the other hand, copious evidence that the development of the early proto-capitalist economy was predicated on a move away from violence in order to protect the private property, arterial trade routes and market nodes – produce, coins, roads, sea lanes, market towns, strong-rooms, banks and so on – that were crucial to the project; the initial impetus to the decline of serious violence was provided by the growing realisation that it was a crucial aid to market-driven prosperity. The complex aspects of the process are explained elsewhere (Hall 2007, 2012), but for our purpose here, to put it probably too simply, we got a bit nicer because it seemed to be helping us to get richer, and, although our sensibilities became accustomed to the pacified life, its maintenance became far too dependent on the promise of permanently increasing prosperity.

England was the first nation to develop early marketisation and merchant capitalism into full-blown industrial capitalism. It had been notably anarchic and violent during the period of socio-political disruption after the Norman invasion, between the late eleventh and late fourteenth centuries. The decline of the murder rate from the late fourteenth century coincided with the Plague, population reduction and the second stage of the development of the early proto-capitalist market economy. This was a period in which nakedly violent politico-economic competition began to be sublimated into a relatively pacified interpersonal and social competition. The crucial symbols signifying social distinction and thus energising actors' struggles shifted from honour, reputation and the defence of land and family interests to the acquisition of symbolic goods in a developing sumptuary consumer culture. Individuals were cast out from the defensive familial and communal units into a precarious, unexplored social hinterland of pure, disembedded symbolic exchange, where, unless one was successful and able to display the symbols of success with convincing style, one ceased to exist in the eyes of all other refugees from the disintegrating traditional social body whose lives were simultaneously being built around the value of these symbols.

In this nascent new world of early social dissolution and marketisation it became ever more difficult to be valued as simply a human being, yet, despite the precariousness of existence, the relative lack of familial and communal support and the ramping up and diffusion of social competition, the individual was expected to behave increasingly in a pacified manner. Libidinal drives, incited and pre-formed as common aspects of the disavowed obscene Real (especially narcissism, envy, deceit and the gambler's and usurer's instinctive calculation, luck and infantile attraction to ways of getting something for nothing), were stimulated as the psychosocial fuel for the nascent market economy, whilst values drawn from the old culture of transcendent idealism were gradually relocated and recast as strategic normative practices designed to restrain these drives, divert them from the transcendental ideal and its politics and sublimate them into symbolically manipulable consumer desires that could be harnessed to the new dynamic economy.

The shift to capitalism's libidinal consumer economy – now seen as funda-mental to the development of capitalism and neglected by older production-based theories – required the systematic destruction of the medieval moral economy, along with all its culturo-legal conventions regulating wages and prices, and the subsequent normalisation of lightly regulated competitive individualism, usury and exploitation. The deracination of traditional forms of law, culture and economics was combined with an upheaval of family and community relations, which cast out the atomised individual into a milieu of unforgiving socioeconomic competition. Central to this process was the diffusion of the laws of primogeniture and entail – confined to the aristocratic stratum in other parts of Europe – throughout the social structure, removing both the security of land and property rights and the guarantee of inheritance for children. The young individual was socially deracinated and cast out to survive in an economically and socio-symbolically hostile outworld, which carved out a libidinal void susceptible to the integration of new ideology at the same time as it stimulated the primary human condition of prematurational anxiety, producing a chronic form to combine with suspicion and resentment, a constant nagging presence across the individual's life-course. The early bourgeois individual was 'incentivised' to become an asocial competitive economic actor in the most psychologically fundamental form.

The cultural consequences were profound; the capitalist project was established alongside the withdrawal of the institutionalised form of unconditional love, which was replaced by a fake benevolentism and sentimentalism. Individuals were thrown out of the frying pan of the violent defence of honour and property to an uncomfortable pseudo-pacified life on the embers of a controlled fire, hopping around and unable to settle. Anxiety, resentment, opportunism, privatism, competitive individualism, a rejection of community and common fate and myriad other emotions were compressed together and sublimated into a fragile pseudo-pacified socio-symbolic form and connected to commodified objects, in order to energise the individual as a competitive actor and harness this energy to the economy. What was created at this epochal point in history was not a rigid social structure but a complex process of loosely structured diffusionary cell division as social units constantly formed themselves only to be split into competitive actors.

The transition to capitalism also undermined the whole traditional culture and society that reproduced the dignity of dependency and interdependency, replacing these constitutive social norms with loose, precarious figurations in which the individual's value became dependent on successful economic performance in competition with others, which is always subject to the logical rules and vagaries of markets. Values that once maintained an erotic relationship to the transcendental ideal and also reproduced relatively fair and stable socioeconomic relations on the ground were deracinated and redeployed to the task of restraining the overstimulated proto-symbolic drives of the obscene Real. Thus values that once inspired human beings to greater things became an irksome fetter, obstructing the instant libidinal gratification that these obscene drives demanded. The libidinisation of the market was present in a growing body of renaissance art and literature (Jameson 2010), but it had to be combined with *la douceur du commerce* (Hirschman 1977), a cultural expression of the pseudo-pacification process's economically functional mode of systematised drive, desire and mollification. By the eighteenth century this had mutated into Hutcheson's 'calm desire for wealth' (Eagleton 2009: 15). The great expectation placed on the capitalist subject was essentially a double-bind comprising the simultaneous commands to succumb to one's overstimulated libidinal drives and compete against others to gratify them, but in pacified, socially acceptable forms, an immensely difficult task for all formal and informal institutions of socialisation.

The traditional control system, once a product of the construction of the super-ego during the Oedipal phase, had to be externalised, bringing upon us the expansion of the detested state apparatus and its rationalised bureaucracy; in a sense, by succumbing to the power and gratificatory pleasures provided by the pseudo-pacification process, and despite the liberal controlologists' constant complaining, we got what we deserved. We saw no genuine, articulated and organised opposition to this process until the Romantic idealism of the late eighteenth century and the proletarian political movements whose heyday stretched from the 1850s to the 1980s (Lea 2006; Hall 2012). The West was swept up in a consumer–capitalist socioeconomic process fuelled by obscene drives and made supple and unstable by the normalisation of systemic infidelity, both required by the logic of what would by the nineteenth century become a globalising system of industrial and commercial exploitation. At its uncontrolled extremities it allies with *death-drive* to become a sociopathic dis-economy populated by a normative 'juvenile psychic apparatus … prematurely and systemically affected by contemporary pharmacological toxicity' (Stiegler 2011: 156). Long processes of individuation, identification and care cannot survive when the dialogic milieu is shorn of meaningful symbols, which over the course of this process were replaced by inherently disposable objects.

Obscene drives were overstimulated by removing the security of community and the creative inspiration of the transcendental ideal and its politics, then re-sublimated and harnessed by the consumer–capitalist economy to fix desire on the symbolism carried by commodified objects. All this overheated libidinal energy had to be contained by a weak and reluctant super-ego reoriented to pleasures rather than restraints, and supported by an expanded external control system. These are the two sets of forces that, held in undialectical tension and refused an articulate political language, constitute the dynamic yet fragile and unstable pseudo-pacification process. From past qualitative research and theoretical work (Winlow 2001; Winlow and Hall 2006; Hall 2007; Hall *et al.* 2008) it is possible to extrapolate further that the pseudo-pacification process creates an infantilised culture locked in the Imaginary and reproduced in the contrived benevolentist and sentimentalist breathing space that was carved out by bourgeois culture between the obscene drive of the Real and the reformulated law of the Symbolic (see Hall 2012). It is, to borrow Bernard Stiegler's term, *pharmacological* in the sense that curative and toxic forces are systematically placed in tension to produce dynamism. The toxic part of the drive is overstimulated as the transitional object is removed and libidinal energy is transferred away from its social task of the care and reproduction of the 'ideal' community to the narcissistic task of identifying with consumer objects, whilst the curative force is re-functionalised as a repressive brake placed on the 'liberated' libido. It fuels, sublimates and pacifies the libidinal economy by sustaining a condition of objectless anxiety and torment in which headless drives can be stimulated to their full power; by no stretch of the imagination can this be named a 'civilising process' or a 'pacifying process'.

For Stiegler (2011), capitalism is essentially a libidinal drive-based economy. The birth of the marketing industry in the USA in the 1920s represented the final triumph of the modernist–capitalist techniques designed to ensure that libidinal energy no longer binds the drives and channels them through pleasurable desire towards the transcendental ideal. The common imagination is entirely short-circuited and its space colonised by pre-packaged imagery

(Adorno and Horkheimer 1992). This engulfing of the imagination is the initial point of repression required to stimulate libidinal energy and incite desire whilst at the same time desocialising and depoliticising the individual; drives do not produce just energy but torment, and the tormented individual seeks a strange hybrid of hostile companionship in adversity; the other should be a friend, but only to share a torment that the self wants to see the other suffer from too. Consumer capitalism operates not by means of 'technologies of discipline' as vehicles for biopower but 'technologies of spirit' – mass media, cyberspace, personalised digital communication, mimetic information flows – as vehicles of *psychopower*; conquering markets to produce new constellations of symbolic objects around which new models of life and subjectivities are formed is now more important than simply increasing productivity (Stiegler 2011). In a libidinal culture, the external control system can function only as the restraining mechanism in the pseudo-pacification process; it is neither primary nor constitutive, therefore 'social reaction' is no longer the central force in criminological aetiology.

The libidinal economy organised and reproduced by consumer culture is highly criminogenic (Hall *et al.* 2008; Mucchielli 2010; Moxon 2011). The subsequent destruction of public power, the creation of political decadence, the negativisation of human rights and their placement on the boundaries, and the hollowing out of transcendental ethical drives from the core of culture all combine to constitute the perfect climate for the rise of public–private criminal partnerships between governmental actors and organised crime. Serious criminal *undertaking* is an attempt to escape the mundane everyday grind and temporal instability of the system – but not the system itself – by levering the individual up to a summit of *special liberty* (see Hall 2012) to gain dis-honorary membership of the ranks of the plutocratic elite, where s/he does not escape but at least controls and benefits from the system. The *criminal undertaker* is an influential role model in difficult or opportunistic circumstances, operating and seeking special liberty in various nodes and arteries of markets and social structures (ibid.).

Post-revolutionary Cuba presents us with an interesting case study of the pseudo-pacification process struggling to stabilise itself with the aid of its various agents in a hedonistic consumer–criminal economy. Since the revolution in 1959 Cuba has been a Christo-communist society that has attempted to reconstruct the link between present, past and future by rebuilding the political community. Libidinal energy has been cathected away from consumer capitalism onto alternative transcendental objects by establishing a heroic cultural hegemony revolving round its legendary revolutionary heroes and the sacrifices they made in the task of combatting evil in the name of the good society. If socialised efficiently, Cuban citizens are indebted to the sacrifices of their ancestors, not to the capitalist banks and media–marketing industry.

Cuba has a long history of heroic struggle. Anti-colonial struggles began in earnest in 1892, with the foundation of the Cuban Revolutionary Party, led by the poet and intellectual José Marti (Villaboy and Vega 2010). However, in the midst of the tough military struggle of the *mambís* against the Spanish colonialists, the USA, in the early stages of its project of cultural, economic and geopolitical domination of the globe, had its eye on the island, and took advantage of the situation. McKinley's government whipped up public sympathy for the independence movement, which legitimised US intervention in 1898. The Spanish signed a peace treaty but no independent state was created, and this hiatus allowed the US Protectorate era to begin. From 1899 the new Republic was tightly controlled by the USA, which dismantled Cuban representative bodies and set up a US-friendly Constitutional Assembly, the central hub in a hegemonic attempt to Americanise the economy and culture. The so-called 'special relationship' that characterised the Protectorate period from 1902 to 1933 essentially became one of neo-colonialism. The Cuban government borrowed $35 million from private US investors, trapping it in a cage of debt, the servicing of which hampered social programmes aimed at combatting poverty, illiteracy and unemployment. From this position of indebtedness a pattern of weak, supine and corrupt liberal or conservative governments was established, largely in the pocket of a partnership of US business oligarchs and government administrators, who embarked on a programme of economic restructuring favourable to US interests, which added mono-cropping and over-dependency on the US sugar market to the debt relation, tightening the USA's political grip on the island.

In the 1920s, inspired by the sacrifices of Marti and others, revolutionary independence movements began to grow again amongst students and intellectuals. The Communist Party of Cuba was founded in 1925, but in the same year Machado's dictatorship was also established. Machado repressed these new movements quite viciously, further consolidating the 'special relationship' with the USA. Nevertheless, strikes and protests burgeoned in the early 1930s, which marked the beginning of a period of long-term political resistance. A fearful and disapproving USA, terrified of the Soviet threat and in desperate need of maintaining markets during the Great Depression, responded by intervening in Cuban politics to enable powerful US financial organisations to penetrate the Cuban economy. The entrance of US ambassador Benjamin Sumner Welles in 1933, following orders to reorganise the traditional power structures in Cuba to facilitate the incursion of US financial operations, coincided with the beginnings of Mafia involvement. The Mafia piggy-backed on the economic incursion and took advantage of the socio-political chaos and the succession of short-lived, supine governments.

The USA sought the socio-political stabilisation of Cuba, but, on the other hand, it did not want to risk independent growth via a strong sugar export trade. In 1934, a reciprocal trade agreement further strengthened dependency by forcing Cuba to accept tariff concessions of up to 60 per cent and the ensuing Costigan-Jones law, granting Cuba 29.4 per cent of the market, stabilised the sugar market at a low level (ibid.). Consequently, in 1935, the US Foreign Policies Association was forced to look for alternative controllable means of developing the economy. The gangsterised libidinal economy that was to follow was not part of the official plan, but, in a situation that required a compromise between ethics, politics and economics, it was clandestinely encouraged by the rapidly consolidating triumvirate of the CIA, US corporations and supine Cuban politicians. Between 1937 and 1940, the financially adept Mafia operator Meyer Lansky built the foundations of a Cuban business empire in the shape of nine casinos, six hotels and, a little later, a race track, which began to generate more profit than the mainstream Cuban economy (Cirules 2010).

When Batista took over in Cuba in 1940, the war effort forced the USA to increase sugar imports. This further enriched the Cuban economy, and from 1943 a period of intensified Americanisation began as transport links were expanded. The liberal politician Grau San Martin returned in 1944, further strengthening the relationship with the USA, maintaining order and guaranteeing sugar production, a situation that was to continue with Prio in 1948. Under these 'tough liberal' administrations corruption flourished and politicians established further economic relations with Cuban and US gangsters, opening up politics to further criminal influences. However, the US government was also very keen to present to its own and Cuba's essentially conservative populations a clean image of their politico-economic involvement; corrupt politics, CIA skulduggery and the expanding libidinal economy arranged by the Mafia were not developments they sought to reveal to the public in too sharp a relief. Batista took advantage of gathering conservative disapproval from both sides of the Caribbean, and took over in a coup in 1952 on a remit to deal with gangsterism. However, it had become integrated in the political economy, so Batista instead focused on creating the impression of repressing and controlling it whilst it flourished and further incorporated itself into the mainstream as a hidden force.

After the Depression and the Second World War, the perennial problems of excess production and surplus capital absorption immediately reared their heads. Any combination of criminalised and legitimised capitalist forces was considered acceptable by the US elite if it could create new 'restructured' markets to absorb the surplus capital desperately seeking developmental outlets and thus postpone for as long as possible the eventual return of recession. The development of the libidinal economy thus took place in the context of neoliberal restructuring, which was imposed on numerous Latin American countries with economically and socially disastrous results. Cuba was dependent on its sugar export trade and imports from the USA. US protectionism and its manipulation of tariffs impeded economic diversification and autonomous economic development, causing the decline of shoes, dairy products, textiles and other industries (ibid.). The US corporate-influenced government wanted economic alternatives on the island that did not threaten the dependency relation and neoliberal restructuring plans, and thus it became one of the largest centres for money-laundering, which boosted the informal economy, which in turn became a normalised aspect of the culture as large sectors of the population confronted even greater impoverishment than they had done under Spanish colonial rule. Large-scale land ownership by sugar producers had collapsed much independent and communal farming, leaving huge areas of disused land. This was another part of the process of systematically under-developing strategic sectors in order to increase dependency. The middle classes did well out of the new leisure economy, but a vast urban underclass and impoverished rural peasantry had grown as 'business' displaced produc-tive agriculture and industry. Such was the socio-political tension caused by economic strangulation and social inequality that even the World Bank, in its Truslow Commission report of 1950, feared trouble, recommending remedial measures of cautious diversification, improved transport, education and poli-tical administration. None of this was ever implemented, an oversight that allowed socio-political tension to increase.

However, despite this mounting tension, the USA was determined to carry on and develop the Cuban economy according to its own ideological, economic and geopolitical interests. During the post-war era investment poured into the US tourist market and it burgeoned. Havana was marketed as a 'rumba heaven', a sub-tropical paradise, a liminal space in which the repressed drives could be 'liberated'. Just below a rather diaphanous veneer of respectability operated a sordid and lascivious consumer culture founded on drink, drugs, sex and gambling. Hotels, casinos and brothels sprang up like mushrooms, fol-lowed by an attendant sub-economy of profiteers ranging from money-launderers to drug suppliers, prostitutes, confidence tricksters, black marketeers and private security operators. The spectacle of movie stars, showgirls, cabaret, casi-nos, sexual affairs and assassinations of government officials, all broadcast by radio, news movies and the new TV apparatus, enraptured populations in the Americas and Europe. The urban poor and the beggars were largely ignored, and the rural poor labouring under the work regimes of the oligarchs were simply rendered invisible. The culturally driven economy became increasingly sordid, but this great reactor, generating immense toxic libidinal energy, also generated huge profits and fuelled rapid urban development; in the midst of such an intense energy field the pseudo-pacification process had to work at its most efficient.

To simultaneously maintain economic restructuring and deal with rising social tension the US government helped place Batista in power; he oversaw an efficiently repressive state that gave the discontented middle classes office and a sense of purpose, and expanded the state sector and the service economy to soak up some of the economically disenfranchised working and peasant classes. The US government also tacitly supported Batista's repres-sion of Fidel Castro's revolutionary forces (Cupull and González 2009). Allen Dulles, head of the CIA, visited Batista in 1955, expressing pleasure at the President's handling of the economic and political situation. However, the political triumvirate knew that at the centre of Havana's economic develop-ment was the legalisation and tacit encouragement of the Mafia's lucrative business activities. They saw Batista as the political key to cooling down and stabilising the vital pseudo-pacification process in order for it to operate at its peak efficiency.

In essence, this economic project demanded a localised suspension of the great historical struggle to civilisation and a departure from the traditional symbolic imagery that structured a whole culture of sublimation that can be sourced back to courtly love, which is still commemorated by Latin American traditions such as *la quincenera*, a symbol of the protected, gradualist transition of teenage girls into social and sexual maturity. Between 1948 and 1959 this suspension was at its most potent, and in the space it carved out a manifestation of the symbolically de-functionalised libidinal economy in its purest form that was allowed to flourish, based largely in Havana. The need to drill straight down to the psychic bedrock of chaotic drives required the rapid clearing a way of the political and symbolic economies and their transcendental idealist objects, an abrupt desublimation moving back from the sophisticated libidinal displacements of politics, aesthetics and productive work to the primitive energy of the drives, fixating them on the 'stupid pleasures' of the consumer economy (Žižek 2008). However, as we shall now see, to act as agents of a pseudo-pacification process operating at such a peak of efficiency and in constant danger of overheating required suitable character and application.

Although they had been operating in Havana since 1933, the Mafia really took off in 1938 when Batista persuaded the government that it was a good idea to increase the city's gaming revenues. Meyer Lansky had been at the centre of Mafia operations from the beginning, and his old school-friend Charles 'Lucky' Luciano joined him in 1947. Lansky operated efficiently, quietly and discreetly, yet his ruthless reputation pervaded business and political circles. He had been born into a respectable middle-class Jewish family in Grodno on the Polish–Russian border, an informal refugee town with a strong Jewish community that had a reputation for fighting back against anti-Semitic attacks. In 1911 the family emigrated to the USA, at a period when US culture was becoming little more than a functional consumerist appendage to its developing production systems (Stiegler 2011). The family eventually settled in New York, and, despite his good academic and conduct record in school, Lansky quickly became involved in the juvenile criminality that pervaded the tough neighbourhood.

Meyer Lansky, it seems, rejected his father's humble values in the way that seems quite common amongst young criminals (Hall *et al.* 2005) and dreamt of being rich (Lacey 1992). He grew up in the criminal milieu of New York's Grand Street, where prostitution, loan sharking, fencing and illegal gambling were rife. Lansky met 'Lucky' Luciano – Salvatore Luciania – as a young boy. In 1921 Lansky left the tool-shop in which he had secured employment to begin pimping and running illegal alcohol, the first steps on the road to becoming a full-time gangster. Very early in his career he learnt to establish relations with corrupt politicians. He admired the well-known 'fixer' Arnold Rothstein, and saw immediately where the power resided in the classic period before organised crime fragmented into the multiple, fluid networks of today;

not in the actual performance of criminal activity but in its central 'business' organisation. He learnt that successful crime was transactional, all about making myriad short-term deals and matching up various fleeting opportunities in a complicated flux of multiple relations before they evaporated (Scaduto 1976). He also followed the norm of being willing to maim and kill in order that 'things should get done'; he became a quintessential ruthless 'undertaker', willing to both risk and perform the infliction of harm on others in the interests of the self (see Hall 2012).

The murder of Rothstein in 1928 opened up a power vacuum. Lansky and Luciano pitched in to the violence and murder that had burgeoned in the chaos, but even in the midst of the mayhem they both knew that whoever could organise a more corporate approach would become very rich indeed (Lacey 1992; Scaduto 1976). Lansky's Mafia associates marvelled at his maths, which he had polished up at night school, and his membership of the Book-of-the-Month-Club. Lansky tended to operate at a more sophisticated and ostensibly respectable level than his Mafia associates; he read basic economics textbooks, paid taxes and often dealt with bank cheques rather than cash. Despite their similar backgrounds and their fervent belief in business and the rights of individuals to financially enrich and defend themselves by any available means, Luciano and Lansky tried to move away from the Capone-style thuggery and libidinal ostentation that prevented the Mafia from developing the veneer of respectability that would allow moves into the realm of legitimate business.

However, from the beginning it became clear that whilst Lansky was suited to the task of becoming the embodiment of pseudo-pacification, with powerful libidinal drives controlled by advanced strategic normative practices, Luciano was not. In their formative years Luciano was always more ostentatious and incautious, less sensitive to public opinion and less aware of the art of stimulating the drives of others as well as himself. Lansky always looked at 'what pulls at the core of a man' (Lacey 1992: 85) – sex and gambling being the favourites, particularly gambling, satisfying the sybaritic barbarian's desire for gratification without effort – but also what can be done to hide, restrain and harness the terrifying libidinal forces he was releasing behind a screen of faux respectability. Additionally, he attracted trust by developing the art of being seen by others to succeed without expending too much effort, using too much violence, making too many mistakes or allowing his raw libido to land himself in trouble, the most effective means of making others feel confident in his ability to get things done.

Luciano was different. Like Lansky, he had learned his criminal trade under Arnold Rothstein, but he was attracted towards the riskier drug market, and by 1921 had become New York's largest importer and wholesaler of illegal narcotics, pulling a rather reluctant Rothstein into the trade. He also established the essential commodity market for bootleg liquor during the Prohibition era and made significant inroads into corrupt labour unions, acting as an arbiter in disputes that were usually settled in terms favourable to management, and, when that failed, supplying strike-breaking thugs. Where Rothstein and Lansky were restrained, Luciano was quick-tempered with a liking for weapons. He favoured enterprise in risky markets, surrounding himself with the accomplices necessary for effective operation, including Lansky, but tending to be mistrustful of them all. He experienced difficulty in the adoption and implementation of the strategic normative practices that are absolutely crucial to a criminal who operates with such a high level of libidinal intensity in most aspects of his criminality. He was attracted to Lansky's restraint and organisational capacity, perhaps because he recognised their absence in his own character, and trusted him more than the others. Luciano tried hard, dressing conservatively, minding his manners in public, setting up numerous legitimate businesses, getting rid of the nickname 'Lucky' and the tattoo, avoiding the mobster joints and cultivating liaisons with politicians, society figures and businessmen. But something burned in him, generating an irrepressible and volatile energy.

The lawless, anarchic Prohibition era seemed to excite Luciano, although everyone was chastened by the infamous Valentine's Day Massacre in 1929, which had considerable repercussions. His high sex drive was difficult to conceal; he invested large sums of money in Broadway musicals largely in order to get amongst the chorus girls. He was a quick-fire serial monogamist and occasional polygamist, occasioned to exercise restraint only when he became worried about a lingering case of syphilis that kept flaring up. He was not as violent or lascivious as Capone, a notably incompetent agent of the pseudo-pacification process, and thus lasted far longer in organised crime. We can suspect a high libidinal intensity but a lower level of restraint than that of Lansky, an early sign that, as an agent of the pseudo-pacification process, Luciano might struggle. Together, however, the pair constituted an effective partnership. With Lansky's help, Luciano reorganised the diverse and chaotic US gangs of the 1920s into the 24 larger and more coordinated business groups that made up the modern US Mafia. However, Luciano could not shake his habit of offending conservative society just that little bit too much. Eventually he was arrested for being involved in the organisation of a prostitution ring. After his trial in May 1936 he was convicted and imprisoned. Lansky attempted to use political contacts to organise his release, but the attempt failed because of unfortunate election results for the principal contact. Luciano was released in 1945 after helping with military operations in Sicily, but he agreed to voluntary deportation to Italy.

During Luciano's time in prison Lansky intensified Mafia operations in Havana. During this post-Protectorate period of political and socioeconomic destabilisation, the foundations of this joint US government/corporate/Mafia operation had to be replaced and strengthened; what had been done politically had to be redone all over again economically. Between 1937 and 1940 the weak liberal state had become extraordinarily pliable and accommodating; they turned a blind eye to the Cuban banks' illegal money-laundering, and by 1949 $1 million per day was flowing into Cuba (Cirules 2010). Lansky was trusted by President Roosevelt to broker political deals, and dissuaded the more hard-line and interventionist Batista from standing for election in 1944, which ensured the return of the pliable liberal Grau San Martin (ibid.). As an agent of the pseudo-pacification process applied locally in an intense and lucrative form, Lansky was performing well. In 1946 Luciano arrived in Havana from Italy via South America. He joined Lansky, whose long-term awareness of Luciano's failure to control the various ways in which his libidinal energy was manifested made for an uneasy partnership. Under Lansky's close stewardship, Luciano was introduced to local dignitaries and the leaders of Mafia families operating in Havana. As an unavoidable by-product of all this social networking, however, Luciano's name was quickly established in the public eye. At an early 'big meeting' in the Hotel Nacional de Cuba prostitution and sex were involved, but the organisers managed to keep it relatively discreet and low key; bodyguards slipped into the background, doors remained closed and no journalists or politicians were invited. Lansky and others ensured that the public face of the vast Mafia leisure industry was represented by established stars – including Frank Sinatra – whose image was that of wholesome, family entertainers, the sanitised idols of the 'bobbysox' generation. Luciano did the circuit of casinos, dances, parties and horse races in a low-key Lansky-like manner, initially keeping his nose clean, and settled in the respectable middle-class Miramar district (Lacey 1992).

However, Luciano's new liaison with society girl Beverley Paterno began to attract journalistic attention. This glitch in the PR exercise was out of Lansky's hands, mainly the fault of an external publicity agent hired by Paterno, whose professional efforts were the source of numerous news items broadcast in Cuba and the USA. In late 1946 Luciano arranged a party in the Hotel Nacional on behalf of an American actress who had flown over to see him. He invited only a small number of his more expectantly hedonistic friends, but the uncontrollable informal PR network made sure that news of the famous star's visit had spread quickly across the island, eventually reaching a Convent School full of teenage girls from wealthy conservative families. Twenty of the girls hired a bus, bought flowers and, chaperoned by a nun, set off to give the actress, whose wholesome romantic movies had captivated the public on both sides of the Atlantic, a reception to show their appreciation. When the party arrived on the ninth floor they were led by an incautious bellhop through a half-open door straight into the detritus from the previous night's party, which had developed into nothing short of an orgy; the room was adorned by drug paraphernalia, empty rum bottles, discarded lingerie, used condoms and naked bodies. A report of the encounter passed from the schoolgirls to the Mother Superior, the Bishop and other bastions of old conservative authority (Cirules 2010). The mask had slipped.

There are allegations that the whole episode had been arranged by the US Commissioner of the Bureau of Narcotics (Sondern 1959), or even that Lansky and the CIA were behind it (Cirules 2010). The US government intelligence services, powerful players in the US Mafia, and of course Lansky, probably wanted rid of Luciano because they simply did not trust his ability to control his libidinal drives, and there was enough of a scandal amongst the conservative old guard in both Cuba and the USA to legitimise their next moves. Luciano had been a major figure in the modernisation of the Mafia, but there was still enough of the bullet-ridden and syphilitic Capone-like barbarism inside him to present a constant threat to both its public image and the stability of its socio-political network and lucrative business operations. His old-school buccaneering demeanour, his drug operations, his hot temper and his unruly libido constituted an embarrassment to the US government as they were attempting to defeat Soviet-style communism and diffuse a post-war cultural hegemony over the globe. Besides, US government officials, bankers and investors by now all had high stakes in the Cuban leisure economy. All parties had been warned by Lansky that a delegitimising climate was brewing in Cuba as the socioeconomic conditions of the poor did not improve and suspicions were increasing amongst conservative and revolutionary forces who shared the same distaste for decadence. It was important enough for the US government to arrange a blockade of pharmaceutical products in order to bully Grau's government into arranging Luciano's departure in 1947. The Mafia's business interests in Havana did not decrease but increased, but they were carried out in a more discreet manner. Luciano's threat to the operation was the unfortunate and intractable fact that he was an amateurish and unreliable operative of the pseudo-pacification process's vital strategic normative practices; he suffered from a surfeit of libidinal drives and a deficit of sublimatory sensibilities and rational calculation.

These business interests were vast, constituting a giant corporate network far different and far more efficient than traditional Mafia operations. In the Batista era, from 1954, the Mafia/CIA/Government triumvirate arranged the consolidation of banks and trusts into a respectable formation, and links with international finance, efficient money-laundering processes and the constant strengthening of the shield of respectability (Cirules 2010). The blurring of the legal and the illegal reached a new level of sophistication in a corporate business network. At the centre was the tourist industry: hotels, restaurants, casinos, nightclubs, recreation centres and resorts. Ancillary businesses included career training for service workers, channels for drug trafficking and clandestine consumption, multiplex gambling – including horses, dogs, charades, boxing, numbers games, slot machines and bingo – precious gems and jewellery, specialised escort and prostitution services and contraband, the latter enhanced by the expansion of duty-free zones in ports and airports. Mafia interests established themselves at the heart of the Cuban economy, not just banking, finance and investment but transport, department stores, refurbished sugar mills, distribution agencies and insurance companies. They also infiltrated and controlled the political and military system by financing political parties and programmes, arms dealing and setting up private intelligence agencies, all organised efficiently by a centralised business administration working closely with US and Cuban deep security states. Luciano, out of time and out of place, was now the last person they wanted.

In 1950 Lansky moved back to live in Havana, immediately reasserting himself at the heart of the vast operation, using his relationships with politicians, military personnel and businessmen in Cuba and the USA to stabilise operational processes. In 1955 Batista legalised business affairs in a network of Cuban banks to facilitate a huge investment of more than $1 billion, also arranging tax, licensing and land ownership concessions on behalf of the Mafia and large US corporations. Lansky's name appeared numerous times in the press, but he avoided the suspicions and scandals that had always hovered over Luciano. Lansky drank milk in public, and wore plain clothes. He did his rounds of hotels and leisure centres, but avoided parties. His 'special meetings' were held behind closed doors and a virtually impenetrable security net in a luxury suite in the Hotel Riviera. Unlike Luciano, he gave vent to his drives and desires alone: he drank Pernod laced with opium alone in his room in the early hours of the morning, looking at the sea through an open window. During the day he toured the city in his car, doing his rounds, quietly, discreetly and punctually. He used a discreet hand-picked chauffeur and bodyguards. He was never seen to entertain prostitutes, showgirls or actresses, and never known to raise his voice in public. He preferred to do as many dealings with Cubans as possible in private, slipping quietly into the presidential palace for meetings with Batista. He sustained a long-term relationship with an equally discreet mistress in Havana, who owned a chain of brothels and supplied discreet high-class prostitutes for himself and visiting business associates, but he was never ostentatious (Lacey 1992).

Lansky was driven by the same obscene Real that drove Luciano, but the former's mode of sublimation and economic harnessing was far more developed, sophisticated and discreet, the embodiment of an individual agent building new markets by operating at the heart of the pseudo-pacification process. In contrast, Luciano broke the process's fundamental social rule. The creation of the pure entrepreneurial space requires the clearing of politics and social symbolism. Because politics are always mired in some legitimation crisis and some form of corrupt practice, the first is easier than the second, and diplomatic moves had to be made towards the Catholic Church and attendant ethico-cultural traditions reproducing *la verguenza*, the modesty and shame on which all civilisations are founded. Such socio-symbolic practices and their resulting subjective sensibilities are essential for intergenerational transindividuation, a process in which the reproduction of the long circuits of reflexive desire into which individuals are collectively bonded is dialogically activated to symbolise and communicate the transcendental ideal (Stiegler 2011). American gangster capitalism proceeded by fostering the illusion that it was not wholly dependent on the stimulation and pacification of obscene drives, and that these ethico-cultural traditions were safe in its hands. In reality the destruction of political infrastructures and processes of cultural reproduction and intergenerational transindividuation are essential to the operation of the pseudo-pacification process and its subsequent economic success. Luciano broke the illusion of suspended disbelief by clumsily manifesting the obscene Real that underlies the consumer capitalist economy.

References

Adorno, T. and Horkheimer, M. (1992) 'The culture industry', in T. Adorno and M. Horkheimer, *Dialectic of Enlightenment,* London: Verso

Cirules, E. (2010) *The Mafia in Havana*, Melbourne: Ocean Press

Cupull, A. and González, F. (2009) *The CIA Against Che*, Havana: Editorial Capitán San Luis

Eagleton, T. (2009) *Trouble with Strangers*, Chichester: Wiley-Blackwell

Elias, N. (1994) *The Civilizing Process*, Oxford: Blackwell

Hall, S. (2007) 'The emergence and breakdown of the pseudo-pacification process', in K. Watson (ed.) *Assaulting the Past,* Newcastle upon Tyne: Cambridge Scholars Press

——(2012) *Theorizing Crime and Deviance: A New Perspective*, London: Sage

Hall, S., Winlow, S. and Ancrum, C. (2005) 'Radgies, gangstas and mugs: imaginary criminal identities in the twilight of the pseudo-pacification process', *Social Justice*, 32 (1): 100–12

——(2008) *Criminal Identities and Consumer Culture*, Cullompton: Willan

Hirschman, A. (1977) *The Passions and the Interests*, Princeton, NJ: Princeton University Press

Jameson, F. (2010) *Valences of the Dialectic*, London: Verso

Johnston, A. (2008) *Žižek's Ontology*, Evanston, IL: Northwestern University Press

Lacey, R. (1992) *Little Man: Meyer Lansky and the Gangster Life*, London: Arrow Books

Lea, J. (2006) *Criminology and History*, from John Lea's Criminology Website: http://www.bunker8.pwp.blueyonder.co.uk/history/36801.htm (Retrieved 11 May 2011)

Moxon, D. (2011) 'Consumer culture and the 2011 "riots"', *Sociological Research Online*, 16 (4): 19

Mucchielli, L. (2010) 'Are we living in a more violent society? A socio-historical analysis of interpersonal violence in France, 1970s–present', *British Journal of Criminology*, 50 (5): 808–29

Scaduto, T. (1976) *Lucky Luciano: The Man who Modernised the Mafia*, London: Sphere Books

Sondern, F. (1959) *Brotherhood of Evil: The Mafia*, New York: Farrar, Straus and Cudahy

Stiegler, B. (2011) *The Decadence of Industrial Democracies*, Cambridge: Polity

Villaboy, S.G. and Vega, O.L. (2010) *Cuba: A History*, Melbourne: Ocean Press

Ward-Perkins, B. (2005) *The Fall of Rome and the End of Civilization*, Oxford: Oxford University Press

Winlow, S. (2001) *Badfellas*, Oxford: Berg

Winlow, S. and Hall, S. (2006) *Violent Night*, Oxford: Berg

Žižek, S. (2008) *Violence*, London: Profile

——(2010) *Living in the End Times*, London: Verso

3 The neoliberal harvest

The proliferation and normalisation of economic fraud in a market society

Jörg Wiegratz

Introduction

The global capitalist economy of the 2010s is characterised by a significant and apparently rising level of economic trickery, fraud and crime in many business sectors – and related to this we often find associated corruption and intimidation. These sectors include not only the trade in arms, drugs and human beings but also industries and sectors such as manufacturing, agro-business, food, supermarkets, pharmaceuticals, hospitals, elderly care, banking, accounting, insurance, marketing, emissions trading, military and telecommunication services, housing and construction (e.g. UNODC 2011; Friman 2009; Levi 2008; Whyte 2007; Black 2005; Callahan 2004).

Notably, fraud has been 'mainstreamed' in the formerly 'purified' Global North: readers of the major newspapers in Britain, Germany and elsewhere are confronted on an almost daily basis with the newest revelation about harmful illegal practices in the corporate sector, from banks and waste management to online ticket sales. In particular, there seems to be an expansion of organised fraud in the everyday economies and markets for legal goods and services. Notably, some of the flagship organisations and big household names of Northern capitalism have been linked to fraud: Goldman Sachs, Deutsche Bank, Barclays, Siemens, Nestlé, News Corp, and so on.

Indeed, the list of contemporary fraud cases is long and remarkable when it comes to the economy; add to that the recent publicised cases of fraud, corruption and crime in the various polities around the globe and the prevalent discourses about predatory and crony capitalism, powerful oligarchies, elite criminality, or moral crisis and bankruptcy. This social reality is a significant analytical puzzle and raises crucial questions. What does the empirical significance of these practices tell us about contemporary capitalist societies? What is the political–economic and normative context in which these practices are embedded? What are the values and norms – and especially moral codes – that shape and govern these practices of elite and non-elite actors, both in the Global North and Global South? What explains the shift, if any, in these practices and their structural underpinnings since the end of the Cold War and the accelerated neoliberalisation of not only global commerce but also many societies around the globe?

The argument of this chapter is that contemporary forms of economic fraud, trickery and deceit can be analysed fruitfully through an understanding of the cultural political economy (CPE) dynamics of a neoliberal market society. In this view, the apparent proliferation and normalisation of fraud is in significant ways an outcome of the extensive neoliberal restructuring and transitions of the past decades, at both the political–economic and normative levels. This includes the re-calibration of the moral underpinning of the economy, society and polity; a process that can be called neoliberal moral restructuring (Wiegratz 2010).

Significant levels of fraud, I argue, are to a large extent an outcome of the extensive and simultaneous changes in both the political economies (PEs) and moral economies (MEs) of a range of social sub-systems – across economic sectors, the state, communities and so on – in the societies that have undergone neoliberal transformations. It is an outcome of the accumulative effect of the interaction of both these changes and their broader repercussions. My own research into these matters in Uganda further suggests that the intensification of fraud is in many ways a manifestation of the political–economic and moral–economic views, interests and priorities of very powerful actors (i.e. political, technocratic and economic elites), both domestic and foreign, as they impact on, dominate and re-engineer the political moral economy (PME) of a country and thus the context and conditions in which others live and work. In other words, fraud trends – and the distribution of the benefits and costs of fraud – are to a significant extent a function of the morals of the powerful (Wiegratz 2010). In this chapter I will attempt to explain what fraud has to do with political moral economy; and in so doing I will address dominant moral norms, power structures and relationships, and matters of power and vulnerability, welfare and harm.

Notably, a number of Western social scientists seem to have been surprised by the extent of the fraudulent underpinnings of the recent financial crisis of the late 2000s and also of much of the contemporary global economy in general. There could be many reasons for this significant analytical neglect of the crucial role of fraud in capitalism (despite Marx's early lead) including: (1) the low level of empirical studies of actual economic practices, while an abstract market and actor model continues to dominate the field (Carrier 1997); (2) the considerable disinterest in investigating micro-level political–economic and moral–economic phenomena at the level of practice; (3) a particular belief in the basic diligence and non-fraudulent orientation and operation of the typical Western capitalist firm and actor, and the pro-honesty tendency of the 'free market' mechanisms (ibid.); and (4) an overall neglect of the study of norms in actually existing capitalist social formations, that is of the actual, operational, practical and latent norms (Boggs 2010; Olivier de Sardan 2008; Streeck 2010) that play a role when people act, and more importantly interact, in order to make a living, survive, escape poverty, be successful, become and remain wealthy and powerful, and so on. In sum, what Western science has not studied as extensively as it perhaps should – especially when it comes to Western economies – is how people, both directly and indirectly, interact with and treat one another in the economic sphere, what the bundles of norms, values, orientations and practices (hereafter: NVOPs) in specific set-ups are, and how social context and NVOPs interact over time.

Had the study of fraud a more prominent place in the social sciences throughout the last century, the recent fraud dynamics would perhaps have come as little surprise, and there would be extensive academic debates given the availability of new and telling fraud cases. Instead, while we have no shortage of scholars discussing the global economic crisis in rather conventional terms, we have – with some notable exceptions – minimal debate about economic fraud; its many facets and implications and what it tells us about structure, agency, social change, power, accumulation, democracy and so on. To a significant extent then, there is business as usual post-2008. This situation prevails while fraud appears to be 'the new normal' in a number of neoliberal societies and has triggered substantial problems for affected individuals and communities.

Given the above, a stronger scholarly engagement with the realities of fraud and the related bundles of NVOPs and power structures would allow us to challenge conventional social science narratives and models about the capitalist market, organisation, actor, practice, culture, society, and sources of wealth, poverty and power. This analytical move is long overdue. Indeed, 'taking capitalism seriously' (Streeck 2010) and investigating its major actual institutional – including moral–economic – properties and dynamics at the level of practice seems not only highly relevant but also fruitful to move various academic debates forward, or rather to revisit apparently settled old issues.[1]

Moralities and moral economies of defrauding (and harming others in the process)

Why should we consider going for a moral economy analysis of fraud? Can there be a moral underpinning to the structures and practices of fraud, or of exploitation, violence and harm? Indeed, we are often told by proponents of the various camps that this is a foolish thing to argue. One claim for instance is that the only relevant or influential norm and aim of action in capitalism that we need know about is profit/income maximisation. In this view, the profit rationale is so powerful among both elite and non-elite actors – i.e. effectively enforced by 'the system' – that a more advanced investigation into the theory and the practice of norms of production and trade is of little worth, or is even misleading and naive because it distracts the analytical attention away from the profit theme. Discussing morals in this context would mean moralising something that is purely economic and can neither be analysed nor challenged via a morality analysis. Hence, our research should be pre-occupied, in this view, with material forces and outcomes. And in any case, morality is an instrument of the powers that be.

This view underestimates or narrows the role of norms (and culture more broadly) in capitalism, both regarding the constitution and reproduction of the capitalist status quo, in driving the system, and in challenging it. Morals can be used by both the suppresser and the suppressed, for various reasons: to justify order, hierarchy, power, privilege, exploitation, injustice, inequality, defrauding, harming and killing, or to challenge and resist these things (Thompson 1971; Trotsky 1973; Gramsci 1971). Morals can be used to justify (and set up and reproduce) specific harm-producing or -intensifying structures, relationships and practices or to challenge them and search for alternatives.

Other views are that capitalism is amoral or immoral, that morals or ethics should not be an economic matter, or that the supposed macro-benefits of wealth and social welfare – and the market competition principle – justify pretty much any (legal) practice however unjust or exploitative.

There are important issues that these views often neglect. For instance, a number of these views are based in some ways on the assumption that morality is only or necessarily about the (objectively) good and desirable, for example an ethical life, about social obligations or care, or about good, virtuous character and altruistic behaviour; and that morality is about acting according to universal, 'agent-neutral principles' (Levine 2007: 148). This overlooks the fact that norms justify and legitimise actions, whether 'good' or 'bad'; harmful, exploitative and socially regressive, or not. In other words, moral norms are not necessarily pro-social.

Unblocking morality research

If one focuses on morality in our thematic context, it is helpful to analytically address morals in a particular way. What makes norms interesting for the study of how capitalism is operationalised and reproduced in a concrete setting – constituted via concrete human relationships, practices, and interactions – is that they coordinate actions with cognition (beliefs, feelings) and, importantly, are socially constituted action justifications (Keller 2006: 169).

Moral norms in particular can be considered as 'standards of interaction concerning others' welfare' (ibid.). They justify or endorse specific practices, and thus specific ways to relate, interact with and treat other human beings and consequently affect their level of well-being. They constitute, govern and express what is regarded as acceptable and unacceptable, proper and improper, legitimate and illegitimate[2] behaviour in the light of moral principles – such as justice, care, solidarity, fairness, decency, reciprocity, authenticity, reliability – in a given country, region, locality, sector or organisation (ibid.: 169–74; Thompson 1971; Scott 1979; Carrier 1997, 2005; Block 2003; Sayer 2007). In other words, moral norms or morality is about how people are *expected* to behave or ought to behave in interactions with other people and also how people *actually* interact with and treat each other, which points to the issue of actual or operative norms or principles that exist in a specific time–space context. A norm gives behavioural guidance: for example, when experiencing condition x do y because of z. A moral norm can then be seen to be about to what extent and in which way the well-being of others matters in a social context where one's actions affect, directly or indirectly, the lives of these others.

Again, one does not need to assume that the kind of behaviour that is expected is pro-social; the moral norm can also be that one should exploit, defraud, harm, mistreat, oppress or eliminate another human being (or social group), for example to survive, to advance or defend one's own power and wealth position or that of one's own social group, corporation, nation, country. For example, generals and soldiers are expected to engage in and are rewarded for dominating and harming others, conquering enemy territory and so on. There are countless analogous examples from non-military contexts too. In our analysis then, to refer to a moral norm or actor, or to a moral economy, does not automatically mean pro-solidarity, honesty, good, social.

Rather, in the context of studying the moral underpinning of the whole spectrum of practice in specific social configurations it is helpful to keep in mind that a moral norm here refers to a standard of interaction that is, in some way, socially derived and learnt. At the same time, the norms are always also interpreted, adjusted, reinvented and circumvented by social actors (Streeck 2009). Thus, which practice is seen to be acceptable and which is not depends on the empirical context.

In this understanding, a harsh, exploitative, brutal or deadly war zone, prison, factory, gold mine or Nazi camp is a moral order or moral economy too; the inter-actor relationships and practices are embedded in or governed by certain standards of interaction and notions of what is acceptable (or proper, legitimate, desirable) practice. For instance, I can (read: it is justified to) exploit, defraud, kill or otherwise harm you – hence, discount or disregard your welfare – because you are, in my or our view, inferior, powerless, sub-human, or, a prisoner, worker, threat, foreigner and so on.[3]

From the above, it follows that to study the morality in economic life, including the morals of fraud, attention needs to be paid to: (1) interactional practices, (2) the action justifications of the actors involved,[4] including how (a) others' welfare is articulated in these justifications and (b) what is considered acceptable, normal, legitimate, good – or unacceptable, bad, illegitimate – practice and how these things are explained, rationalised or defended, and (3) the broader context of political and moral economies in which these actions and justifications are embedded.

In this reading, analysis of the moralities of actually existing economic practice, in capitalist or non-capitalist systems alike, presumes that all practice has a moral underpinning, or, in other words, is informed by notions of both standards of interaction regarding others' welfare and of what constitutes acceptable/unacceptable practice.[5] All actors are then moral actors. Our identities, motives, actions and relationships have a necessary moral connotation. They are informed, shaped and underpinned by a set of moral norms, principles, understandings, reasoning, valuations, preferences, choices and relationships. And, all economies are moral economies in the sense that all economic orders, relations and practices have moral dimensions, preconditions and implications (Thompson 1971; Block 2003; Sayer 2007).

Thus, analytically speaking, the existence of fraud (or exploitation, intimidation, violence) in a concrete case does not mean the absence of moral norms but, on the contrary, signifies the presence of particular moral norms, views and codes which need empirical investigation. Equally important then, the analytical issue is not erosion or decline of morals (or norms generally), but the change or transformation of morals, that is, for instance, the shift from pro-social moral norms to pro-self-interest moral norms, and so on.

My argument is therefore that moral norms (and their specific content) shape the level, form and characteristic of, for instance, exchange, surplus appropriation, exploitation, fraud, injustice and violence as well as cooperation, solidarity, fairness in an economic locality. In other words, in the daily reproduction of capitalist structures by way of social practice, the issue of moral norms as defined above comes in centrally: the norms[6] that shape how one thinks about, values and evaluates the welfare of other human beings with which one interacts to make a living, income or profit. By definition then, changes in levels and forms of fraud signal not just a change in the political economy but also the moral economy of a place. Moreover, in a given social situation, there is usually a variety of *categories* of norms at play, including official, professional, social and practical norms (Olivier de Sardan 2008). Also, norms in a given economic structure and locality are not homogenous or always explicit and conscious (Zigon 2008), but rather diverse, contested and changing over time.

Consequently, and to come back to my earlier point, the normative structure that shapes economic practices in day-to-day interaction, thus constituting capitalist structures of accumulation, exploitation, fraud, cooperation, trust and so on, is likely to be more complex and nuanced than the basic imperative to maximise profits. Put simply, the profit assumption alone does not tell us if, when and to what extent an economic actor should be honest or dishonest, considerate or inconsiderate, uncooperative or cooperative, open or secretive, benign and fair or callous; use legal or illegal, violent or non-violent, environmentally destructive or sustainable means of generating income from an economic structure, relationship and interaction. At the minimum, the objective of profit making has to be operationalised – i.e. broken down or translated – by historically situated actors into more specific norms which 'fit' their life and the concrete context of their social interaction.

Further, the profit motive could be expressed and rationalised in different ways and thus point to different normative, political–economic and socio-cultural underpinnings. It can generally come with a mix of other norms that can, for instance, radicalise or moderate, and in any way qualify the profit rationale; I need/want to make money/take advantage of you because of x, or y, or z. It is thus useful to think of a multidimensional bundle of norms – and values, orientations, beliefs, ideas – that plays a role when it comes to the underpinning of economic practice, including cooperative or fraudulent practice.

Following from that, I argue that we get a better analytical footing regarding the cultural political economy of morals within capitalist social systems if we understand these norms to be about: (1) what is seen as acceptable, justified and normal and what is not, and (2) the interaction standard regarding the welfare of others. There can then be norms that suggest that it is acceptable and proper to deceive others and pay little or no regard to their welfare in the process. Thus the analytical imperative for the study of capitalist relationships and practices is not just to 'follow the money' (as in *The Wire*) but also to follow the norms. To better understand, reconstruct and predict the manner, form, regularity and logic of specific practices, one needs to get an analytical grip on the normative underpinnings of a situation. This includes the specific conditions that are attached to a norm and thus trigger norm-conforming behaviour and set exceptions or conditions as to when the norm does not apply.

Finally, I use the term moral economy to refer to the context-specific combination of social actors, relationships, NVOPs (including moral norms as defined above), structures, relationships and distribution of power, structures of inequality, of welfare and harm, of wealth and poverty, among other things. Various moral and other principles – as well as relevant political and other factors – shape what is regarded as acceptable and unacceptable practice for the social actors in a particular moral economy (Thompson 1971; Carrier 2005). Importantly, neoliberal moral economies differ in key aspects from non-neoliberal moral economies. In any case, as Watson (2005: 179ff.) notes:

> Patterns of behaviour within market arenas are shaped by prevailing social institutions, which in turn reflect the dominant political orientation of society ... What counts as acceptable behaviour is related to political decisions about dominant social institutions in a society in which the market is embedded.

Thus you can't have a moral economy without a political economy. Elements of what is commonly understood as the political economy (class relationships, distribution of power, conflict patterns, the state, regulation, policies, etc.) are actually also components of the moral economy. Equally, elements of the moral economy (i.e. NVOPs) are components of the political economy. A specific moral economy is underpinned by a specific political economy, and so on. Thus, a term like political moral economy (PME) rather than moral economy (that is linked with a particular reading of E.P. Thompson's work) could reflect this empirical situation. In any case, it is crucial to study, more than we have to date, actually existing moralities as both an empirical and political phenomena.

Of course, the principle argument about the moral economy of economic fraud – or generally the normative underpinning of harmful social practice – is well established in criminology and there is an important literature into relevant aspects (e.g. Wikström 2010; Karstedt *et al.* 2006; Hall *et al.* 2008). However, it seems that in moving forward, the study of the moral economies of fraud has to consider, more than to date, some of the key political–economic and moral–psychological aspects of the theme, become more fieldwork based and study relevant dynamics in the countries of the Global South. Taken together, the above could enhance theory building significantly.

Towards a history of the norms of social practice in capitalist social configurations

From what we have so far, it follows that the normative and political–economic underpinning – in short, the political moral economy – of the whole spectrum of regular social practice in capitalist social configurations needs to be studied and explained: from 'good' to 'bad', from intimidation, fraud and violence to cooperation, honesty and trust. Key questions are: What is the bundle of norms, values, orientations and practices (NVOPs) – and the corresponding institutions – that overtly or covertly support, endorse and legitimise structures, relations and practices of hard bargaining, exploitation, intimidation, deceit, crime and violence in social formations? What are the NVOPs and institutions that promote practices of moderation, self-restraint, mutuality, fairness and cooperation in economic contexts? Why and how do the practices and their normative underpinning change during social transformations, and what are the relevant political–economic aspects?

A final point: historically, specific forms of capitalism require, produce and thrive on specific NVOPs; for instance, values that express what is a desirable goal (e.g. to be powerful, rich, independent, successful, dominant, or, show concern for the welfare of others) and norms that legitimise and endorse certain practices (e.g. to engage in fraud, to repress, exploit and harm another human being, or to be other-regarding and cooperative).[7] Hence, capitalism in its different phases – from slavery, colonial, imperial, fascist capitalism up to Fordist, social–democratic, neoliberal, American, Anglo-Saxon or Asian capitalism – was enabled, operationalised and reproduced by particular norms, values, orientations and practices and thus based on specific normative orders or regimes. For example, white supremacist racism, religion, Eurocentrism, modernity, enlightenment, paternalism, elitism, careerism, materialism, instrumentalism, cynicism, militarism, brutality, violence, obedience, conformity, discipline, rationalism, bureaucracy and so on (e.g. Losurdo 2011; Blackburn 2010; Rediker 2008; Engelhardt 2007; Zinn 2005; Bauman 1989).

Analytically, we are looking at a centuries-long continuum: the spectrum of structures, relationships and NVOPs in capitalist social configurations. In all phases, there was variation in the dominant NVOPs – or political moral economies – according to specific places and their power structures and relations. This is to say that there were dominant NVOPs while other, non-dominant NVOPs were also in existence. Powerful structures and actors, directly and indirectly, tended to favour, advance and spread norm *a* rather than norm *b*, and therefore work against and destabilise norm *c*, and so on. Moral economy researchers should have a lot to learn from revisiting the history of (1) capitalist (and other forms of) moral restructuring and (2) the political moral economy of harming others in the course of the last centuries. What then is the link between the NVOPs that are becoming dominant under neoliberal–capitalist conditions and the contemporary prevalence of fraud? Let us look at some aspects of the normative underpinning and dynamics of neoliberal capitalism.

Neoliberal transformations: marching towards the market society

Neoliberal reforms can be interpreted to aim at the emergence and con-solidation of market societies characterised by free-market capitalist social relations, corresponding subjectivities, the hegemony of capital and a set of respective dominant NVOPs. The restructuring thus targets not just the economy, but also the polity, society and culture in the respective countries. It is an ambitious programme of global social engineering (Harrison 2005, 2010). The reforms have to undermine, overwrite and displace – as far as feasible – pre-existing non-neoliberal NVOPs among the population, and to foster neoliberal NVOPs. Countries undergoing neoliberal transformations can be conceptualised as marching towards this ideological end point: market society. The cultural political economy study of neoliberalism as a cultural programme tries to focus on the simultaneous restructuring of the normative and political–economic underpinnings of society.

Building on our earlier discussion, it can be argued that neoliberal moral restructuring in particular is about changing what is regarded as acceptable and unacceptable, proper and improper, legitimate and illegitimate, or praiseworthy and blameworthy behaviour in the light of moral principles. Re-engineering morals entails changing the criteria by which people evaluate their own and each other's actions,[8] and reordering the power structures and relations, or the relative power of actors and social groups, in a particular social space, so as to foster neoliberal morality proponents and agendas. This process has top-down, bottom-up, intra-top and intra-bottom dimensions.

Though there will be variations from case to case, neoliberal moral restruc-turing is arguably about making the self-interest principle the hegemonic or overriding moral norm. In addition it is about fostering dimensions of a blatant '*homo economicus*' including cost–benefit calculus, individualism, and dis-position and behaviour to maximise utility, instrumental rationality, egoism, low other-regard and empathy, opportunism and cunning and an emphasis on transaction-based relations and disregard for the common good (e.g. Slater and Tonkiss 2001; Harrison 2005; Ferguson 2006; Giroux 2008; Streeck 2009). Key pillars of the neoliberal moral economy are money availability, wealth accumulation, consumption, individual preferences, choice, self-interest, freedom, the power of capital.

A major moral code of the neoliberal doctrine is: maximise your own self-interest (utility) in every situation and you will maximise social welfare (Beckert 2005). Rationalise, calculate and maximise your business; do not consider other-than-gain imperatives. Neoliberal doctrine links self-interest, acquisitiveness and ruthlessness at the micro-economic level to welfare at the macro-economic and societal level (ibid.). Social welfare is the unintended macro-level consequence of the micro-level self-interest maximisation of autonomous individuals. Unrestrained self-interest is seen to be beneficial for social welfare; no other moral motivation or reflection is required.

As regards the actors who are the 'drivers' of change, their actions and/or the processes that they set in motion are in part intended but also unintended, conscious and unconscious (Streeck 2009). At the same time, processes of neoliberal change are interwoven and interact with other, both newer and older forces of transformation: urbanisation, technological change, modernisation, commodification, secularisation, population growth, and so on.

Neoliberal reforms in the country that I have studied the most, Uganda, but also elsewhere, have targeted almost all social sub-systems: banking, agriculture and other economic sectors, collective economic institutions such as cooperatives, the political system, general administration, business regulatory institutions, the police and judiciary, the education, health and arts systems. Via restructuring these societal systems and institutions, the deeper aim and effect of the reforms is to restructure the systems and relationships of authority and power the structure of the sources and distribution of power and wealth, the context in which people have to live, the systems of thoughts, feelings and actions, subjectivities, sensitivities, sociabilities, families, communities, NVOPs, beliefs, language, discourse and judgment criteria (see Harrison 2010). This and other research work (e.g. Reiner 2007; Hall *et al.* 2008) suggests that there is a strong link between these neoliberal reforms and the fraud/crime trends in the restructured societies. I will now highlight a few findings from my research in Uganda and then briefly conclude.

The case of neoliberal Uganda: the hardening of moral economies

This research sought to advance the study of the normative underpinnings, dynamics, effects and repercussions of neoliberal policies, programmes and transformations. It investigated (a) the various sites, actors, processes, outcomes and implications of the neoliberalising of the moral–economic structure, and (b) the ways in which normative restructuring is intertwined with political–economic restructuring in a local setting. It explored how the structures and NVOPs that impact on inter-personal relationships and interactions in a local economy were reshaped in the course of neoliberal transformations.

The analysis of the process of neoliberal moral restructuring focused on how the reforms have changed the moral economy of agricultural trade in eastern Uganda. The study explored which NVOPs were promoted, directly and indirectly, by the reforms and how these have interacted with and reshaped the prevailing NVOPs. The chiefly interview-based research tracked, explained and interpreted the changes in the NVOPs by exploring people's experiences and views regarding the changing moral economy of trade. The relationships between people's orientations, motivations, actions, action justifications and explanations and the respective wider existing action context (widespread poverty, unemployment, economic crisis, inequality, insecurity, power asymmetries, state corruption and violence) were also explored.

The key finding was that the foreign-induced reforms and their effects have negatively affected the trade relationships and practices between smallholder farmers and traders (including middlemen, brokers and larger domestic and foreign companies) in the study area. Liberalised market transactions were characterised by higher levels and changing forms of 'malpractice', and a modification of their moral underpinnings. There was a significant level of deceit, intimidation, violence, corruption, 'riding the system', and a specific way to view and act upon the vulnerability of other human beings. Practices based on honesty, fairness, cooperation, solidarity and long-term considerations came under pressure.[9]

The specific structure and operations of neoliberal moral economies, in interaction with neoliberal political economies, contributed to the (re-)production – and often deepening – of poverty, vulnerability, uncertainty, inequality and specific structures of exploitation, abuse and violence in economic relationships. A major change was the re-calibration of various power structures and relationships in a social configuration, especially between (very) powerful and (very) weak actors. Neoliberal transformations heightened the vulnerability of many actors, and changed (or reinforced) the way in which certain powerful actors in the respective economic settings (a) perceive, think about and act upon the vulnerability of weaker actors and by extension social groups, and (b) view and exercise their own power in this context. This had repercussions for what certain powerful actors regarded as normal and acceptable economic practice, i.e. the normal rate of bluntness and/or deceit.

The research identified particular views of the relationship between a vulnerable and a powerful person that were significantly fostered and institutionalised due to neoliberal changes: how one views and acts in a situation of power and vulnerability; how the powerful actor could or should use his/her power; whether, when and why any restraint should be applied, and how to feel about these matters. In some research sites, vulnerability of others was increasingly seen as a business chance to make more money – also often involving the use of deception, theft, intimidation, extortion, etc. Significant poverty and financial pressures, and/or material and social ambitions underpinned these views. Mechanisms of moral disengagement (Bandura 2002) were evident in some of the interviews with traders: actions were justified in a specific way, the consequences ignored or played down, the victim dehumanised, the blame shifted, and moral responsibility displaced and diffused. Moral economies of survival were common: Many people reported that the difficult economic situation they were in forced them to drop their previous moral commitments and engage in deceptive trade at times; and they regretted this. Others had fewer emotional concerns about the effects of their deception on others.

The various action logics were embedded in a particular perception of the national and local political economy and moral economy, specific arguments about (1) the available and optimal options and feelings of the powerless,[10] (2) one's own and the other's (moral) agency, and (3) who deserves what, when and why in the economy. Notably, as the market society evolves, there is also a complex differentiation, fragmentation and individualisation (e.g. according to economic experiences, including the exposure to fraud) in the perception, understanding of and reasoning about moral issues and related NVOPs; this impacts on action justifications.

Within this context, deception and fraud has increased across many economic sectors: from the bank, microfinance, telecommunication and health, to the agro-industry sectors. There were notable vertical and horizontal knock-on and reinforcement dynamics within and across the various political moral economies. For instance, as large coffee buying firms step up fraudulent practices or as fraud and corruption increase in the police, bank, land regis- tration and road building offices, in standards and other business regulatory agencies, in schools, hospitals and factories, the financial pressure to deceive each other rises among those at the bottom of the capitalist 'value chain', i.e. when already defrauded (by the large buyer, traffic police, etc.) the village coffee trader and peasant have to fight over their shares of the remaining 'surplus'. Indeed, the mentioned neoliberal shifts have profound implications for the political–economic and normative structures in which many poor and vulnerable actors have to earn their living, reproduce livelihoods and try to survive and stabilise or improve their economic and social conditions. Importantly, a neoliberal dimension was in one way or another always present in the investigated fraud cases; thus, the reference to 'the neoliberal harvest' in the title of this chapter. This is to indicate that the contemporary intensification of fraud that can be observed in Uganda and elsewhere is a systemic repercus- sion of the planting and now blossoming of neoliberal–capitalist 'seeds' in their various forms in almost all sub-systems of a society. In Uganda's case, the significantly neoliberalised socio-economic, cultural and political structures, among others, provided a fertile ground for the spread and institutionalisation of a number of specific action justifications (some of them pre-existing) that in turn fostered fraud trends further.

Notably, the state apparatus regularly (and often violently) suppressed efforts of various actors – from farmers to workers and formal opposition groups – to de-neoliberalise their local and national political moral economies. Furthermore, recent state actions to address some of the escalating fraud and 'malpractice' trends (e.g. via the Uganda National Bureau of Standards and various crackdown-type task forces) had mixed results. Not surprisingly, these measures have their own effectiveness issues as well as political–moral–economic tensions and dynamics: renewed state violence, intimidation, corruption and organisational infighting, and (further, deepened or renewed) cycles of uncertainty, insecurity, injustices and impoverishment for many of the affected already poor were a regular feature of them.

An empirically informed theory of capitalist systems of economic interactions?

The study showed how crucial and fruitful it is for social scientists interested in matters of moral economy, fraud and economic practice generally to detect the actual norms, read action justifications, and their social making, via qualitative empirical research. Notably, the reported trends in Uganda are not unique to that country; we find them in other countries too. More generally, the findings confirm what Streeck (2009: 27–9, emphasis in original) considers to be key characteristics of the 'typical' capitalist actor and neoliberal–capitalist action norm:

> 'Opportunism with guile' … represents the normalized ethos in the enactment of institutions in a historical context, in which a competitive breach of solidarity is in principle socially licensed and can never in any case be prevented or ruled out, and where restricting competition is fundamentally less legitimate than engaging in it … Actors in capitalism, therefore, given their characteristic non-traditionalist restlessness, appear *constitutively devious* from the perspective of the institutions that are supposed to govern them. The typical rule-taker in capitalism is a rule-*bender*: He reads rules entrepreneurially, i.e., 'in bad faith,' incessantly looking for ways of interpreting them in his favor. Typical capitalist actors are rational–utilitarian exploiters of gaps in rules, in a culture that fundamentally approves of innovation in rule following, if not in rule violation, and has few legitimate means to enforce informal traditional standards of good faith. Creative enactment or non-enactment of rules may, after all, be an important source of profit, and can routinely be justified as a necessary preemptive defense against elimination by competition.

Equally, taking advantage of and gaining at the expense of others can be seen to be a core pillar of a capitalist normative structure (Streeck 2010: 21–2); embedded, normalised and reproduced in a culture:

> In which rational–egoistic advantage-seeking at the expense of others cannot be morally condemned and, if successful, is in fact entitled to the admiration even of those who find themselves left behind … Competition exists where there is a social license for actors to try to improve their position at the expense of others. A license to compete implies a license to behave in a way that is the opposite of solidarity. Capitalist political economies are characterized by the fact that they hold out very high rewards to actors who skilfully and innovatively breach norms of solidarity in order to enrich themselves, even if this means impoverishing others who are less successful.

We can find plenty of examples of the above-mentioned spirit among the global neoliberal business and political elites: take only Lehman Brothers and other investment brokers who, according to their own accounts, sold their risky and eventually useless products preferably to the old, weak, relatively poor, 'stupid', 'naive'. This became known as the prevalence of the NINJA ('No Income, No Job and No Assets') loans to weaker actors in the context of the subprime crisis. It is worthwhile to investigate the years-long making – from top to bottom – of the political moral economies of this and similar cases. It would be an important contribution to our understanding of the actual NVOPs – and respective dynamics – in capitalist organisations and societal structures and the role of the political economies in the making of the moral economies.

Concluding remarks

'Neoliberal' moral codes seem to be widespread across the global economy and to underpin many cases of economic crime therein. Importantly, contrary to popular discourse, neoliberalism is not 'dead', 'bankrupt' or 'collapsed'. The market society project has for the most part not been abandoned by the rulers and elites that continue to govern our political moral economies. The longer-term and deeper-level dynamics and repercussions of the unfolding of the market society project are not behind us, but ahead of us. Overall, our collectives continue to march, by design and default, towards advanced market societies; plenty of seasons of neoliberal harvests seem yet to come. However, the market society project is contested, increasingly on normative or cultural grounds. There are struggles for non-neoliberal and non-capitalist moral economies; they usually face opponents, especially at the political–economic side of the conflict.

Given this, the research from Uganda and elsewhere shows (see also Thompson 1971): moral and political–economic (or material) structures and dynamics are interrelated; moral issues are intertwined with power issues. To reproduce one's morals one needs resources, including money. To undermine the dominant societal position of the morals of others (i.e. socially regressive actors), one needs to destabilise, weaken and dry up their sources of power, that includes their financial but also cultural and symbolic power; the new movements from Occupy to UK-Uncut (i.e. anti-tax evasion protests) have translated this insight into praxis.

Notes

1 The remaining part of this chapter draws on Wiegratz (2010).
2 Or, right/wrong, good/bad, praiseworthy/blameworthy, responsible/irresponsible, permissible/forbidden, normal/abnormal behaviour. I will refer to the 'acceptable/unacceptable' pair in the remaining text. Implicitly, the pair then refers to the other pairs mentioned here too.
3 Note that this analytical approach – i.e. to conceptualise a factory, a war zone and so on as a moral order and moral economy as well – is part of a descriptive not prescriptive morality analysis.
4 This can also be called the respondents' moral universe or 'moral cosmologies' (Slater 2010: 283).

5 Economic relationships and practices are also always moral because of the inter-connectedness of people's welfare and the well-being–harm nexus; practice always affects others' welfare.
6 And therefore also: the moral assumptions, understandings, meanings, sentiments, distinctions, valuations, reasoning, preferences, choices, principles, frames and logics.
7 See Schwartz and Bilsky (1987) on values.
8 I owe this point to James Carrier.
9 The term 'malpractice' is used as a heuristic tool to group and analyse practices that are characterised by negotiation and transaction relevant deception, trickery, manipulation, intimidation or use of force, theft and corruption in market affairs. Note that economic fraud was existent in the country's pre-neoliberal phase of capitalist restructuring too; most respondents however were of the view that the fraud (and corruption) level in neoliberal Uganda is historically unprecedented and respective NVOPs more institutionalised than in the past.
10 E.g. inform yourself, learn the market, sharpen or toughen up, join the game, try your luck.

References

Bandura, A. (2002) 'Selective moral disengagement in the exercise of moral agency', *Journal of Moral Education*, 31: 101–19

Bauman, Z. (1989) *Modernity and the Holocaust*, Ithaca, NY: Cornell University Press

Beckert, J. (2005) 'The moral embeddedness of markets', Max Planck Institute for the Study of Societies (MPIfG), *MPIfG Discussion Paper*, 05/6, Köln: MPIfG

Black, W.K. (2005) *The Best Way to Rob a Bank is to Own One*, Texas: University of Texas Press

Blackburn, R. (2010) *The Making of New World Slavery*, London: Verso

Block, F. (2003) 'Karl Polanyi and the writing of the Great Transformation', *Theory and Society*, 32 (3): 275–306

Boggs, C. (2010) *The Crimes of Empire*, London: Pluto Press

Callahan, D. (2004) *The Cheating Culture*, New York: Harcourt

Carrier, J.G. (2005) 'Making rough places plane: moralities and economies in environmental conservation in Jamaica', paper for Moral Economy Conference, Lancaster University
——(1997) 'Introduction', in Carrier, J.G. (ed.) *Meanings of the Market*, Oxford: Berg

Engelhardt, T. (2007) *The End of Victory Culture*, 2nd edition, Amherst: University of Massachusetts Press

Ferguson, J. (2006) *Global Shadows*, Durham: Durham University Press

Friman, R.H. (ed.) (2009) *Crime and the Global Political Economy*, London: Lynne Rienner

Giroux, H.A. (2008) *Against the Terror of Neoliberalism*, Boulder, CO: Paradigm

Gramsci (1971) *Selections from the Prison Notebooks*, New York: International Publishers

Hall, S., Winlow, S. and Ancrum, C. (2008) *Criminal Identities and Contemporary Culture*, Cullompton: Willan

Harrison, G. (2005) 'Economic faith, social project, and a misreading of African society: the travails of neoliberalism in Africa', *Third World Quarterly*, 26 (8): 1303–20
——(2010) *Neoliberal Africa*, London: Zed

Karstedt, S., Levi, M. and Godfrey, B. (2006) 'Introduction' to special issue 'Markets, Risk and "White-Collar" Crimes: Moral Economies from Victorian Times to Enron', *British Journal of Criminology*, 46 (6): 971–5

Keller, B. (2006) 'The development of obligations and responsibilities in cultural context', in: L. Smith and Vonèche, J. (eds) *Norms in Human Development*, Cambridge: Cambridge University Press

Levi, M. (2008) '"Organised fraud": unpacking research on networks and organisation', *Criminology and Criminal Justice*, 8 (4): 389–420

Levine, A. (2007) *Political Keywords*, Oxford: Blackwell

Losurdo, D. (2011) *Liberalism: A Counter-History*, London: Verso

Olivier de Sardan, J.-P. (2008) 'Researching the practical norms of real governance in Africa', The Africa Power and Politics Programme (APPP), *APPP Discussion Paper*, 5, London: APPP

Rediker, M. (2008) *The Slave Ship*, London: John Murray

Reiner, R. (2007) 'Neo-liberalism, crime and justice', in Roberts, R. and McMahon, W. (eds) *Social Justice and Criminal Justice*, London: Centre for Crime and Justice Studies

Sayer, A. (2007) 'Moral economy as critique', *New Political Economy*, 12 (2): 261–70

Schwartz, S.H. and Bilsky, W. (1987) 'Toward a universal psychological structure of human values', *Journal of Personality and Social Psychology*, 53: 550–62

Scott, J.C. (1979) *The Moral Economy of the Peasant*, New Haven, CT: Yale University Press

Slater, D. (2010) 'The moral seriousness of consumption', in 'Panel discussion: Critical and Moral Stances in Consumer Studies – Juliet B. Schor, Don Slater, Sharon Zukin and Viviana A. Zelizer', *Journal of Consumer Culture*, 10 (2): 274–91

Slater, D. and Tonkiss, F. (2001) *Market Society: Markets and Modern Social Theory*, Cambridge: Polity Press

Streeck, W. (2010) 'Taking capitalism seriously: towards an institutional approach to contemporary political economy', *Socio-Economic Review*, 9 (1): 137–67

——(2009) 'Institutions in history – bringing capitalism back in', *MPIfG Discussion Paper*, 09/8, Köln: MPIfG, also published in Morgan, G. *et al.* (eds) *The Oxford Handbook of Comparative Institutional Analysis*, Oxford: Oxford University Press

Thompson, E.P. (1971) 'The moral economy of the English crowd in the eighteenth century', *Past and Present*, 50: 76–136

Trotsky (1973) *Their Morals and Ours*, 5th edition, London: Pathfinder Press; first published 1938

United Nations Office on Drugs and Crime (UNODC) (2011) *Estimating Illicit Financial Flows Resulting from Drug Trafficking and Other Transnational Organized Crimes*, Research report, Vienna: UNODC

Watson (2005) *Foundations of International Political Economy*, Basingstoke: Palgrave

Whyte, D. (2007) 'The crimes of neo-liberal rule in occupied Iraq', *British Journal of Criminology*, 47 (2): 177–95

Wiegratz, J. (2010) 'Fake capitalism? The dynamics of neoliberal moral restructuring and pseudo-development: the case of Uganda', *Review of African Political Economy*, 37 (124): 123–37

Wikström, P-O. (2010) 'Explaining crime as moral action', in Hitlin, S. and Vaisey, S. (eds) *Handbook of the Sociology of Morality*, New York: Springer

Zigon, J. (2008) *Morality*, Oxford: Berg

Zinn, H. (2005) *A People's History of the United States: 1492–Present*, London: Harper Perennial

4 Theorising the prison–industrial complex

Ioannis Papageorgiou and Georgios Papanicolaou

In the following pages we aim to take a closer look at the idea of the 'prison–industrial complex' (PIC). While we propose to query this idea from a theoretical viewpoint, our interest in it is underpinned by significant political concerns. An entire stream of radical, academic and activist work appears to rely on this idea in order to make sense of and mount a critique against the growth of the penal state and the explosion of racialised prison populations in the United States (e.g. Davis 2003). According to this idea, recent transformations in penality and the corresponding patterns of development of the penal apparatus in that country can be understood on the basis of an increasing convergence of interests between big capital, criminal justice bureaucracies and policy makers. In so far as the administration of criminal justice presents entrepreneurial opportunities and profit increasingly overtakes considerations of justice as its commanding rationale, a swelling penal apparatus not merely consolidates but rather amplifies the social, racial and spacial divides engendered by neoliberalism, and feeds upon them.

While its proponents defend this approach vigorously, on the basis of both theoretical considerations and empirical evidence, it appears that the idea sits rather uneasily with other commentators on penality. Of course, the ideological ascendancy of the right allows conservative commentators to take a derisory approach, labelling all work on the prison–industrial complex as 'laughable left-wing nonsense peddled by Marxist goofballs and other passengers in the clown car of academic identity politics' (Goldberg 2011). On the other hand, among the wider critical group that does regard the contemporary transformations of penal apparatuses as deeply disturbing, reactions towards the PIC thesis range from scepticism over the significance of the available empirical evidence (e.g. Parenti 2008) to outright rejection on grounds of projecting a misplaced and 'conspiratorial vision' of penal realities (Wacquant 2009b).

Now, no one today, at least those in the latter group, refutes the fact that repressive apparatuses have assumed an alarming centrality in the management of the social consequences of unbridled neoliberalism. While interrogating why and how this should have happened is a formidable task that invites theoretical debate, the fact that a considerable number of active and consciously radical prison activists rely on the idea of the PIC to organise thought and action points to a theoretical challenge and is politically pertinent, too. At the core of that thesis is the claim that the mechanisms sustaining the reproduction and growth of penal apparatuses appear to stand in an organic relationship with core systemic economic processes. The existence of an economic apparatus that can be understood in terms of an 'industrial complex' at the heart of the contemporary political economy of punishment would entail dramatic transformations of penal modalities. What sort of tendencies and contradictions are inscribed into such development? If such are the characteristics of penality today, how does one organise against it? What kind of oppositional, alternative social visions and strategies are possible?

In what follows we attempt to situate and unpack theoretically the debate on the PIC by surveying both the arguments put forward by its proponents and the criticisms directed against it. We find that the concept of a prison–industrial complex firmly deserves a place within an analytical framework that captures the modality of the integration of the repressive and economic apparatuses under mature neoliberalism, provided that one recognises that what is captured by it is a tendency, rather than a rigid economistic teleology, in the development of contemporary advanced capitalist societies.

A prison–industrial complex?

The entire debate on the birth and development of the prison–industrial complex has a distinctively American flavour. Private sector involvement in punishment in that country has by no means been a modern-day development (Conley 1980), but developed in the 1980s after a combination of conditions proved particularly conducive to a closer intertwining of 'tough-on-crime' and profit-seeking agendas. With public fears about crime driven to hysterical levels and prison populations reaching new record high numbers every year, criminal justice emerged as a new market for the defence and other industries and as a highly attractive field for investment for ascending Wall Street finance. Private sector interest bore the promise not only of addressing public concerns about crime, but also of job creation particularly in economically decimated areas. Unsurprisingly then, prison began to appear as 'the juiciest pork in the barrel' for politicians across the political spectrum (Paulette 1994).

While accounts of these emerging interrelations published in the mainstream financial press pointed favourably to new business opportunities, some scholarly work, diverging from the mostly technical debates on prison privatisation that intensified in the 1980s, began to raise questions about their extent and consequences in penal policy making in the USA. In an important article Lilly and Knepper (1993) explored the emerging articulation of a subgovernmental national policy network in the US penal system, comprising private companies, federal agencies and private professional organisations. The emergence of this 'iron triangle' of interests in the field of punishment occurred in a fashion similar to that of the 'military–industrial complex' (MIC), the policy network that has shaped the political economy of warfare in the USA following World

War II (Koistinen 1980), and to which we shall return soon. They thus found evidence that what they called the corrections–commercial complex showed 'signs of becoming a fixture within the national policy area of punishing' (Lilly and Knepper 1993: 161) and they raised concerns about its potential to skew sentencing and, more generally, criminal justice policy, in a more punitive direction that would sustain the involvement of private business in punishment.

Cases illustrating how the penal 'iron triangle' works have been picked up at different times by critical commentators (e.g. Parenti 1996; Lotke 1996), and they all highlight what the implications of its existence are for penal policy and prison regimes in practice. For example, following the introduction of 'three strikes' in California, exploding prison budgets and prison populations consolidated the contracting of prison labour to private firms, a possibility that was reinstated legally in that state in 1991 after it had been abolished in the late nineteenth century. Such contracted-out prison labour would engage in work from shovelling hog manure to assembling circuit boards to making telephone reservations and data entry for minimum wage or less (out of which prison authorities would deduct the cost of room and board). Performed by a 'captive workforce' lacking any rights or say over work conditions, prison labour appeared to be a good deal for private business aiming to cut down on labour costs, even though the financial gains for prisons were not necessarily high enough to cover the costs of their operation. Thus the key development in this respect for those commentators had less to do with the implications of prison labour for state budgets and more with private profiteering at the expense of prisoners' rights and conditions: 'a few firms will be making out like … bandits. In the meantime prisons are rapidly becoming maquiladoras in our midst' (Parenti 1996: 14).

The preceding observations should suffice to indicate that, in fact, there are at least two possible ways in which the question of the prison–industrial complex can be raised within critical considerations of penality. When treated as an idea used in the interrogation of the interweaving of private, policy and professional interests, the PIC has been primarily intended to capture config-urations of governance within a country's political economy of punishment; accordingly, questions of undue influence, perhaps corruption, and distortion or circumvention of established institutional processes in a democratic polity come to occupy the centre-stage. On the other hand, when the preponderant concern is the social purpose of incarceration and the experience it involves for imprisoned populations, the idea of a PIC can be used primarily to underscore the implications of the former regime for questions of justice and rights that intrinsically relate to punishment. It goes without saying that these two uses are not mutually exclusive. Rather, they are inextricably connected. However, to interrogate the theoretical status of the PIC as a concept within an analysis of the political economy of punishment can differ from using it for the purpose of providing a useful, and, as we shall see, rather established point of reference for making sense of the disparate manifestations and impli-cations of entrepreneurialism in punishment. In the latter context, a concept can perfectly function while being in a practical, or at any rate less theoretically elaborate, state.

The distance between what can be schematically[1] labelled as theoretical and activist-oriented discourses accounts for the state of the debate on the question of the PIC within the critical camp. This is not too hard to show when one considers the variations of its use in the literature. There is a minimum common denominator whereby the PIC is understood as the interweaving of private business and governmental interests, serving to increase the profitability of private corporations and at the same time expand social control, while the pronounced rationale lies with crime-fighting (Goldberg and Evans 2009). This is similar to the approach taken by Julia Sudbury (2002), who also understands the prison–industrial complex as an intricate web of relations between state penal institutions, politicians and profit-driven prison corporations. In Angela Davis's account, the PIC is extended to involve corporations, government, correctional communities and media (Davis 2003: 84), in a fashion echoing Dyer (2000), who sees in the PIC a 'political and economic chain reaction' that involves a symbiotic and profitable relationship between politicians, corporations, the media and state correctional institutions. It is clear that referring to 'interweaving', 'intricate web of relations' or 'symbiotic profitable relations' allows space and flexibility for a construction of analyses on the basis of specific cases exemplifying the reality against which a polemic is raised. But this inductive logic also denotes the practical state of the concept.

Consider conversely the point of departure for criticisms against the idea of a PIC. Wacquant (2009b: xx) openly denounces the PIC as a 'conspiratorial vision framing the activist myth', whereby a shadowy malevolent and omnipotent centre consisting of industry giants providing surveillance and punishment and private operators acting in cahoots with correction officials and politicians weave a deliberate plan to push for limitless carceral expansion aimed at exploiting the booming captive workforce. He also rejects the idea that the expansion of the PIC is dictated by some systemic need – however, one may note that nowhere in the accounts criticised (see Wacquant 2009b: 320, note 11) is the concept of the PIC constructed at levels of specificity adequate enough to allow a critique on these terms. This very same problem allows more sympathetic commentators to raise doubts about the empirical soundness of the concept: Parenti (2008), for example, approaches the PIC as a broadly Keynesian stimulus, whereby both the expansion of public spending on prisons and the direct involvement of the private sector via prison privatisation and exploitation of prison labour result in a profitability boost. But while he finds no strong empirical support for the idea constructed on these terms, the theoretical issue is by no means settled.

Complications also arise from the fact that in a significant number of accounts wherein it is being defended most vigorously, the idea of the PIC understood as an economic mechanism by no means occupies the centre-stage of the argument, at least not in the sense that the sudden and unbridled growth of punishment for profit has sprung from an inner dynamic or necessity of capitalism. Consider Angela Davis's work, which is rather characteristic of this tendency. Davis does embed a discussion of the PIC within an overarching abolitionist argument – the message of her powerful *Are Prisons Obsolete?* (2003) is exactly about a society without prison, a prospect which the emergence of the PIC and the fact that incarceration develops a distinctively capitalistic dimension makes acutely distant. But the key argument of the book involves not capitalism, but slavery, fully laden with the racial dimension it has involved in the USA: incarceration in this sense is a distinctively capitalist continuation of slavery, an idea that is inevitably underscored by the fact that more than 60 per cent of the US prison population are non-white men and women (see West 2010). By means of an investigation of the connection between race and the early penitentiaries, theoretical priority is thus reserved for the connections between prison, slavery and racist segregation and exploitation, rather than class exploitation. This preoccupation becomes clearer when Davis deals with the gendered aspects of prison – the preferential victims of modern prison are women of colour.

Furthermore, adding to the rather confusing state of the debate is the fact that while discussions pointing to the idea of a PIC can be clearly found in the older stream of radical criminology in the USA, the link is nowhere made explicit in the more recent literature. Consider, for example, how, in assessing the implications of the establishment of the federal Law Enforcement Assistance Administration in 1968, Quinney (1977: 107) spoke in no uncertain terms of the emergence of a criminal justice–industrial complex. He began from the idea that 'the state, under late capitalism, must establish the framework for capital accumulation and foster the conditions for maintaining the capitalist system'. In this context, he understood the emergence of a political economy of criminal justice as one of the fundamental characteristics of advanced capitalism. A characteristic of this is the growth of a criminal justice–industrial complex, consisting in an involvement of industry in the planning, production and operation of (state) criminal justice programmes (ibid.: 117). According to Quinney, the state in its efforts to stimulate capital accumulation and stabilise the social order, forms an alliance with the monopoly sector of the economy: 'the state provides the structure for the economic development of the monopoly sector; and the state, in turn, depends on the monopoly sector for its economic well-being as well as the services and technology for maintaining social stability' (ibid.: 117). Quinney's line of thinking was shared very explicitly by others working within the radical current at the time (see, e.g. CRCJ 1977); yet more recent work appears reluctant to invoke and capitalise upon this heritage.

Thus a certain opportunity is lost, in the sense that the idea of a PIC and the repressive reality it aims to capture cannot be effectively connected with a wider theoretical framework that, particularly in the USA, has been consistently concerned with the analysis of post-World War II imperialism. Rather, the PIC seems to be a concept that somehow is taken for granted, and mostly acts as a shortcut for denouncing exploitation, social injustice and the corruptive influence of big capital in democratic policy making. This results in obvious analytical links being very loosely exploited: for example, Goldberg and Evans (2009) do relate the proliferation of prisons in the USA with present-day imperialism and neoliberalism, but the explanatory mechanism offered is merely that prisons constitute a repressive solution substituting for social welfare under the neoliberal model for the minimal state. Davis (2003) also refers to globalisation to account for the rise of the PIC in the 1990s: it was globalisation that fuelled on the one hand the de-industrialisation of the economy and on the other the dismantling and privatisation of welfare institutions. In turn, the expansion of the prison system and incarcerated populations, both domestic and migrant, made punishment appear ripe for investment and exploitation. The question of globalisation is also raised by Gilmore (1999), who sees in the PIC a variety of Keynesianism, whereby the carceral apparatus supersedes the military and becomes key to the profitability of individual investors and the domestic economy as a whole, while at the same time being instrumental for managing surplus and marginalised populations. The PIC is (correctly) understood as a certain shield against the consequences of globalisation, but the necessary links to state theory remain all too limited.

It should be evident from the above discussion that the idea of the PIC is, in fact, used to accommodate a number of concerns regarding contemporary penal realities. It is thus no surprise that it appears a rather woolly concept. In so far as the PIC is understood as an apparatus of ideological and political domination, it is taken to account for the perpetuation of racial and ethnic inequality and discrimination. This is certainly the case in the USA, but this is a reality experienced in other Western countries in so far as the expansion of penal apparatuses is fuelled by the criminalisation of migrant populations (Wacquant 1999, 2009b). Thus while the prison has always been understood as a weapon against the poor and the marginalised, the emergence of the PIC can be understood as a new instrument of political domination either directly, through the criminalisation of domestic and international informal economies, or indirectly, through the centrality of prison in the symbolic divisions engendered by the new discourses of insecurity. On the other hand, to the extent that the PIC is understood as an economic apparatus, it is seen as the quintessence of exploitation and profiteering. Not only does it feed upon a population whose civil and legal status is severely truncated and which is thus vulnerable to exploitation and abuse whether in the form of wage or in the form of living conditions. It also lays the conditions for its perpetual expansion by virtue of the very transformation of prison into an economic apparatus, firmly embedded in local, national and international economic circuits (Dyer 2000). These two conceptions of the PIC are complementary – in so far as the conditions of its reproduction as an economic apparatus depend on its political function to expand and intensify punishment. One wonders whether the concept of the state itself is somehow superseded by the concept of a 'penal state'.

State of a debate

Since, as we have attempted to show so far, the reception of the idea of the PIC within the critical camp is marked by either a tendency to invest too much in it or a straightforward dismissal, our way of proceeding to unpack its theoretical challenges passes first through a closer consideration of the latter tendency. Considering the grounds on which the use of the idea is met with scepticism is likely to point to both its shortcomings and its strengths with more clarity.

As mentioned previously, Christian Parenti is among those who turned their attention very early to the manifestations of the emergence of a prison–industrial complex. He has recently moved on to evaluate more thoroughly the state of play in his *Lockdown America* (2008), where he organises, from within a critical perspective, his misgivings about the idea of the PIC primarily around the strength of the empirical evidence on the existence and significance of the PIC. In the 1990s he had queried for-profit prison labour (Parenti 1996), which at the time was heralded by politicians and others as an excellent solution to the economic burdens created by exploding incarceration numbers. A number of states had allowed prisons to contract out labour resulting in prisoners involved in work ranging from restocking the shelves of Toys-R-Us in Chicago and data entry in Ohio to building and fixing circuit boards for an IBM and Dell subcontractor in Texas and testing blood for medical firms in Arizona. Even then, he found that prison labour was not taking off, even though prison labour was contracted under extremely favourable terms for the industries involved. More ominously, not only did the operation of private business in the prison system not result in increased efficiency overall, but rather it has been associated with serious incidents of violence and abuse which have had an impact on its public image and prospects.

In *Lockdown America* Parenti (2008) furthers those objections by beginning from the assessment of the idea that the PIC can be seen as a form of Keynesian stimulus via public spending and prison privatisation. While carceral expansion has presented considerable business opportunities, the economic circuits that emerged around it cannot be shown to be more significant than any other private investment in the public domain and thus fully justify talk of a prison–industrial complex. What must be remembered here is that a typical starting point for this discussion is the claim that the prison–industrial complex was to supersede – to some extent – the military–industrial complex (MIC), that is, the policy network that is almost universally acknowledged to have commandeered ever-growing defence budgets in the post-World War II USA (Pursell 1972; Koistinen 1980; Hossein-Zadeh 2006). Additionally, although profit-driven interests for investment in prison contracting-out did and continue to exist, private sector involvement is still hindered by public reaction, including the resistance of prison officers' trade unions. Thus Parenti refutes the hypothesis that the expansion of the PIC balances the downsizing of the military–industrial complex, as spending on incarceration has continued to be negligible when compared with the US military budget, and the growth of the PIC cannot be compared, both quantitatively and qualitatively, with the role of the MIC in the post-war US economy. Parenti is, of course, directly addressing a key point argued by those defending the idea of a PIC most vigorously, and therefore the lack of strong empirical support for the latter dictates a scepticism for the thesis in its totality. However, one would be justified to wonder whether this kind of empirical comparison between the American warfare machine and the nascent prison industry is a sound point of departure for analysis.

Wacquant's critique appears to be of a different kind, and it is certainly hostile to the idea of a prison–industrial complex. Wacquant is nowadays recognised as one of the most forceful and sophisticated critics of contemporary penality, and he has presented a comprehensive explanation of the rise of the penal state as the result of a neoliberal strategy for the management of poverty (Wacquant 2008, 2009a). He understands contemporary transformations of penality as a partially commercialised, carceral–assistential organisational form which spearheads what he calls the nascent liberal–paternalist state, and whose mission is to 'surveil and subjugate and if need be chastise and neutralise the populations refractory to the new economic and moral order' (Wacquant 2009a: 83–4).

Now, within this framework, the idea of a PIC is thoroughly rejected as irreparably reductionist, on four main grounds. First, the idea of the PIC is judged to be based on a conspiratorial vision of history, in so far as it reduces the explanation of a contemporary twofold penal and social transformation into an explanation of an industrialisation of incarceration. In other words, the explanation of the change cannot be based on the changing scale of incarceration alone, nor on the economic motives potentially associated with this development. Economically, Wacquant claims, carceral inflation began well before the acceleration of capital mobility, let alone globalisation, and, incidentally, other countries whose levels of economic internationalisation are comparable to those of the USA have only experienced modest rises in prison populations. Politically, the growth of incarcerated populations cannot be a product of racism and discrimination alone, since due process and safeguard concerns have become much more important since the 1970s. Additionally, he claims that underpinning this transformation is a political logic, not an economic one: the penal system offers little scope for profiteering and, at any rate, privatisation is ubiquitous in the USA – this implies that some involvement of private industry is inevitable, due to American political tradition. Echoing Parenti, Wacquant also asserts that quantitatively prison labour is insignificant vis-à-vis the total prison population, and, at any rate, the output of prison labour as a percentage of GDP is negligible. In addition, the PIC erroneously brings together under the same analytical vein the military–industrial complex and penal transformation: whereas MIC depends on a highly centralised administration and policy making, the American penal system is highly decentralised and lacks an overarching philosophy of punishment. Finally, Wacquant finds that the PIC tendency refuses to acknowledge the fact that a welfarist logic (still) exists within the penal system: not only is there increased judicial oversight, but there has also been an increasing rationalisation and professionalisation of the confinement such that it has now become a key mechanism for the provision of otherwise unavailable or hard to get social services such as education and medical services or mental health provision and so on (Wacquant 2009a).

In considering the above objections to the idea of a PIC, we must return to our observation that the discussion on the PIC occurs at different registers, with activists mounting a critique of the PIC stressing particular issues, whereas more academically styled discussions allow for more balanced theses. Thus while Parenti's analysis mounts a successful critique of the PIC thesis on a point-to-point basis, it does not constitute a wholesale criticism of the idea. Rather, he criticises the tendency of the PIC literature to emphasise the exploitative and profiteering logic of the system, when in reality both the output and the economic contribution of the PIC are rather marginal and under constant challenges. It is in this sense that the idea that the PIC can be viewed, especially in the post-Cold War period, as a substitute of the MIC is untenable. Incidentally, in this respect, both Parenti's and Wacquant's criticisms of the PIC are very similar, that is, empirical, not theoretical in nature. Coming to Wacquant's objections, one cannot fail to note that at the level of the narrative of the social transformation of American labour and inner city, *both his and the PIC thesis largely coincide.* To put it simply, there seems to be a fundamental agreement as to the fact that the social change that has fuelled the widening and deepening of the control the carceral and correctional apparatus exercises over the American poor has its roots in the changes ignited by the systemic crisis of the late 1960s–1970s (Sudbury 2002).

This is not the place to engage in an extensive evaluation of Wacquant's overall project and argument. Ultimately his aim is to produce a wider theory of the penal state as a primary aspect of a new stage in the development of the state under neoliberalism. However, the approach towards the new role of the penal apparatus as an organisational form that primarily exercises a racialised and gendered form of social control contradicts his own terms. The primary aspect of the social change his narrative refers to is the disappearance of blue-collar jobs as the upshot of a globalised economy (Wilson 1997); if this is so, 'neoliberalism' cannot be understood as an abstract social force and development, but rather as a process primarily defined by *class conflict* and a project aiming to *restore class power* (Harvey 2007). Wacquant's patent reluctance, for theoretical reasons, to acknowledge class and class struggle as a factor forcefully underpinning the development of the (neo)liberal–paternalist state contradicts his own narrative of that development. In the absence of a considered analysis of 'neoliberalism' in relation to class interests, power and struggle, Wacquant's own criticisms of the PIC thesis as conspiratorial prove a boomerang: such a reading of *Prisons of Poverty,* which is rife with accounts of policy exports, transfers and transnational propaganda for the neoliberal penal policy recipe made in the USA, is, in fact, possible. But why do such ideas possess such power of conviction, and why there, why then?

The preceding point helps to highlight an important weakness of the PIC thesis itself, given that it has, after all, emerged from within an explicitly radical stream of thought. That weakness relates to the low priority given to class struggle as a formative condition of the PIC. This weakens the import of the recurrent reference to globalisation, monopoly capitalism and the mobility of financial capital: is it plausible to think that *class* struggles did not play a role by either causing this transformation or by resisting it, and thus to relegate to a secondary plane this major aspect of social transformation in the period of reference (1970s and 1980s) and the ongoing systemic over-accumulation crisis? In fact, the relative absence of such analysis appears to inform the peculiar sense of linearity or fatalism of an economist flavour in the overall PIC argument, in so far as the link between the economic developments of the last quarter of the twentieth century, the emergence of the PIC and its implications is constructed as direct and unmediated. It understands economy as an autonomous, self-fuelled system: once capital has seized a social domain, the evil consequences are inescapable.

Positioned between the two extreme points of full endorsement and outright rejection, Parenti's approach offers a constructive way forward, in so far as he does construct a class-theoretical argument. In this light, he acknowledges class struggle as the key in understanding the over-accumulation crisis of the 1960s and 1970s, the capitalist class strategy to circumvent labour and popular militancy and ultimately the swelling of the penal apparatus as a ruling class solution towards the containment of surplus populations. But what is missing is a consideration of the specific processes through which such a solution has been consolidated into hegemonic strategy. Put differently, what is absent, and this is an interesting characteristic of the entire debate, is a comprehensive analysis of *the state* as the locus where the class contradictions are condensed, and transformed into hegemonic strategies, specific policies and concrete apparatuses.

Towards a revision

In what way, then, is it possible to assign the concept of the PIC an appropriate theoretical place where it can operate *within* and not *in lieu of* a theory of the capitalist state?

A possible starting point is perhaps the observation that the distant origin of the idea is not found in the political armoury of critical social theory, but, rather, it was US president Dwight Eisenhower, who, in his 1961 farewell speech, issued a warning about the dangers the existence of the military–industrial complex involve for democratic policy making.[2] As the centrality of military spending for post-World War II US growth was already an undisputed fact, Eisenhower was primarily referring to the possibility of unwarranted influence and its capacity to skew public policy in favour of big industry interests.

As Davis (2003) remarks, it was opportune for left activism to capitalise on a warning issued by the establishment itself, and the message does appeal to both the social and democratic sensibilities of a wider audience, in so far as what is involved is a subjection of society to the logic of money making and profit maximisation and a distortion of the democratic process, which disenfranchises the interests and concerns of the majority of the citizenry potentially. But such an *overpoliticised* conception of the prison–industrial complex, reflecting essentially liberal sensibilities and concerns, cannot be transplanted into radical theory without qualifications.

From a theoretical viewpoint, there is, within the radical tradition, no difficulty associating the idea of an 'industrial complex' with a long stream of analyses on monopolies, their role and, more importantly, their relationship with the state. This is an observation that goes back to early analyses of finance capital and imperialism, and it is also a problematic that gained renewed relevance in the context of the crisis in the 1970s: the formation of a 'social–industrial complex' was seen by O'Connor (1973) as a solution for the long-term stability of the system, namely for raising productivity by restraining costs and prices and increasing production and profits in the monopoly sector of the economy and for ameliorating the fiscal crisis in the state sector. Economically, O'Connor (1973: 63) notes, the social–industrial complex implies vast new government subsidised investments in various social areas; socially, it implies the creation of new class alignments; and politically, the complex requires a realignment of the political system.

On the above terms, it is difficult to deny that a *process* of creation of a prison–industrial complex in the United States (and elsewhere) has been taking place: alongside booming incarceration figures, spending on public safety as a GDP percentage of civilian government consumption and investment in the USA has doubled since 1969, from about 8 per cent in 1969 to about 15 per cent in 2007 (Holleman *et al.* 2009), while total civilian government spending has in the same period remained stable on average at around the 14 per cent mark. This indicates an increasing involvement of the state in the production and consumption circuits associated with public safety, including the carceral apparatus. It is also clear that private business is part of these circuits as well, and increasingly so, given the trends involving privatisation, contracting-out and other methods contributing to lowering the fiscal costs of the system. Even the tendency towards managerialism within the carceral apparatus creates ample opportunity for extensive interlocking between the correctional bureaucracy and private business. One would have to examine the composition of decision-making bodies and whether their membership is exclusively drawn from the carceral bureaucracy. In other words, evidence about the existence and extent of the PIC cannot be reduced to the quantitative indicators typically used in the literature, such as turnover and output and others used, for example, by Parenti.

An example about the uncertainty surrounding the quantitative extent of a complex's growth is the older literature regarding the emergence of a medical–industrial complex (Relman 1980; Navarro 1978, 1975; Bodenheimer *et al.* 1975) in the 1970s. In these older debates processes similar to those associated with the emergence of the PIC were identified: in the example of the medical–industrial complex these were, among others, the overuse and fragmentation of services; a heavy emphasis upon the use of technology; so-called cream-skimming (meaning risk-avoidance by the private component of the complex); and, finally, the exercise of undue influence on national health policy (Relman 1980). But what are these, if not processes reflecting both economic and political rationales and conditions, whose persistence and diffusion, in the absence of effective political organisation and resistance of subordinate classes, may amount to a complete takeover of a social domain by business interests (Szasz 2001)?

It follows that one would not need to see in the PIC the *replacement* of the MIC. Like Davis (2003: 206), who notes the symbiotic relationship between the two complexes, we would suggest that these are parallel processes, whereby different domains of public sector activity are colonised by big business. The examination of this process and also the temporal variance in the emergence of the particular industrial complexes, suggests that what in fact is involved here is a *tendency*, rather than a rigid economistic teleology, in the development of the system. The challenge, therefore, is to develop an analysis that both theoretically and *politically* is capable of recognising the import of economic, political and ideological class struggles for the crystallisation of such tendencies and contradictions into concrete policies and apparatuses within given social formations and particular conjunctures. The PIC, therefore, does not exist because it stems from an inherent authoritarian essence of capitalist political power, but is, rather, a concrete correlate of a balance of forces in the field of class struggle. More specifically, the coagulation of ruling class interests into particular apparatuses is a historical process contingent on the efficacy of subordinate classes to resist and advance their own interests (Poulantzas 2000).

Our suggestion is that the usefulness and political efficacy of the idea of the PIC will depend on the extent to which its theoretical understanding and interrogation as a particular apparatus will be embedded in a wider class–theoretical perspective of the state. For us, the rise of the PIC is inextricably related with the form of the state that emerged as a ruling class response to the intensification of the class struggles in the period of the ongoing over-accumulation crisis.

Notes

1 This distinction is strictly as a presentational device, and by no means is it intended to reflect on the scholarly value of the accounts we consider here.

2 'This conjunction of an immense military establishment and a large arms industry is new in the American experience. The total influence – economic, political, even spiritual – is felt in every city, every statehouse, every office of the federal government. We recognize the imperative need for this development. Yet we must not fail to comprehend its grave implications. Our toil, resources and livelihood are all

involved; so is the very structure of our society. In the councils of government, we must guard against the acquisition of unwarranted influence, whether sought or unsought, by the military–industrial complex. The potential for the disastrous rise of misplaced power exists and will persist. We must never let the weight of this combination endanger our liberties or democratic processes. We should take nothing for granted. Only an alert and knowledgeable citizenry can compel the proper meshing of the huge industrial and military machinery of defense with our peaceful methods and goals so that security and liberty may prosper together' (Eisenhower 1972).

References

Bodenheimer, T., Cummings, S. and Harding, E. (1975) 'Capitalising on illness: the health insurance industry', in V. Navarro (ed.) *Health and Medical Care in the US*, Farmingdale, NY: Baywood

Conley, J.A. (1980) 'Prisons, production and profit: reconsidering the importance of prison industries', *Journal of Social History*, 14: 257–75

CRCJ (1977) *The Iron Fist and the Velvet Glove*, Berkeley, CA: Centre for Research on Criminal Justice

Davis, A.Y. (2003) *Are Prisons Obsolete?* New York: Seven Stories Press

Dyer, J. (2000) *The Perpetual Prisoner Machine*, Boulder, CO: Westview Press

Eisenhower, D.D. (1972) 'Farewell address,' in C.W. Pursell, Jr (ed.) *The Military–industrial Complex*, New York: Harper and Row

Gilmore, R.W. (1999) 'Globalisation and US prison growth: from military Keynesianism to post-Keynesian militarism', *Race and Class*, 40: 171–88

Goldberg, E. and Evans, L. (2009) *The Prison–industrial Complex and the Global Economy*, Oakland, CA: PM Press

Goldberg, J. (2011, 28 November) 'The real prison industry', *Newsday.com*, http://www.newsday.com/opinion/oped/goldberg-the-real-prison-industry-1.3350716 (accessed 30 March 2012)

Harvey, D. (2007) *A Brief History of Neoliberalism*, Oxford: Oxford University Press

Holleman, H., McChesney, R.W., Foster, J. B. and Jonna, R. J. (2009) 'The penal state in an age of crisis', *Monthly Review*, 61: 1–17

Hossein-Zadeh, I. (2006) *The Political Economy of US Militarism*, Basingstoke: Palgrave Macmillan

Koistinen, P.A.C. (1980) *The Military–industrial Complex*, New York: Praeger

Lilly, J.R. and Knepper, P. (1993) 'The corrections–commercial complex', *Crime and Delinquency*, 39: 150–66

Lotke, E. (1996) 'The prison–industrial complex', *Multinational Monitor*, 17: 18–21

Navarro, V. (1975) 'The political economy of medical care', in V. Navarro (ed.) *Health and Medical Care in the US*, Farmingdale, NY: Baywood

——(1978) *Class Struggle, the State and Medicine*, London: Martin Robertson

O'Connor, J. (1973) *The Fiscal Crisis of the State*, New York: St. Martin's Press

Parenti, C. (1996) 'Making prison pay', *The Nation*, 287: 11–14

——(2008) *Lockdown America*, London: Verso

Paulette, T. (1994, 12 May) 'Making crime pay: triangle of interests creates infrastructure to fight lawlessness'. *Wall Street Journal*, A1

Poulantzas, N. (2000) *State, Power, Socialism*, London: Verso

Pursell, C.W., Jr. (ed.) (1972) *The Military–industrial Complex*, New York: Harper and Row

Quinney, R. (1977) *Class, State, and Crime*, New York: Longman

Relman, A.S. (1980) 'The new medical–industrial complex', *New England Journal of Medicine*, 303: 963–70

Sudbury, J. (2002) 'Celling black bodies: black women in the global prison industrial complex', *Feminist Review*, 70: 57–74

Szasz, T. (2001) *Pharmacracy*, Westport, CT: Praeger

Wacquant, L. (1999) '"Suitable enemies": foreigners and immigrants in the prisons of Europe', *Punishment and Society*, 1: 215–22

——(2008) 'The place of prison in the new government of poverty', in M.L. Frampton, I.H. López, and J. Simon (eds) *After the War on Crime,* New York: New York University Press

——(2009a) *Prisons of Poverty*, Minneapolis: University of Minnesota Press

——(2009b) *Punishing the Poor*, Durham, NC: Duke University Press

West, H.C. (2010) 'Prison inmates at midyear 2009 – Statistical tables', Washington, DC: Bureau of Justice Statistics, US Department of Justice

Wilson, W.J. (1997) *When Work Disappears*, New York: Vintage Books

Part 2

Issues in environmental criminology

5 But is it criminology?

Rob White

Introduction

'But is it criminology?' This was the first question I was asked a couple of years ago when presenting a paper on climate change and paradoxical harm at a critical criminology forum. That particular paper explored how some solutions to the problems associated with climate change are, in turn, generating new forms of social and environmental harm.

The first response to the presentation was, as described, to question its validity and location in and as 'criminology'. But, I replied, wasn't I dealing with matters of harm? Isn't one of the briefs of critical criminology to extend our understandings of what is harmful beyond that of the formally 'criminal'?

And what can be more harmful than global warming? Indeed, climate change is the greatest challenge facing planet Earth. So why wouldn't criminologists engage with the notion of environmental harms and environmental crimes? Why wouldn't we examine harms and crimes perpetrated by corporations, aided and abetted by nation-states, and by global agencies, some of which are indifferent to their victims (especially in developing countries) and many of which are engaged in chronic recidivism? Isn't this the stuff that at least a 'critical' criminology is made of?

In retrospect, I guess a more adequate response to the initial query would have been to question the relevance and seeming importance of the question. That is, why and how does it matter if what I was doing is criminology or not? Interestingly, in answering this question for myself I discovered that I needed to both reject and affirm criminology. This chapter attempts to explain why this is the case and how I came to this conclusion.

Biography, structure and agency

In pursuing an answer to the question 'but is it criminology?' I needed to ask several further questions. Namely, what is it that intellectuals actually do? How do we engage in the intellectual labour process? And, what are the implications of this for what we produce?

In recent years a lot of specifically criminological attention has been placed upon the idea of 'desistance'. Across different topic areas, from juvenile justice to drug and alcohol diversion, homelessness and offender rehabilitation, this notion has underpinned efforts to get individuals to stop their offending behaviour and to basically carve out a new lawful life for themselves. This burgeoning literature has grappled with the complications surrounding 'structure' and 'agency'. When all is said and done, at least at an abstract theoretical level, most would agree that the exercise of agency is situational, dependent upon personal biography and contextually shaped by what is occurring in the wider labour market, educational sphere, and public and private welfare and health provision. Desistance is a desired social project in so far as it entails future conformity (often described in terms of pro-social behaviour) and, thereby, enhanced life chances.

Simultaneously, there has been greater attention given to the idea of transgression, particularly in the literature associated with cultural criminology. Here agency is explained and celebrated in terms of the structural positioning of 'deviants' and their conscious responses to imposed orders of varying kinds. Breaking the law and breaking with convention are basically celebrated, and analysed in terms of dominant ideologies, economic insecurities, heavy-handed coercive force on the part of the state, and restricted opportunities to find oneself in the context of oppressive or limited emotional spaces. Deviance is an understandable individual project in so far as it entails resistance to expectations and social processes in the here and now.

What do these observations have to do with the question at hand? First, they alert us to the continuing debates within criminology regarding how best to conceptualise the relationship between structure and agency. This is central in fact to much of both mainstream and critical criminology. Personal biography is meshed with social circumstance, but how is individual agency exercised in any one particular instance? It all depends upon the exchange between structurally given propensities and personal history.

Second, the observations above highlight some of the tensions within criminology between those who desire to assist people to break from the criminal justice system, and those who interrogate why it is that certain people engage in behaviour that brings them to the notice of that system in the first place. Each approach is critical of the more right-wing law and order approach to criminality. Yet each offers something quite different to the political project of progressive social change.

Turning the structure–agency lens upon ourselves may provide some insight into why it is that some criminologists find it hard to 'desist' from criminology, while others revel in the notion of 'deviance' from the criminological mainstream. In reflecting upon this we return once again to the relationship between biography, social circumstance and active choice. To understand the nature and politics of my engagement in the study of environmental harm, for instance, requires that we unpack the key elements underlying this engagement. In doing so I hope, as well, to consider the matter of where the doing of criminology fits into the equation.

Analytically, I approach the study of environmental harm from the point of view of historical materialism. To understand environmental harm it is essential to ask basic questions about the mode of production in any given society, and how the mode of production shapes the particular economic, political and cultural organisation of a society. As Marx and Engels put it, social being determines social consciousness. That is, the mode of production in material life determines the general character of the social, political and spiritual processes within any particular society. The material conditions and material activity of humans determines not only the way in which the physical existence of individuals is reproduced but also the ways in which individuals express their life – their ideas, cultural forms, political structures and so on.

Thus we are historical beings, whose lives are constructed and constrained in and through the specific ways in which production is organised in any particular epoch. While to be human is to engage in production-in-general, specific forms of production are historically determined by the development of the means of life at any one point in time. In this way, the Greek gods who offer explanation of lightning and thunder disappear into myth upon the advent of electricity.

Accordingly, questions of agency must be located historically and empirically in the context of given structural relations. The goal of progressive social science is to understand how social life is shaped by these structural relations, in order to expand the scope and potential for human agency. For most of us, agency is generally pitched at individual or personal choices about things over which we as individuals have some measure of control. But the 'choices' exercised tend to be based upon private goals linked to our immediate social, economic and political circumstances. For example, how we act is made possible by the cultural and material resources already on offer and much of what we do takes place within the context of the choices inscribed within existing social relations and institutions. Agency beyond this is agency that is consciously directed at modifying, reforming or transforming aspects of the existing social order. This kind of agency is linked to social change, including fundamental shifts in the overall social order.

These statements about structure and agency are not simply about the world 'out there' – they are about the world 'in here', and as such are applicable to each of us as individuals and members of collectivities. In other words, biography and the personal are directly implicated in this worldview. Agency refers to the exercise of will and conscious action on the part of human subjects. My particular agency is influenced by particular institutional contexts and the interplay between my evolving position within the class structure and what it is that I choose to do with my time, energy and resources. To put it differently, my decisions – for example, to engage in study of environmental harm – are always already shaped by my social circumstance. Why should I be any different to the 'offenders', the 'victims', the 'perpetrators' and the 'authorities' that are so often the central object of criminological study in general? Indeed, a brief analysis of intellectual labour illustrates precisely this point.

The material basis of intellectual work

The kind of work that criminologists do reflects particular ideological and political dispositions on the part of the people doing it. But what criminologists do is also very much bound up with the conditions under which intellectual labour, in general, is undertaken. Intellectual histories of criminology and sociology point to the ways in which the institutional base of particular disciplines or fields shape the general character of academic work. Thus, for example, social research in the United States was of direct service to the military, the corporate sector, state bureaucrats and social workers, and, accordingly, sociology's dominant ideological character in the 1950s through to the 1970s tended to be predominantly conservative. The foundations of British and Australian criminology likewise were constructed first and foremost as a service discipline for state agencies, especially given the importance of the state's crime control apparatus as a key site or institutional domain for much criminological work.

Conversely, the emergence of critical and reflective criminologies that challenged correctionalism and the generally conservative nature of 'mainstream' criminology were associated with political struggles in the 1970s. This questioning of the status quo stemmed from action around such issues as prison abolition, police misconduct, indigenous rights, racism and women's liberation. Furthermore, the 'radical tinge' within Australian criminology over the last 25 years or so coincided with the establishment of criminology within the tertiary education sector. Thus the development of academic criminology as a bona fide programme of study and research within universities opened the door to progressive, critical work, although in recent years the nature of this space has been rapidly altered. This is manifest, for example, in the commercialisation and privatisation processes that we have witnessed across the educational and criminal justice domains. This has been accompanied by pressures to undertake academic work that is 'safe' and policy-oriented, rather than critical and socially challenging.

Where does my current work on environmental harm fit into this picture? To answer this we have to appreciate the difference between critical criminology in the 1970s and early 1980s, and criminology in the twenty-first century. For example, the work of Australian left-wing criminologists in the 'radical era' was largely informed by two key influences. First, many critical criminologists were directly engaged with and had practical ties to reformist groups such as prisoner action groups, feminist collectives and indigenous rights activists. Second, many likewise were members of, or fellow travellers with, militant socialist organisations – including the Communist Party of Australia (CPA), the Socialist Workers Party, and the International Socialists right through to the Socialist Left of the Labor Party. Importantly, 'socialism' was not just a slogan, it was often and usually linked to education in the basic concepts and principles of Marxism. This was not simply an academic exercise. It involved reading the works of Marx, Lenin, Gramsci, Mao, Trotsky and others directly, and discussing the relevance and significance of revolutionary leaders, movements and events for understanding and acting within the Australian context. The detachments from its working-class base and the movement of Marxism into the academy may have been in train, but the separation between academic and movement was not quite complete. Regardless of academic specialisation our reading was dominated by political rather than 'academic' texts.

By the late 1980s and into the 1990s, intellectual life took on a different character in the academy. The demise in Australia of the CPA and its publication *Tribune*, once a staple diet for the Left on campus, left a huge hole in radical politics and radical education. In its heyday the CPA had over 30,000 active members, trained and educated militants in the fight for a new society. Socialist parties of the Left, such as the CPA, were important in socialising a whole generation of activists into using the concepts of class analysis and learning the lessons of revolutionaries throughout history and across the globe. It also exposed them to the possibilities and pitfalls of the new social movements that were also emerging at the time. The fall of the Berlin Wall and the demise of the Soviet Union in 1989, however, presented further difficulties for socialist politics. The association of Marxism with Stalinism, and the failure of Soviet-style communism, reinforced the discrediting of Marxism and its proposed alternatives to capitalism. The conclusion that these vitiate Marxist explanation and critique of capitalism was not only illogical, given the substantive concerns of Marxism, it was intensely ideological, as evidenced in popular proclamations at the time that neoliberal capitalism constituted the 'end of history'.

The diminished presence and influence of the Left radical parties and party factions generally was reinforced by the intellectual attractions of 'postmodernism' in academic circles. Regardless of the specific contributions and detractions of postmodernism, it nevertheless served to both reflect and fuel a nihilistic and pessimistic political mode on campuses across the country. Moreover, the obtuseness and 'Frenchness' of the new language proved seductive for those wishing to prove their cleverness at abstract theorisation of 'the text'. This demanded little else than cynicism and disavowal of values and principles – and certainly nothing in the way of concrete political action. Class was soon gone as a way in which to frame the world. The 1970s radical academic basically morphed into the 1990s careerist, a transition that demanded incessant criticism but precious little commitment.

One consequence of these transitions is that relatively few of the younger criminologists today have actually read original socialist texts – such as the *Communist Manifesto*, the *German Ideology*, the *Eighteenth Brumaire*, the *State and Revolution*, *Prison Notebooks*, *What Is To Be Done*, *Capital*, *Theories of Surplus Value* – and certainly not in the context of activist politics. Of the academic generation of the last decade, some may be good at talking about grand narratives, but less so at actually reading them. If you want social revolution, then study revolution in practice.

Meanwhile, mainstream social science floundered around the class question – sometimes by dismissing it altogether, and sometimes by privileging individualism as a key concept over and above class. At any rate, very few in academia today learn 'class' in the same way that it was learned in the previous era. It is not that class has gone away; but our basic understanding of class and class analysis has been altered. In its stead there developed approaches that more often than not were antagonistic to Marxist class analysis, or that wished to sever any connection with the class politics of socialism.

Today, critical criminology badly needs a reassessment and re-substantiation of the importance – indeed, the centrality – of class analysis. This is not to denigrate or belittle the consciousness of complexity in contemporary social analysis, especially in the light of 30 or more years of theorising intersections. However, too often the mode of intersection analysis itself ends up striving to achieve an equality of concepts, rather than reflecting the hegemony of class in our lives. Wherever we live in the world today our lives are dominated by the capitalist mode of production – in one form or another we all now live in a global capitalist society. This is the determining aspect of our lives from the point of view of production, consumption and community. It is this that structures the basic material resources that underpin what we do, when we do it, with whom we do it, and how we do it. Class as a lived relation predominantly shapes as well as interacts with other key facets of our social being.

Other social divisions in society are not class-based divisions per se. However, the nature of these divisions is nevertheless shaped by the structural relations of class in particular ways. In other words, inequality and discrimination are, in part, sustained by practices and decisions based upon class interests. This has long been recognised in socialist politics, as evidenced in the nineteenth-century commentaries of Engels on the family and the *Communist Manifesto* itself. Contemporary discussions of women's oppression, and discrimination relating to indigenous peoples and ethnic minorities, likewise have to address the different class resources within each of these communities and social categories. Social divisions that reflect unequal gender, ethnic and race relations are thus themselves intersected by significant class cleavages.

While 'race' or 'gender' oppression cannot be reduced to explanations that subsume this oppression simply under 'class exploitation', it needs to be acknowledged that the class structuring of gender, ethnicity and race at the level of lived experiences is central to an understanding of economic and social inequality. To put it differently, the different dimensions of sexism and racism are inextricably intertwined with the development and extension of capitalism on a world scale. The economic, ideological and political relations of oppression are thus inseparable from the context of capitalism within which they exist. Ultimately, capitalism is essentially hostile to the promotion of human rights and personal empowerment, and to alternative social arrangements and philosophies that can result in a more inclusive and humane society.

The study of environmental harm

The social, political and cultural changes described above are, of course, experienced in a very personal way as they ebb and flow through institutional systems and intellectual fields. They affect people as thinking, emotional, political and physical beings. Each individual is a site for competing demands on our time, energy and resources, and these are impacted upon by diverse kinds of workplace-related pressures and practices. Be this as it may, what makes intellectual labour in criminology 'intellectual' hinges upon how each criminologist responds to the conditions and authority structures of their work. The institutional context of intellectual labour has no small part in influencing the extent to which subversion of authority, dissent from dominant power structures and the telling of alternative 'truths' features in our everyday work. We do what we can do, under circumstances not of our own making.

Enter 'green criminology'. A distinctive, critical 'green criminology' has emerged in recent years that takes as its focus issues relating to the environment and social harm. Much of this work has been directed at exposing different instances of substantive environmental injustice and ecological injustice. It has also involved critique of the actions of nation-states and transnational capital for fostering particular types of harm, and for failing to adequately address or regulate harmful activity. Given the pressing nature of many environmental issues it is not surprising that many criminologists are now seeing environmental crime and environmental victimisation as areas for concerted analytical and practical attention.

The key question for green criminology is how to conceptualise the causes and nature of environmental harm arising from human actions. In responding to this question, it becomes clear very quickly that political economy is at the heart of the exploitation of humans, nonhuman animals and environments – that capitalism, in particular, demands profitable use of such as a means to assign value. The perspective of political economy is grounded in recognition of different social interests, different forms and types of social power, and clear distinctions being drawn between exploiter and exploited, and oppressor and oppressed.

It is at this point that the activism and literature of the 1960s and 1970s finds purchase by informing, at least implicitly, many of the conceptualisations of harm and what to do about it propounded in the 1990s and 2000s. Consider for example the following statements:

> The materialist conception of history starts from the proposition that the production of the means to support human life and, next to production, the exchange of things produced, is the basis of all social structure: that in every society that has appeared in history, the manner in which wealth is distributed and society divided into classes or orders is dependent upon what is produced, how it is produced, and how the products are exchanged.
>
> (Engels – *Socialism: Utopian and Scientific*)

> Life is not determined by consciousness, but consciousness by life.
>
> (Marx and Engels – *The German Ideology*)

> The conclusion we reach is not that production, distribution, exchange and consumption are identical, but that they all form the members of a totality, distinctions within a unity. Production predominates not only over itself, in the antithetical definition of production, but over the other elements as well.
>
> (Marx – *Grundrisse*)

Political economy is intrinsically concerned with power relations that are ingrained in dominant institutional arrangements. In today's world, the capitalist mode of production presents as the foundation of global economic development, a phenomenon that inexorably bears within it the imperative to expand, and in so doing exploit in every way imaginable the natural and human resources of the planet. The moments of our mutual destruction lie within the social and technical relations of advanced capitalism.

> Production thus not only creates an object for the subject, but also a subject for the object. Thus production produces consumption (1) by creating the material for it; (2) by determining the manner of consumption; and (3) by creating the products, initially posited by it as objects, in the form of the need felt by the consumer. It thus produces the object of consumption, the manner of consumption and the motive of consumption.
>
> (Marx – *Grundrisse*)

> Everything which the political economist takes from you in terms of life and humanity, he (*sic*) restores to you in the form of *money* and *wealth*, and everything which you are unable to do, your money can do for you: it can eat, drink, go dancing, go to the theatre, it can appropriate art, learning, historical curiosities, political power, it can travel, it is *capable* of doing all those things for you; it can buy everything; it is genuine *wealth*, genuine *ability*. But for all that, it only likes to create itself, to buy itself, for after all everything else is its servant.
>
> (Marx – *Economic and Philosophical Manuscripts*)

> The worker is only permitted to have enough for him (*sic*) to live, and he (*sic*) is only permitted to live in order to have.
>
> (Marx – *Economic and Philosophical Manuscripts*)

Production and consumption within the capitalist mode of production are subversive of basic needs, and disrespectful of the subject status of humans, of nonhuman animals and of specific environments. We are alienated from Nature, from ourselves, and from taking responsibility through the routinised and largely unconscious everyday regimes of work and shopping. Individualised guilt and blame, however, exist within the wider field of structured patterns of consumption that intertwine at the existential level to promote a deep desire to consume in particular ways.

> The philosophers have only *interpreted* the world, in various ways; the point, however, is to *change* it.
>
> (Marx – *Theses on Feuerbach*)

> The 'dangerous class', the social scum, that passively rotting mass thrown off by the lowest layers of old society may, here and there, be swept into the movement by a proletarian revolution; its conditions of life, however, prepare it far more for the part of a bribed tool of reactionary intrigue.
>
> (Marx and Engels – *The Communist Manifesto*)

> National differences and antagonisms between peoples are daily more and more vanishing, owing to the development of the bourgeoisie, to freedom of commerce, to the world market, to uniformity in the mode of production and in the conditions of life corresponding thereto.
>
> (Marx and Engels – *The Communist Manifesto*)

> The ideas of the ruling class are in every epoch the ruling ideas: i.e., the class which is the ruling *material* force of society, is at the same time its ruling *intellectual* force. The class which has the means of material production at its disposal, has control at the same time over the means of mental production, so that thereby, generally speaking, the ideas of those who lack the means of mental production are subject to it.
>
> (Marx and Engels – *The German Ideology*)

The struggle over ideas is materially related to the production (and distribution) of information, and how specific sections of the population construe their social interests relative to others around them. Greenwashing, extensive use of public relations, and mobilisation of public opinion in favour of particular industrial policies to the detriment of the ecologically sound and environmentally just, reflects the power of the dominant industries and classes in contemporary intellectual life. Developing counter-hegemonic strategies and propaganda is vital to challenging the ruling ideas of the present era.

> Men (*sic*) make their own history, but they do not make it just as they please; they do not make it under circumstances chosen by themselves, but under circumstances directly encountered, given and transmitted from the past. The traditions of all the dead generations weigh like a nightmare on the brain of the living.
>
> (Marx – *Eighteenth Brumaire of Louis Bonaparte*)

Climate change demands urgent action now, if planetary well-being is to be assured into the future. The ideological and coercive interventions of the ruling classes have the consequence of diverting action and attention from the development of meaningful and systemic alternative pathways for humanity. For both those who advocate for change and those resisting it, however, we have not only the collective weight of the past but the ecological limits of the present to contend with.

From nineteenth- and twentieth-century radicals and revolutionaries we have an intellectual platform that still serves us well. Analysis of the fundamental nature of the state, social movements, finance capital, the changing nature of imperialism – these and more are central to not only past understandings but contemporary events.

Consider for a moment the proposition that humans are at the stage in our history where global environmental catastrophe is nigh upon us and unless we deal with the environmental crisis as a universal problem then humanity as a whole is at risk. There are common human interests that need to take priority over any other kind of interests if we are, as a species, to survive. However, while everybody on the planet has a common interest in the survival of the human race, the specific class interests of business, of transnational companies, of corporations, mean that they are not willing to implement or enact strategies and policies that would, in fact, further the common human interest. In other words the reason why we are not fixing up the planet, even though it is to the advantage of all that we work together in our common interest, is that specific class interests intrude upon the process whereby planetary well-being might be prioritised.

The problem, however, is that we are running out of time. This makes the affirmation of the old-fashioned socialist agenda even more urgent. Environmental harm is immediately implicated in and a manifestation of wider class processes. It is symptomatic of basic divisions in society that at their core revolve around the private ownership and control of the means of production. The crucial political challenge is to view entrenched social injustice and ecological destruction as lying within the system of capitalist rule, and to struggle against this rule. This can be achieved through concrete action toward equitable distribution of the social surplus through democratic ownership and control of community and natural resources. It can involve the contesting of the class nature of the state apparatus, informed by a broad agenda of democratic control in accordance with the interests of subordinate classes and social groups. It can be done by reiterating old ideas – 'from each according to their capacity, to each according to their need' – that ought to find increasing public resonance in a world beset by gross inequality and environmental crisis.

Coming back to me

Self-identity is part of the intellectual process as much as particular types of knowledge acquisition and development of specific expertise. Intellectuals are often placed in contradictory and precarious situations in regard to how their work is defined and, indeed, used by others. At this point we therefore return to the matter of structure and agency.

What is happening in the world of academic research provides a situational context for the interplay between structure and agency. Who produces knowledge, who controls it, and the uses to which it is put, are all sites of contestation involving complicated institutional pressures and many different kinds of choices on the part of the intellectual. The challenge is to find the spaces within which to pursue progressive criminological work, in a period of sustained work pressures and restricted funding opportunities. How we identify and use the 'subversive spaces' afforded to us within the academic sector is partly a matter of political philosophy, and partly a matter of time. The first speaks to the notion of ideology and strategic alliances within the field and with fellow travellers outside of criminology as such. The second goes to the heart of the material conditions shaping the working lives of criminologists. The issue of resources (money, time, staff and funds) is especially pertinent to those who wish to undertake transformational research in a period witnessing the disappearance of public funds and the rise in political sensibilities around environmental issues.

All of this requires a basic resolve that what we are doing is right, and is on the right track. This is where self-identity and biography once again come into the equation. For myself, the ethical foundations for study of environmental harm were laid way back in my childhood, a time in which I was imbued with Judeo-Christian values, some of which – like 'do unto others as you would have them do to you' – still resonate strongly today. A stint with a 'far left' political party helped expose me to both the literature on revolution and the experience of activist politics. Reading the 'classics' makes so much more sense when read as an activist and not just as an academic. Out of these dual influences – the ethical and the engaged – emerged a particular sense of 'right' and 'wrong', and a trajectory that ultimately led to concerted action around environmental issues.

My job as an academic has meant that my particular intellectual labour has been heavily circumscribed as well as enormously facilitated by the fact that I work within a tertiary educational institution. There are 'rules to the game' that apply to all of us if we are to continue working within this sphere, rules that likewise shape what we write about, how we write about it, and for whom we write. Similarly, I am employed as a 'criminologist' that, in turn, carries with it certain expectations in terms of teaching, research and administrative duties. It is my field of work, as well as a field of study. It is in the light of these material realities that I say my intellectual labour is 'heavily circumscribed'. But it is also 'enormously facilitated' by the resources available, the publishing outlets, the public speaking opportunities and by a general atmosphere that even today still allows for a modicum of 'free' thought.

How we use this 'relative' freedom is at the fulcrum of how and where our intellectual labour fits into the broad political economy. The Gramscian notion of organic intellectuals refers to thinkers who are connected closely to grassroots working-class and social movements and who reflect the social interests of the less powerful. This can be juxtaposed with those who are mouthpieces for the ruling classes and the handmaidens of the state. Critical criminology is 'against criminology' precisely due to the preponderance of so much of the latter within conventional criminology. The world may be burning up, villages destroyed by toxins and wild animals butchered, yet mainstream criminological and criminal justice attention rages about working-class offenders getting drunk and into punch-ups on the weekend. We need to 'desist' from certain types of criminology. This is about priorities and social interests.

However, the idea of independent thinking is also what defines the intellectual. We need to be subversive about the ideas of the ruling classes, but this extends as well to the dominant institutions, the dominant paradigms, and to ortho-doxy generally (including 'radical' orthodoxy). For progressives, the political project is to make a new and better society, to garner a safe and secure future for our children and our children's children, and to ensure the widest possible biodiversity and climatic stability. It is about social, ecological and species justice. As with other sources of useful knowledge, even conservative types of criminology can be mined for what is most suited to this political agenda without dictating the contours of the project itself. Marx and Engels, for instance, were experts at extracting from bourgeois economics and all manner of mainstream science, anthropology, sociology and history that could readily aid revolutionary goals and objectives. As a 'field', criminology is well placed for just this kind of melding together of information, ideas and data from many different kinds of sources. We need to be 'deviant' when it comes to self-righteous attitudes and prescriptive/proscriptive approaches to knowledge. This is about openness and synthesis.

Conclusion

This chapter has provided a critical reflection of my own study of environ-mental harm, and the intellectual traditions and trajectories that have informed this work. Key concerns have included the nature of the intellectual and political project, and the synergies between my own intellectual development and the relevance of this to my subsequent work on environmental harm.

What continually strikes me in undertaking intellectual and political work of this kind is the ways in which activists and academics before me (and alongside me) have struggled with the issues, and approached the challenges of trying to understand and change the world around them. Stretching the limits and pushing the boundaries are how such contributions are sometimes described by mainstream criminologists and academics. Yet, it seems to me that informed and challenging political analysis is intrinsically multidisciplinary, is usually eclectic in its sources, and is driven by concerns that are always already intended to go beyond the status quo. A fusion of 'old' ideas and 'new' circumstances is surely part of this process as well.

6 Critical green criminology, environmental rights and crimes of exploitation

Nigel South and Avi Brisman

Introduction

The proposition put forward here is that the pursuit of social justice and human rights must be bound up with a regard for ecological justice and the protection of the environment. In this respect, this chapter builds upon work describing the environmental and social injustices afflicting communities of the poor and the powerless around the world (e.g. Bullard 1990, 1994), on the recent recognition in criminology and sociology of the importance of human rights (e.g. Cohen 2001; Turner 2006; Green and Ward 2000), and on the development of a 'green' perspective in criminology (e.g. Lynch 1990; South 1998; White 2008; Sollund 2008; Walters 2010). While green criminology has, to a large extent, always been a critical endeavour (e.g. Lynch and Stretesky 2007; Ruggiero and South 2010a, 2010b; Walters 2010), we bring these together to provide a critical green criminology concerned with crimes of exploitation and domination that argues for the need to recognise and strengthen the link between human and environmental rights.

A critical criminology of exploitation and domination

Critical criminology has a long-established commitment to exposing exploitation and domination and to exploring broader conceptions of 'crime' than normally associated with the 'core' of the field, including an array of harms not necessarily proscribed by law (see e.g. Barak 1994: 255; Carrington and Hogg 2002; Henry and Milovanovic 1996, 2003; Kauzlarich and Friedrichs 2003; Michalowski 1985, 1996, 2007, 2010; Platt 1975; Schwartz and Hatty 2003). As Barak (1994: 254–5) notes of this 'core', while 'the past fifty years [have seen] ... an expansion [of] the "acceptable" boundaries of criminological focus to include the criminal behavior of the powerful, beginning with the professional, white-collar, organized, and, most recently, corporate criminals ... ', mainstream or core criminology has retained a 'legalistic state definition of crime' and pursued 'investigation and analysis confined to legally proscribed behaviour and control'. Critical criminology, on the other hand, has engaged in a much broader inquiry: social injuries or harms caused by exploitation and domination do not lie beyond its analytic gaze simply because the acts and consequences are not prohibited by law (see e.g. Beirne 1999; Brisman 2008, 2011a; Burns *et al.* 2008; Halsey and White 1998; Michalowski 1985, 2007, 2010: 8; Walters 2007, 2010; White 2008). In other words, critical criminology, as Barak (1994: 255) argues, 'has not confined itself to studying legally defined crime ... [I]t has studied harmful and injurious behavior that may or may not be sanctioned by particular nation-states' definitions of illegality, but that are recognized in the "higher" criteria established in various international treaties, covenants, or laws.' The gross harms, as well as the legally defined crimes, associated with the over-exploitation of the planet and environmental resources, may increasingly fall within such higher criteria (Beirne and South 2007; Brisman *et al.* 2013; South and Beirne 2006) although these too may have an unhelpful narrowness of vision that misses the impact of the everyday injuries of over-consumption and the generation of waste affecting our environment (Agnew 2013; Brisman 2011b, 2011c; South 1998).

For Michalowski (2010: 9), a 'critical criminology formed around a broad vision of social injury is well suited to the challenge of pursuing social justice in the twenty-first century' and he suggests that '[w]hile domination remains [a challenge] ... within the advanced capitalist states ... the dominion that advanced states exert over those situated lower in the global class structure is an even graver challenge to the ideals of social justice that animate critical criminologists of all flavors'. Domination and exploitation, however, do not follow from the actions of advanced capitalist states alone; they also occur at many points across the class structure of the global periphery as a result of actions by the governments and elites of the developing world (see e.g. Messer 1993: 234). It is in response to such external and internal sources of power that the principles and language of *rights* are articulated as a local and global basis for action and accountability. As Macklem (2007: 581) points out: 'human rights protect essential characteristics or features that all of us share despite the innumerable historical, geographical, cultural, communal, and other contingencies that shape our lives and our relations with others in unique ways. They give rise to duties that we owe each other in ethical recognition of what it means to be human.'

Human rights and the protection of the environment

Conceptions of rights pre-date the twentieth century (Benton 1998), but the internationalisation of human rights protection did not occur until after the atrocities of World War II (Hunter *et al.* 2002: 1288; Shestack 2000) with the 1948 Universal Declaration of Human Rights (UDHR). The internationalisation of environmental protection began 24 years later with the 1972 Stockholm Declaration of the United Nations Conference on the Human Environment (Brisman 2011d). There are numerous ways of looking at rights and the environment, for example, in terms of environmental rights as expressed in various international treaties; seeing property rights as environmental rights; instances where human rights regimes incorporate environmental rights; or the case of the 'public trust doctrine' (arguing that much private land is held subject to the right of the state to ensure use in the 'public interest') (Sax 1970). Rather than sketch out the different arguments for the various sources and conceptions of environmental rights, we turn to Hiskes (2009) as a springboard for highlighting what environmental rights might mean or imply, and how human rights and environmental protection are intertwined.

Hiskes (2009) highlights four relevant discourses. First, human rights jurisprudence is not as powerful, but contested – in certain conditions, the 'War on Terror' being a notable example, rights may be disputed, suspended or redefined. Second, environmental rights as expressed in some national laws and constitutions, albeit with the recognition that expression is one thing but ensuring protection and prosecuting violations is another. Third, discourses around the rights of future generations – the principle that we must have regard for inter-generational justice and a duty to our children and their children, and so forth. This is a powerful and both rationally and emotionally persuasive position but it is also a wide-ranging commitment (embracing, for example, mitigating climate change, eradication of transmitted diseases, establishing food security and so on) and therefore not attractive to those favouring 'business and politics as usual'. Fourth, Hiskes argues that environmental rights should be seen *as* human rights. This also is not straightforward. White (2007: 35), for example, asks whether environmental rights should be considered 'an extension of human or social rights (e.g. related to the quality of human life, such as provision of clean water)' or indeed whether human rights should 'be seen as merely one component of complex ecosystems that should be preserved for their own sake (i.e. as in the notion of the rights of the environment)?' Rather than take a position, White (2007: 40–1), assumes the perspective that 'any decision about a particular environmental issue very much depends upon situational factors, community norms and values, and available technologies and techniques'. While this suggests a case-by-case approach that balances cultural, subsistence and environmental considerations, White (2007: 41) also stresses the importance of recognising our 'interconnectedness and human obligations to the non-human world' and argues that '[e]cological justice demands that how humans interact with their environment be evaluated in relation to potential harms and risks to specific creatures and specific locales as well as the biosphere generally'.

Principle 1 of the 1972 Stockholm Declaration of the United Nations Conference on the Human Environment recognises that both the natural and the human engineered features of our environment are essential to well-being and to the enjoyment of basic human rights and to the right to life itself:

> Man has the fundamental right to freedom, equality and adequate conditions of life, in an environment of a quality that permits a life of dignity and well being, and he bears solemn responsibility to protect and improve the environment for present and future generations.

As Clark (2009: 130–1) explains, the Stockholm Declaration led to the Aarhus Convention of June 1998, signed by 35 nations and the European Community. More formally known as the United Nations Economic Commission for Europe Convention on Access to Information, Public Participation in Decision-making and Access to Justice in Environmental Matters, this is an international agreement granting the public rights regarding access to information, public participation and access to justice in governmental decision-making processes regarding matters pertaining to the local, national and trans-boundary environment. Importantly, the definition of 'the public' employed here includes the often-overlooked sector of non-governmental organisations (NGOs). These are often the organisations campaigning on behalf of those who need to know more, need to participate (either to provide legitimacy or to register protest) and need a right to remedy (Clark 2009: 130–1). Their role and activity has been particularly (though not exclusively) important in developing and transitional nations. In these contexts, a key goal is sustainable development which, according to the Centre for International Environmental Law (2002; cited in Clark 2009: 132) 'should include such factors as increased accountability of governments, increased participation of citizens and the strengthening of local democracy'.

The positive impact of liberal democracy on environmental safeguarding is not as unequivocal as one might hope however and, of course, much green criminology draws attention to the harms to the environment that are common in contemporary democratic states with economies based on corporate capitalism. Dryzek (1996: 108) concludes that if 'two or more decades of political ecology yield any single conclusion, it is surely that authoritarian and centralised means for the resolution of environmental problems have been discredited rather decisively'. On the other hand, Ward (2008: 406) argues that 'while Dryzek correctly summarised the theoretical debate, the existing empirical evidence is far more ambiguous. My analysis suggests that liberal democracy can be given [a] more positive report, although green theorists will no doubt remark on the numerous ways in which it could do better.' On this basis, even with reservations about the effectiveness of democracy as a force for environmental protection, compared to all but the most benign dictatorship that might be concerned with environmental issues and human rights, states *without* benefit of accountability, participation and strong democracy are frequently loci of some of the most egregious human and environmental rights violations (however one conceives of those rights). According to Alario (1993) dictatorships in Brazil and Chile brought about both human rights violations and a legacy of environmental destruction as a result of the colonisation of land by large corporations, forced eviction and migration of indigenous peoples, and the destruction of lands and native cultures.

Today, as Clark (2009: 129; see also Newell 2001) observes, the forces that follow from the global flow of capital, increasing multinational trade and competition across borders with reduced trade restrictions, all put increasing pressure on corporations to lower environmental standards and to collude in the violation of the rights of activists seeking to protect the environment (see also Leader and Ong 2011; Landman 2006). This is a late modern 'world in motion' that Aas (2007: 283) describes as being 'permeated by transnational networks and flows of goods, capital, information and cultural symbols, as well as potentially risky individuals and substances' and nowhere is the cumulative and damaging effects of this more evident than in the profiteering that comes from the exploitation of the mineral, plant and wildlife wealth of developing nations by global capital and the corporations of the developed world. This is a process of profiteering that makes a mockery of moral philosophy by claiming 'rights' to indigenous knowledge, by patenting the genetic or pharmaceutical products of plants of local origin, and by pursuing the mining of ores and felling of timber to meet demand in the ever-expanding consumer markets that span the world, in advanced as well as emerging economies (South, 2007). This has been described as the 'resource curse' of developing nations.

The resource curse of developing nations

Wenar (2008: 3) defines the phenomenon of the 'resource curse' (also referred to as the 'paradox of plenty') in the following way:

> Economists have noticed a peculiar phenomenon in some less developed countries, which is a symptom of the violation of property rights that concerns us. They have named this the resource curse. Economists have found that many countries rich with natural resources are full of very poor people. For many less developed countries, natural resources have become an obstacle to prosperity instead of its foundation. The resource curse afflicts many countries that derive a large portion of their national income from exporting high-value extractive resources such as oil, natural gas, and diamonds. Less developed countries that gain a large portion of their national incomes from these extractive resources are subject to three overlapping 'curses.' They are more prone to authoritarian governments, they are at a higher risk for civil conflict and they exhibit lower rates of growth.

The 'resource curse' of various countries with mineral, plant and wildlife 'wealth' has led to the exploitation of their environmental inheritance and destruction of the legacy that should be left for future generations. This exploitation contributes to what Wenar (2008: 2) describes as a 'system of global commerce' built upon laws and agreements that are 'little more than a cloak for larceny' generating both legal and illegal trades in diamonds, timber and wildlife that bring little or no return to indigenous peoples but that do produce huge profits for organised crime groups, corrupt governments and unethical corporations. In addition, there is a longer-lasting and profound effect of intergenerational ecological injustice (Weston 2012). This offends one of the key principles of sustainability:

that we look at the earth and its resources not only as an investment opportunity, but as a trust passed to us by our ancestors for our benefit, but also to be passed on to our descendants for their use. This notion conveys both rights and responsibilities. Most importantly, it implies that future generations have rights too. These rights have meaning only if we the living, respect them, and in this regard, transcend the differences among countries, religions, and cultures.

(Weiss 1992: 19–20)

Both human rights and the principle of environmental sustainability are entwined and need to be upheld across national, religious and cultural divides.

The case of the Democratic Republic of Congo (DRC) is a now well-known example of a country affected by the 'resource curse'. Rich in mineral resources, including gold, the country has suffered ceaseless conflict for nearly two decades involving six countries, felt the effects of genocide in neighbouring Rwanda and internally seen ongoing factional warfare between the Congolese army, 'defence forces' and 'rebel units'. According to a UN expert panel, this had led to 'highly organized and systematic exploitation' (UN 2002: 10, para. 52) involving, *inter alia*, rebels and government forces profiting from the trades in mineral ores (gold, coltan, tin, tungsten), subjecting civilians to massacres, rape and extortion, and using forced labour and coercing children into the role of soldiers. Taylor (2011: 30) reports cases of rape victims in eastern DRC being forced to work in conditions of slavery in mines producing coltan, gold and tin ore, used for jewellery, mobile phones and laptops. In addition, while it was traditionally the case that women were engaged in farming, the fields are in forests that are now occupied by rebels and growing food has become too dangerous:

'If you choose to get food from the field you have to accept that you're going to be raped,' said Patience Kengwa, 30, who works at Kamituga gold mine. She fled her village, Luliba, after being raped five times in two and a half years. Now she pounds rocks and carries heavy sacks, earning between 50 cents and a dollar a day.

(Taylor 2011: 30)

Dominique Bikaba, director of Strong Roots, an environmental charity that works with miners to improve their conditions, has condemned the situation in the following terms: 'These girls and women are working in the mines in conditions of slavery. They earn less than a dollar a day and are often forced to work harder than they are physically capable of working' (quoted in ibid.).

Further evidence of the ongoing exploitation of people and resources, and the challenges arising, is provided in the work of several NGOs including a report by DanWatch[1] (an NGO specialising in investigative journalism on corporate ethics) on cobalt mining in the DRC:

Cobalt mining ... also involves a wide range of human and labour rights abuses. Working conditions in the mines are often dangerous and unhealthy, workers often have no safety equipment and many serious accidents injure and kill workers. Children account for approximately 10 per cent of the work force in the informal mining sector, and in some regions children perform dangerous work underground. In some cases, security forces and armed groups have forced children to do mining work, especially in the conflict areas in the eastern part of the country. Local people's basic rights to health, water and development have also been violated by mining activities in DR Congo leading to a range of serious environmental hazards. The extraction of metals generates a massive amount of waste. For instance, one ton of copper produces 110 tons of waste and 200 tons of overburden from blasting away the soil and rock. This waste can contain toxic substances polluting the environment and affecting local communities. Many companies do not clean up when closing down mining operations. Local ore processing plants also create severe air pollution and are in some instances placed close to vital water tables with drinking water supply for local communities, creating a risk of water contamination. Another health risk is related to radioactivity, because copper and cobalt ores and waste material sometimes contain high concentrations of uranium, which both can affect the mining workers and spread into the environment and ecosystems ... Mining has also led to violent crackdowns on protests from small-scale miners and surrounding communities.

(quoted in Schönsteiner *et al.* 2008: 1–2)

In addition to the obvious immediate harms to humans, such mining practices adversely affect the food chain and water supply of other species and plant life. Species harms and violations also occur because the tantalum/ coltan mining areas also cover national parks that are home to the endangered mountain gorilla (Nellemann *et al.* 2010). Here ground clearance for mining has led to the gorilla population halving in recent years as their food supply has been disrupted or lost; at the same time, the displacement of the human local population has led to their impoverishment and to hunting gorillas to slaughter for 'bush meat' to consume and to sell to miners and rebel armies.

Local and global denial and lack of accountability

In recent years, the number of international agreements relating to preservation of the environment and prohibitions relating to environmental crime has increased (Fouchald *et al.* 2008, 2009). A critical green criminology itself reflects a growing awareness and momentum around these issues. At the same time, however, a well-known pattern of global and local denial of the problem overall as well as in terms of accountability and responsibility mirrors all of this (see Cohen 2001; Markowitz and Rosner 2002), producing rationales for non-compliance, the opening up of loopholes and means of evasion, the emergence of new commercial (legal or illegal) opportunities and incentives to commit offences regardless.

The persistence of market and state behaviour in this way is influenced by the structure of international project financing (Leader and Ong 2011), which may allow banks to declare a corporate commitment to green and ethical values while subsidiary companies engage in deals that break both the spirit and detail of laws and agreements. If fined, these subsidiaries internalise costs and blame. Projects are financed to yield a profitable return in ways that incentivise rapid completion and the cutting of corners: health and safety, human rights and environmental protection are impediments to such timetables. The costs entailed for any acts of transgression of rules and laws are simply factored into operating budgets and, if these transgressions are noticed by the wider world, into budgets for public relations and marketing campaigns as well. Meanwhile the consequences of environmental degradation are externalised.

All of this has even wider significance if we consider the responses of financial operators to environmental harms. For example, we might wonder why it is not perceived as more rational to exercise stewardship over the environment than to continue to diminish its capacity to supply the market. Degradation of the environment and climate change may pose the most catastrophic threats imaginable, involving disruptions and indeed extinctions, affecting societies and their underpinning financial systems and markets on a global scale.[2] Yet the turn of investment toward prevention and preparation is not greatly evident. In light of recent financial failures, it is not inappropriate to recall that criminologists with an interest in corporate crime have pointed out the negative consequences of the 1980s 'Big Bang' deregulation of City of London finance market operators and similar relaxation of controls internationally. In response, financial services achieved enormous growth and the 'bonus culture' embedded itself in the elite circles of corporate business (Croall 2011: 341–2). This was the situation that led to the celebration and selling of 'financial innovations' designed to 'help the richest' accompanied by 'labour savings innovations' that had the effect of limiting employment opportunities when, as Baddeley (2010) points out, what societies actually need are 'innovations with wider benefits for ordinary people and workers; innovations targeted at minimising the negative consequences of environmental damage, for example'.

Conclusion

The current system of control and enforcement actually depends on models of deregulation (the market will provide effective and efficient remedies) and 'legislative balancing acts' (agencies charged with encouragement of compliance in the course of doing business are also charged with prosecuting and penalising in cases of offending) that are not fit-for-purpose – if that purpose is supposed to be meaningful. In addition, the systemic problems of 'regulatory capture' and the 'trivialisation' (De Prez 2000) of actions and consequences that often follow legal debate about mitigation occur at the levels of both transnational crime and local offending. The 'soft law' instruments that do exist and operate can, as Huisman (2010: 56) observes, 'contribute to creating generally accepted social norms regarding the protection of human rights by corporations' but 'the worst offenders are not compelled to take part' while 'increasing numbers of corporations affiliated to the UN Global Compact initiative do not comply with their reporting obligations'. Huisman (2010: 59) rightly draws attention to the 'ambiguity and ambivalence' underlying the issues at stake here. Both market suppliers and product consumers can readily justify behaviours that are so easily presented as legitimate and normal, whether licensed mining or buying mobile phones and laptops or gas-guzzling vehicles (Brisman 2004, 2009). In this context of ambivalence and ambiguity, there is a need to continue to develop a critical green perspective that throws further light on the crimes of environmental exploitation and their consequences as well as on the human rights infringements that many remain ignorant of or prefer to ignore.

Notes

1 Commissioned by DanChurchAid and Roskilde Festival Copenhagen and published in 2008 but strangely no longer available on the DanWatch website. It is however summarised at various locations including that of the sponsor DanChurchAid: http://www.danchurchaid.org/projects/denmark-old/campaigns-old/roskilde-festival/bad-connections
2 See: http://news.yahoo.com/blogs/sideshow/next-great-depression-mit-researchers-predict-global-economic-190352944.html

References

Aas, K. F. (2007) 'Analysing a world in motion: global flows meet the "Criminology of the Other"', *Theoretical Criminology,* 11 (2): 283–303

Agnew, R. (2013) 'The ordinary acts that contribute to ecocide: a criminological analysis', in N. South and A. Brisman (eds) *The Routledge International Handbook of Green Criminology,* London: Routledge

Alario, M. (1993) 'Environmental policy enactment under the military', *International Journal of Contemporary Sociology,* 3: 222–30

Baddeley, M. (2010) 'Review of J. Stiglitz (2010) *Freefall: Free Markets and the Sinking of the Global Economy*', *Times Higher Education,* 25 February. http://www.timeshighereducation.co.uk/story.asp?storycode=410474

Barak, G. (1994) 'Crime, criminology, and human rights: toward an understanding of state criminality', in G. Barak (ed.) *Varieties of Criminology,* Westport, CT: Praeger

Beirne, P. (1999) 'For a nonspeciest criminology: animal abuse as an object of study', *Criminology,* 37: 117–47

Beirne, P. and South, N. (eds) (2007) *Issues in Green Criminology,* Cullompton: Willan

Benton, T. (1998) 'Rights and justice on a shared planet: more rights or new relations?', *Theoretical Criminology,* 2: 149–75

Brisman, A. (2004) 'Double whammy: collateral consequences of conviction and imprisonment for sustainable communities and the environment', *William & Mary Environmental Law & Policy Review*, 28 (2): 423–75

——(2008) 'Crime–environment relationships and environmental justice', *Seattle Journal for Social Justice*, 6 (2): 727–817

——(2009) 'It takes green to be green: environmental elitism, "ritual displays", and conspicuous non-consumption', *North Dakota Law Review*, 85 (2): 329–70

——(2011a) 'Advancing critical criminology through anthropology', *Western Criminology Review*, 12 (2): 55–77

——(2011b) 'Examining potential tensions in green criminology: green corrections, rights regimes, and individual-level eco-deviancy/environmental delinquency'. Paper presented at the 13th Annual Justice Studies Association Conference, Chestnut Hill College, Philadelphia, PA (10 June)

——(2011c) 'Green criminology, zemiology, and relational justice in the anthropocene era'. Paper presented at the American Society of Criminology Annual Meeting, Washington, DC (16 November)

——(2011d) 'Stockholm Conference, 1972', in D. Chatterjee (ed.) *Encyclopaedia of Global Justice*, Vol. 2: 1039–40, Heidelberg: Springer

Brisman, A., Beirne, P. and South, N. (2013) 'A guide to a green criminology' in N. South and A. Brisman (eds) *The Routledge International Handbook of Green Criminology*, London: Routledge

Bullard, R. (1990) *Dumping in Dixie: Race, Class and Environmental Quality*, Boulder, CO: Westview

——(1994) *People of Color Environmental Groups*, Flint, MI: Charles Steward Mott Foundation

Burns, R., Lynch, M. and Stretesky, P. (2008) *Environmental Law, Crime, and Justice*, New York: LFB

Carrington, K. and Hogg, R. (eds) (2002) *Critical Criminology*, Cullompton: Willan

Clark, R. (2009) 'Environmental disputes and human rights violations: a role for criminologists', *Contemporary Justice Review*, 12 (2): 129–46

Cohen, S. (2001) *States of Denial*, Cambridge: Polity

Croall, H. (2011) *Crime and Society in Modern Britain*, Harlow: Longman Pearson

De Prez, P. (2000) 'Excuses, excuses: the ritual trivialisation of environmental prosecutions', *Journal of Environmental Law*, 12: 65–77

Dryzek, J. (1996) 'Strategies of ecological democratisation', in W. Lafferty and J. Meadowcroft (eds) *Democracy and the Environment*, Cheltenham, UK: Edward Elgar.

Fouchald, O.K., Hunter, D. and Xi, W. (eds) (2008) *Yearbook of International Environmental Law*, Oxford: Oxford University Press

——(eds) (2009) *Yearbook of International Environmental Law*, Oxford: Oxford University Press

Green, P. and Ward, T. (2000) 'State crime, human rights, and the limits of criminology' *Social Justice*, 27 (1): 101–15

Halsey, M. and White, R. (1998) 'Crime, ecophilosophy and environmental harm', *Theoretical Criminology*, 2: 345–71

Henry, S. and Milovanovic, D. (1996) *Constitutive Criminology*, London: Sage

——(2003) 'Constitutive Criminology', in M. Schwartz and S. Hatty (eds) *Controversies in Critical Criminology*, Cincinnati, OH: Anderson

Hiskes, R. (2009) *The Human Right to a Green Future: Environmental Rights and Intergenerational Justice*, New York: Cambridge University Press

Huisman, W. (2010) *Business as Usual?* The Hague: Eleven International

Hunter, D., Salzman, J. and Zaelke, D. (2002) *International Environmental Law and Policy*, New York: Foundation Press

Kauzlarich, D. and Friedrichs, D.O. (2003) 'Crimes of the state', in M.D. Schwartz and S.E. Hatty (eds) *Controversies in Critical Criminology*, Cincinnati, OH: Anderson

Landman, T. (2006) *Studying Human Rights*, New York: Routledge

Leader, S. and Ong, D. (eds) (2011) *Global Project Finance, Human Rights and Sustainable Development*, Cambridge: Cambridge University Press

Lynch, M. (1990) 'The greening of criminology: a perspective on the 1990s', *Critical Criminologist*, 2 (3–4): 11–12

Lynch, M. and Stretesky, P. (2007) 'Green criminology in the United States', in P. Berine and N. South (eds) *Issues in Green Criminology*, Cullompton: Willan.

Macklem, P. (2007) 'What is international human rights law? Three applications of a distributive account', *McGill Law Journal*, 52: 575–604

Markowitz, G. and Rosner, D. (2002) *Deceit and Denial*, Berkeley: University of California Press

Messer, E. (1993) 'Anthropology and human rights', *Annual Review of Anthropology*, 22: 221–49

Michalowski, R. (1985) *Order, Law and Crime*, New York: Random House

——(1996) 'Critical criminology and the critique of domination: the story of an intellectual movement', *Critical Criminology*, 7 (1): 9–16

——(2007) 'Who's the criminal here? Social injury and immigration politics on the U.S.–Mexico border'. Paper presented at the 35th Annual Conference, Western Society of Criminology, Phoenix, AZ

——(2010) 'Keynote address: critical criminology for a global age', *Western Criminology Review*, 11 (1): 3–10

Nellemann, C., Redmond, I. and Refisch, J. (eds) (2010) *The Last Stand of the Gorilla: Environmental Crime and Conflict in the Congo Basin*, A Rapid Response Assessment. United Nations Environment Programme, GRID-Arendal. Accessed at: http://www.grida.no/publications/rr/gorilla/.

Newell, P. (2001) 'Managing multinationals: the governance of investment for the environment', *Journal of International Development*, 13: 907

Platt, T. (1975) 'Prospects for a radical criminology in the USA', in I. Taylor, P. Walton and J. Young (eds) *Critical Criminology*, London: Routledge & Kegan Paul

Ruggiero, V. and South, N. (2010a) 'Critical criminology and crimes against the environment' *Critical Criminology*, 18 (4): 245–50

——(2010b) 'Green criminology and dirty collar crime', *Critical Criminology*, 18 (4): 251–62

Sax, J. (1970) 'The public trust doctrine in natural resource law', *Michigan Law Review*, 68 (3): 471–566

Schönsteiner, J., Kazimova, R. and Leader, R. (2008) 'Collaborative agreement between the Democratic Republic of Congo and the Chinese Enterprise Group, signed April 22nd, 2008: an analysis'. Prepared for Global Witness NGO, unpublished paper, Business and Human Rights Project, School of Law, University of Essex

Schwartz, M. and Hatty, S. (2003) 'Introduction', in M. Schwartz and S. Hatty (eds) *Controversies in Critical Criminology*, Cincinnati, OH: Anderson

Shestack, J.J. (2000) 'The philosophical foundations of human rights', in J. Symonides (ed.) *Human Rights*, Aldershot: Ashgate

Sollund, R. (ed.) (2008) *Global Harms*, New York: Nova Science Publishers

South, N. (1998) 'A green field for criminology? A proposal for a perspective', *Theoretical Criminology*, 2 (2): 211–33

——(2007) 'The "corporate colonisation of nature": bio-prospecting, bio-piracy and the development of green criminology', in P. Beirne and N. South (eds) *Issues in Green Criminology*, Cullompton: Willan

South, N. and Beirne, P. (eds) (2006) *Green Criminology*, Aldershot: Ashgate

Taylor, D. (2011) 'Congo rape victims forced to work in mines', *The Guardian*, 3 September, p. 30. Available at: http://www.guardian.co.uk/world/2011/sep/02/congo-women-face-slavery-mines.

Turner, B. (2006) *Vulnerability and Human Rights*, University Park: Pennsylvania State University Press

UN (2002) *Interim Report of the Panel of Experts on the Illegal Exploitation of Natural Resources and Other Forms of Wealth of the Democratic Republic of the Congo*, United Nations Document S/2002/565/22 May:1–19. Accessed at: http://www.unhcr.org/refworld/pdfid/3d0471ad4.pdf.

Walters, R. (2007) 'Crime, regulation and radioactive waste in the United Kingdom', in P. Beirne and N. South (eds) *Issues in Green Criminology*, Cullompton: Willan

——(2010) 'Toxic atmospheres: air pollution, trade and the politics of regulation', *Critical Criminology*, 18 (4): 307–23

Ward, H. (2008) 'Liberal democracy and sustainability', *Environmental Politics*, 17 (3): 386–409

Weiss, E. (1992) 'In fairness to future generations and sustainable development', *American University International Law Review*, 8 (1): 19–26

Wenar, L. (2008) 'Property rights and the resource curse', *Philosophy and Public Affairs*, 36 (1): 2–32

Weston, B. (2012) 'The theoretical foundations of intergenerational ecological justice: an overview', *Human Rights Quarterly*, 34: 251–66

White, R. (2007) 'Green criminology and the pursuit of social and ecological justice', in P. Beirne and N. South (eds) *Issues in Green Criminology*, Cullompton: Willan

——(2008) *Crimes Against Nature*, Cullompton: Willan

Part 3
Researching crime and deviance

7 Stalking the margins of legality

Ethnography, participant observation and the post-modern 'underworld'

Craig Ancrum

Context

What follows is a reflective account of the feelings and experiences that developed as a result of my role as an ethnographic researcher for the book *Criminal Identities and Consumer Culture* (Hall *et al.* 2008). My main goal is to suggest that criminology attempts to free itself from the stultifying institutional and disciplinary forms of control that seek to divorce criminologists from 'the real world'. I will claim that it is vital that our discipline is willing to risk an authentic encounter with this real world, and that it begins the process of transforming what, under the current system, is deemed 'ethical', 'proper' and 'achievable'. The end point of this process is an empirical criminology unimpeded by restrictive bureaucratic control but one that has ethics at the heart of its practice.

The methods and ethical practices I outline in the pages that follow will, inevitably, be criticised by those criminologists who are paralysed by either traditional social sciences' objectivism and abstracted empiricism or liberal–postmodernist social sciences' fetishistic relativism, pluralism and perspectivism. In this chapter I claim that it is only by risking a genuine encounter with the real world that we can approach the truth of crime, criminal markets and criminal motivations. I will also suggest that the ethical frameworks imposed upon us by our institutions and discipline increasingly transform 'ethics' from an emotional concern with what is right to a mere restrictive framework of control that must be negotiated (see Winlow 2012). In unpredictable research environments the engaged ethnographer has no choice but to marginalise the formal world of ethics committees and methodological guidelines and proceed under the somatic guidance of his or her own ethical code as it interacts with the ethics and values of the researched community.

My model for a transformed ethical ethnography, driven by a desire to fully immerse myself into the cultural and professional practices of a criminal group, is unlikely to find approval in the standard research methods text-books. My initial claim is that the entire edifice of the contemporary social scientific research methods framework is polluted by a liberal ideology that has achieved such dominance that it is no longer conceived as 'ideological'.

The fundamental issue at stake here is one of distance: we are exhorted into maintaining academic integrity by remaining separate from the polluting influence of the real world, and, by the same token, we remain 'ethical' by ensuring that our influence on the lives of real people is as close to nought as we can make it. My claim is that if we are to truly know the 'real world' in our time we must close this distance, accept our own common humanity and become fully immersed in the world as it is.

To close this distance effectively we should consider adopting a critical ultra-realist ethnographic framework that is unafraid to draw close to the horrors and pleasures of everyday criminal life and depict them for an academic audience without the usual affirmative left–liberal romantic veneer. We should neither appreciate nor condemn (see Winlow and Hall 2006), but, by representing and explaining empirical reality and its underlying Real as faithfully as possible, we can push past the established dogmas of left- and right-wing variants of liberalism and provide the raw material that can be used to drive new explanatory intellectual agendas in the social sciences.

Introduction

Ethnographies of 'closed groups' are the empirical foundation of modern criminology. From its earliest anthropological origins the ethnographic method has provided scholars with detailed and focused narratives of the realities of criminal life. Drawn as an undergraduate to the early studies of Sutherland, Merton, Whyte and others, I was impressed by the immediacy of these historic texts and their ability to capture a reality I intuitively felt to be true. They delivered insights and revealed nuances that were lacking from the policy-oriented and, frankly, quite dull Home Office studies and liberal depictions of 'disenfranchised youth' that formed the basis of my undergraduate syllabus. Discovering the work of Hobbs (1995), Winlow (2001), Armstrong (1998) and others only served to reinforce this conviction and my attachment to ethnography.

These vivid and vibrant accounts of active criminals and individuals involved in a vast spectrum of illegal and semi-legal opportunistic and entrepreneurial endeavours rang true with my own experiences. Having been excluded from school at the age of 15 I had gradually become embroiled in the local area's criminal marketplace. Shoplifting, commercial burglary and drug deals became the norm as I struggled to gain a foothold in the precarious economic maelstrom that was Thatcher's deindustrialising Britain in the early 1980s. The voices of the actors in *Badfellas* (Winlow 2001) and *Bad Business* (Hobbs 1995) were those of my friends who had given up the pointless charade of attempting to earn a legal income and refused to submit themselves to a dispiriting existence of 'just getting by'. Instead they had 'diversified' and become attuned to the rapidly changing postmodern criminal marketplace. The life histories discussed in these books mirrored closely the insecure and hazardous biographies of many of the criminal contacts I have developed during my career as an ethnographer. My own familiarity with criminal culture (Ancrum 2011) encouraged me to believe that I could see the reality that lay beyond abstract criminological theories. As Fleisher (1995) so astutely remarks, these theories are merely 'abstract constructions about behaviour that criminologists, for the most part, have never seen'.

Whilst studying as an undergraduate, this lack of experience was immediately apparent in the attitudes to crime held by many of my tutors, who were resistant to any distraction from their clichéd or romanticised view of criminal behaviour (Ancrum 2011). For these academics, crime was either a result of social exclusion, poor parenting or committed for a 'buzz'. Worst of all was the common view that criminality was a form of resistance: sticking up two fingers to an authoritarian regime, rebelling through crime against a hopeless situation and existential oppression. Employment was often seen as the 'answer' to the crime problem, alongside education and that mythical beast, 'rehabilitation'. Even in my early days as a student I found this kind of narrative totally divorced from my experience of criminal cultures. The continuing prevalence of this romantic narrative should prompt critical criminologists to rethink the intellectual foundations of their discourse (see Hall 2012), and this task can be aided by a growing commitment to ultra-realist criminological ethnography (Winlow and Hall 2006; Treadwell 2012; Briggs 2012).

Those academics who *have* witnessed crime as an actual lived experience imbue their narratives with a realism that appears beyond those academics who *have not*. When Philippe Bourgois (1996) talked of college-educated intellectuals who were too afraid or too elitist to engage with violent, drug-using criminals in a non-judgemental manner he was perhaps overstating the case. However, not every academic or researcher possesses, or is willing to develop, the cultural competence to engage freely and comfortably with active criminals. This is not necessarily a problem for the discipline of criminology. Not every criminologist must be an ethnographer driven by a desire to reveal the gritty reality of the contemporary criminal cultures. However, I would ask that those who do have this ability and desire should be given the autonomy and the encouragement to engage ethnographically with the real world as they find it.

The move towards ever-increasing managerialism and greater accountability means ethics boards now fail to consider the actual ethical basis of any research project, and instead concern themselves only with the administrative task of sifting and sorting research projects and dividing the 'allowed' from the 'not allowed'. Ethics has degenerated into risk management (Winlow and Hall 2012). It is now becoming evident that we are in danger of discarding the tradition of engaged ethnographic inquiry in favour of 'safe' studies of crime which fit the demands of an academia fettered by managerial imperatives and policy-driven rationales. To abandon or restrict the use of ethnographic methods means that we deny ourselves the opportunity to access the types of empirical data that can renew the intellectual vitality of our discipline and help produce the new theoretical frameworks that academic criminology sorely needs. I believe that the ethical procedures of the social sciences have borrowed far too heavily from those of the hard sciences, and that our debilitating concerns with objectivity or pluralism have prevented our discipline from making the advances that might allow us to move away from 1960s radicalism and produce a new critical account of crime, deviance and harm that is firmly rooted in twenty-first century neo-capitalism (Hall *et al.* 2008; Hall 2012). Furthermore, we must come to terms with the fact that it's sometimes necessary for researchers to 'skirt the fringes of the law' in the pursuit of original and unique data. In truth we should be less concerned with our public image as objective or pluralist social scientists, and more concerned with advancing our intellectual understanding of contemporary crime and deviance.

Hopefully, by offering this brutally honest and graphic depiction of life in the field some interest in ethnographic method may be rekindled. In addressing the flaws and exposing the stifling bureaucracy attached to ethics procedures, I seek not to attack or castigate but to reason for a comprehensive and inclusive approach to criminological research methods that recognises the complexity of criminal life and the difficulties researchers face when attempting to untangle it.

Carville

Consumerism is the economic foundation of the contemporary global economy, and as such it has played a considerable role in the transformation of community, solidarity, and civil codes and cultures. Anxiety and envy drive the cultures of postmodern consumerism (Hall *et al.* 2008) and herald a new order of individualisation and the emergence of a predatory winner/loser society (Beck 1992). The erosion of traditional forms of working-class culture, employment and identity have had a profound effect upon what were reasonably stable and functional industrial locales in the north of England. Many of these places now suffer a tangle of social problems reflective of rising hopelessness, insecurity and economic and social redundancy (Hall, 2002; Taylor, 1999; McAuley 2007). Carville is one such locale. There is now sufficient evidence to prove that the onset of the neo-capitalist consumer merry-go-round has transformed what was once a reasonably well-organised place of 'working class male culture and biographies rooted in collectivism and shaped by the rhythms and structures of the industrial economy' (Hall *et al.* 2005: 1). The unpredictability and growing enmity that now characterise these male-dominated spaces are a clear indication of the aggressively corrosive nature of the post-industrial winner-takes-all economy, an economy that has no use for a mass industrial working class and no time for the social detritus left behind.

The rapid withdrawal of industrial employment has clearly impacted negatively, but not just on the economic well-being of these places. This crucial transformation in processes of capital accumulation has also blighted local cultures and transformed the habitus of the industrial working class (Winlow 2001). There is growing evidence to suggest (Levi and Maguire 2002) that a sharp increase in levels of drug-related crime, intimidation and violence followed this crucial shift in the legitimate economy, and this is certainly true in Carville.

For Carville the demise began in the late 1970s and early 1980s, with increasing foreign competition, privatisation and rocketing domestic inflation. Quickly, the town's shipyards closed and in so doing denied local working-class families traditional forms of employment (Rae and Smith 2001). When Beck (1992: 139) wrote of the importance of having a trade in industrial society, and further claimed that 'wage labour and an occupation ha[d] become the axis of living', he was also attempting to draw our attention to the loss of stabilising aspects of culture in the post-industrial period. In particular, the traditional anti-utilitarian elements of working-class culture, especially those of collectivism and solidarity (see Winlow 2001; Winlow and Hall 2006), began to subside as our political leaders pushed us towards an era defined by the dominance of the global free market. In a parallel development, criminal cultures also began to transform in line with the new requirements of the market. Serious violence rose considerably (Reiner 2007), and mutating forms of professional and organised crime became increasingly important in defining the nature and operation of criminal markets throughout Carville.

Little has changed in the town since we began our initial research (circa 2006). A walk down the high street illustrates the precarious economic condition perfectly. The large retail chains have long since moved on, and, fast food outlets aside, the once thriving thoroughfare is now a succession of charity shops, cut-price food stores and 'booze and fag' shops. On the housing estates groups of young men gather outside bookmakers' offices or, for those with the funds, around the snooker tables of the local and now rather dilapidated working men's club. The irony of the venue's title is not lost on those who line the bar. Others spend the day lost in a fog of cannabis smoke or, for those who rely on the sale of drugs, 'running around' sorting out supply and payment. Just as in Bourgois's (1996) study of illegal drugs markets in El Barrio, sizeable sums of money are circulating in the area, despite the obvious poverty of many of its inhabitants.

Drug sales dominate the town's shadow economy. Heavily adulterated cocaine, amphetamines and home-grown skunk cannabis account for the bulk of trade. The cannabis trade in Britain has been transformed by the increase in demand for this strong and pungent form of the drug. Where previously most of the country's supply of poor quality 'soap bar' cannabis was imported from Morocco via Spain and Amsterdam, the majority of 'weed' smoked in the UK is now grown here (Hough *et al.* 2003).

This has provided opportunities for some of the area's inhabitants to become 'skunk farmers'; with an ounce selling for upwards of £150, this can be a very lucrative venture. It's also an undertaking that carries considerable risk. Aside from the obvious threat of detection by the police, growers run the risk of 'being taxed': having their produce, profits and equipment stolen or appropriated by other criminals. The practice of taxing is not restricted to cannabis growers; criminal predators are now commonplace and are happy to use extreme violence to boost their reputations and defend their market share. Dut, a committed criminal who I spent a lot of time with as we built the empirical foundations of *Criminal Identities and Consumer Culture*, offers the following account:

> You've got to watch your back, like. I know a good few lads have had their crops took off them. What can they do? Some nasty cunt, tooled up, tells you he's having it, what the fuck you gonna do? Nowt, that's what!

This 'taxing' of the weak and vulnerable in a reconfiguring and violent criminal hierarchy is now commonplace in Carville. Entrepreneurial forms of crime developed rapidly as Carville was forcibly transformed from a functional industrial community to a wasteland of neoliberalism, but 'the hidden power of a violent reputation' (Winlow 2001: 165) is crucial for those criminal businessmen trying to defend or expand market share and also for violent predators who simply extort payments from those who operate in all the tiers of the market.

Most of the people I interviewed for *Criminal Identities and Consumer Culture* remain heavily involved in crime, and, in the midst of the current double-dip depression, the majority have seen their fortunes decline since we completed the fieldwork for the book. Stevie, who was once a relatively successful cannabis and cocaine dealer, is now eking out a living as a shoplifter and selling skunk in £20 bags from his doorstep. Most of his symbols of consumer success that we highlighted in the book have vanished, and he has been unable to keep up the payments on the flash car he bought during the high times. He cites the reason for his fall from grace firmly on the increasing competiveness and ruthlessness of the criminal market:

> It's too hard mate, every fucker's a dealer, too much competition for punters. It's too tricky finding good gear as well, it's all shit, coke anyway, can't grow 'green' coz there's nowhere safe, you've got cunts trying to tax you left, right and centre. [They are all] plastic fucking gangsters, but they're crazy. It's all fucked.

So not only are opportunities for legitimate employment severely restricted, there is little room in the area's criminal markets for all but the most ruthless or well connected. The individuals trapped in a cycle of crime and poverty in Carville bear little resemblance to the 'noble working classes' that is such a clear feature of pious, benevolentist middle-class liberal accounts of the poor. Real poverty and the constant background static of threat, conflict and competition is the unpalatable reality of these ex-working class social spaces, and it is producing cultures and subjectivities fit for its demands. There is no solidarity, no community spirit and no sense of collective destiny or common purpose.

Instead, growing enmity and a deeply anxiety-inducing social competition defines the lives of those who occupy Carville's rougher estates. For the criminals I spoke to, the prospect of rehabilitation or regular employment was laughable. Those who chose this path were 'mugs' willing to throw their life away for an income so low that it couldn't service even the most meagre consumer expectations. As Dut explains:

> It's like the bloke next door to me Mam. Worked for the council his whole life. What's he got to show for it? Fuck all! Not even a fucking Ford Fiesta. Never goes abroad or nowt. What kind of life is that?

Despite the liberal trope of the great 'crime drop', crime in areas like Carville is rocketing. The latest crime figures for the town show burglary is up 12 per cent. Drug crime has risen by 10 per cent. Anecdotal accounts offered by a number of the area's major criminals suggest that the scale of unreported drug-related crime is unprecedented. Only 'legitimate people', or people with something to gain, phone the police if they've been the victim of a crime. For low-level criminals like Dut and Stevie, threats, violence and theft form part of their everyday social reality. Low-level theft and small-scale drug sales are, for them, the only realistic means of making a living, and their own crimes, and the crimes committed against them by others, are unlikely to be integrated into the latest regional crime statistics. Stevie elaborates

> Violence happens all the time that nobody hears about. Stabbings and people popping shots off at each other and that, never makes the news half the time, nobody grasses, nobody calls the bizzies; you sort it yourself don't you? I know lads that have stitched up their own wounds rather than go to hospital and have the police nosing about.

In Carville's clubs and pubs, on the street corners and outside the off-licences and bookies, the illegal marketplace is the economic foundation of life. Consumer dreams of rapid upward social mobility remain powerful, but many of the young men on the estate recognise that crime and violence are the only obvious routes to consumer spending and social status. Crime in Carville is not merely the phenomenological product of a sensationalist media and an authoritarian government joining forces to whip up a moral panic. Rather, it is the very fabric of everyday life for a significant portion of the population. It erodes those things that make civilised social life possible and reinforces the area's fractious and highly competitive cultures. It is an area where violence and a person's capability for using it are highly valued and where the sale and exchange of illegal drugs is the dominant commercial activity. For those involved, crime is a ruthless and hyper-competitive arena and there is much more than money at stake. Status, acceptance and personal safety often depend on the ability of the individual to perform adequately on the streets and in the area's dominant trades. Throughout my research I encountered men willing to use serious and lethal violence. The use of knives and firearms was common, and many of those I spoke to knew someone who had died as a result of violence. This is the reality of life in Carville today.

Living in the field

Ethnographers, to be successful, usually have to navigate a whole host of obstacles in order to achieve and maintain access. Methods textbooks discuss the slow and steady process of building trust, negotiations with 'gatekeepers' and a slow but steady integration into the particular 'closed group' they are trying to engage. Researchers often discuss the elaborate charades deployed to gain admittance and the days spent hanging around the margins, hoping for eventual acceptance.

However, I have been able to bypass most of this. I have lived in Carville all of my life, and I possess extensive personal knowledge of the values, nuanced meanings and practices of local criminal cultures. I have known some of the area's celebrity gangsters since childhood. It was not difficult for me to arrange interviews with key players in the criminal marketplace, and from the outset they were forthcoming and happy to help me with my research. I also observed some of the area's most active criminals as they performed their daily routines. This included actual criminal offences, performed entirely without consideration of my presence. In the same way as both Armstrong (1998) and Winlow (2001), I was lucky enough to be able to observe law-breakers in an entirely naturalistic way simply by associating with my usual circle of friends and acquaintances. There were many occasions when valuable research could be gathered without even leaving the house. On one occasion, a respondent arrived at my front door fresh from burglarising a chemist's shop with a bag full of stolen prescription drugs to show me. Another, just out of prison following a ten-year sentence for armed robbery, was the subject of a 'hard stop' by armed police officers as he pulled away from my front door. While these events were always illuminating, I did often worry that I would come to the attention of the police. My anxiety about this was not unjustified.

One sunny August morning I awoke to the sound of the Regional Crime Squad smashing through my front door. After being manhandled from our bed, my wife and I were shown a warrant relating to cocaine and other class 'A' drugs. The police officer informed me that I had been seen 'in all the wrong places, with all the wrong people'. Despite the huge pressure this placed upon myself and my family, this negligent intrusion further established my credentials and affirmed my place in the local criminal culture. I had come through this challenge and, in the eyes of those I was researching, behaved admirably. I hadn't betrayed anyone and I kept my mouth shut. I took a minor cannabis possession charge, and continued onwards.

As Winlow (ibid.) and others have noted, those involved in illegal activities have little to gain from allowing academics admittance to their lives. My access was enabled by close personal relationships with key stakeholders in the local economy, but I realised that I may, at some stage, be called upon to 'get my hands dirty'. I occasionally found myself in a position of committing minor illegal acts. These were often quite trivial. Close friendships were at stake, and my response reflected the nature and balance of these friendships rather than a basic utilitarian cost/benefit analysis or a deadly fear of the opprobrium of my colleagues. My ethical response to these issues reflected the complexities of my own identity and biography and often the deep affection in which I held my respondents. For example, on occasion I helped one of my key respondents to 'bosh' his cocaine and weigh it out into one-ounce bags. 'Boshing' is the process whereby powdered cocaine is diluted with a cutting agent, in this instance lactose, in order to maximise profits. Doing this reaffirmed our relationship in a way that transcended my own academic concerns, but nonetheless proved that I was willing to place myself in the same precarious legal position as my respondents. In my view, the benefits gained from these activities were invaluable. Any issue of trust or suspicion was at once removed by my involvement in this minor activity, and the reciprocity upon which our relationship was founded was immediately reaffirmed.

Polsky (1971) famously suggested ethnographers should be 'fully immersed' in the researched culture. Blumer (1969) has also noted that empathy and critical insight are of paramount importance in ethnographic research. My own long-term research has these two principles right at the heart of my work. I do not want to simply turn up, grab as much usable data as I can and then disappear from the lives of my respondents. I am in it for the long haul, and I am willing to go through the highs and lows that accompany all meaningful relationships. I try to avoid negative value judgements and instead seek to understand the deeply complex reasons that underlie the criminal behaviours I witness with such regularity. I empathise with respondents greatly, even when that means offering what might appear to be academic critique. In my view, a deep commitment to representing the world as it is helps the researched community in the long term. Middle-class left liberals, even some of my own colleagues, often set themselves up as the heroic defenders of 'the working class', and refuse to countenance any suggestion that the post-industrial wastelands of the north-east display anything but a stoical, hard-but-fair, community spirit. For me, trying to distract academic discourse from the harsh reality of life in Carville would be intellectually naive and politically counterproductive. It is only when we understand and accept how far things have fallen that we can begin the political process of putting things right. We could go so far as to argue that the constant denial of the reality of life in Britain's deindustrialised wastelands is itself the product of a liberal strategy to prevent the return of calls for the sort of uncompromising politics and economics required to effect a real socio-cultural transformation in these locales (see Hall 2012 for a discussion).

It was easy for me to fit into the culture of those I was observing because, after all, this was *my culture*. Agar (1980: 456) suggested that 'to be knowledgeable is to be capable of understanding what is going on, on the basis of nominal cues'. He stressed the importance in fieldwork of being able to look beyond words for what Geertz (1975) termed 'the intentionality which distinguishes the wink from the twitch'. I was certainly not going to be one of Fleisher's (1995) 'scholars who have not spent enough time on the streets around their subjects to understand the cultural and semantic nuances of the culture'. In the vernacular of my friends and respondents 'I knew the dance' before the fieldwork had even begun. I knew when to ask questions and when to shut up. In a cultural setting where it's frowned upon to discuss 'graft', I knew that there were many issues that needed to be approached with caution. I went through the often elaborate conversational rituals as that was what was expected of me. It was not that my respondents were always unwilling to discuss sensitive topics. Indeed, it became clear that many of them were in fact keen to do so, but in the right place at the right time. Rather, one had to acknowledge the parameters of accepted speech and interaction in these settings. One could not simply ask a man with a reputation for extreme violence about his relationship with his mother. One had to approach these things sensitively, and be fully willing to reciprocate in order to encourage respondents to talk freely about sensitive topics.

Little Legs was one of my most high profile criminal contacts and he is an extremely unpredictable and violent man. Little Legs has been linked to a number of local murder enquiries, and for many young criminals in Carville, he is the beacon of criminal and consumer success they are so keen to emulate. His name had been linked to a number of big criminal cases, and I was very keen to establish the extent of his involvement. Of course, my detailed knowledge of the culture and the individual ensured that I avoided direct discussion of these events and restricted my questions to less sensitive topics. In this way, and despite missing out on useful factual information, I continued to learn more about Little Legs: about his life, his motivations and his views on his occupation and the region's criminal cultures. Perhaps more importantly, I was able to retain Little Legs as a key respondent, and one who I can return to over and over again with my developing research projects.

I did on occasion feel a sense of betrayal whilst recording field notes and submitting text for publication. Walcott (1995: 14) wrote of field research ultimately involving betraying those involved 'no matter how well-intentioned or integrated the researcher'. There were times when reading back data provoked feelings of considerable guilt. To be a 'grass' in Carville is to be the lowest of the low. I often felt like an 'academic grass'. The prospect of my observations being publicly available was daunting to say the least. Despite rigorous measures imposed to shield the participants and disguise their identities and so on, the possibility that my work could be read by law enforcement was not a pleasant one. Jayne Fountain (1993) discusses the experience of paranoia in her study of high-end cannabis dealers, and many other ethnographers have reflected upon this as an outcome of the ethnographic research process.

These anxieties are related to the emotional connections we make with our respondents, and the internal debate we have about how our research might affect them is a fundamentally ethical and often deeply subjective process. We make judgements about what is and what is not acceptable after long and often tortuous soul-searching, and we do all of this without the dismal administrative oversight of institutional ethics committees.

'Surely you aren't going to ignore acts of criminality?'

This is a quote from the chair of my institutional ethics committee in response to a proposal to study the drug-using habits of young people in Carville. For me, this quote encapsulates the difficulties faced by criminologists who wish to begin empirical work with active criminals. It seems difficult for many academics to see the purpose of engaging with criminals on their own terms, and to do so without immediately informing the appropriate authorities is often deemed to be entirely 'unethical'. But these short-sighted moralists are not the only impediment to serious ethnographic research. As many have acknowledged, criminology appears oriented to minor acts of criminality and civil disorder, and often displays a squeamish reluctance to engage with those criminals who are engaged in more destructive crimes. With regard to ethnographic practice, when do we say enough is enough? The answer of course is entirely subjective. We all have our own limits of moral tolerance and I have no intension of offering a prescriptive assessment here. As Winlow and Hall (2012: 402) claim 'Criminology is suspected of being more ethically problematic at a deeper level because it exists at the forefront of moral condemnation.' We certainly need to be a little more open to the possibility of exploring in a non-judgemental manner some aspects of serious crime. I am not advocating the abandonment of ethics in relation to criminological enterprise. Rather, I am suggesting that we need to recalibrate our understanding of 'ethics' in the hope of making that discourse more philosophical in nature, more considerate of ethics proper, and less concerned with dry managerialism. I have attended many ethics committee meetings, and at these meetings ethics has never been discussed in any real sense. The abiding sense I have taken from these meetings is a desire on the part of the committee to apply the formula, and in so doing reduce the consideration of research ethics to the status of a mere administrative task (ibid.).

Ethics committees are particularly wary of covert methods, and this appears to be partly related to their administrative obsession with 'informed consent'. The institutional need to defend against litigation is palpable, but one can also discern an obvious middle-class liberal bias here, as if all individuals are similarly able to understand, digest and rationally determine an appropriate response when faced with a researcher keen to get a signature on their informed consent documentation. Of course, approaching active criminals in this manner is usually unthinkable. My research and my place within the wider community would've immediately come crashing down if I had attempted to gain this kind of informed consent. Ethics committees are now complicit in the process of stripping away the last vestiges of academic professionalism. The assumption is that I cannot be trusted to engage in an ethical way with those I seek to observe and interview. While there is a strong case for forms of institutional ethical oversight, it also seems that we need to develop a more informed 'real world' understanding of the realities of ethnographic enterprise. Of course, to me, engaging ethically with my research covertly is at the very forefront of my mind. I want to protect my respondents as much as possible from external scrutiny, and I would happily sacrifice my research in order to achieve this. To assume that I am profoundly instrumental and willing to harm my respondents in order to get data, and that I need to get ethical clearance from colleagues who often have no knowledge of criminal cultures and no interest in the practical nature of my research before I can proceed in an ethical manner is a troubling indication of the restrictive, cynical and paternal nature of contemporary research governance.

So, I claim that we actively need covert research methods if we are to advance intellectually from this point. We also need to develop new forms of ethical oversight that is less administrative, moralistic and cocksure in their certainty of what is ethical and what is not.

Conclusion

It's abundantly clear that, in recent years, criminology has cut itself adrift from its rich ethnographic history and is sailing perilously close to the jagged rocks of abstracted empiricism. Too often we take the easy road in academic criminology. We opt for safe empirical studies in institutional settings that neatly avoid any disturbing encounters with the real world and produce anodyne, superficial data. We concern ourselves with racking up safe publications and gaining promotion to the next rung on the ladder. We avoid unpalatable truths and instead meekly accept the prevailing academic frameworks that have been doing the rounds since the 1960s. What we need is a renewed interest in revealing the often painful realities of crime and violence in our urban areas. We must dispense with the unworldly affirmative liberal assessment that negates the harms of crime and attempts to defend criminals from 'labelling', which is a politically driven attempt to prevent the truthful 'thick description' at the representational heart of criminological research. A perfect example of this can be found in Craine's (1997) work, in which he talks of a researcher who failed to discover any evidence of individuals committed to a life of crime on the notorious Meadowell estate in the north-east of England. Instead, the researcher discovered an organic and self-supporting community in which crime played a negligible part. This kind of narrative is representative of the most obscene form of ideological mystification in contemporary criminology. If we are serious about renewing the intellectual vitality of our discipline, two things need to take place. One, we need to develop new intellectual frameworks that are respectful of the accomplishments of the past but that are willing to offer a new account of the world as it is today. The first step in this process is to once again borrow innovative ideas and concepts from cognate fields. And two, we need to rejuvenate the empirical base of the discipline with ethnographic data that reveal the hard truths of the contemporary crime problem. To do this, we must abandon instrumentalism, careerism and liberal ideology and commit ourselves once again to the difficult task of gathering hard-to-reach data.

References

Agar, M. (1980) *Professional Stranger*, New York: Academic Press

Ancrum, C. (2011) '"Knowing the dance": the advantages and downfalls of a criminal biography', *Enhancing Learning and Teaching in the Social Sciences (ELiSS)*, 3 (3)

Armstrong, G. (1998) *Football Hooligans*, Oxford: Berg

Beck, U. (1992) *Risk Society*, London: Sage

Blumer, H. (1969) *Symbolic Interactionism*, London: Prentice Hall

Bourgois, P. (1996) *In Search of Respect*, Cambridge: Cambridge University Press

Briggs, D. (2012) *Crack Cocaine Users*, London: Routledge

Craine, S. (1997) 'The black magic roundabout: cyclical transitions social exclusion and alternative careers', in R. MacDonald (ed.) *Youth, the 'Underclass' and Social Exclusion*, London: Routledge

Fleisher, M. (1995) *Beggars and Thieves*, Madison: University of Wisconsin Press

Fountain, J. (1993) 'Dealing with data', in D. Hobbs and T. May (eds) *Interpreting the Field*, Oxford: Oxford University Press

Geertz, C. (1975) *The Interpretation of Cultures*, New York: Basic Books

Hall, S. (2002) '"Daubing the drudges of fury": men, violence and the piety of the hegemonic masculinity thesis', *Theoretical Criminology*, 6 (1): 35–71

——(2012) *Theorizing Crime and Deviance*, London: Sage

Hall, S., Winlow, S. and Ancrum, C. (2005) 'Radgies, gangstas and mugs: imaginary criminal identities in the twilight of the pseudo-pacification process', *Social Justice*, 32 (1): 100–12

——(2008) *Criminal Identities and Consumer Culture*, Cullompton: Willan

Hobbs, D. (1995) *Bad Business*, Oxford: Oxford University Press

Hough, M., Warburton, H., Few, B., May, T., Man, L., Witton, J. and Turnbull, P. (2003) *A Growing Market*, York: Joseph Rowntree Foundation

Levi, M. and Maguire, M. (2002) 'Violent crime', in M. Maguire, R. Morgan and R. Reiner, *The Oxford Handbook of Criminology*, Oxford: Oxford University Press

McAuley, R. (2007) *Out of Sight*, Cullompton: Willan

Polsky, N. (1971) *Hustlers, Beats and Others*, Oxford: Oxford University Press

Rae, I. and Smith, K. (2001) *Swan Hunter*, Newcastle: Tyne Bridge Publishing

Reiner, R. (2007) *Law and Order*, London: Routledge

Taylor, I. (1999) *Crime in Context*, Oxford: Polity

Treadwell, J. (2012) 'White riot: the English Defence League and the 2011 English riots', *Criminal Justice Matters*, 87 (1): 36–7

Walcott, H. (1995) *The Art of Fieldwork*, Lanham, MD: Altamira Press

Winlow, S. (2001) *Badfellas: Crime, Tradition and New Masculinities*, Oxford: Berg

——(2012) '"All that is sacred is profaned": towards a theory of subjective violence', in S. Hall and S. Winlow (eds) *New Directions in Criminological Theory,* London: Routledge

Winlow, S. and Hall, S. (2006) *Violent Night,* Oxford: Berg

——(2012) 'What is an ethics committee? Academic governance in an epoch of belief and incredulity', *British Journal of Criminology,* 52 (2): 400–16

8 A phenomenological account of deviance and risk on holiday

British youth and the consumer experience in Ibiza

Daniel Briggs

Introduction

As the sun starts to set on another day in San Antonio, Ibiza, I get talking to a group of young men (aged 19–20) in a nearby bar. The night is still young as we all take large gulps of beer from our pint glasses. During our focus group, they laugh about beating up 'some random guy' and how they paid for another 'random' to have sex with a prostitute because they couldn't pay for it themselves. Here Charlie who is unemployed, recounts tales of cheating on his girlfriend by sleeping with five girls:

CHARLIE: 'When the cat is away, the mouse will play' [awkward pause] … it's not that I don't love her but I am young and stuff. How can I be in Ibiza and not live it to the full potential? There's girls there walking around in hot pants.
AARON: I saw less than that, boy.
OTHER BOYS: Yeah, yeah, yeah.
DAN: What you're saying is to fully experience Ibiza one has to, or is expected to …
CHARLIE: Well in my opinion, yeah. I had a girlfriend, it wasn't that I didn't care about her but I just felt like I am in Ibiza, I'm gonna have fun.
DAN: Do you feel bad? Be honest.
CHARLIE: A little bit if I am honest. It wasn't because I was drunk. I hate people that say 'I was so drunk'.

[A short time later, after we have all had a few shots of tequila]:

DAN: How do you work out what a 'good' night out is?
AARON: How fucked I get and who I end up with at the end of the night. That is what I base it on.
DAN: [to Charlie] How do you feel about that?
CHARLIE: Well I just think the more money you spend, the better it is.
GERALD: Before I went out [last night], I had 14 pints during the day.
DAN: What did you have on top of that?
GERALD: Don't know because we just stopped off bar by bar.

DAN: You can't even tell me how much you drank.

GERALD: No way bruv.

It's easy to get a sense of what the 'holiday' means for this group of young working-class men from south London. The narrative highlights general hedonistic attitudes to the holiday which include drug use, risk-taking, sex, violence and a clear departure from home–life responsibilities. The social occasion, boisterous group dynamics and an emphasis on 'taking advantage' of the opportunities presented to them are also evident. Also apparent is an undivided dedication to consumption highlighted in Charlie's words: *'I just think the more money you spend, the better it is.'* One could easily assume that these narratives echo the general stereotypical view of young British holiday-makers abroad in places like Spain (Andrews 2005). However, in this chapter I will argue otherwise. I would like to direct attention to young British holidaymakers and their consumerist attitudes but also frame their behaviours within an aggressively commodified social context that endorses and amplifies the group's deviance and risk-taking, cashes in on their desire for indulgent hedonism, and leaves them almost penniless by the time they return home. In doing so, I will attempt to identify the manner in which class-based gender identities engage with and contribute to the structure and content of alcohol-based leisure markets.

I am doing this for several reasons. First, because the existing literature that addresses British youth and their deviant actions abroad is devoted to survey research, subcultural analyses or distant participant observation strategies; there seems to be no serious effort to document how these environments are subjectively experienced and interpreted by the people who holiday there. Second, I am interested in providing a detailed, first-hand account of the nature of commodified excess among male British tourists in Ibiza. By definition, Geertz (1973) would suggest that such an approach is 'an elaborate venture *in*', and that's why I also drank alcohol with them and participated in their group activities. It's disappointing that some colleagues thought I was just 'going on holiday' or undertaking a 'dream research trip' just because this fieldwork took place in a leisure zone which celebrates all the hedonistic wonders of the night-time economy (NTE). For me, this fieldwork was not 'fun', and, in fact, opened up raw self-reflexive feelings of what it means to *be* in this post-political age. Acting as a researcher and experiencing life with British holidaymakers in San Antonio only confirms to me how debauched, vulgar and dangerous consumer culture can be.

I turn first to the literature surrounding young British consumers and NTE because the group's familiarity with 'going out', 'getting wankered' and other aspects of consumption relate closely to the UK leisure landscape. Specifically, the gendered holiday abroad represents a bizarre continuation and exaggeration of concerns, goals and group dynamics regularly seen in Britain's strangely conformist and Bacchanalian youth drinking cultures. I then discuss the importance of the social occasion: the holiday. This temporal period represents a 'time out of time' (Bakhtin 1984) for these young people, a time that encourages participants to abandon normative components of their home selves, and regular routines and responsibilities. Against this background, individual moral boundaries appear to become more malleable, a process that appears to be encouraged and reinforced in group interaction, shared culture and forms of talk. The following section provides a contextual narrative on the hyper-real and commodified nature of the social context of San Antonio, paying particular attention to the dedicated NTE space called the West End Drinking strip ('drinking strip' hereafter). I draw all these dimensions together using interview data, field notes and informal conversations with a group of working-class young men whom I met in San Antonio. I claim that their actions and experiences over the course of their holiday reflect three key elements: first, the manner in which the ideology of possessive consumerism (see Hall *et al.* 2008) shapes their desires for a holiday 'blowout'; second, how the desire for a 'blowout' finds form in the incessant offers, inducements and opportunities to experience indulgences that exist beyond the boundaries of usual social experience; and third, as a consequence of these elements, the manner in which chances for deviance and risk-taking multiply.

Young British consumers and the NTE

The transition to late modernity has witnessed massive social changes across the social structure partly produced by the economic transition from 'Fordist' to 'post-Fordist' economies. It is argued that this shift led to the reinvention of major Western cities from flagging post-industrial town centres to sites that facilitate engagement in a culture of leisure and excessive consumption (Hayward 2004; Hayward and Hobbs 2007). This, some indicate, has led to increased social, cultural and spatial segregation as well as to the exclusion of working-class and lower-income populations from participation in the new consumer economies.

One aspect of these changes is the shift towards leisure-oriented NTEs that enable the construction of identities and lifestyles characterised by a high incidence of crime and disorder (Winlow and Hall 2006). At the same time, commentators note increased branding of excess in these spaces (Hobbs *et al.* 2005) and important changes in attitudes to excess such as a 'new culture of intoxication' (Measham and Brain 2005). Therefore, certain forms of crime and antisocial behaviour are associated with dynamics intrinsic to the burgeoning NTE, as well as changes in the culture of intoxication among British youth (Winlow and Hall 2006). It is within these social spheres that youth risk-taking has become more pervasive (Hayward 2004) and this certainly appears to be appealing for many.

The holiday

Another social arena that seems to provide a playground for risky behaviour and excessive consumption is the holiday (Andrews 2009; Briggs *et al.* 2011b). Indeed, it is well documented that British youth engage in increased alcohol, drug use and sex during their 'holidays' at various European nightlife destinations (Bellis *et al.* 2003). Among British youth, Spain is a popular overseas holiday destination (Govern de les Illes de Balears 2008), particularly the Balearic Island of Ibiza. Research points to the popularity of its club music (IREFREA 2007), 'crazy' party scene and relatively easy access to illegal substances (Bellis *et al.* 2003). However, Ibiza's hippy origins, 'club scene' and other distinct features of the 'white island's' tourist pull are no longer exclusive to the elite (Hayward 2004). Visiting Ibiza, and being able to say one has 'done the big clubs', 'gone Ibiza' or 'done Mambo'[1] are now available to a significant portion of working-class Britons (Andrews 2005). This is predominantly because different groups of British youth can now take advantage of cheap international airfares and package holidays. However, statistics show the numbers of British tourists visiting Ibiza have significantly dropped over the last decade: from 700,000 in 1999 (Fomento del Turismo de Ibiza 1999) to 570,000 in 2007 (IREFREA 2007). This may be because there is increased competition with 'new cheap beach destinations' and the local government seems to be moving towards the promotion of other areas of tourism such as cycling and golf – perhaps in the hope of altering the image of Ibiza as a place of drugs, alcohol and general transgression (Payeras *et al.* 2011).

Consumer excess, transgression and phenomenology

Consumer culture and its role in facilitating and promoting consumer excess and transgression in the NTE is well documented (Winlow and Hall 2006; Hayward and Hobbs 2007). In the context of the holiday, perspectives of the carnivalesque (Bakhtin 1984) and the quest for immediate satisfaction of desires (Bataille 1957) in the absence of work help us see the ways in which we subjectively engage with the appealing otherness of the holiday. Identity perspectives are also potentially significant given that young people go abroad on these holidays and engage in these activities to create memories which become significant in processes of identity construction (Briggs *et al.* 2011a).

In this chapter, I want to complement these perspectives with descriptions of the practice and experience of excessive consumption, risk and deviant transgression in the context of British youth in Ibiza. In doing so, I am therefore more interested in giving priority to description over explanation because I want to bring readers close to the lived reality of British youth abroad and their risky consumption practices. In this way, I have found Michael D. Jackson's (1996) endorsement of phenomenology and detailed descriptions of 'lived reality' a useful position to adopt (see Tutenges 2010). I turn now to the aims and methods of the study before contextualising the findings and presenting my empirical data.

Aims and methods of the study[2]

These data are drawn from three short ethnographic studies examining youth risk-taking with British youth abroad in Ibiza, Spain, in July 2009, July 2010 and June 2011. Observations were conducted in bars, clubs, beaches and general touristic areas. These areas were public and activity was observed that would have happened without intervention or influence from researchers. We used a combination of overt and covert roles (Briggs 2011), recording low-inference descriptors (field notes) as well as thoughts, impressions and summaries of conversations (Geertz 1973). In 2009, a scoping exercise was undertaken on the island; in 2010, 17 open-ended focus groups (Griffin *et al.* 2009) were undertaken in Ibiza (n = 97, aged between 17 and 31); and, in 2011, 15[3] were conducted (n = 72, aged between 17 and 35).

When the research team arrived in San Antonio it became obvious that we would have to collect data from individuals who were intoxicated in some way. Indeed, had data collection remained restricted to non-substance using groups, the sample size would have been small and researchers would have developed a skewed picture of the holiday 'experience'. As others have done in the context of researching youth drinking cultures (Briggs *et al.* 2011a) we drank alcohol with participants to establish credibility, rapport and trust.

Informal conversations were also undertaken with local businesses, bar owners, strippers, taxi drivers, prostitutes, PR workers, police and tourist representatives about their perceptions and experiences of British youth abroad. All participants were given pseudonyms. Once transcribed, interview and observation data were categorised thematically, with the key areas of investigation providing the overall framework for coding. Analyses were inductive, which meant that themes emerged from the data rather than being hypothesised. The research was funded and granted ethics approval by the University of East London's Ethics Committee.

The social context of San Antonio

Addressing the social context is imperative if we are to understand how risk and deviance arise in holiday resorts like San Antonio. Data indicate that this space actively endorses and promotes alcohol consumption, drug use, sex and violence (Bellis *et al.* 2003). Indeed, in the 'drinking strip', where most of my data collection was undertaken, tourists can take advantage of numerous bars, clubs, takeaway outlets, restaurants, strip clubs and all the familiar sites of entertainment in the UK NTE (Measham 2004). This particular space is quite strategically designed and concentrated in one area of San Antonio to maximise consumer spending. It is made up of only one main pedestrian road and a few intimate alleyways either side. Such is this concentration that one need not drift too far to find the next site of attraction. At night, young female and nearly naked PRs march up and down the drinking strip advertising various DJs, nightclubs or special events that populate the nightlife calendar. There are also young male PRs, but they generally wear more clothes. In this way, the drinking strip in San Antonio predominantly caters for the male, heterosexual gaze (Pritchard and Morgan 2000), and it constantly showers visitors with tempting opportunities for excess (Andrews 2009; Tutenges 2010) which resonates with working-class British youth who often stay in or nearby the resort and are found in this social space.

In general, there is no regulation of this space; the police only seem to appear to arrest or move prostitutes on. There are private security guards outside a few clubs and bars, and while they quickly resort to violence to resolve disorder, they often let the same troublemakers in the next night (Briggs *et al.* 2011a). As the night progresses, this social space swells with young British tourists; in particular, male groups lose their friends, get into fights and/or wander off and are at the mercy of other socio-commercial pressures that occupy the same landscape (Hayward and Hobbs 2007; Briggs *et al.* 2011b). My field notes give the reader an idea of how intense this space is and the ways in which potential punters are constantly roped into deals on alcohol, drugs and sex:

> [The time drifts past 1am. I walk down past the strip and pass a hen party. I am stopped again]:

PR WOMAN (PRW): Are you coming in again?
DAN: Again? We haven't been in yet? How did you remember us?
PRW: Yeah, come in for some drinks.

> [As I look down, once again, at the streets, they are strewn with drink bottles, sick, waste, half-eaten burgers, chips and all manner of rubbish. Suddenly, we are dragged over once again]:

LIVELY PR MAN (LPRM): Come in here to have a drink. Get two free shots as well, guys. [Physically shepherding me in] What would you like to drink?
DAN: We're coming back, calm down.
LPRM: Come down now, come on, come in.
DAN: No.
LPRM: Try it now.
DAN: Er, NO.
LPRM: [As if nothing has happened] Ok, guys enjoy your night.

> [30 seconds later – Chirpy PR man (CPRM) approaches us]:

CPRM: Two drinks and a shot for €8.

As I show in the next section, most British youth in this resort intentionally seek out the 'drinking strip', as this appears to act as a springboard for the night out. However, once they are there, it seems they are completely at its commercial mercy.

Findings: on holiday with the Southside Crew

The Southside Crew are a group of four friends from a coastal town in the UK. They have known each other since school and three of the four now work together. They relay their experience in the clubs back home where they used to be *'proper on it'* most weekends; *'pills, coke, the lot'*. Since settling down with families and/or partners, they say the opportunity doesn't present itself as much. At home, they confess to getting into fights, mostly with each other. All four have been in trouble with the law; Popeye has served two years in prison for cocaine dealing and C-Dawg three years for grievous bodily harm (GBH). On their return to the UK, Jay and Streetfighter face a court case for fighting outside a nightclub. Last year, two of the four went to Magaluf, another holiday resort on the island of Majorca, together. They say they have come to Ibiza for a 'blowout', and because of the 'name' and the superclubs – which they can't really afford to go to so end up most nights on the 'drinking strip'. They had also come away with 14 other friends who were staying in another hotel.

When I met them at 3 p.m., they had arrived in Ibiza at 10.30 a.m. that day but had been drinking without a break from 6.30 a.m. What I think the field notes and interview data highlight are the 'lived experiences' of the holiday, and the ways in which the Southside Crew display a ravenous desire to consume whatever is on offer to them. However, it also shows the way in which the commodified social context, and the players of this social scenery, actively and continuously shape the potential for and nature of deviance and risk-taking.

Holiday intentions: meeting the Southside Crew

I walk along the San Antonio bay and look for groups of men to approach for interview. I go straight for a group of four guys sitting in a beach bar. Fortunately, they are quite welcoming and allow me to sit with them. The music pumps out as the sun shines down on their half-naked bodies while they cheer and sip cold pints of beer. They struggle to remember how much they drank on the plane, where they stopped since arriving and where they are staying. They concede to needing vodka red bulls to pick them up during those moments where their drinking has started to flag. As another pint arrives, they argue with the waiter, saying that they are owed a 'free shot', and eventually seem to bully him into bringing them over. They then recount tales of sex from Magaluf, high five and hug me before we move on to talk about girlfriends:

STREETFIGHTER: It's a holiday mate. I love my girl, I love my baby.

POPEYE: Clearly not.

STREETFIGHTER: But I am away, I need to get fucking something. If I don't have sex on this holiday I am going to go back more frustrated, more angry.

C-DAWG: And he'll end up taking it out on the missus [then laughs].

DAN: [To Popeye] What do you think of this?

POPEYE: Terrible.

STREETFIGHTER: It's best to be honest mate.

POPEYE: Seriously, your girlfriend is pregnant.

STREETFIGHTER: But you don't get a fuck when your missus is pregnant.
POPEYE: That's why I think its terrible. [A young woman in a thong bikini walks past] Cor, look at the tits on that.

The irony of Popeye moralising Streetfighter on his confessional desires for sex only to pick his jaw off the floor while watching a girl in a bikini walk past. Despite their home relationships, two concede that there is a little competition to chalk up as *'many shags as possible'*. Some young women walk past with makeup and fake tan melting down their faces and legs; they try to sell us club tickets but, perhaps because they don't take the boys' fancy, there is little interest. After C-Dawg recounts a tale of being ambushed by a *'black bird'* for a €5 *'blow job'* in Magaluf, we get on to the subject of bodies and they all concede to strict diets prior to the holiday. Popeye thinks that girls approach him because of his body[4] and this seems to be confirmed for him as we are once again approached by PR girls, vying for us to part with our money to attend their bar party. The Southside Crew all downplay drug use, saying they used to do that when they *'was younger'*. Despite this, it emerges that Jay just bought weed from an African man; he says *'it don't count.'* When the bill finally arrives, they argue and claim they have been ripped off but the anger quickly diffuses as their mouths drop open as half-naked girls walk past in bikinis. Jay says *'fuck it'* and throws a bunch of euros on the table.

Commercial temptations and ideologies of consumption

We stumble out of the bar at around 4.45 p.m. and they permit me to continue recording. We walk slowly in pairs down the road, distracted by different attractive women trying to pry us into bars or sell us tickets to help shape our 'night out'. Jay practises his kickboxing techniques on me and shows me ways to kill people, while Streetfighter whispers in my ear about how he 'pulls women'. He tells one PR woman he will *'fuck her senseless in his apartment.'* *'Charming'* she says. He tries again only to have little success:

JAY: Nice arse.

[The girls passing by walk on unimpressed]

STREETFIGHTER: [To me] Mate, you have to push the birds out here.

[One PR woman approaches us]

PR WOMAN: Hi guys we just want to let you know what is going on Thursday ... [Hands out leaflets for a pre-party 'booze cruise']
STREETFIGHTER: Nice face. Pretty.
JAY: Then to our hotel to party or you could come pre-party?

STREETFIGHTER: We will fucking smash you up, fuck you, all sorts.
PR WOMAN: Eugh, that's disgusting. That's vile.

[All the lads laugh while Streetfighter remains serious about the offer]

Streetfighter's technique seems just to be to approach everyone woman with the same blunt offer for sex. The flirting continues and Popeye takes the lead. In fact, whenever attractive women walk past, our conversations cease in favour of gorping at the flesh on offer. However, the fact that we are now semi-mobile seems to make their advances for sex more brash and direct, but also our potential as 'commercial targets' more vulnerable. Thirty seconds later another PR couple approach us with tickets for Eden.[5] There is almost no interest until the possibility of 'pulling women' is presented:

PR WOMAN (PRW) 1: How many of you are there?

[She starts wrapping free entry wrist bands around our wrists]

PRW 2: Come over, Mark Wright from The Only Way is Essex[6] will be there!
POPEYE: [Sarcastically] Oh great. You're just trying to sell me something.
STREETFIGHTER: All they are is a pretty face. They all want to sell something.
POPEYE: [As the wrist band is carelessly wrapped on his wrist] Looks like we're going to Eden tonight.

[An Irish PR man (IPR) comes along]

IPR: Plenty of pussy in Eden tonight.
JAY: Fuck it, I'm gonna pay for everyone.
PRW 1: I'll sort your tickets out then because we also have Professor Green.[7] Its gonna be really good guys. [IPR imitates having sex with a girl from behind and laughs about how he claims he pulled two young women in a night the other night]
PRW 2: I guarantee you, you will pull in there tonight.
IPR: Oh mate, you gonna find some hot pussy in there [laughs to himself]. Want to see my cock?
JAY: I'm gonna go, I'm paying. I don't give a fuck how much. Tell me. I have unlimited money.

Burgers, beers, sangria and sambuca, everything

We eventually drift towards the town centre and eventually settle in a café at the dock area. The waiter comes over and gets upset because we have our t-shirts off; he stands there unimpressed by our brash behaviour:

JAY: [Gesticulating] I want a jug of San Mojito, what's it called? That drink which the Spanish drink.

DAN: Sangria.

JAY: Right, I want five shots of Sambuca.

POPEYE: Are you going to get fucked up?

JAY: Lets get minging [extremely drunk].

DAN: [Matter of factly] Yes, but lets also remember what the time is.

JAY: [To the waiter] And I want five pints of beer.

DAN: I don't think there is room on the table.

JAY: I also want five shots of tequila.

WAITER: Food?

JAY: I want a massive chicken. Just a chicken. Massive chicken [gesticulates as if to suggest the chicken should be the same size as the plate].

POPEYE: I just want a burger no salad.

DAN: This is crazy.

While we wait for the drinks, they wolf whistle at women in bikinis and I admire their designer sunglasses and swimming attire. Jay says my next 'survey' should be on *'looks and image'* as men will do *'anyfuckingthing to get cut* [look toned].' Popeye concedes to spending £300 on a pair of jeans for his holiday, £62 on a pair of shorts and £300 on a watch. I have little to compare and play down my Primark short-sleeved t-shirt which hangs from my shorts. It is about 6 p.m. We get on to the topic of religion and politics and Streetfighter tries to avoid the subject, partly because of how he feels about war in Iraq. The discussion seems to make him angrier and he stands up, and shouts for his drinks. All the drinks arrive at the same time and dominate the table. *'Its gonna get messy'* says Jay. Even though I don't remember anyone ordering tequilas, we knock them back. As more PR girls come over, glasses are chinked again as we down a cupful of sangria.

The food arrives and we eat like savages; while I benefited by having a breakfast, for my new friends this is the first meal of the day. Conversations die away between large mouthfuls, and intermittent gulps of whichever drink is in front of us. Although we finish the food, there still remains a substantial amount of alcohol on the table so I am encouraged to down as much beer as possible with them and slam down the pint glass. We leave the restaurant and the order of the night seems to shift once again as we are stopped by more PR men telling us how much 'pussy' there is in their bar/clubs on the drinking strip. As we stumble very slowly to the hotel, Jay takes off his swimming shorts and runs naked as fast as he can towards the hotel.

At the hotel …

When I arrive at Jay's room to check he is OK, the door is slightly ajar. There he lies naked in a pile on the bed while a small, paint-stained CD player hammers out loud music. He awakes and tries to get himself together for the night out. He stumbles over to the safe to get the rest of his money but has forgotten the code. Frustrated he reaches to a zip pocket on his shorts where he hopes to find some reserve euros. Shortly after, Popeye enters and is ready to go and invites me to his room which he shares with C-Dawg. They show me their CDs, put on *'some tunes'* and do little funky dances. They both seem quite sober despite the volume of alcohol they have drunk. As we are leaving, Streetfighter comes in dressed in white shorts and vest. We move from the balcony where C-Dawg and Streetfighter practise their Spanish on passers-by. As our flip-flop steps echo around the hall, we descend to the all-inclusive bar they have paid for but rarely use. We have a few beers and more PRs descend to try and get us into Eden even though we have the wristbands. They, like the others, boast about *'fucking loads of pussy'* in their clubs. C-Dawg returns with six beers and we are forced to down them quickly because the others have decided we are leaving.

To the drinking strip

After petty arguments of whether we should take a taxi or walk, Popeye starts walking and we all follow. As we pass the bars, the music booms out across the small road. The night has begun. On the way down, we are separated several times and tempted by new offers for drinks and entertainment. As we pass a drunk man, passed out on the pavement, Popeye dares C-Dawg to put his 'cock' in the man's hand. We walk past a higher proportion of African men and some instead of offering sunglasses directly offer drugs: *'hey del boy, pills, weed, coke'.*

As we get to the 'drinking strip', we start to walk up the lazy incline. It is 9.30 p.m. On the promise of 'women' and free shots, we are persuaded to enter a bar/club but the dance floor is empty and it almost kills their mood. Suddenly a beer and shot are thrust into my hand. We send cheers and sink our shots. Outside we meet an annoying PR man who slaps our backs and tells stories how he has *'shagged loads of women'*. He offers us €40 tickets for 'Clubland' – a bar crawl where you pay for your own drinks, are led by *'pretty birds'* and get access to a water party in Es Paradis and wet t-shirt party in Eden. However, we already have free entry to Es Paradis because of the wristbands so we are really paying €40 for semi-naked women to march us around, lead us to places where we pay for our own drinks and let us into Eden. However, C-Dawg and Jay are very keen and move to muster up support from the others.

The PR man directs us further up the strip to his friend who will sell us tickets. As we walk up the hill, we are then offered laughing gas for €5 by two young women wearing next to nothing. Streetfighter wants to go back down the strip but Jay moves in for Clubland tickets. We reach the 'man' who seems completely wired on drugs; his eyes move around like jolty discs. He takes some money from C-Dawg and more from Jay and then hurriedly puts €160 in his pocket, taking little care about folding the money. When Popeye catches up with us and realises they have bought tickets for a bar crawl in which they have to pay for their drinks, he is not happy: *'oh for fuck's sake man, a walk around a few bars'*. There are some awkward moments as C-Dawg and Jay try to persuade Popeye that it is worthwhile because they'll be led around by pretty women. The 'man' talks the experience up and immediately tries to usher us into a bar where the bar crawl starts. I join them in the bar without paying. Quite quickly I am welcomed and start dancing:

C-DAWG: Danny boy!!!
DAN: C-dawgy boy!
C-DAWG: [Puts his arm around me] Lets dance baby.

> [We all get a drink and I end up dancing in puddles of alcohol and sick on the floor.]

C-DAWG: [Shouting] Danny boy!
DAN: [Laughing to myself and looking down at my beachwear which I have had on all day] I smell very bad. [C-Dawg laughs]
DJ: Are you people ready?
CROWD: YEAH!!!
DJ: Lets get fucking twatted!!!! [Drunk]

The host girls who are to lead us around start to dance with the lads who reciprocate by grinding their bodies up against their skinny bikini figures. I jump around in the puddles and my flip-flops fill with the mixture of sick and alcohol. Professor Green takes the stage and shouts *'MAKE SOME FUCKING NOISE!!!!'* There are some high fives and hugs which include me. C-Dawg says *'it's gonna be a good night'* but then realises that his expensive new shoes are already ruined in the alcoholic vomit. We are led out of the bar by the women in bikinis and high heels. They all hold flags as if to symbolically lead the way for the debauchery which is to follow. The lads follow mesmerised as if the pied piper is leading the way. As we move to another bar, we lose Jay but I find him quite happily and aimlessly wandering the streets.

It is now about 11 p.m. The same female dancers dance on the tables around the bar and seem to completely mesmerise Streetfighter. There is barely time to have a drink before Professor Green says that we should move on. The red-dressed female dancers go to the street in formation with a pair of big banners and a security guard. We follow them and reach the next bar where some young women walk around selling shots and others have a kind of booze-sprayer which they try to foist on people. While the others dance, Streetfighter chats with one of the booze-sellers, even getting to hug her and touch her bottom a little. But when she sees that he is not interested in buying anything she quickly moves away. On the dance floor, people crash together, jump around and everything is rather chaotic.

As we are led away to the next bar by the red-dressed females, our group breaks up along the drinking strip. C-Dawg and Popeye continue in pursuit of the red-dressed females while Jay and Streetfighter walk into KFC. They quietly eat from their bags of food, which is not a pretty sight. Gnawed chicken legs fall to the ground and their faces and fingers glisten with the fat. After eating, they sit on some benches. Jay is so drunk that he almost falls off several times. Then three Brits in their late twenties sit nearby and scowl; one of them says something insulting in our direction and walks over in a threatening manner. There are some angry exchanges but Jay gets up and walks towards the clubs. *'Take a piss'* Jay says and stumbles across the street, taking several minutes to unzip his trousers before staggering over to a rubbish bin and urinating in it.

Meanwhile, Streetfighter continues and is now 100 metres ahead of us. Jay collapses again, this time on a bench. It is only 500 metres to Es Paradis but it takes us about 40 minutes to arrive. They then stand staggering in front of the entrance of the club. One of the doormen gives a sceptical look and shakes his head, but they are permitted to enter. Ten minutes later, the two of them waddle out and head towards Eden, which is situated on the other side of the street. They explain that Es Paradis is *'crap and empty'*. We stand in front of the entrance and again the doormen look sceptically at my two companions.

We walk inside and there are only around 50–60 guests in the giant club. They each pay €12 for a vodka red bull but as Streetfighter takes a sip of the drink, he tips it over. Then a female photographer comes around, perhaps working for the club. Streetfighter tries to reach out for her bottom and gives a grunt but she jumps away. Suddenly Jay gets up to leave, having barely sipped his drink. However, Streetfighter leaves his visa card lying on the bar and I pick it up and hand it to him. He nods gratefully. When we get outside we can't see Jay, and Streetfighter seems perplexed without his friends. I take a seat to take stock, and Streetfighter disappears. I walk back to the drinking strip but can't find him or any of the others. It is about 1 a.m.

The next day …

I find them the next day, late in the afternoon lying on the beach, playing with the sand. They reiterate how it was a 'great night'. So what happened after I lost them? It seems Jay could not remember where he went or how he got back to the hotel. He thinks he got in at 2 a.m. but C-Dawg says he *'got lost'*. Popeye stayed with C-Dawg but found some of his 14 mates and got in about 6.30 a.m. C-Dawg left for the hotel but was approached by a prostitute, had no money, 'ran back to the hotel' to get some money but then couldn't find her. He finished the night slamming tequila shots on his own until about 4 a.m. He too couldn't remember how he got back to the hotel. Streetfighter? Well …

STREETFIGHTER: Got sucked off by two black birds.
DAN: Oh yeah? What down the West End?
STREETFIGHTER: Yeah.
C-DAWG: Yeah, I almost paid for a hooker on the way home.
STREETFIGHTER: Well it was going to be for €40 because it was two of them but I didn't have money.

DAN: You didn't have money?! So what did you give them?

C-DAWG: Give them dick!!!

STREETFIGHTER: They sucked me off a bit, I shit myself then I just told them to piss off afterwards.

DAN: [Disbelieving] You shit yourself?

C-DAWG: [Laughing] Too much drink mate.

STREETFIGHTER: I don't know how it happened mate but as I was cumming [ejaculating] I shit myself [starts to smile]. I had shit everywhere, all on my white shorts.

DAN: I wouldn't put that on Facebook.

STREETFIGHTER: Stuff like that stays on holiday, mate.

Discussion

In this chapter, I have tried to complement the literature surrounding British youth on holiday and the deviant and risky activities in which they participate. I wanted to go beyond surveys (Bellis *et al.* 2003), subcultural considerations (Malbon 1999) and distant forms of participant observation (Andrews 2005, 2009) to bring the reader closer to the 'lived experience' (Geertz 1973) of this particular culture. I tried to do this by taking a phenomenological angle and by spending time with these young people, drinking, dancing and parading myself half-naked through the drinking strip of San Antonio in an effort to glean subjective meaning. The way in which I did this is akin to others working in the sphere of substance-using youth cultures (Briggs *et al.* 2011a). For me, this was no 'holiday', no opportunity to either indulge or take advantage of the social occasion as an excuse to get drunk. I went into this fieldwork with the intention of revealing just how raw the holiday experience is and what it means to this group of working-class men whose post-industrial habitus shapes their attitudes toward leisure and the hopes for the holiday.

The chapter shows that holiday deviance and risk-taking should be seen as a commodified and strangely postmodern extension of Britain's liminal night-time drinking cultures. I have also tried to draw out the crucial importance of the culturo-economic context in which these excessive consumer behaviours take place, and the ways in which the desire for extreme experiences collides with the logic of the market. The Southside Crew are regular players in the UK NTE, restricting sessional substance use to weekends (Measham 2004), and often getting into fights (Winlow and Hall 2006). Their class-based habitus and culturally framed expectation of orderly disorder and irregular social comportment in Britain's NTE shapes their attitudes towards the drinking strips of San Antonio as a social field (ibid.; Bourdieu 1993). Their experiences in Britain's NTE also helps to pattern their desires as they formulate a dream-like image of what the perfect holiday experience may hold for them.

Their attachment to expensive branded consumer goods suggests a democratisation of excessive consumerism, but this should not be read as a form of liberation and instead appears to reflect both the post-industrial economic requirements of neo-capitalism and the postmodern ideological injunction to enjoy (Žižek 1999; Hall *et al.* 2008). The Southside Crew can still say they 'did the clubs' even though they didn't quite have the holiday capital to, as they say, 'do Ibiza properly'. It may not necessarily matter though. This is because there is an inclusive, carnivalistic spirit (Bakhtin 1984; Winlow and Hall 2006) on the San Antonio drinking strip (Briggs *et al.* 2011b) and therefore there is little spatial or cultural exclusion. So if they can't be the celebrity in the club, swanking it up in the VIP lounge and throwing money at expensive cocktails, they can be the 'crazy person' on the drinking strip where many forms of misbehaviour are not simply permitted but subtly encouraged. Either way, it will be a tale to tell (Briggs *et al.* 2011a).

This is because the holiday occasion is a special time in which the absence of responsibilities and routine are celebrated (Briggs *et al.* 2011a) and this helps loosen the boundaries of the home 'self'. This is further encouraged by the group dynamics in which many travel to Ibiza and mutually reaffirm the centrality of sex, drunkenness and hedonistic abandon (Briggs *et al.* 2011b). The Southside Crew, like many British youth holidaying in San Antonio, drastically increase the use of illegal substances and engage in a rather different and broader range of risky behaviours (Bellis *et al.* 2003). The holiday thus functions as an almost cathartic 'time out of time' (Bakhtin 1984), where, in the absence of work, there is clear enjoyment in being 'wasteful' (Bataille 1957), particularly evident in the way Jay and Streetfighter continued to party even though they could barely walk. This is because the everyday home life of these young people is subjected to the demands of necessity (Tutenges 2010): some get up early in the morning during the week to study, work or look for a job, while others have what they say are stressful family commitments and other associated obligations that form part of their normative non-holiday identity. Indeed, as Ferrell *et al.* (2008: 41) observe:

> Late modernity with its trajectories towards uncertain work, immediacy, short term hedonism, NTEs and mediated aggression pushes the subterranean lust for kicks ever more to the surface.

This is especially the case for this cohort of working-class British youth. They don't have the resources to 'party' regularly like the elite, but while on holiday they focus on the consumption and destruction of resources – most notably money, time and health – in ways that copy the expressive waste of the leisure class (Veblen 1994) and suggest a desire to recreate the self in the image of the boundless celebrity consumer that is so central to popular culture (see also Hall *et al.* 2008). The chapter therefore complements the existing literature on contemporary alcohol-based leisure culture as a driver and facilitator of excess and transgression (Bauman 1988; Hayward 2004). This culture results in situation-specific risk-taking and forms of deviance that, as we have seen, is immediately appealing to those involved (Hayward and Hobbs 2007).

For example, it is noticeable that Jay's initial rejection of drug use loses its connection to his normative identity and moral being in the strange cultural atmosphere of the holiday and results in him taking two Es on one night. Similarly, Popeye's narrative in our focus group was one of a committed partner and father, averse to drug use and who, over the course of his holiday, took an E while on a bungee jump ride and had sex with a girl on the last night. The pliability of moral accounts of themselves shouldn't surprise us. The Southside Crew were bombarded with offers of drugs almost everywhere they went. As the field notes of the Southside Crew show, sex was being sold as a commodity in San Antonio – as a promise for capital exchange if one attends the clubs or goes into the bars. Leading this market assault were the PRs who made continuous sales references to the lure of 'pussy' which validates the male consumer view that women exist to be 'fucked': this logic lives in their point of sale, their branding, and the way they commodify it, thereby transforming women from a subject into object.

Therefore while San Antonio seems to represent a gendered landscape (Andrews 2005) designed for the male gaze (Pritchard and Morgan 2000) where both young British men and women play out their gender roles (Andrews 2009), payments are made with the expectancy that sex will be the end result. The direct and blunt sexual advances of the Southside Crew often resulted in instant rejection from other female tourists and this appears to redirect their thirst for sexual conquest towards those working in the sex entertainment sphere. If it is not the bar crawls led by half-naked women, there are open markets for strippers, lap-dancers and prostitutes.

Much deviance in this context should be understood in relation to the poorly regulated nature of the aggressive hedonistic consumption that sustains the island's legitimate and quasi-legitimate economic spheres. San Antonio, and the drinking strip in particular, offer unbridled consumption and excess. The blame for the perceived cultural ills that are associated with British youth tourism on the island should not be laid at the door of tourists themselves (Winlow and Hall 2006), especially given the economic benefits this tourist sector bring to Ibiza (Armstrong 2004). Local government may be concerned about the image of the island, but it has yet to turn down the business opportunities provided by the annual influx of young British hedonists (Payeras *et al.* 2011). So by combining a familiar NTE of ultimate paradise with aggressive marketing, culturally framed individual intentions for a holiday 'blowout', group dynamics which promote a continuous flow of pressured spending for collective 'enjoyment' (Mewhinney *et al.* 1995) and a social context which is designed to drain money from those who grace its shores (Armstrong 2004; Garratt 1999) makes for haphazard spending, deviance and risk-taking (Winlow and Hall 2006). The holiday 'experiences' therefore not only leave 'good memories' but also become the receipt of the holiday transaction; something which is extracted regardless.

Acknowledgements

The author would like to thank all the young people who participated in the research; and Tim Turner, Keith Hayward, Ruth White, Lauren Holdup, Sébastien Tutenges, and Paul Brindley for assisting with the project. The work was funded by the University of East London Research Framework and gained ethical clearance from the University of East London's Ethics Committee.

Notes

1 Café Mambo is a well-known sunset café/chillout zone where tourists watch the sunset and pay for the privilege in the swanky cafes and bars nearby.
2 For a detailed discussion of the sampling strategies and ethical procedures see Briggs *et al.*, 2011a.
3 We base this number on data collected by Daniel Briggs and Sébastien Tutenges.
4 Popeye takes steroids and rarely eats carbohydrates so he can sustain his figure.
5 Eden is a nightclub in San Antonio. It is one of the smaller clubs in Ibiza and regulars of Pachá and Amnesia say it is lower down the list of 'clubs to visit'. It caters to the San Antonio market.
6 *The Only Way Is Essex* is a reality TV programme.
7 Professor Green is a UK music artist.

References

Andrews, H. (2005) 'Feeling at home: embodying Britishness in a Spanish charter tourist resort', *Tourist Studies*, 5 (3): 247–66
——(2009) '"Tits out for the boys and no back chat": gendered space on holiday', *Space and Culture*, 12 (2) 166–82
Armstrong, S. (2004) *The White Island*, London: Bantam Press
Bakhtin, M. (1984), *Rabelais and His World*, Bloomington: Indiana University Press
Bataille, G. (1957), *Eroticism*, London: Marion Boyars
Bauman, Z. (1988) *Freedom*, Buckingham: Open University Press
Bellis, M., Hughes, K., Bennett, A. and Thomson, R. (2003) 'The role of an international nightlife resort in the proliferation of recreational drugs', *Addiction*, 98: 1713–21
Bourdieu, P. (1993) *The Field of Cultural Production*, Cambridge: Polity Press
Briggs, D. (2011) *Crack Cocaine Users*, London: Routledge
Briggs, D., Turner, T., David, K. and De Courcey, T. (2011a) 'British youth abroad: some observations on the social context of binge drinking in Ibiza', *Drugs and Alcohol Today,* 11: 26–35
Briggs, D., Tutenges, S., Armitage, R. and Panchev, D. (2011b) 'Sexy substances and the substance of sex: findings from an ethnographic study in Ibiza, Spain', *Drugs and Alcohol Today*, 11 (4): 173–88
Ferrell, J., Hayward, K. and Young, J. (2008) *Cultural Criminology: An invitation*, London: Sage
Fomento del Turismo de Ibiza (1999) *Ibiza tourist statistics*, Fomento del Turismo de Ibiza (Department of Tourism for Ibiza): Palma Majorca, Spain
Garratt, S. (1999) *Adventures in Wonderland*, London: Headline
Geertz, C. (1973) *The Interpretation of Cultures*, London: Fontana

Govern de les Illes de Balears (2008) *Dades informatives 2007: El turisme a les Illes Balears*, Palma de Majorca: Govern de les Illes de Balears (Government of the Balearic Islands)

Griffin, C., Bengry-Howell, A., Hackley, C., Mistral, W. and Szmigin, I. (2009) '"Every time I do it, I absolutely annililate myself": loss of self-consciousness and loss of memory in young people's drinking narratives', *Sociology*, 43: 457–76

Hall, S., Winlow, S. and Ancrum, C. (2008) *Criminal Identities and Consumer Culture*, Cullompton: Willan

Hayward, K. (2004) *City Limits*, Glasshouse: London

Hayward, K. and Hobbs, D. (2007) 'Beyond the binge in "booze Britain": market-led liminalization and the spectacle of binge drinking', *British Journal of Sociology*, 58 (3): 437–56

Hobbs, D., Hadfield, P., Lister, S. and Winlow, S. (2005) 'Violence and control in the night-time economy', *European Journal of Crime, Criminal Law and Criminal Justice*, 13 (1): 89–102

IREFREA (2007) *Tourism and Violence in Nightlife*, Brussels: European Commission

Jackson, M.D. (1996) 'Introduction: phenomenology, radical empiricism and anthropological critique', in M.D. Jackson (ed.) *Things as They Are: New Directions in Phenomenological Anthropology*, Bloomington: Indiana University Press

Malbon, B. (1999) *Clubbing*, London: Verso

Measham, F. (2004) 'The decline of ecstasy, the rise in "binge" drinking and the persistence of pleasure', *Probation Journal*, 54 (4): 309–26

Measham, F. and Brain, K. (2005) '"Binge drinking", British alcohol policy and the new culture of intoxication', *Crime, Media, Culture*, 1 (3): 263–84

Mewhinney, D., Herold, E.S. and Maticka-Tyndale, E. (1995) 'Sexual scripts and risk-taking of Canadian university students on spring break in Daytona Beach, Florida', *Canadian Journal of Human Sexuality*, 4 (4): 273–88

Payeras, M., Alcover, A., Alemany, M., Jacob, M., Garcia, A, Martinez-Ribes, L. (2011) 'The economic impact of charter tourism on the Balearic economy', *Tourism Economics*, 17 (3): 625–38

Pritchard, A. and Morgan, N.J. (2000) 'Privileging the male gaze: gendered tourism landscapes', *Annals of Tourism Research*, 27 (4): 884–905

Tutenges, S. (2010) *Louder! Wilder! Danish Youth at an International Nightlife Resort*, Copenhagen: Department of Sociology, Copenhagen University

Veblen, T. (1994) *The Theory of the Leisure Class*, London: Constable

Winlow, S. and Hall, S. (2006) *Violent Night: Urban Leisure and Contemporary Culture*, Oxford: Berg

Žižek, S. (1999) *The Ticklish Subject: The Absent Centre of Political Ontology*, London: Verso

9   Easy money

Cultural narcissism and the criminogenic markets of the night-time leisure economy

Oliver Smith

Introduction

The night-time leisure economy (NTE) has been the focus for a number of research projects within the social sciences over recent years. Several studies have drawn attention to the close relationship the night-time economy shares with crime and deviance. This chapter attempts to draw attention to the cultural and criminogenic outcomes of commodified night-time leisure and, in so doing, I hope to identify the socially deleterious effects of aggressive twenty-first century consumer capitalism.

This chapter will argue that marketised, night-time alcohol-based leisure economies encourage forms of crime that go beyond the violence on the night-time high street and entrenched illegal drug markets that contribute to these leisure experiences. Rather, some committed consumers develop a cultural, aesthetic and emotional attachment to the night-time economy that both reflects and exacerbates ontological insecurity. This 'insecurity' is closely related to the fear of cultural inconsequentiality that might otherwise result from the inability of consumers to access these hedonistic consumer circuits. For the group of people on which I will focus, getting drunk at home before going out in order to save money – a practice known as 'pre-loading' – is not a viable solution. It is within the marketplace of the city centre that facets of identity are presented, and for some individuals the cultural practice of buying rounds of drinks, 'chasers' or 'shooters' is key to the ways in which identity is presented within these arenas and its links to their sense of status and identity.

The research presented here also reveals that for some committed consumers of this leisure economy, illegal drug markets can offer a route to 'easy money', although fear of becoming known as a drug dealer outside of a 'safe' client base of friends, acquaintances and linked outsiders prevents a full immersion into the underworld of the bona-fide dealer. For some of my respondents, the less risky option is to occupy a more positive role as a 'facilitator', able to reliably and consistently procure drugs for people at short notice. These para-criminal identities are often presented as being temporary, victimless and as an appealing alternative to 'real' criminality or, perhaps worse, failing to generate the money necessary to fully commit to commodified night-time leisure practices.

This work draws upon data collected as part of a larger project on the cultural and aesthetic attachments that people form to the alcohol-based night-time leisure economy. Comprising participant observation and in- depth interviews with dedicated adult consumers aged between 30 and 40, a picture emerges that suggests high levels of cultural infantilisation that surpass what has previously been referred to within sociological literature as 'emerging adulthood' (Arnett 2000) or 'prolonged adolescence' (Cote 2000). The following pages will attempt to outline the processes that contribute to what Slavoj Žižek (1991) would describe as the reorientation of the cultural superego, and how this is reflected in the deep commitment shown to the immediate pleasures of the NTE, which is viewed in this context as a microcosm of broader consumer culture. After establishing the ways in which consumer markets 'capture' the maturing individual, the experience of relative deprivation, perhaps better conceived of in terms of a Lacanian lack, or absence is considered (Hall *et al.* 2008). This lack, this nagging and enduring sense that something is missing, is felt by individuals within the precariat (Standing 2011). Specifically, this study involves those who may have once been considered working class and the new proletarianised lower middle class, all of whom are forced to wrestle with job and income insecurity. This sense of lack is heightened in a process closely linked to the relentless cultivation of desire. Here, respondents found themselves 'squeezed', to use the popular parlance of our times: driven to consume more as a means of addressing their sense of subjective incompleteness, but also forced to deal with job insecurity and declining incomes. For some, this 'squeeze' encourages the subject to be increasingly mindful of the criminal opportunities offered by the NTE.

Identity and the NTE

The past few years have seen a proliferation in media and academic accounts of alcohol-related violence, drug use and antisocial behaviour centred on the night-time leisure economy of the United Kingdom. Documentaries such as Channel 4's *Party Paramedics* depict the night-time high street as dangerous, drug-fuelled and alcohol sodden, with presenters and commentators both expressing distaste and bafflement at the displays of drunkenness, hypermasculinity and aggression that unfold in front of them with mesmerising predictability. The city centres depicted in these TV shows are now ubiquitous across the UK, products of the deregulation of public space in order to stimulate and facilitate local growth and development (Winlow 2009) and progressively more relaxed licensing laws, culminating in the 2005 move to round-the-clock drinking hours. Designed to provide revellers with more choice in venue, autonomy over when to leave the pubs and clubs and to promote a more relaxed, 'Mediterranean' model of alcohol consumption, the net effect appears to have been to increase competition within an already crowded marketplace, where two-for-one drink deals are plentiful and idealised outdoor tapas dining, or cappuccino-sipping experiences are notably absent.

The development of night-time, poorly regulated leisure spaces has encouraged many young people to invest heavily in this particular aspect of the non-work identity. But involvement in this leisure space does not reflect their organically formed choice of leisure practice and 'identity', and their practice in these spaces is not necessarily transgressive or resistant to the dull normality of capitalist realism. Rather than resisting the seductions and compulsions of the market, social behaviour in the NTE seems to suggest conformity and incorporation, albeit covered in a thin veneer of radicalism and otherness (see Winlow and Hall 2006). True forms of resistance to consumer capitalism are rare, and throughout the research there emerged little sense of political commitment or radicalism within the commodified arenas of Britain's NTE.

The current form taken by the NTE is indicative of broader societal change affecting young people today. A number of commentators (Winlow and Hall 2009a; Bauman 2005) suggest that traditional forms of friendship and community are being radically and perhaps permanently changed. Social identity that may have traditionally been tethered to employment, class and location, now appears to be giving way. Here, beneath the shadow of the neoliberal project, we witness the establishment of multiple 'identities' and aspects of self that are easy to construct, easy to modify and above all easy to discard. As Bauman (2005: 11) suggests:

> [This] trend is self-sustained and self-invigorating. The focusing on self-reform self-perpetuates; so does the lack of interest in, and the inattention to, the aspects of common life that resist a complete and immediate translation into the current targets of self-reform.

Although Simmel (1957) suggests that individuals occupy a number of diverse social circles relating to family, nationality, work and leisure throughout the course of their lifetime, data presented here indicate that the conditions of liquid modernity (Bauman 2005) has the effect of compressing this process, to the extent that we now occupy a number of different circles through the course of one day. The ability of individuals to bring alternative facets of personality to the fore in an attempt to present a range of 'identities' to different audiences in different social situations appears to result in an almost regimented compartmentalisation of the various facets of their lives and identities. Winlow and Hall (2006: 29) claim that, for the working-class youth that form the basis of their research:

> life can be clearly compartmentalised and judged according to the instrumental utility and potential benefits and pleasures of each sphere. Work is unimportant aside from the fact that it provides the funds for other, more pleasurable spheres of personal activity.

These more pleasurable spheres of personal activity for many consist of the night-time leisure economy, an arena that allows the structuring of identity in relation to a complex dynamic of consumer symbolism and incorporation. Through the creation and the maintenance of 'coolness' (Heath and Potter 2006), the individual is encouraged to imagine themselves as distinct from the mundane and homogenised cultures of consumerism and corporate leisure through complex processes involving specialist knowledge and understanding, rooted in an abstract symbolism. The night-time city centre provides the savvy consumer with seemingly limitless opportunities to stake a claim on individuality – myriad ways in which they can travel an alternative route or turn their back on conventionality in a way that inspires respect or envy in others (see Hall *et al.* 2008). 'Coolness' can also be linked to identification with certain bars, drinks and consumption behaviours, which suggest distinction and freedom from the restrictions of corporate leisure or workaday mundaneity. For the committed consumers I studied, this notion of 'cool' was always connected to a lifestyle rooted in adroit consumer choices, hedonistic practice and studied inebriation. Respondents, such as Michelle, a single mother in her mid-thirties talked of being 'left out of the loop' if they failed to persistently partake in 'nights on the town':

> People drop off the radar if they don't go out. There's the fear that if you keep saying no to people then they stop asking. If you keep turning people down, they will assume you are going to say no every time and you drop out of the loop.

It is of course too simple to reduce this concern and nagging anxiety to the effects of peer pressure. At the heart of the anxiety surrounding failure to indulge in the commodified hedonism of the night-time high street lies the principle of symbolic exchange. Indeed, Žižek (2000) and Winlow and Hall (2009b: 289) might link consternation at 'dropping off the radar' to the very nature of consumer capitalism:

> The economic imperative to constantly expand the consumption of symbolically loaded goods that drives consumer culture has diminished prohibitions on enjoyment and the gratification of hedonistic desires. This major cultural shift has reconfigured the way we experience the guilt directed at us by the ferocious superego; we are no longer quite so guilty about gratifying ourselves, but far guiltier about missing opportunities to do so.

Most respondents were in their late teens in the early 1990s, a time identifiable as the genesis of what we now understand as the NTE in Britain, a new city centre space structured in relation to a commercialised hedonism predicated on consumption of a rapidly increasing number of branded beverages, venues and experiences. 'Identity' for some then becomes inextricably bound up within the specificities of their experience of the night-time economy. The processes of identity formation that were synonymous with Fordism were inaccessible to the vast majority of young adults and so a significant proportion of the socially included and economically active sections of this age group have spent the best part of two decades looking to the commodified hedonism of the NTE to source alternative symbolic and biographical narratives. As Malbon (1999: 183) states, with regard to the 'clubbing' scene of the 1990s, the appeal of the night-time economy lies in its promise to offer what he refers to as 'experiential consuming':

> A form of consuming in which nothing material is 'taken home', but which can nevertheless produce important memories, emotional experiences and imaginaries (remembered imaginations) that can be sources of identification and thus of vitality.

Malbon is suggesting that stories and experiences gleaned from participation in the night-time economy are integral to the creation and maintenance of 'identity'. Little wonder then that, for these individuals, there is scant incentive to adopt a more traditional version of adulthood and renounce the pleasures of youth when we consider the importance placed upon identity creation within the night-time economy.

Cultural infantilisation

Hollands (see also Cote 2000) suggests that young consumers are experiencing obstructions in their transition to adulthood, structural obstacles that result in prolonged periods of 'post-adolescence'. In order to better understand and contextualise these claims it is useful to revisit the Freudian model of infantile narcissism, a concept reinvigorated in recent years by Slavoj Žižek. I use this phrase in the psychoanalytic rather than the common pejorative sense, and my analysis here in no way implies a simple suggestion of childish selfishness among this group. Rather I want to use the body of work associated with infantile narcissism to create a more nuanced analysis of subjective psychological responses to the manifold pressures that bear down on individuals inhabiting our post-political age.

Processes of identity creation and maintenance appear to take place against the backdrop of an 'infantilist ethos' (Barber 2007) which serves to generate attitudes, desires, habits and preferences that seem to not only legitimise, but also encourage, childishness among adult consumers. Keith Hayward (2012) draws attention to this process with an astute deconstruction of the advertising industry. Introducing the notion of 'life-stage dissolution', he highlights the bi-directional processes of 'adultification' and 'infantilisation' as problematising the ability of young people to differentiate and disassociate themselves from the generation before them, resulting in an increased commonality of interchangeable cultural experiences between different generations. Undoubtedly, these forms of cultural infantilisation can be witnessed in bars, clubs and off-licence sales on a global scale. Consider, for example, the market success of alcoholic drinks that negate what might be viewed as the 'adult' element of consumption of alcoholic drinks – the taste peculiar to alcoholic beverages. The process of 'learning to drink' is avoided through drinking alcopops, bottled beverages with relatively high alcohol content, but presented in a host of fruit flavours. 'Corky's' shots are a further example – flavoured and branded almost as confectionery items, which appeal to this cult of the inner child (Barber 2007). Venues themselves are able to offer a route into childish abstraction, such as 'Skool Disco' club nights where adults are encouraged to dress in school uniform. Similarly, the 'Reflex' and 'Flares' bar chains offer themed bar experiences based on the 1980s and 1970s respectively, where the cult of a falsely remembered teendom is encouraged through the use of era-specific music, dressing-up of customers, and cheap, commodified decor.

Infantilisation as a social process then, induces childishness in adults, as well as maintaining those elements of childishness within children who are 'growing up'. The maturing individual is diverted from taking on traditional adult concerns, instead entering a form of biographical stasis, the pause button pressed during a period in which they are most susceptible to consumer symbolism and marketing messages (Barber 2007; see also Hall *et al.* 2008). In turn, capitalism is nourished by the creation and exploration of new markets and committed consumers, enabling its seemingly inexorable progression and expansion. The following section will address consumer society, drawing upon elements of theoretical psychoanalysis in order to describe and explain the cultural and aesthetic attachment that some adult consumers retain in relation to the pleasures of the NTE.

The unconscious and consumer society

Many commentators within the social sciences have positioned the individual as in control of a system of signs, imbued with the freedom to choose and reinvent themselves through the myriad opportunities proffered by the benevolence of consumer capitalism. This (mis)respresentation of the consumer and the consumerist dynamic is simplistic, framed by a particular ideological framework that appears unwilling to relinquish its attachment to a raw Cartesian subjectivity. From this analytical viewpoint the unconscious roots of desire are largely ignored, which results in a failure to account for those forces that might explain just how individuals become ensconced within the complex folds of consumerist society. Indeed, the process of assimilation may be traced back into childhood, and the formation within the unconscious of a very specific mode of identification with external objects and signs, which in turn contributes to an interminable desire of consumer goods and their associated symbolism. Key to the perpetuation of the processes of capitalism however, is the continuation of this desire and pursuit of the new throughout the life course (see Hall *et al.* 2008; Fisher 2009). This process is destined to self-replicate, not least because of the inescapable truism that desire itself can never be realised.

Earlier forms of capitalism were characterised by functional symbolic orders with a system of moral regulation and reality-testing mechanisms, which allowed the maturation process to take place unfettered in the vast majority of individuals. As the maturation process evolved, the unconscious, with its associated infantile narcissistic demands tended to be displaced onto other and more mature concerns such as art, politics, science and love (Hall *et al.* 2008).

Hall *et al.* (2008) suggest that consumerism hijacks the maturation process, steering it away from objects and signs that appeal to the mature individual or those that are not overtly supportive of consumer capitalism. Politics is boring, history best left in the past. Furthermore, the role of capitalism cannot be ignored when exploring how society has been transformed through the reorientation of the superego (see Žižek 2000). In its latest manifestation, capitalism has been pivotal in reducing the level of emphasis on prohibition within the social order. The processes behind the 'commodification of everyday life' (Baudrillard 1984) essentially undermine traditional forms of authority and emphasise the importance of enjoyment, a fact drilled home hundreds of times a day by advertising billboards, magazine advertisements, commercial breaks and, increasingly, viral and internet marketing. A plethora of advertising media preaches messages unimaginably far-removed from the ideology of the 'work ethic' with its central tenets of delayed gratification. This ideology was tethered to the notion that 'not leisure and enjoyment, but only activity serves to increase the Glory of God, according to the definite manifestations of His will' (Weber 1996: 157). Enjoyment *had* to be denied in order to ensure that the work, necessary for the functioning of the socioeconomic system, would be completed and production maximised. As such the superego operated efficiently, ensuring that should the individual deviate from the prescribed mantra of delayed gratification and sociability, the burden of guilt would weigh heavy. Under consumer capitalism however, economic growth is assured only through the development and exploitation of new and niche markets, a process that necessitates the dismantling and reconfiguration of the superego.

For Lacan, the ideal-ego is conceptualised as the narcissistic, idealised self-image of the subject – the image that the individual identifies with, that which they would like to become, while the ego-ideal is the agency that the individual is attempting to impress with their ego-image. According to Lacan, the agency of the ego-ideal that ushers the individual toward moral growth and maturity forces the denial of the law of desire through adopting the demands of the socio-symbolic order. The superego then, through mechanisms of excessive guilt and shame, exerts pressure on the individual as the law of desire has been betrayed. It is this process that led Lacan to note that 'the only thing of which one can be guilty is of having given ground relative to one's desire' (Lacan 1992: 314).

While the superego induces the individual to interminably seek out the new and desirable from the alluring window displays of the consumer epoch, the very structure of capitalism expedites and facilitates the ability to obey the injunction to enjoy. This accomplishment is relatively simply achieved through the realisation of the credit-based economy that has dominated the UK and much of the Western world for the last 30 years. As we mature within a consumer society, the processes that we would expect to take place are rendered impotent by the very fact that the Symbolic Order is made up of innumerable stylised resemblances of the individual's ideal ego. For committed adult consumers within the night-time alcohol-based leisure economy, the city centre is an arena of competitiveness and anxiety, humming with the potential for violence and humiliation as well as the imaginary social capital that is to be gleaned from participation in this particular cultural field. The overarching desire experienced by some to present themselves as youthful, successful and fun individuals reflects a durable insecurity that is no longer contained by the certainties of the modern symbolic order. The search for cultural capital and the illusory promise that a great night out will quell the underlying sense of lack or anxiety results in feelings of guilt being stirred in the event that they are unable to access these consumer markets through constraints of finance or family commitment.

Neoliberal global capitalism and the reoriented superego with its compulsion toward bounded enjoyment exist within a state of mutually supportive harmony, as the 'individual feeling compelled to enjoy' becomes an integral factor in global consumer capitalism (see Hall *et al.* 2008). Consumer culture is able to exploit the fact that the mirror stage maintains a grip on the individual throughout the process of maturation – the child develops a desire to model itself upon whichever 'imagined' other most clearly recognises and reflects back to its imagination and ego. The inherent resistance to entering the symbolic order provides a juncture of weakness that consumer culture, with its arsenal of marketing weapons, is able to exploit. It is now that we can appreciate the mechanisms that lie behind the observations of a whole swathe of commentators such as Barber (2007), Cote (2000) and Virilio (2005). In order to successfully corrupt the 'natural' maturation process, the trappings and allure of consumer culture must be prominently displayed and celebrated. Consumer markets like the NTE must appear to the subject as the most 'competent other', the most capable and desirable reflection of wholeness or completeness to young people in the early, formative and vulnerable stages of the life course.

Each of the imagos – those images and mythical scenarios churned out by the machinations of global media – promise to complete the individual and provide a recovery of the narcissistic identity; however this is little more than a mirage, the sense of incompleteness remains and the individual is exposed to another shifting imago that appears certain to deliver on its promises, only for that to fail as well. It is in this way that the individual becomes firmly ensconced within the contextual environment of consumer markets. Consider alcohol advertising. Who doesn't long for the camaraderie, the friendship and loyalty depicted by advertisements that enquire as to whether or not we have a 'WKD side', or depict a narrative culminating in a show of solidarity and brotherly action that assures us that 'You know who your mates are'. As Hall *et al.* (2008: 81) surmise:

What we can see clearly here is a process of identification that allows the most potent and competent aspects of the contextual environment into which the infant experiences the early stages of its development to capture its emotional allegiance in a form that endures across the life-course. The structural essence of the series of images, as a pivot of successful performance, can therefore represent the central value that the agents of liberal capitalism's symbolic order wish to promote: the master-signifier of the rugged, 'off road' hyper-individualist competing in the market and eschewing all forms of collectivism and collectivist politics – the attractive, exciting but essentially apolitical and immature reluctant citizen known as the 'cool dude'.

In the void created by the absence of the traditional symbolic order, narcissism blossoms and the individual is encouraged to progress into an adult life which is filled with objects and language that actively reinforce identity based on their ideal ego, rather than to continually challenge it through the social prohibitions, laws and demands of more traditional forms of maturation.

This psychosocial explanation of failure to transcend consumer markets, of which the NTE is a convenient example, indicates that we are witnessing something more complicated and profound than a simple, creative engagement with leisure opportunities. In fact, as I shall illustrate in the following section, the symbolism and allure of meaning and identity that is tantalisingly promised by the NTE has the potential to open avenues of criminality for individuals experiencing a more piercing sense of relative deprivation and increased levels of precarity in the face of rising costs and falling wages being experienced by many of these consumers. These individuals are utilising criminal opportunities in a way that cannot be described or explained in simple Mertonian terms of innovation.

Precarity and the NTE

The NTE then, is more than a straightforward leisure destination of choice. Imbued with cultural significance and meaning, its more committed consumers are unlikely to forsake it in the face of underemployment, financial obligation or the strains of expenses associated with a consumer lifestyle. The research upon which this work is based takes place against a backdrop of global financial crisis, a process that had been building throughout the 1990s as an increasing percentage of people found themselves drawn into a precarious existence characterised by labour insecurity, insecure social income and the distinct lack of a work-based identity. Interviewees were for the most part in employment, although the majority had a history of low-paid, insecure jobs and even those with vocational or academic qualifications could not lay claim to the traditions of social memory, reciprocity and parallel biography that would protect them from the pervasive sense of alienation and instrumentality that is synonymous with employment under neoliberalism.

For individuals who are unlikely to consider their identity in terms of geographic or labour communities, identity creation can be subjectively understood as an almost vocational, craft-based activity, facilitated by the seemingly vast array of lifestyle signifiers at their disposal. Commercialised leisure in the pubs and bars of the night-time high street is ground into everyday life and laden with symbolic meaning, becoming central to belonging and the creation of a sense of self. While aspects of their life that may once have been tied to the symbolic order are relatively underdeveloped, a discernible sense of anxiety, tension and pressure reflect the reality of our fragmented, individualised and increasingly atomised social order. For some, identities that are presented and cultivated within the context of the NTE have been years in the making and are often viewed as too valuable to be simply discarded as the weakened injunctions of the modernist symbolic order attempts to draw them away from commodified hedonistic excess.

An exemplar of commitment to participation within the night-time economy in the face of more traditional commitments can be seen in Billy, a 40-year-old joiner. He has a reputation for being on the drinking 'scene' for as long as anyone can remember, and I had been told a number of anecdotes relating to his hedonistic exploits before our meeting, stories that abounded with sexual conquest, superhuman absorption of hard drugs and sometimes violent interludes. I recognise him as a character I have seen at last orders in a number of pubs in town, still dressed in his work attire, from his high-visibility vest down to his dusty and dirty steel toe-capped boots, holding court at the bar. I am sitting at the bar with him on this occasion, at around 7 p.m. on a Saturday night, and he sits opposite me, grey-haired, overweight and in a checked shirt with jeans and smart-casual trainers, smelling strongly of freshly applied aftershave. Our conversation revolves largely around the 'good old days' before marriage, kids and a weighty mortgage that he procured at the height of the market. He is married with two children under 8 years old, and explains to me that having a 'massive night out' and 'getting fucked up' stops him getting depressed about financial pressures that are facing him as a consequence of the downturn in the construction industry. He finds himself drawn towards supplementing his income through selling illegal drugs, and the imperative to maintain his active presence within the NTE loosens the adhesive of the traditional symbolic order that continues to demand that he adopt the role of father and family man:

> Just as an example right, take hanging doors. In a big block of flats, offices or whatever, a few months ago I would have been looking at forty quid a door, I'd turn up and the door would be right there, someone would have put it right there for you and all I had to do was hang it and move onto the next one. I was making serious money, and that's just hanging doors, you know. These days, the guys that would set up the doors for you, just go and get them and lean them up against the wall or whatever, their jobs are gone, and I get paid 10 quid for hanging a door.

I have to go and get the door myself, lug it up a load of stairs or whatever then hang it, before moving onto the next one. Seriously, some
weeks, I am making about 175 quid. It's hardly fucking worth it. I can
make fucking loads more than that selling gear [cocaine]. I could make a
phone call now, and go and get some really good shit, cut it and shift it
all tonight, make about 300 quid.

For Billy, the prospect of denying the injunction to enjoy, of curtailing his full
participation in the night-time leisure economy, is unthinkable. He appears to
attribute enormous importance and meaning to his continued participation
within the NTE, and an awareness of the financial commitment that this entails
opens up the possibility of dealing drugs in order to leave his leisure time unaf-
fected. The £300 that Billy talks of is in all likelihood an exaggeration. Further
conversation suggests that he limits the risk by selling only to people that he
knows, friends, acquaintances and others who have a link to him.

Billy is not a unique figure within the dataset. Jase is a 38-year-old white
male who, although officially registered as unemployed, occasionally works as
a labourer for a kitchen-fitter, and he has seasonal work at music festivals,
preparing the site and general manual labour. Home is a bedsit above a
takeaway, and his largest outgoing is experiential consumption within the
night-time economy. For Jase, the cash-in-hand work from the kitchen-fitters
dwindled as the financial crisis worsened, creating a cashflow problem that
has been eased through drug-dealing. Jase appears to be less circumspect than
Billy with regard to carefully cultivating a client base, and on the occasion we
meet for an interview in a city centre bar Jase is in possession of 5 grams of
cocaine, ecstasy tablets, and a couple of grams of MDMA powder. Some is
pre-ordered and will be dropped off later that evening, while the rest he will
keep on him and hope to sell throughout the course of the night. His hands
never leave his phone as he receives and sends brief, staccato-like text messages. Once he has delivered the pre-ordered drugs, he will reduce the risk of
prosecution as a drug dealer by only having an amount that could reasonably
be interpreted as 'for personal use'.

I'm skint. No way could I afford to go out and get pissed if I wasn't
selling ... people want it and I can get it, so I don't see the problem really.
It's not like I'm out robbing houses like our kid [his brother]. I've never
stolen anything in my life, well, never robbed anyone anyway, so all I'm
doing is earning a bit of cash. People know I can get them anything they
want – scag, coke, anything. I don't rip people off like a lot of proper
serious dealers out there. I've got contacts from when I was proper into it
before, so I get a good deal and don't have to sell weak shit.

Jase talks about renewing a number of contacts from when he was involved in
drug dealing in a much more serious way, and the link between his 'capture'
within the night-time economy and his criminal activity is clear. His clothing

is all branded, and I notice he owns the latest model of iPhone. He doesn't own a car or go on expensive holidays, although his financial commitment to the NTE is not insignificant.

Billy's and Jase's growing involvement in local drug markets gives us some initial insight into what we might call the criminogenic drive that appears to undergird the night-time leisure economy. By supplementing their meagre incomes with drug dealing, they are running a serious risk of incarceration. Both men spoke of their reluctance to get involved in the drug market, Billy through alluding to his commitment toward his daughters, and Jase toward the fact that he had previously been involved in the trade but for the past few years had 'gone straight', as legitimate work was plentiful and the money was good. However, both mentioned the 'easy money' associated with selling drugs, and I suspect that the social capital associated with being able to supply drugs to friends and acquaintances also held some allure.

The desire to be constantly involved in and associated with night-time leisure markets also results in other forms of deviance. Sarah, a 32-year-old who works for the local council, provides an alternative, though no less instructive example:

> We are definitely starting to feel the effects of the cuts at our place. You could say I'm lucky to still have a job really. We're working longer hours but the take home at the end of the month is getting smaller. People are not going to sit back and see their pay drop like that, they'll get it back somehow. I use my own car for work, and petrol has gone up, but we still get the same allowance for using our own cars, that hasn't gone up at all. I've started being more creative with my mileage sheets, just a couple of miles here and there, not enough so that you could really notice if you checked against Google maps or anything, but it adds up, pays for a new top or a night out which otherwise I just wouldn't be able to afford.

These acts should not be interpreted as reflexively railing against an oppressive and unjust system, a considered form of resistance, of protest at individual impotence in the light of the governmental agenda of austerity and drops in real wages. Rather it is bizarrely conformist in its nature, indicative of the extent to which these individuals have been captured by consumer capitalism's obscene totality. Beneath the criminal act is the conformist desire to maintain an active presence within the consumer circuits of the NTE, and failure to do so comes with the existential threat of cultural irrelevance to peers that drive their sense of self-worth and identity.

Conclusion

This chapter has drawn upon the example of the NTE in order to build upon an understanding that has been at the centre of the critical project in criminology for some time: that consumer capitalism is inherently criminogenic. Whereas previous epochs were characterised by a recognition and understanding of social and cultural location, we find ourselves embedded within an age characterised by global capitalism and its associated consumer markets. As the only available option, capitalism acts as its own counter-position, even producing its preferred forms of dissent (Hall and Winlow 2007). Analysis reveals quite clearly that there can be no resistance at the point of consumption in the NTE. Rather, capitalism's powerful seductive imagery often induces consumers to rush towards expressive consumerism in an ill-considered way, and at the expense of those traditional aspects of the symbolic order that might have compelled the individual to have a settled career, family and relatively independent identity by the time they hit their thirties. For many respondents, failure to partake in these markets, to avail themselves of all the opportunities proffered by the commodified night-time high street is accompanied by the profound fear of cultural obscurity. Capitalist ideology creates this deep dread of social irrelevance, and in so doing pushes the anxious individual back to the arena of expressive consumerism. For some, this inducement is so powerful that normative social attitudes that forbid criminal activity are suspended or negotiated. Somehow, the anxious subject must generate the income necessary to experience life where it matters most. Where this insecurity is compounded by increased levels of precarity associated with diminishing levels of income and security in post-crash Britain, it is likely that a growing number of individuals will find themselves drawn toward criminal opportunities that allow them to avoid losing their foothold within the consumer marketplace.

References

Arnett, J.J. (2000) 'Emerging adulthood: a theory of development from the late teens through the twenties', *American Psychologist*, 55 (5): 469–80
Barber, B. (2007) *Consumed*, New York: Norton
Baudrillard, J. (1984) *In the Shadow of the Silent Majorities, or, the End of the Social, and Other Essays*, New York: Semiotext
Bauman, Z. (2005) *Liquid Life*, Cambridge: Polity Press
Cote, J. (2000) *Arrested Adulthood*, New York: New York University Press
Fisher, M. (2009) *Capitalist Realism*, London: Zero
Hall, S. and Winlow, S. (2007) 'Cultural criminology and primitive accumulation: a formal introduction for two strangers who should really become more intimate', *Crime, Media, Culture*, 3 (1): 82–90
Hall, S., Winlow, S. and Ancrum, C. (2008) *Criminal Identities and Consumer Culture: Crime, Exclusion and the New Culture of Narcissism*, Cullompton: Willan
Hayward, K. (2012) 'Pantomime justice: a cultural criminological analysis of "life stage dissolution" ', *Crime Media Culture*, 8, 2: 213–29
Heath, J. and Potter, A. (2006) *The Rebel Sell*, London: Capstone
Lacan, J. (1992) *The Ethics of Psychoanalysis*, New York: Norton
Malbon, B. (1999) *Clubbing*, London: Routledge
Simmel, G. (1957) 'Fashion', *American Journal of Sociology*, 62 (6): 541–58
Standing, G. (2011) *The Precariat*, London: Bloomsbury

Virilio, P. (2005) *The Information Bomb*, London: Verso

Weber, M. (1996) *The Protestant Ethic and the Spirit of Capitalism*, Los Angeles, CA: Roxbury

Winlow, S. (2009) 'Violence in the night-time economy', in F. Brookman, M. Maguire, H. Pierpoint and T. Bennett (eds) *Handbook of Crime*, Cullompton: Willan

Winlow, S. and Hall, S. (2006) *Violent Night: Urban Leisure and Contemporary Culture*, Oxford: Berg

——(2009a) 'Living for the weekend: youth identities in northeast England', *Ethnography*, 10 (1): 91–110

——(2009b) 'Retaliate first: memory, humiliation and male violence', *Crime, Media, Culture*, 5 (3): 285–304

Žižek, S. (1991) *For They Know Not What They Do*, London: Verso

——(2000) *The Ticklish Subject*, London: Verso

10 Atrocity exhibitions

Experiencing violence as student training

Audra Mitchell

Introduction

Educational field trips – field trips taken primarily to support the development and learning processes of students – are becoming an increasingly common feature of specialized training in disciplines such as peace and conflict studies, security studies, human rights and development (Mitchell 2011; see also Ng 2006). Increasingly, postgraduate programmes in these fields are expected to provide 'field experience' in places designated as 'war zones' or '(post-)conflict zones'. In many cases, a core component of such field trips involves direct contact with people perceived to be directly involved in, or affected by, acts of violence – that is, groups of people identified as 'victims' and/or '(ex-)combatants'.

Why do students (as well as educators and potential employers) view these encounters as valuable? Moreover, what are the ethical implications of seeking direct contact with 'perpetrators' or 'victims' of violence? To explore these questions, I undertook a study of 42 postgraduate students enrolled in 13 different postgraduate training programmes in the disciplines mentioned above (or cognate disciplines) at two major UK universities. Drawing on this project, I begin by analysing my respondents' conceptualizations of violence before they undertook educational field trips – that is, what exactly they expected to 'experience' in the field. I argue that most of my respondents sought to enhance their *experiential* understanding of the phenomena by encountering empirical evidence of it in the 'field'. Then, I discuss two inter-linked motivations, both of which relate to the perceived imperative to gain different kinds of 'experience'. The first relates to the demand for technical 'experience', and 'field' experience in particular, generated by potential future employers – predominantly major international organizations (IOs) and international non-governmental organizations (INGOs). The second is personal and existential: many of my respondents viewed these encounters as a means of breaking through the 'virtual' processes of knowledge formation in which they perceived themselves to be ensconced, and gaining access to a 'real' world hitherto unavailable to them. In so doing, they sought to make sense of distant, fragmented and seemingly abstract atrocities by exposing themselves to evidence of violence and constructing internal narratives and schema from it – much like the protagonist of J.G. Ballard's (2006) *The Atrocity Exhibition,* to which the title of this chapter refers.

Taking these motivations into account, I conclude by assessing some of the ethical risks raised by the demand for contact with the 'real' people perceived to be 'victims' or 'perpetrators' of violence.

Methodology

Educational field trips have become an integral tool for training future 'international' workers and thus for translating scholarship in international studies into 'real-world' impact. Yet there is little discussion within international studies on the nature of the field trip in teaching and training. There is a handful of reflexive and detailed studies that engage with the practical and ethical risks of fieldwork more generally, but they tend to focus on facilitating more effective research and reducing risks to individual, professional researchers and their subjects (see Sriram *et al.* 2010). Sometimes, ironically, such studies produce an idealized image of the fearless fieldworker (see Nordstrom and Robben 1995), thus fetishizing the 'field' and the experiences it is expected to offer. In other cases, they offer apologias for damaging actions taken on field trips, which urge researchers to learn from the quandaries or mistakes of the author (see Bourgois 2001). Although attentive to the ethical dilemmas of field research and highly self-critical, these studies focus exclusively on individual, professional researchers. They do not engage with the ethical dilemmas of undertaking fieldwork for purely *educational* purposes, rather than as part of an independent or commissioned research project.

To explore these issues, I conducted interview-based research with 42 postgraduate students recruited from two UK universities. Participants were enrolled in 13 separate postgraduate (MA/MSc) programmes in peace and conflict studies, war/security studies, human rights and development. In order to protect the anonymity of respondents, the universities remain unnamed and I have only explicitly mentioned the site of field trips where these cannot be traced to a specific university or degree programme. These programmes were selected because they placed a strong emphasis on practical skills training and fieldwork. Respondents were nationals of a range of countries; the largest single group was from the UK and Ireland, with a plurality of participants from Scandinavia or Northern Europe, Central Asia, Southeast Asia, the Middle East/West Asia, Latin America and Western Africa. They undertook field trips in a range of countries in Southeast Asia, East, West and South Africa, Western and Central Asia, and Latin America. Moreover, participants represented an age range from 21 to 56.

During the period in which interviews were carried out, all participants took part in an educational field trip to a place they or their instructors designated as a 'post-conflict zone' or 'post-war' zone. Most trips took place in countries in which a formal international intervention and/or peace agreement had taken place or was in progress. Participants took part in field trips of two kinds: student-led field trips, in which the student planned and undertook the trip independently, with the remote guidance of an academic adviser; and 'guided' field trips, in which students took the trip as a class, under the direct supervision of an academic and/or 'field' guides. Of my sample of 42, 25 participants took part in student-led field trips, and 17 participated in guided field trips. All field trips were between one week and two months in length and were intended to contribute solely or primarily to the production of a thesis or project required by the course of study. In all cases, the field trip consisted primarily of qualitative interviews with two categories of research subjects: those perceived as 'victims' and/or 'perpetrators', or other intended beneficiaries of international intervention; and their intended benefactors (IO and INGO workers, government officials, and so on). This chapter focuses primarily on accounts of encounters with the first category of research subjects – as did, overwhelmingly, the discussions of my respondents.

Violence and experience

In this study, I sought to engage my respondents in the discussion of 'violence', focusing my respondents' attention on the concrete social and material phenomena that they hoped to encounter. In the first interviewing sessions, I asked my respondents to explain any pre-existing conceptions, or formative images of violence that they used in planning their field trips, in particular in the selection of their research subjects – that is, in identifying 'victims' or 'perpetrators' to interview. Importantly, very few could describe violence in abstract terms, and most struggled to come up with definitions. For the most part, my respondents sought to engage with the concept of 'violence' by describing evidence of somatic or bodily injury. There was a general consensus that whilst psychological harm was important, the presence of physical harm was necessary in order to distinguish between 'normal' crime and the kind of systemic violence with which peace and conflict studies is concerned. This is reflected in the answer given by this respondent:

> there has to be some visible harm. Now that can be psychological, but my first initial reaction to violence is usually physical ... I understand violence at the primary level as being like, literal, physical.

Following from this assumption, my respondents sought to identify people and places associated with 'violence' by assessing evidence of bodily harm or the potential to inflict it. For instance, when asked how he would identify a context of 'violence', this respondent simply replied: 'Deaths. Guns ... When you see that almost 100,000 people died, it says it's violent.' These succinct answers suggest that empirically verifiable information about the effects of violence was necessary to these participants' understanding of the phenomena.

By focusing on the material, empirically measurable manifestations of violence, my respondents were able to construct categories thereof. The main way in which they engaged with these categories was to place them within conceptual hierarchies, some implicit and others explicit. In particular, my respondents seemed most able to articulate their notions of violence when asked to discuss the processes of 'triage' (Dillon and Reid 2010) undertaken by potential intervenors to determine the seriousness of an act of violence and the necessity of response. In other words, although they were largely unable to give an account of what violence is, they were surprisingly forthcoming in offering determinations of which 'kinds' of violence were 'worse' than others. Consider the comments of this respondent, who was planning to take part in a group field trip:

> I think you should have a hierarchy ... you should [prioritize] rape, because it's not just a physical, but also psychological form of violence ... [then] physical violence, is more worse than verbal violence.

For her, certain abstract categories of violence were implicitly understood to be inherently worse than others, based on perceptions of their impact upon the individual victim. On the other hand, for this respondent, who was planning a field trip to Rwanda: 'The worst type of violence is systematic ... for example, the violence in Rwanda, or for example, suicide bombing.' In this case, the intent of 'violent' actors was used as a means of categorizing and hierarchizing violence. For others, inherent qualities related to the victims were considered most important in understanding violence, as this respondent's comments suggest: 'I think violence against civilians to me is the most violent violence ... when you look at children being killed and babies ... to me, that's violent violence.'

Others made hierarchical distinctions between 'kinds' of violence that caused death and those associated with other harms, as these two respondents suggest:

> I think the worst form of violence is ... loss of life ... That's irreplaceable when you lose a human being ... And the effects on the family and friends.
> it's [a life lost to violence] not replaceable and it doesn't achieve anything. I mean it's a completely useless thing to do.

The second quote in particular is interesting because it conveys dismay at the idea of life being lost 'for nothing', or 'wasted' by violence. This attitude reflects distinctly Western secular notions of violence, which deny its meaning-making qualities and view the loss of individual lives as a wasteful form of destruction (see Taylor 2007; Asad 2003).

However, for many of my respondents, the experiential dimensions associated with violence were equally constitutive. For instance, the sense of the threat of violence, or willingness of certain actors to behave violently, was considered crucial. This respondent argued that violence can be assessed in terms of a: 'proven readiness to ... resort to violence, and armed violence. [How] can you define it as a peaceful society when every village has armed policemen, armed soldiers?'

Moreover, for these two respondents, fear of violence based on the capacity of specific actors to inflict bodily harm was sufficient to designate a particular context as 'violent':

> There is the aspect of the fear ... [violence] might happen again, even if it's not a violent society anymore, at the surface. Because it has been, for a while, a very violent society.
>
> People still feel somehow threatened. But not by the war now, by other things like routine violence, or like small-scale criminality [and] insecurity, or abduction.

In both of these quotes, violence is presented as a distinctly experiential phenomena, one that can only be understood through its psychological, physical and emotional effects on human beings. This, I shall argue below, had an important impact on the kind of contact my respondents sought: they wished to obtain direct, experiential knowledge of the 'real' people and places they associated with violence.

This brief discussion suggests that, despite the lack of unity in terms of conceptions, definitions and understandings, all of my respondents believed that violence was an *experiential* phenomenon. Only when discussing concrete, empirical ways of knowing violence could they create categories and hierarchies to help them grapple with the phenomenon. Moreover, they shared the implicit belief they could obtain access to knowledge of violence experientially, through *direct contact* with those who had been involved in or affected by it. I shall argue that this is premised on the desire to obtain two kinds of 'experience': professional or technical experience deemed necessary for gaining a foothold within IOs and INGOs; and personal, even existential experience intended to enhance my respondents' sense of 'reality'.

Becoming 'international'

The first explanation relates to the professional aspirations of my respondents, the vast majority of whom expressed an explicit desire to work with or for a major IO, INGO or governmental department with responsibility for international affairs. Aspiring 'internationals' face increasingly fierce competition to obtain entry-level positions – or even unpaid internships – in the IOs and INGOs of their choice. This is largely due to the increasing popularity of these jobs, and the rapid professionalization and technocratization of humanitarian, development and other organizations. Indeed, according to Christophe Girod, a long-serving official within both the UN and the International Committee of the Red Cross (ICRC), speaking in 2011:

It has become a competitive market. It has become a business ... I remember when I joined [the ICRC], you were asked to have a university degree, to know how to drive a car, to be motivated ... and we had a week test before signing the contract, which was in Geneva. And if you had no experience, you would have it on the job ... now, the ICRC would ask 'do you have any humanitarian experience? If you do not, you cannot join'. So now [applicants ask] 'Where can I get my international experience?'

As these comments reflect, the rapid professionalization of 'international' work, and heightened demand for work in this 'industry', has led to ever more exacting recruitment criteria on the part of 'international' employers. Indeed, Rony Brauman, one of the founders of Médicins Sans Frontières, claimed in 1999 that 'he might not be accepted by MSF were he to be evaluated according to the agency's contemporary standards' (Rieff 2002: 3–4).

In response to this trend towards professionalization, educational programmes in applied fields of international studies are increasingly expected (by students and future employers alike) to provide their graduates with concrete 'experience' of working in 'field' conditions. According to Edgar Ng, who has researched development degree programmes of this kind:

the overwhelming focus [of these programmes] is on equipping students with the 'tools of the trade' ... Indeed, one cannot help but wonder whether they are created largely to capitalize on the demand for more development administrators.

(Ng 2006: 132)

I agree with Ng that the production of skilled, technocratic practitioners is an important element of the programmes in question. However, in addition to technical training, these programmes are often expected (by students and potential employers) to provide something more: 'experience' of working in a 'war zone', 'conflict zone' or other site deemed relevant. This expectation is related to the desire of IOs and INGOs to employ individuals who are both technically and emotionally prepared for work in contexts assumed to be risky or dangerous. From employers' perspectives, this emphasis on 'experience' often translates directly into recruitment criteria. Severine Autessere comments on this particular requirement in a recruitment document issued by the UN integrated bureau for a consultancy post related to conflict analysis in the Democratic Republic of Congo (DRC) saying that it required:

A Masters in conflict studies or political science, ten years of experience in management of peacebuilding programs, knowledge of French, and analytical synthesis skills. Country expertise was not required; instead, the terms of reference mentioned that 'knowledge of the DRC and/or of countries in transition would be a plus'.

(Autessere 2011)

This observation raises an important point: although the post in question was highly area-specific, the specifications did not call for *specific* knowledge of the DRC. Rather, it demanded quite substantial 'experience' (ten years) of working either there or *someplace like it*. This illustrates an important assumption embedded in these criteria: that experience of working *anywhere affected by 'violence' or 'conflict'* can translate to competence in any other context designated as such. It also tends to reify 'violence', 'conflict' and places associated with them as homogenous phenomena of which one can become 'experienced' through contact. This helps to explain the desire of many students to visit areas that they, their instructors or potential employers designate as a 'conflict zone' or 'war zone' – whether or not they have a particular interest in that specific country.

Moreover, this enthusiasm to visit 'war zones' or 'conflict zones' is driven by the social premium placed on danger and risk in the internal culture of major IOs and INGOs. As Michael Barnett argues, within large IOs such as the UN, one's aptitude and sense of seniority is often directly associated with having been in 'dangerous' places, and particularly at sites of 'violent conflict' (Barnett 2010). Consider, for instance, this comment on a blog created by several international aid workers to satirize the professional culture in which they work: 'Untreated PTSD [post-traumatic stress disorder] is straight-up street cred of the sort that makes newbies green with envy in the first week after a mega disaster' (SEAWL 2011). Although presented in a tongue-and-cheek manner, this quote reflects the popular notion that 'experience' in dangerous places is necessary to attaining credibility and status within the social and professional circles of 'international' workers. This, in turn, makes 'dangerous' places more attractive to aspiring 'internationals'. It also heightens their desire to interact with *people* directly affected by, or involved in violence or conflict.

For many respondents, not having 'direct experience' of violence was considered to be a severe disadvantage, both in terms of their chances of obtaining employment and their ability to carry out work in a 'field' context. This issue arose repeatedly in the discussions amongst my participants, many of whom felt that those who had 'direct experience' of violence were better able to understand and approach work in the 'field' than those who had not. According to this respondent, who was interviewed before a field trip to South Africa:

> for someone like me that grew up in the UK and hasn't ever really had to deal with things like that, I think it's important for us to *experience* it … if I'm learning a language, and I intend to fully learn the language, I have to go to the country, to learn the language. So I don't see why it should be any different for this, for conflict.

Similarly, for this respondent (also from the UK) who was planning a field trip to Kosovo:

> I feel like because I have limited experience of it, I'm in a bit of a delicate position in terms of being useful to the people that I'm working for … it would be disingenuous to practise in a field that you have no experience of.

These comments reflect the respondent's sense that she was disadvantaged in the 'international' career stakes, and in her ability to interact effectively with her research subjects by her lack of 'experience'. Indeed, the notion of 'experience' is crucial here. The term refers not only to the technical knowledge associated with undertaking certain competencies or using job-specific skills. Crucially, it also relates to the personal experience of encountering 'violence' or evidence thereof – that is, of obtaining the formative experiential sensation of being in direct contact with it. This, I shall argue, is integral to the second form of 'experience' sought by my respondents.

Getting 'real': gaining exposure to violence

Beyond the desire to gain skills that would help them to attain desired careers in the future, many of my respondents sought contact with people and places they associated with violence as a means of exposing themselves to distant atrocities and gaining a sense of the 'reality' of violence. The association of 'violence' with 'the real' is a potent yet ambiguous one. According to Slavoj Žižek (2002), contemporary 'Western' society is mired in a sense of virtual unreality (or perhaps sur-reality) which its members attempt to temper by seeking encounters with the 'Real'. This term refers to the Lacanian notion of an underlying, ultimately disruptive element of the human psyche which counters the 'virtual' world of socio-economic constructs in which modern life takes place. As Žižek argues, encounters with events framed as 'violent' often represent the 'Real' for individuals living in modern, 'Western' societies. Yet the way in which we understand the 'Real' is ambiguous. Commenting on the event of the bombing of the World Trade Center (WTC) buildings in 2001, he argues that:

> while the number of victims – 3000 – is repeated all the time, it is surprising how little of the actual carnage we see – no dismembered bodies, no blood, no desperate faces of dying people … in clear contrast to reporting on Third World catastrophes, where the whole point is to produce a scoop of some gruesome detail: Somalis dying of hunger, raped Bosnian women, men with their throats cut.
>
> (Žižek 2002: 13)

This, he claims, is because the implication of experiencing the 'real' in a virtual world is that 'precisely because it is real, that is, on account of its traumatic/excessive character, we are unable to integrate it into (what we experience as) our reality, and are therefore compelled to experience it as a nightmarish apparition' (Žižek, 2002: 19). Thus, even for individuals living in a society whose media, educational apparatuses and socio-economic structures are saturated with images and ideas of 'violence', 'the understanding of war among people who have not experienced war is now chiefly a product of the impact of these images' (Sontag 2003: 19). Thus, no matter how thoroughly one may study it, the phenomenon of 'violence' may seem unreal – that is, intangible, unintelligible and unrelatable. Indeed, relating to 'victims' or 'perpetrators' of violence through personal contact was crucial to many of my respondents, who hoped to enhance their sense of commitment to humanitarian work through such contact. Indeed, as Luc Boltanksi claims, contemporary humanitarianism is predicated upon a belief that strong commitment to helping others must be obtained through forms of psycho-social development that 'can only be actualized in situations in which those who do not suffer meet and come face to face with those who do' (Boltanski 1999: 6).

For many of my respondents, gaining access to 'real' evidence of violence was perceived as a means of breaking through the 'virtualized' forms of knowledge they believed to be conveyed through formal, academic teaching and written or audio-visual resources. Indeed, a large number of respondents suggested that this kind of knowledge was inferior to that obtained through face-to-face interactions. This was not, on the whole, due to the fact that the *factuality* or bias of these sources was called into question (although several participants alluded to this); far more frequently, it was suggested that only information gleaned through *experience* – that is, as a participant or 'victim' in an act deemed to be 'violent' – was valid. As such, when attempting to find even initial information on the regions where they were conducting fieldwork or research, many participants demanded contact with people who had 'seen' or 'experienced' what they perceived as 'violence':

> The people who are suffering, those who are the victims, those who actually … yeah, those who are the victims, they can be great resources of information.
>
> I actually rely so much on locals, because I think from locals you can get a really good perception and perspective of what actually happened to them.

In particular, this respondent suggested that face-to-face encounters with perpetrators of violence would enable him to engage in a critical analysis of the knowledge gained from other sources:

> My only experience of an ex-combatant is what I might have seen on YouTube, or what I might have seen on television. So even though of course you do have some experience, but it's *removed* … You've just been presented with information and then you digest what someone else has, you know, presented to you.

In this regard, the experiential element of the encounter with perpetrators of 'violence' was used instrumentally to enhance theoretical learning and enable critique of it.

However, for many of my respondents, the experiential elements of these encounters were considered to be ends in themselves. Simply put, encounters with 'violence' were expected not only to make specialized knowledge about violence and conflict more 'real', but in fact to make the world more 'real'. This was articulated in a number of different ways. For instance, many of my respondents claimed that face-to-face interactions made the events and people they had studied in their courses suddenly appear real. This is reflected in the comments of these respondents:

> Just walking through that gate on the first day [of the field trip] was interesting ... suddenly I got off the air conditioned bus and it was so *real* ... and I just wasn't really prepared.
>
> Before we took the trip to Sri Lanka ... it seemed unreal. But as soon as they started talking, it all came ... true. It has *happened* ... it was significant, to realize that it's *real*.

The words of the latter respondent are particularly illustrative: only when she had seen the places and people affected by the episodes of violence she had been studying did they seem to her as if they had actually happened. Indeed, this kind of analysis was often applied to violence as an ontological and theoretical category. As discussed above, my respondents expressed a variety of expectations about the qualities and categories of different 'types' of violence. However, many respondents suggested that their experience in 'the field' confounded these preconceived notions of violence. For instance, this respondent remarked after returning from a field trip that

> Violence is something really, really, really out of my conception. Because I also come from an absolutely non-violent environment. I never saw war directly, and I never experienced violence in my family ... to me, I couldn't imagine them fighting – I couldn't imagine them, like, holding a gun or killing some people.

In other words, until she met individuals who were directly involved in or affected by violence, this respondent could not conceive of people actually engaging in violent acts. Although she had theoretical ideas of what violence was and how it might be enacted, she felt that she was not able to conceptualize it as a form of action undertaken by, and against, real people until she came face to face with the evidence of this.

Finally, a number of my respondents argued that violence, and particular episodes of violence, only became real once they took on a personal dimension – that is, once they become real 'to' my respondents. In other words, the concepts of violence expressed above only made sense when violence 'became' a phenomenon that could potentially affect them directly. Consider the comments of this respondent, who was planning a field trip to Somalia:

> If you don't really know that you're going to take a flight to Somalia next week, you say 'hmm, why not?' ... but I think it is then another thing when you know 'next week I'm going to a place where people might shoot you quite easily just because you're walking around there'.

For her, the awareness that she may be exposed personally to violence or danger made the phenomenon seem more 'real' to her even before she took her trip. Likewise, for this respondent, the sense of being close to someone who had the potential to harm her had a similar effect: 'Interviewing the ex-combatants ... that was the first time I personally had been in a real situation where I might face aggression or violence or whatever.' She claimed that the proximity to individuals who had the potential (or at least the perceived potential) to engage in violence enhanced her sense of the reality of violence. For both these respondents, the degree to which they might themselves become victims of violence was deemed necessary to understanding the nature of this phenomenon. This suggests that the pursuit of contact with 'violent' individuals and victims of 'violence' has a deeply existential element: my respondents felt able to understand the 'realities' of the world, and their own understanding of it, through direct contact with the 'realities' of violence.

Discussion and conclusions

In this chapter I have argued that students who take part in 'field' experiences in contexts of violence seek particular kinds of 'experience' that help to make 'real' both their career aspirations and their sense of self – including their internal understandings of distant, external atrocities. I want to conclude by assessing the ethical advantages and risks of this approach – for all parties.

On the one hand, face-to-face interactions between students and individuals they associate with 'violence' can encourage critical reflection about the nature of violence and the way in which international actors (and educators) approach it in theory and practice. Indeed, as discussed above, the encounter with 'real' people involved in or affected by violence provided opportunities for my respondents to think critically about the schemes, tropes, categories and hierarchies of violence discussed in the first section. Moreover, it enabled them to place these 'real' people at the centre of their learning processes, and thus to think reflexively about the effects of policy and the research that drives it.

On the other hand, however, the relationship between my respondents and their research subjects often raised ethical dilemmas for the former, particularly in relation to the potential for extractive or exploitative dynamics. Simply put, many of my respondents felt acutely aware that they were treating their research subjects instrumentally, as objects for their own learning processes. A major theme of the discussions revolved around whether or not this could be justified in terms of the outcomes of educational field trips. After returning from a group field trip, this respondent remarked that: 'It almost looks like we're going in looking for suffering just to feed on.' This respondent's experiences in the field imbued him with a deep sense of guilt and shame. He was shocked by the eagerness of his colleagues – and himself – to extract 'traumatic' experiences from victims of violence in a detached and insensitive way, by the fact that he derived satisfaction out of this. Similarly, these respondents, who had undertaken a group field trip to a demobilization, disarmament and reintegration (DDR) camp reflected on their experience as such:

P1:   It feels like a zoo – both us observing them, and them observing us …
P2:   Yes, it was like going to a zoo. We were going there observing these people like they were not actually people … just because they were ex-combatants. So I felt really, really bad.

One of these respondents even described being so emotionally upset by the experience that she 'blacked out' and could not remember most of what occurred while she toured the DDR camp. This set of quotes suggests that the respondents felt that both they and their research subjects were dehumanized by the encounter.

For many respondents, these feelings of deep unease arose from their awareness of the potentially exploitative nature of their interactions. This was articulated in two main ways: first, discomfort at their own lack of professional training and its impact on research subjects; and second, the sense that the research they conducted was purely for their own individual benefit. The first problem is reflected in this post-field trip discussion:

P1:   I think for me, one of the most important experiences was the interview that we did with those young women [victims of 'violence'] … when we walked in, we saw that they had so much to offer and … we were told they would be a good source. And then we kind of pressed them for information …
P1:   Yeah, I got *so* uncomfortable … think that we should've stopped talking to them, or done the interview in reverse and asked the questions at the end that would have eased them in, at the start. Not jumped in and tried to get the information we wanted. And I was surprised that some people didn't realize that, and kept pushing and pushing.

These respondents reflected with obvious regret upon a group dynamic in which they felt they had exploited their research subjects, at the expense of their ethical principles. This was not, however, generally the result of crass insensitivity; on the contrary, it tended to derive from excitement and the desire to 'learn by doing'. As this respondent put it:

> We were *so* keen to talk to somebody, that I think people just forgot the effects … I think the main thing that came out of the whole trip for me was the importance of balancing your desire to get information with potential distress that that can cause in the people that you're researching with.

The respondent quoted above learned a valuable lesson – but only through an experience that was damaging both to her and her research subjects. This highlights an important dilemma: my respondents needed to learn how to conduct ethical research, but they were expected to learn this by practising on living human subjects, in a way that compromised the very ethical principles they sought to master.

Similarly, these respondents, who were interviewed after returning from a group field trip, felt that their lack of ability to benefit their research subjects directly rendered the dynamic exploitative:

P2: I felt quite exploitative in a lot of situations ... these people were giving their time to me, answering questions that they might feel very uncomfortable with, and I wasn't [well enough] prepared to ask them in a particularly sensitive or accommodating kind of way.

P3: Well, I would agree with that ... the whole purpose of this trip was to build research skills, not to publish research that's going to help them [research subjects]. This was a very, very *selfish* research trip. We had nothing to give back at all. We weren't there to research development theory. We weren't there to provide [the information] back to NGOs ... we were there to build our own personal experience of doing field research. The purpose of the trip wasn't to do something constructive for them – [it was] to do something constructive *for us* ... there's a very small potential that it will be something that an IO or an NGO can actually do something constructive with.

The discussion between these two respondents illustrates the ethical bind that my respondents found themselves in. On the one hand, they needed to gain practical experience of fieldwork in order to enhance their knowledge and to succeed in their studies and careers, but on the other, they were aware that the likelihood that this experience would directly benefit others – in particular the *specific* individuals they had encountered in the field – was minimal.

This analysis suggests that whilst there are good professional and personal reasons for students to seek contact with 'real' people affected by and involved in violence, these encounters also have significant ethical costs for both students and their research subjects. They run the risk of fetishizing 'victims' and 'perpetrators', and of treating them as objects for the instrumental self-development of students. In the cases discussed above, my respondents were torn by the feeling that their desire to obtain experience could potentially harm or exploit the very people whom they hoped these learning experiences would enable them to benefit in future. This suggests that the desire to gain 'experience' of violence comes with significant ethical costs for all parties. Given the employment pressures and socially mediated desires for 'real' knowledge discussed above, it is unlikely that the demand for such encounters will decrease. Therefore, it is crucial that educators, potential employers and students think critically about the motivations for seeking direct experience of 'violence' and ways of minimizing the ethical impact for all involved.

References

Asad, T. (2003) *Formations of Secularity*, Stanford, CA: Stanford University Press

Autessere, S (2011) 'We, the international community: understanding how international peace interventions operate in practice'. Paper presented at the PRIO/PACSA conference 'The Local in Global Understandings of War and Peacemaking: Anthropological and Interdisciplinary Perspectives'. Nicosia, 1–3 September

Ballard, J.G. (2006) *The Atrocity Exhibition*, London: Harper Perennial

Barnett, M. (2010) *The International Humanitarian Order*, London: Routledge

Boltanski, L. (1999) *Distant Suffering*, Cambridge: Cambridge University Press

Bourgois, P. (2001) 'The power of violence in war and peace: post-Cold War lessons from El Salvador', *Ethnography*, 2 (1): 5–37

Dillon, M. and Reid, J. (2010) *Killing to Make Life Live*, London: Routledge

Mitchell, A. (2011) 'The field trap: ethical dilemmas of escaping the ivory tower'. Paper presented at the 2011 Millennium Conference 'Beyond the Ivory Tower: Theory and Practice in IR', London School of Economics, 22–23 October

Ng, E. (2006) 'Doing development differently' in P. Darby (ed.) *Postcolonizing the International*, Honolulu: University of Hawaii Press

Nordstrom, C. and Robben, A. (1995) *Fieldwork Under Fire*, Berkeley: University of California Press

Rieff, D. (2002) *A Bed for the Night*, London: Vintage

Sontag, S. (2003) *Regarding the Pain of Others*, London: Penguin Books

Sriram, C., King, J., Mertus, J., Martin-Ortega, O. and Hermann, J. (eds) (2010) *Surviving Field Research*, London: Routledge

Stuff Expatriate Aid Workers Like (SEAWL) Blog (2011) '#84: Being enigmatic', *Stuff Expat Aid Workers Like*. Available: http://stuffexpataidworkerslike.com/ (accessed 9 October 2011)

Taylor, C. (2007) *A Secular Age*, Cambridge: Harvard Belknap

Žižek, S. (2002) *Welcome to the Desert of the Real!* London: Verso

11 'You only get what you fight for'

Understanding the backlash against the US battered women's movement

Molly Dragiewicz

I understand that if I resist what I'll get back. I get that, I don't feel like that's a conflict, that's just what it is. (R2)[1]

Introduction

While feminist demands for sweeping social changes in order to ameliorate men's violence have been largely ignored, efforts to institutionalize emergency assistance for abused women are pervasive and highly visible. In the United States, 'awareness' of the problem is nearly universal. Politicians from both major parties regularly declare their condemnation of domestic violence. University students don ribbons and paint T-shirts to 'break the silence' and show solidarity with survivors. The Violence Against Women Act (VAWA), passed in 1994, outlined a federal policy agenda on the issue. Feminist concepts, language, and concerns, largely drawn from survivors, have been institutionalized in law and discourse, even if 'not to the degree sought by groups of activists involved in the process' (Dobash and Dobash 2001: 189). In this context, it is easy to forget that violence against women was not always such a high-profile issue. For critical scholars, it is easy to become mired in theoretically based critiques of contemporary responses to violence and abuse, resulting in disengagement from action on these key issues.

Drawing upon interviews with 35 advocates working within the mainstream battered women's movement I identify foundational themes for theorizing about the backlash against the battered women's movement in the United States. The advocates' accounts of support for and resistance to work to end violence against women provide a rich source of information about what has changed, and what has not, over the past 40 years. The respondents' narratives point to key pressure points in the struggle to address violence against women as well as the need to expand the focus of contemporary criminological theory beyond the social construction of deviance and responses to it. We also need to study and organize around the backlash: the response to the response.

Literature review

Critical criminologists have devoted considerable attention to previously under-studied social harms. They have dedicated sustained effort to understanding how repressive forms of social control are deployed and maintained through formal institutions, from mass media to law, and informal relations, such as those between peers and family members. Violence against women has been an important focus for such work. Critical criminologists have made important contributions to theory and methodological improvements to measuring violence and abuse (Dobash and Dobash 2001; Mooney 2000). Significantly, critical work on woman abuse has long questioned the extent to which it is actually a deviant behavior. Rather than being a manifestation of deficient collective efficacy, woman abuse, and the failure to intervene in it, may in fact be an expression of social organization and hegemonic community values (DeKeseredy and Schwartz 2009; Mooney 2000). In other words, men's violence against women may represent a transgression of some social norms *and* a reassertion of others (Dragiewicz 2008).

Despite critical contributions to the field, violence against women has sometimes been awkwardly positioned within the scholarship on deviancy (Carrington 2002; Dragiewicz 2010). Scholarship on the social construction of crime has targeted the gratuitous criminalization of deviance and delinquency in the service of conservative politics. As Carrington (2002: 126) has argued, early radical theories were 'primarily interested in the expressive, rather than the instrumental qualities of deviance'. While the shift to a focus on the social construction of deviance through criminalization was a major contribution to critical criminology:

> Only the experience of those doing the criminalising (i.e. the state) seemed to matter. Within these kinds of critical frameworks, the lines between the victim and offender were almost meaningless. The offender was the victim of some overarching structure of class, sexual, or racial exclusion, domination, repression, or oppression.
>
> (Carrington 2002: 127)

In other words, many criminologists emphasized the process of criminalization over victims' experiences of crime. Criminologists' accounts of male offenders as feckless victims of an authoritarian state are remarkably similar to those produced by antifeminist men's groups who complain about persecution based on false accusations of violence (Dragiewicz 2008, 2010, 2011). Even more problematically, a similar narrative is articulated by male batterers who have had repeated encounters with police and men who murder intimate partners. Work with survivors and advocates in the mainstream battered women's movement points to the need to turn our attention to the response to the naming of men's violence against women as deviant, the criminalization of the deviant act, and responses to both.

Battered women's movement work to improve the application of existing laws to men's violence against women sits uneasily alongside critiques of the prison–industrial complex. Feminist work to draft new laws has undoubtedly contributed to the more generalized encroachment of state surveillance and control (Currie 1990) and violence against women has historically been used to justify funding for law and order initiatives (Pleck 1987). Perhaps the most blatant recent example of this is US justification of the war in Afghanistan as being about rescuing women from patriarchy (Ayotte and Husain 2005). One unintended consequence of the institutionalization of criminal justice responses to woman abuse is the disproportionate criminal justice system involvement of women and men of color and poor women and men (INCITE! 2003; Wood 2005).

Despite these serious problems, the battered women's movement has had a profound impact on the interrogation of men's violence and inadequate responses to it. Naming men's violence against women as a social problem has been no small feat. Naming the violence has posed a preliminary challenge to patriarchal gender norms. While this is a necessary first step toward changing the culture that produces violence, there is more to be done. Accordingly, I propose that we need to expand our focus beyond the social construction of deviance, and responses to it, and study the reaction to that response. Indeed, the criminalization of diverse types of behavior by discrete groups has been taken up very differently. Lamenting the creeping encroachment of the neoliberal capitalist state doesn't really get at these differences, nor do descriptions of the disproportionate impact of law and order campaigns on the most marginalized populations. In the current cultural environment where the normative position is ostensibly antiviolence, critical analysis of the dynamics of the backlash against the battered women's movement can help to illuminate the abstruse values and structures that continue to engender violence.

Historical developments

Just as the context of individual acts is required to understand the nature of violence and abuse, consideration of the political history of the battered women's movement is a prerequisite to understanding critiques of contemporary responses to woman abuse. The earliest theories of woman abuse were developed out of the dual practices of feminist consciousness-raising and supporting battered women in the absence of a state response. As such, early feminist theories about woman abuse were empirically grounded in the experiences of many women with abusive men.

Feminism facilitated the conceptualization of men's violence against women as a social problem requiring a collective response. One early article in a medical journal put it succinctly, 'Assertion of women's rights has created the climate for exposure of the previously hidden facts of wife abuse' (Gayford 1975: 196). From the beginning, multiple varieties of feminist theory proposed various relationships between patriarchy and men's violence against women (Schechter 1982: 40). Accordingly, there has never been a singular, monolithic feminist theory of woman abuse. Nor has there been a feminist consensus on the one best approach to ending violence against women. However, early work in the battered women's movement did focus on a few key areas. When Del Martin wrote *Battered Wives* in 1976, she concluded:

> After having reviewed all the supposed options open to battered women, I have reached the conclusion that the creation of shelters designed specifically for battered women is the only direct, immediate, and satisfactory solution to the problem of wife-abuse. Victims and their children need refuge from further abuse; any other consideration – such as the need for counselling or legal advice – is of secondary importance.
>
> (Martin 1981: 196)

This analysis was based on the realities of the time. Systems that did not yet recognize men's violence against female intimate partners as a public social problem could not respond appropriately to the violence. Reflecting on the beginnings of the battered women's movement, Schechter (1999) wrote:

> Because so few institutions heard us in those early days – or took the violence seriously – we in the battered women's movement worked as outsiders. Our resources were almost non-existent. We started to house women on our pluck and courage. A shelter for battered women was a totally new and creative phenomenon that we designed, managed and maintained, and that required a tremendous amount of energy to sustain. Our early advocacy for battered women with the police and courts led us to be sharp critics of victim blaming and unjust responses and to design new and ingenious legislative and administrative innovations with our allies.

Schechter (ibid.) identified three priorities of the early work: '1) securing shelter and support for battered women and their children, 2) improving laws and the police and court response, and 3) changing public consciousness about violence against women through education.' The battered women's movement has made remarkable progress toward meeting these goals over the past 40 years.

As Tierney (1982: 207) observed, 'wife beating has received increasing attention in recent years, not because it has become more widespread, or because the public has become more concerned, but because social movement organizations (SMOs) have effectively mobilized resources to aid battered women'. Services designed specifically to meet the needs of battered women developed out of the particular constellation of needs shared by many survivors. Although early services were provided by organizations like 'suicide or mental health crisis hotlines, rape crisis centers, organizations aiding families of alcoholics, or homes for transients, now independently operated battered women's organizations are the norm' (Tierney 1982: 208).

Significantly, Tierney (1982: 208) noted that '[s]ince 1975, the movement has made substantial headway in three areas, besides emergency shelter: legislation, government policy and programs, and research and public information'. Publications from 1976 identified 20 resources for abused women. By 1978, the US Commission on Civil Rights identified 300 such organizations (ibid.). This growth coincided with the influential 'second wave' of the women's movement. Despite the proliferation of resources in the 1970s, efforts to secure a federal law on 'domestic violence' were unsuccessful at the time. However, funding for services to battered women was already beginning to be incorporated into government programs like Victim Witness (ibid.).

In 2010, the National Network to End Domestic Violence (NNEDV 2011) identified 1,920 local domestic violence programs in the USA. NNEDV's 24-hour census, conducted on September 15, 2010, gathered information about these programs. The study had a 91 percent response rate and found that 70,648 victims were served in one day while an additional 9,541 requests for help went unmet due to lack of resources and 60 percent of the unmet requests were for shelter. In addition, local programs answered 22,292 hotline calls and the National Domestic Violence Hotline answered 1,230 calls.

Domestic violence organizations reported feeling the effects of the recession and concomitant retrenchment of public spending, with 77 percent of programs reporting funding cuts during 2010. However, funding from the American Recovery and Reinvestment Act also benefited 854 local programs, allowing them to maintain or add 1,384 victim advocacy jobs during the same year. Despite budget cuts, 82 percent of programs reported an increase in demand for services in 2010 (NNEDV 2011).

NNEDV's census points to both the rapid expansion of services for survivors of violence and the persistent need for these resources. Contemporary efforts to end violence against women comprise disparate approaches and institutions. As in the beginning of the movement, practitioners, scholars, attorneys, and survivors continue to differ on the best ways to prevent and respond to violence (Schechter 1982: 40). There continues to be considerable debate and disagreement among feminists over the efficacy and desirability of involvement from state institutions including, but not limited to, the criminal justice system (INCITE! 2003). One part of this debate is over the concept of backlash.

Theorizing backlash

Backlash has been alternately defined as 'resistance to attempts to change the status quo' (Sanbonmatsu 2008: 634) and efforts to roll back past changes (Faludi 1991). Mansbridge and Shames (2008: 625) argue that 'when a group of actors disadvantaged by the status quo works to enact change, that group necessarily challenges an entrenched power structure'. Accordingly:

> Movements do not advance in linear progression; they are marked by successive periods of definition, progress, consolidation, backlash,

redefinition, regrouping, new support, and on and on. A movement is a shifting, ever-becoming entity, not an event that is won or lost.

(Sancier 1992)

Backlash is a response to a threat to existing hierarchies of power and privilege rather than simply the ebb and flow of change (Mansbridge and Shames 2008). In this sense, antifeminist backlash is not just a 'countermovement' as some have portrayed it (Crowley 2009). This conceptualization misses the key component of power that shapes the emergence of backlash as well as its effectiveness. Accordingly, the ways in which power is deployed in backlash efforts are of central interest.

There is a growing body of scholarly work on antifeminist backlash (Chafetz and Dworkin 1987; Chesney-Lind 2006; DeKeseredy 1999; Dragiewicz 2011; Faludi 1991; Laidler and Mann 2008). This literature describes backlash tactics, attempts to assess its impact, and counters inaccurate claims. To date, however, the concept of backlash has been loosely defined and minimally theorized in criminology. Although feminist criminologists write about back-lash, we rarely define what it means. With the exception of a few critiques of the concept,[2] the interdisciplinary work on understanding the particular nature of backlash in order to counter it comes mostly from organizational psychology and, more recently, political science (Mansbridge and Shames 2008).

Sylvia Walby (1990: 23) wrote, 'few writers on gender consider issues of historical regress in the position of women … or even the social forces which oppose advance. … I think this is a serious gap in feminist scholarship. Men and some women have actively and effectively opposed feminist demands'. To date, little empirical consideration has been devoted to the specific dynamics and effects of backlash against the changes wrought by the battered women's movement. Jalna Hanmer (2001: 9) noted that, 'resistance to identifying violence against women as crime, as serious, as worthy of agency intervention, has been examined in health, housing, social services and policing services. Resistance by informal contacts, and the actions taken by the women and men involved, has received less attention'.

Woman abuse and state responses to it are located at the intersection of profound cultural anxieties about crime, law, gender, economics, knowledge, and the family. The research literature on woman abuse has grown exponentially since the beginning of the battered women's movement. Elizabeth Castelli (2004: 2) described the landscape of gendered violence as, 'the myriad structures of domination and exchange that sustain frameworks of violence: global and local economic inequalities, patterns of (forced and voluntary) migration, transnational trafficking in small arms, institutional and ideological structures that continuously legitimate violence as the default response to a situation of conflict or hostility'.

Despite antifeminist objections to 'the politicization of violence against women by feminists', there would be no scholarship on 'domestic violence', no prosecution of wife beaters, no shelters for battered women and their children, and no consideration of woman abuse at custody determination if not for feminist activism. Calls for the imposition of gender-blind approaches to violence in the name of 'neutrality' or 'fairness' ignore centuries of patriarchal law and culture that condone violence as a justifiable, if sometimes illegitimate means of controlling women. Furthermore, especially at the present time, they arise in opposition to the effective deployment of feminist conceptualizations of woman abuse as a gendered problem intricately tied to power differences between women and men. As Dobash and Dobash (2001: 187) wrote:

> Perhaps the most important first step in the process of social change is the very act of creating new visions and thinking new thoughts. ... Thus, it is important to acknowledge that while it may now be generally agreed that it is unacceptable for a man to use physical or sexual violence against his female partner, this is, in fact, an extraordinary departure from thinking of the recent past. This is a change of great magnitude.

Although a minority of scholars argue that patriarchy and gender are not important factors in violence against women, this is a marginal position. Discourses from human rights to public health have institutionalized conceptualizations of violence as highly gendered.

Methodology

This study used semi-structured interviews to gather information about support for and resistance to antiviolence work. A convenience sampling method was used, with invitations to antiviolence advocates to participate extended online via listserv for prevention advocates, antiviolence advocates, scholars, and lawyers. The invitation encouraged recipients to forward the call for volunteers to anyone else who might be interested in the study. Volunteers were interviewed until responses reached thematic saturation. The sample consisted of 35 interviews conducted and transcribed between 2007 and 2009. Interviews ranged from 52 minutes to over two and a half hours, with an average of approximately an hour and a half. Transcribed interviews were coded using MAXQDA, a qualitative software analysis package.

The average age of respondents for this study was 59, and the age range was from 30 to 67. Thirty-one of the respondents were Caucasian, and four identified as mixed race, including a mix of Caucasian, Asian, Native American heritages. Thirteen respondents had a Juris Doctor, 15 had Master's degrees, five had PhDs, two had some college, and one had a university degree and some graduate classes. Respondents were from 20 different states. For respondents who reported salaries, the annual average was $49,000. Two respondents reported being retired and working on a volunteer basis. A few respondents noted that their income fluctuates from year to year due to consulting work. Thirty of the respondents were female and five were male. Seven respondents identified as lesbian or queer, and 28 identified as straight or heterosexual. Respondents averaged 22 years in the field, ranging from nine years to more than 40 years. The sample included clinical law professors, practicing attorneys, battered women's shelter staff, state coalition staff, national advocacy organization staff, university antiviolence program staff, child counselors and therapists, government antiviolence program staff, and independent advocates. Most of the respondents had had more than one job working on antiviolence projects prior to their current position.

Findings

> Yeah, there's resistance. (R7)

While the larger study looked at a range of issues related to support for and resistance to battered women's movement work, this chapter is focused on advocates' understandings of the backlash against their work on violence against women. In response to a question about whether respondents experience resistance to their antiviolence work, the most common response was 'absolutely'. While all respondents indicated experiencing or observing some forms of resistance to their work, the level and impact of resistance varied widely according to respondents' specific professional locations. Respondents differed about whether there was a change in the level of resistance to their work, with some remarking that resistance had increased and others describing changes in the ways that resistance is manifested.

Respondents identified six key types of resistance: resistance to acting on legal and policy changes; victim blaming; discrediting women/feminists; individualization; changing the subject; and direct attacks and threats.[3] These types of resistance are related to advocates' perceptions about the factors contributing to the backlash. The picture of backlash that emerged from the interviews was remarkably clear. Advocates described a rising tide of awareness of 'domestic violence', generally understood as men's violence against women, and increased condemnation of it. As one advocate put it, 'We used to be pushing everybody and there are a lot of people we don't have to push anymore' (R1). At the same time that awareness and disapproval of men's violence against women were on the increase, pressure points emerged where resistance to antiviolence work was especially fierce. For example, 'it changed over time. But I would say that with specifically my own evolution, our evolution as a program, overall I'd say in the world as I see it today, I see support for antipatriarchal work has been an issue. Constantly getting worse' (R5). In other words, the resistance that this advocate saw was focused on recognition of patriarchy as contributing to violence rather than resistance to recognizing the violence itself as a problem. Another respondent said of resistance, 'it is more frequent, it's worse, there are more tactics' (R8).

Respondents' explanations for why there has been a backlash against battered women's movement work reflect the two definitions of backlash described above. Some respondents saw the backlash as efforts to roll back advancements in the protection of abused women. Others saw the backlash as a constantly evolving effort to prevent change in the first place.

Backlash as effort to maintain the status quo

Advocates' descriptions of the backlash as an effort to maintain the status quo included a few primary forms: resistance to challenging individual authority figures; resistance to cultural-level changes to prevent violence; and resistance to the deep implications of work to end violence on a personal level. The first variation on this theme is resistance to antiviolence work that challenges the authority of high-profile or powerful community members. For example:

> I was getting some flak in the legal community before I left because in the last year [I was there], my office represented thirteen victims whose perpetrators were attorneys in the community. That nobody else would take. And of those, three of the victims were from the same attorney. And I've represented sports figures, caught flak for that, represented against attorneys, caught flak for that, represented against doctors in the community, caught flak for that, against military officers, caught flak for that. (R2)

Challenging authority figures came at a cost for some of the advocates, including facing harassment from individuals and retaliation from professional organizations. However, many of the respondents observed that pushing the boundaries of standard practice is a necessary part of systems change.

> Another thing I think we need to accept is that probably three times out of five, force is the way that they're going to decide they have to change. It's awful, those of us that have been around counselors a lot like to think of ourselves as enlightened, know that shouldn't be the case, but the fact of the matter is in many institutions in our criminal, civil justice system and law enforcement etcetera, that's what it takes. You have to do this so that's what it takes. (R2)

Another example of efforts to maintain the status quo can be seen in this response in which the implications of social change for individuals are considered:

> I really think that the reason why is that people are too afraid of what would happen if they really looked at making a change in things. Sort of grab them with the underlying issues that ... would ... result in some pretty fundamental changes to how we order our lives how we relate to one another, you know the personal relationships ... and that's scary to people. I mean that calls into question who makes decisions and how we make them and how we co-raise our families and you know, all those things come into question. ... And I also think that people want to make a distinction between us and them. And that if you sort of accept sort of

my view of what causes violence against women that you don't get to say it would never happen to me ... I think that that's really sort of the pearl behind, sort of the crux of why people are like this. (R9)

In this example, the respondent identifies interpersonal implications of social change related to antiviolence work. Resistance to the very social changes sought by feminists is identified as a source of backlash. The respondent also mentions individual-level resistance to thinking about the nature and causes of violence against women. Victim-blaming explanations for woman abuse enable the maintenance of belief in a safe, just world. In other words, if violence against women is the victim's fault, it can never happen to me.

Backlash as effort to reverse changes that have been made

Other respondents described backlash as an effort to roll back the changes that have come about as a result of battered women's movement work and the institutionalization of antiviolence policies. For example:

Yes from the batterer's perspective and in terms of what about the resistance in men I think it's that there is, and it's hard to articulate, but it's like for a millennium men have had the premier spot in the universe and all of a sudden women are starting to be vocal and heard and dealt with so there is this whole bunch of people going, 'wait what about me?' and 'I used to be first and I want to be first again!' and so there's this whole pushback from the patriarchy on that one. The other one is a pushback on women who are finding their voice and I think that's where it is coming from. (R1)

This example points to resistance to women as authorities on violence and abuse, whether as survivors or scholars. The legitimization of women's authority as producers of knowledge about violence and abuse was a frequently mentioned location of backlash efforts. One advocate explained resistance to changes in the common knowledge about violence against women this way:

Because I think we are winning. That's why I think these vitriolic pockets are popping up is because we are winning and that's what causes resistance and backlash and if we weren't winning we wouldn't be having all of this crap. Some resistance is just bureaucratic crap but the fathers' rights things and the custody stuff is all because we have been getting our way and we are getting people to understand and if not the word feminism at least the concepts of it and we settle for that because at least it's something. (R1)

This quote references organized resistance to feminism in general and battered women's movement work in particular as a response to the institutionalization of feminist understandings of violence.[4] Many respondents named areas where state responses to woman abuse needed improvement, including multiple critiques of the unintended outcomes of recent changes. However, the overall impression was that, at the very least, battered women's movement work had forced fundamental changes in influential discourses on woman abuse.

> Whatever it may be, the more effective, when you make good laws that are there that require them to do the right things in the court systems, the better we get, the more effective we become, the stronger the resistance gets. I think in the past we challenged, we got some good things through and we challenged things to some extent and we got people angry and upset enough the politicos thought they needed to make changes. Then they settled right back down into the same comfortable groove but the really fairly thin veneer over it of change. And now we're getting to the point where we're starting at least in [this state], and I think nationwide too, threatening them with you really are going to have to fundamentally change your system, and that's bringing about a huge lash out, which really we should expect. (R2)

As this respondent indicates, advocates aren't surprised that the call for system change provokes a strong reaction. Rather than being paralyzed by reports of incomplete reform, unintended consequences, or efforts to circumvent the changes that have been made, advocates reported the need to keep working. In fact, despite occasional reports of increased crankiness due to certain forms of resistance to their work, many respondents indicated that it had made their work stronger and smarter, and had reinvigorated them for sustained struggle.

Discussion

The interviews illustrate that despite the ascendancy of awareness of violence against women, competing interests and values have shaped the assimilation of this problem into the machinery of social control. Martha McMahon and Ellen Pence (2003: 71) remind us that:

> Much of the battered women's movement's work has been to challenge the social sanctioning of male violence in the private sphere and to end the protections afforded such male privilege by the criminal justice system and other institutions. Every effort we have made has met with resistance and claims that we seek to establish a double standard. We have consistently fought against such efforts to obscure women's realities.

Efforts to resist feminist-informed approaches to violence against intimates are not unique to the United States. Similar campaigns are underway in many countries, and a scholarly literature is emerging on the situation in Australia (Flood 2010; Murray and Powell 2009); Canada (DeKeseredy 1999; Dragiewicz and DeKeseredy, forthcoming); India (Basu 2011); and the United Kingdom (Hester 2009).

While 'governments typically try to reintegrate disaffected groups or their leadership into the power structure and direct them to less politically disturbing forms of behavior' (McMahon and Pence 2003: 62), feminist efforts to (1) secure shelter and support for battered women and their children, (2) improve laws and the police and court response, and (3) change public consciousness about violence against women through education have all been at least partially accomplished (Schechter 1999). Because of the success of efforts to de-normalize men's violence against women, at least at a surface level, the backlash against the battered women's movement has been forced to use more subtle and indirect tactics. Advocates' stories can help us identify the contradictory social values around violence that we need to understand to craft more effective campaigns to end violence in the short and long term. In addition, advocates' stories can sensitize us to similarities and differences in these efforts across time and place.

Castelli (2004: 2) has observed that, 'theorizing always takes place in time and space, situated in history and in particular places of enunciation'. In the contemporary context, efforts to reclaim the ground ceded to the battered women's movement are well underway. As scholars who study crime and responses to it, we can contribute to addressing the backlash as well as the violence itself. This preliminary study points to some key themes for theory development on backlash as efforts to preserve the status quo and roll back the changes that have been accomplished. Despite the tendency for feminists and other critical criminologists to engage in merciless critiques of our always imperfect engagement with the state, the study of backlash can help us understand what is working and to what extent.

Antiviolence advocates are doing what critical criminologists say we want to do: foregrounding the experiences of those most affected, developing theories of violence that stand up to the test of reality, and engaging with the people who can actually affect systems. This work is rife with perils and possibilities, but it is essential given that so many women utilize state resources, especially the police (Hutchison and Hirschel 1998). Blaming advocates, activists, or scholars for failing to end men's violence against women inside of 40 years or for the unintended outcomes of their work is not the most useful focus for our energies. Neoliberal notions of equality and neutrality have definitely been taken up by backlash forces, but the impurity of critical or feminist theory or discourse is not the primary cause of violence against women. Likewise, the perfect words or theory will not end violence against women. Any tool that we devise will undoubtedly be used against us. This does not mean that we can throw up our hands and walk away.

Directions for research and policy

The findings from this study suggest several directions for future research. First, comparative research on the dynamics of backlash against groups doing antiviolence work with different groups of women and men is needed to develop a more comprehensive understanding of backlash. Different communities experience resistance in very different ways. Second, theory testing will be necessary to see if the themes emerging from this study apply on a larger scale. Third, respondents working in different institutional locations described different dynamics and effects of backlash, so future studies could focus more closely on the particular dynamics of each field. Finally, future studies should compare resistance to antiviolence work to the backlash against other social movements to promote a better understanding of their similarities and differences.

The study findings point to the need for continued systems advocacy even as work to reform and change social systems moves forward. The reality is that many social institutions affect abused women's lives and their ability to leave abusers, protect themselves and their children, and support themselves. While critique and caution around the institutionalization of antiviolence work is productive and necessary, these can contribute to theoretical paralysis and inaction. As early advocates noted, meeting the basic safety and survival needs for abused women and their children continues to be of paramount concern. It is neither timely nor safe to move on from this basic function of advocacy for abused women. Finally, it is clear that continued research and public education efforts are needed to promote a more nuanced, holistic understanding of violence as an abuse of gendered power as well as a location for the expression of race and class inequality. Respondents articulated a changed landscape wherein violence against women is denounced, but there is still plenty of work to do to prevent it and respond effectively.

Acknowledgements

I would like to thank all of the people who volunteered their valuable time to talk with me about their experiences.

Notes

1 All identifying information has been removed or disguised to protect the privacy of the respondents.
2 See Chunn *et al.* (2007) and Newson (1991) for critiques of the concept of backlash.
3 For an in-depth discussion of these themes, see M. Dragiewicz (forthcoming).
4 The 'custody stuff' referred to is in reaction to legal requirements that violence and abuse be considered at custody determination. These policies were created at the behest of feminist antiviolence organizations which were concerned about women being forced into joint custody arrangements with abusers.

References

Ayotte, K.J. and Husain, M.E. (2005) 'Securing Afghan women: neocolonialism, epistemic violence, and the rhetoric of the veil', *NWSA Journal*: 112–33
Basu, S. (2011) 'Realigning family: Indian men's movements, family law, and family violence', presented at the South Asian Masculinities Invited Symposium, Oxford, OH

Carrington, K. (2002) 'Feminism and critical criminology', in K. Carrington and R. Hogg (eds) *Critical Criminology,* Portland, OR: Willan Publishing

Castelli, E.A. (2004) 'Feminists responding to violence: theories, vocabularies, and strategies', in E.A. Castelli and J.R. Jakobsen (eds) *Interventions,* New York: Palgrave Macmillan

Chafetz, J.S. and Dworkin, A.G. (1987) 'In the face of threat: organized antifeminism in comparative perspective', *Gender and Society,* 1 (1): 33–60

Chesney-Lind, M. (2006) 'Patriarchy, crime, and justice: feminist criminology in an era of backlash', *Feminist Criminology,* 1 (1): 6–26

Chunn, E., Boyd, S. and Lessard, H. (2007) *Reaction and Resistance: Feminism, Law, and Social Change,* Vancouver: UBC Press

Crowley, J.E. (2009) 'Fathers' rights groups, domestic violence and political counter-mobilization', *Social Forces,* 88 (2): 723–56

Currie, D.H. (1990) 'Battered women and the state: from the failure of theory to a theory of failure', *Critical Criminology,* 1 (2): 77–96

DeKeseredy, W.S. (1999) 'Tactics of the antifeminist backlash against Canadian national woman abuse surveys', *Violence Against Women,* 5 (11): 1238–57

DeKeseredy, W.S. and Schwartz, M.D. (2009) *Dangerous Exits: Escaping Abusive Relationships in Rural America,* New Brunswick, NJ: Rutgers University Press

Dobash, R.E. and Dobash, R.P. (2001) 'The politics and policies of responding to violence against women', in J. Hanmer and C. Itzin (eds) *Home Truths about Domestic Violence: Feminist Influences on Policy and Practice – A reader,* New York: Routledge

Dragiewicz, M. (2008) 'Patriarchy reasserted: fathers' rights and anti-VAWA activism', *Feminist Criminology,* 3 (2): 121–44

——(2010) 'A left realist approach to antifeminist fathers' rights groups', *Crime, Law and Social Change,* 54 (2): 197–212

——(2011) *Equality with a Vengeance,* Boston, MA: Northeastern University Press

——(forthcoming) 'Tactics of antifeminist backlash: The view from advocates for abused women', in K. Carrington, M. Ball, E. O'Brien and J. Tauri (eds) *Crime, Justice & Social Democracy: International Perspectives,* London: Palgrave Macmillan

Dragiewicz, M. and DeKeseredy, W.S. (forthcoming) 'Claims about women's use of non-fatal force in intimate relationships: a contextual review of the Canadian research', *Violence Against Women*

Faludi, S. (1991) *Backlash,* New York: Crown

Flood, M. (2010) '"Fathers' rights" and the defense of paternal authority in Australia', *Violence Against Women,* 16 (3): 328–47

Gayford, J.J. (1975) 'Wife battering: a preliminary survey of 100 cases', *British Medical Journal,* 1: 194–7

Hanmer, J. (2001) 'Domestic violence and gender relations: contexts and connections', in J. Hanmer and C. Itzin (eds) *Home Truths about Domestic Violence,* New York: Routledge

Hester, M. (2009) *Who Does What to Whom?* Bristol: University of Bristol, Northern Rock Foundation

Hutchison, I.W. and Hirschel, J.D. (1998) 'Abused women: help-seeking strategies and police utilization', *Violence Against Women,* 4 (4): 436–56

INCITE! (2003) 'Critical resistance: INCITE! Statement on gender violence and the prison–industrial complex', *Social Justice,* 30 (3): 141–51

Laidler, K.J. and Mann, R.M. (2008) 'Anti-feminist backlash and gender-relevant crime initiatives in the global context', *Feminist Criminology,* 3 (2): 79

McMahon, M. and Pence, E. (2003) 'Making social change: reflections on individual and institutional advocacy with women arrested for domestic violence', *Violence Against Women*, 9 (1): 47–74

Mansbridge, J. and Shames, S.L. (2008) 'Toward a theory of backlash: dynamic resistance and the central role of power', *Politics and Gender*, 4 (04): 623–34

Martin, D. (1981) *Battered Wives*, revised edn, Volcano, CA: Volcano Press

Mooney, J. (2000) *Gender, Violence and the Social Order*, New York: Palgrave

Murray, S. and Powell, A. (2009) 'What's the problem? Australian public policy constructions of domestic and family violence', *Violence Against Women*, 15 (5): 532–52

National Network to End Domestic Violence (NNEDV) (2011) 'Domestic violence counts 2010: a 24-hour census of domestic violence shelters and services', Washington, DC: National Network to End Domestic Violence. Retrieved from: http://nnedv.org/docs/Census/DVCounts2010/DVCounts10_Report_BW.pdf

Newson, J. (1991) 'Backlash against feminism: a disempowering metaphor', *Resources for Feminist Research*, 20 (3/4): 93–7

Pleck, E. (1987) *Domestic Tyranny*, New York: Oxford University Press

Sanbonmatsu, K. (2008) 'Gender backlash in American politics?' *Politics and Gender*, 4 (4): 634–42

Sancier, B. (1992) 'Whose backlash is it, anyway?' *Affilia*, 7 (3): 5–7

Schechter, S. (1982) *Women and Male Violence*, Boston, MA: South End Press

——(1999) 'New challenges for the battered women's movement: building collaborations and improving public policy for poor women'. Retrieved from: http://www.mincava.umn.edu/documents/nwchllng/nwchllng.html (accessed 16 June 2011)

Tierney, K.J. (1982) 'The battered women movement and the creation of the wife beating problem', *Social Problems*, 29 (3): 207–20

Walby, S. (1990) *Theorizing Patriarchy*, Oxford: Basil Blackwell

Wood, J.K. (2005) 'In whose name? Crime victim policy and the punishing power of protection', *NWSA Journal*, 17 (3): 1–17

Part 4

Issues in contemporary crime and deviance

12 Drifting on and off-line

Humanising the cyber criminal

Craig Webber and Michael Yip

Introduction

> we are free to choose our lifestyle for a while, and most of us are here because
> we like what we do or what we get from it[1]
>
> (_cracker_)

Hackers and hacktivists were a rare breed when the original series of National Deviancy conferences took place. Now they are ubiquitous in the media, the folk devils of late modernity. Cybercrime is now a central concern of crime control, from the rise of online activism, labouring under the awkward neologism hacktivism (Jordan and Taylor 2004); to the writers of viruses, Trojans and worms; the hackers stealing data and the carders buying and selling stolen credit cards and using them to buy goods and services (Taylor 2005; Yar 2006). Hacking is now a central concern of government and law enforcement (The Stationery Office 2010). Carding (Peretti 2008), the trading of stolen credit card details, is one of the main profit-driven cybercrimes currently taking place and the topic of this chapter.

Our interpretation of what a hacker is has changed and become universally thought of in negative terms. Several connotations have now become commonplace. A hacker is a deviant; someone who infiltrates your privacy, a lurker, a hidden presence. However, hacking, or cracking as it used to be known, was an activity that had more positive, creative associations. Recently, the British government minister responsible for education, Michael Gove, highlighted the lack of programming skills in computing courses for young people. At about the same time, a cheap programmable computer came onto the market. The computer can be programmed by budding App designers of the future, or parents misty eyed for their old BBC Micro. Programming computers, designing new software and using a device for a purpose that it was not originally designed for is the definition of hacking (Taylor 2005). In much the same way that all young people become demonised, so all hackers become demonised, a classic case of moral panic. However, in the original formulation of moral panic, Cohen argued that an activity that had been witnessed previously was repackaged by the authorities and the media as new and unique (Cohen 2002). To what extent does hacking fall into this category? Is there really nothing new about it? We will argue that hacking is a combination of the new and the old, that there is something new and unique about it, it is a truly borderless crime, but there is also something familiar about those who engage in it.

By looking at online carding forums we approach the subjects of this activity as having a life that drifts between the online and the offline world and challenges preconceptions about the mythical hacker. One of the most interesting developments in organised crime is the use of social networking tools to facilitate like-minded individuals through the creation of discussion forums: an 'Underground Facebook'. Therefore, this chapter explores the myths and representations of cyber criminals. In order to understand cybercrime we need to interrogate older theories, draw on them and expand them but, more than this, we also need to actively and unself-consciously engage in literatures from outside our comfort zone. Since the end of the Deviancy conferences in 1973, and the rise of realism in the 1980s, theoretical experimentation has gone out of fashion to be replaced with rational choice, routine activities and target hardening (Young 2011). Yet, critical criminology in the 1970s was the epitome of theoretical synthesis and trans-disciplinary integration. The rise of cultural criminology has demonstrated that there is still room for a critical criminology that is situated in opposition to the technical controlling forms of the discipline such as crime science (Ferrell *et al.* 2008). Now, more than ever, theoretical synthesis and the broadening of the available literatures is possible since the world of Google replaced the card indexes of the old libraries (Webber 2007, 2010). Computer science and social science can be combined[2] as long as openness and innovation remain hallmarks of academic practice.

Our concern in this chapter is not with the sociology of credit card use, or of consumerism per se. There is a small literature on the former (see for example Ritzer 2001), and a more weighty literature on the sociology of consumption (e.g. Hayward 2004; Hall *et al.* 2008). Our interest is in those who engage in the practice of carding, the trade in stolen and false credit cards. Very little academic research has been conducted on this activity (for exceptions to this see Wall 2007; Yar 2006). No one has yet used online forums as a dataset to understand the activity from a criminological perspective. Most work in this area derives from law enforcement, journalism, computer science or the security industry. The most in-depth study so far is by journalist Misha Glenny (2011) on the creation of several of the early discussion forums such as Dark Market and Cardersplanet. Glenny's book is an example of what can be achieved by good journalism in an era when the profession is under fire, for, ironically, widespread hacking of phones and other nefarious trade crafts. However, Glenny's book did not have access to the kind of data we have, namely the forums that were set up to allow carders and other cyber criminals to engage in communication and, most important of all, business.

Deconstructing the duality of cybercrime: beyond real and virtual

So, how do we begin to understand this activity from a criminological perspective? Mike Presdee (2000) suggested that Mikhail Bakhtin's (1984) concept of the second life of the people was a way to explain the duality of life on the Internet. A similar concept from Jonathon Raban's book *Soft City* (1974) describes the duality of the city with a hard structural city of urban planners, politics and policing plans (Hayward 2004). The soft city is one where people live and make meaning from the structural properties of the hard city. This is often innovative, challenging of authority and a deviation from the intentions of the city's planners. Ferrell, Hayward and Young (2008) note that this is one of the driving ideas behind cultural criminology: 'the *lived experience* of crime, transgression and social control' (2008: 80). This approach is seen to be in contrast to the rational choice perspective and sociological positivism. The Internet, likewise, has its spaces of conformity and deviance. Much of our lives are now spent in front of screens, so much so that it has come to represent a place in its own right.

However, perhaps this overstates the case. The virtual versus the real is a common duality that has come under increasing criticism. Katja Franko Aas has joined others in questioning the binary of virtual and real, of technical and social. Utilising Baudrillard's (1994) argument that the virtual, or simulation, is real, and that the real is no longer real, she applies this concept to criminology's understanding of cybercrime. She notes the 'hype and hyperbole surrounding the alleged exceptionality of the virtual' (Aas 2006: 164). For example, Manuel Castells prefers to talk about 'the culture of real virtuality' (1997: 10). Certainly, this has been evident in criminology with an emphasis on the real. Similarly, the architecture of the web makes structural accounts appealing. Also, there is no doubt that carding is an organised crime, with specific roles that link and find meaning with others in a network. We wish to explore this side of the phenomenon *and* the other side: the human being who buys and sells stolen cards for the myriad reasons they have to do this. Following Katja Franko Aas, we also want to move beyond description and rhetoric and begin to understand the way that the online and the offline interact. Other ways to look at this might be to define the differences as a structure/agency problem, with the security industry and computer science generally taking the structural route of mapping the networks and roles. One of the myths that has become part of the stereotype of cybercrime is the cyber criminal (hacker, carder, malware writer, etc.) as technical geniuses able to transcend the original intention of a technology. Although, clearly there are those with high technical ability, increasingly the skills are becoming outsourced so that programmes can be bought online that can do the job that used to be a more bespoke occupation. Consequently, we will present the world of cybercrime as a complex interaction of the technical and the mundane. What we are proposing is a way to move away from computer science and the security industry's approach to cybercrime, whilst still accepting its value, and harking back to the tradition of humanising the deviant that was central to the sociology of deviancy and the original National Deviancy Conferences.

The problem of researching cyber-deviance: moving beyond the structural approach

Too often computer science and the security industry also takes a technological approach that explores the architecture and security properties of the systems being exploited by hackers, and how to disrupt these networks: effectively, a structural approach. However, it has been argued by Aas (2007: 296) that criminology also:

> Seems to be, theoretically and methodologically, somewhat ill-equipped for analysing and researching the relevance of the emerging 'space of flows'. There is therefore a need to develop concepts and methodologies that are sensitive to the complexities of the global.

The concept of a 'space of flows' derives from Manuel Castells (2000) and is seen as oppositional to the space of places. The latter was seen as still being the predominant space wherein communication, experience and social and political control took place. But, in the network society, the space of places was itself being taken over by the space of flows as communications networks overtook the role of territorial organisation. The space of flows takes place in the computer-mediated (inter)network of informational capitalism. One company can effectively marginalise a village, a town or a country by deciding to locate a business anywhere in the world so long as electricity and communication systems allow the setting up of a computer network. Businesses that are truly within the informational sphere are not as reliant on the natural resources that derive from the natural ecology of a region, or the need to store and transport large items (Negroponte 1996). Of course, one could argue that the canals and railways of the Industrial Revolution did the same to towns and villages in that era. A town without a train station could be cut off from the accumulation of capital in much the same way as Castells describes. The difference, however, is the connection of space and time; literally the information age has allowed vast quantities of data to be transferred increasingly fast (Negroponte 1996). Castells argues that the network society, and the specific form of informational capitalism to which it gives rise, has resulted in several features that differentiate it from industrial capitalism. This networking logic is at the roots of major effects in our societies. Using it:

- capital flows can bypass controls
- workers are individualised, outsourced, subcontracted
- communication becomes at the same time global and customised
- valuable people and territories are switched on, devalued ones are switched off.

The dynamics of networks push society towards an endless escape from its own constraints and controls, towards an endless supersession and reconstruction of its values and institutions, towards a meta-social, constant rearrangement of human institutions and organisations (Castells 1997: 15).

Castells usefully provides a framework that allows for the analysis of this new form of organised crime. Carding, we will argue, certainly reflects the characteristics identified by Castells as forming the information age. We would also argue that this is not to deny the utility of criminological theories that are more at home in the space of places, rather than the space of flows. Indeed, that is one of the key arguments in this chapter, there needs to be a theoretical space of flows linking the different theories that were developed for different eras. One such is from Jock Young, darling/devil of the NDC, depending upon your position, and still courting controversy. His book *The Criminological Imagination* (2011) is a thesis that sets out to discredit the quantitative approach to crime. We have sympathy for a lot of the arguments; if Young had the intention of provoking a reaction, he succeeded. We would argue, however, that one approach does not negate the other; both can live together, and have done, even when C. W. Mills – the inspiration for Young's recent book – was writing (Webber 2010). The data we will discuss later certainly show that synthesis, and not oppositional dualism, is the only way to make sense of the very human experiences of carders. What follows, therefore, is an outline of the structure of the economy of carding. This will be added to later by following a necessarily limited series of discussions showing the various motivations, regrets and justifications of those engaged in carding.

Cybercrime and the structure of the underground economy: forums as networks of trust

Over the last decade, the nature of cybercrime has transformed from vandalism to being profit-driven and the main force behind this paradigm shift is the rise of carding, a type of identity theft. Carding involves the unauthorised use of credit and debit card account information to fraudulently purchase goods and services (Peretti 2008: 6). Those in the business, the carders, are the individuals who bring money into the 'cybercrime ecosystem', characterised by a specialised labour division (Wall 2008: 43). These include hackers, spammers, phishers, malicious software (malware) authors, vulnerability finders, money mules, drops and cashiers (Thomas and Martin 2006). Most often, only ephemeral relationships akin to the arm's length 'market relationships' often seen in enterprises (Uzzi 1997: 41) exist between these 'cybercrime entrepreneurs'. Together, they give rise to a dark web of offenders, more often referred to as the underground economy (Thomas and Martin 2006) – less like Raban's (1974) soft city, more a dark city akin to a cyber-Chicago in the 1920s and 1930s. Failed and failing states, mainly from the former Soviet Union, produced eager recruits for these forums (Glenny 2011). Like the concentric zones of Ernest Burgess (1925) and Shaw and McKay (1942), they entered sites that would seem initially disorganised and where trust in new members was set to low by default. As is well known in criminology, this theory was criticised by Edwin Sutherland (1939), who suggested that rather than social disorganisation, it was differential association that was behind criminal behaviour. People learn how to commit crime and, getting better at it, some move up the deviant meritocracy. These forums demonstrate that both explanations are relevant. Forum members can gain knowledge of how to 'do' carding, demonstrate their trustworthiness and possibly move up the scale and into more respected positions. Just like the new inhabitants of Chicago as they moved out of the city and into the suburbs; wealthier, respected, trusted. To further understand how carding drives profit-oriented cybercrime, it is best demonstrated by following the propagation of demand and supply for different types of goods and services triggered by a carder.

The objective of a carder is simple: to steal financial information from a large number of victims. Although carders can steal credit cards from the offline world, only the Internet can provide a large enough pool of potential victims that makes carding most feasible and financially sound. In the following, we focus on a carder aiming to steal credit card details from other Internet users.

There are three main ways in which credit card details can be stolen: hacking, eavesdropping and phishing. To steal credit card data by hacking, a non-technically competent carder would pay for the help of a skilful *hacker* in order to gain access into one or more database(s) of Internet-enabled systems and steal the stored credit card data. An example of this type of data theft is the Sony hacking case in 2011.[3] In order to steal credit card data flowing through the network, there are two options for a carder. First, one could hire a *malware author* to produce specifically designed malicious software (malware) to eavesdrop on computers and steal the targeted type of credit card data entered in the web browser by the unsuspecting victims. Alternatively, one could purchase ready-made malware generator toolkits such as Zeus[4] or SpyEye.[5] Furthermore, a carder would pay *botnet herders*. These are people in control of botnets, or compromised computers, sometimes referred to as zombie machines. The aim is to install the malware on large networks of zombie machines allowing the carder to collect a large quantity of credit card data. It is important to note that the *malware authors* would in turn require the expertise from *vulnerability finders* who are experts in finding undisclosed vulnerabilities in popular software applications such as Internet Explorer so that the malware authors can write software to exploit those vulnerabilities.

Indeed a carder could choose the last and by far the easiest option, by luring unsuspecting users into providing such information voluntarily. However, even this requires the expertise from others, namely *phishers* and *spammers*. The *phishers* are the specialists in setting up campaigns to get unsuspecting victims to give up their banking details. If the phisher did not possess the expertise, it would be necessary to hire a *rogue web designer* to create websites designed to mimic the targeted financial institutions, such as online banks, payment processors and auction sites. Visitors to these fake websites are tricked into trusting the website as genuine and would instinctively attempt to login using their credentials, only to have their credentials stolen (Dhamija *et al.* 2006). However, to steal a large amount of credentials, one would need to draw a sizeable traffic to these fake websites. To achieve this, a phisher would draft email messages designed to socially engineer victims into clicking the link to the phishing website, which is embedded in the email, and then hire a *spammer* for mass mailing. The *spammers* usually have control over a large number of compromised computers and they are needed because mass mailing requires intensive computational power. With the help of the spammers, the web addresses of the phishing websites are mass mailed to millions of Internet users whose email addresses have been harvested or stolen by hackers.

Assuming the carder has successfully stolen a sizeable quantity of credit card data, he would then need to use them to make a financial gain. Two common options are chosen at this stage: use the stolen credit cards to purchase goods from online shops or, if direct access to bank accounts is possible, the carder could take money out of those bank accounts by simply going to an ATM with a fake card carrying a magnetic strip with the stolen information (Peretti 2008). However, the main problem the carder faces at this stage is the need to obscure the true source of the money, which requires money laundering. If the carder wants to purchase goods from online shops, he would hire *drops* that would provide him with a mail address to which the purchased goods could be delivered and then forwarded to the carder. On the other hand, if the carder wishes to take money directly out of stolen bank accounts then he would need the help of money mules who would (most often unknowingly) accept and forward proceeds of fraud using their own bank accounts for a small percentage of the transferred fund.

Trust among thieves?

As outlined by von Lampe and Johansen (2004), trust is an essential social process in criminal networks. However, trust is made almost impossible by the anonymity offered by the Internet and has become a major problem in the underground economy. In 2002, a clever solution was borrowed from business and implemented in the underground economy: escrow. Escrow is a system to overcome the problem of dishonest traders, also known as *rippers* (Franklin *et al.* 2007). These rippers would sell stolen data which no longer work, and sell the same set of stolen data to two or more buyers meaning that the resulting cards were not only useless, but that many buyers might be risking arrest. Carding forums were created to minimise this problem, although they could not eradicate it. Forums are also set up with roles and responsibilities in a hierarchy (Yip 2011). At the top are the administrators who are mainly responsible for the overall direction and management of the forum. Then, moderators are responsible for monitoring activities on sub-forums. Reviewers are responsible for reviewing the quality of the products from prospective sellers, also known as vendors. If the products are found to be legitimate then the vendor would gain a status called *reviewed vendor*. This is the trust mechanism in place to minimise the problems of the rippers. But, in addition to trust being gained through successive sales of working cards or data, the introduction of a system of escrow led to the rapid expansion of carding (Glenny 2011). Escrow allowed a seller to provide the escrow officer with a sample of the cards, and the buyer to hand the escrow officer the money for safe keeping. Once the escrow officer was satisfied the card details were working, they would then release the money to the seller and arrange for the rest of the 'dump' to be passed on. This increased the level of trust that pertained among these carders and the offence rapidly took off after its introduction. This system of ensuring fair play turned carding into an industry.

Carding: a super highway to Merton's 'American Dream'?

What can we learn from forums? The forums that form the core data in this chapter have never been studied academically before. They are a unique record of the conversations, business deals, tutorial sessions for self-improvement, and the residual human anxieties of those engaging in the buying and selling of stolen credit cards. It is where the offline and the online merge. They are no longer in existence since the forums, and the computers upon which they were stored, were taken down. We do not have the space here to discuss the intricacies of the methods, methodology or ethics of collecting the data. There is a small, but growing literature on researching on the Internet and forums in particular, as well as the ethics of doing so (King 1996; Hine 2000). However, most of the ethical considerations common to this form of research relate to 'live' forums, what some have referred to as 'lurking', but which might be better described using the more familiar term, non-participant observation. The forums discussed in this chapter are all historical and no longer active, akin to documentary research.

Carding forums and the continuing relevance of traditional criminological accounts

According to Symantec's cybercrime report on 2011, global cybercrime has an estimated worth of $388bn and is thought to be larger than the entire global underground market of marijuana, cocaine and heroin combined. With the anonymity, instantaneity, networking and global reach afforded by the Internet (Wall 2008), it can be said that cybercrime appears to be an easy way to quick money. Using discussions between the carders on a well-known carding forum called ShadowCrew[6] (Glenny 2011), we examine the perceptions, fears and triumphs of the carders themselves and get a glimpse of their way of life.

Forums are generally accessible to all, but carder's forums often have the additional element of an invite-only system of allowing only those most trusted to go through to other areas. These forums are also venues for the discussion of topics that have a more mundane, offline, quality, such as where to buy illegal drugs or what protein shake is best for muscle gain. These forums provide an insight into the life that is lived outside the confines of the carders' computers and outside the purpose of the forum's original creation. There are exchanges that raise questions about the morality of the theft of credit cards; rivalries explored and status negotiated; fame sought despite the dangers of raising one's head above the firewall. In these exchanges we get a sense of humanity and see crime and deviance beyond the business of credit card exchanges. They exhibit what Matza and Sykes (1961) termed subterranean values – rather than their opinions and values being located in a distinct group separate from mainstream, ethical values, they instead exist as part of a continuum. They also act as a subcultural group in resistance to authority, and similar to the Birmingham School analysis but rather than the usual class-based location these forums are marked by a distinctly mixed demography of participants (Hall and Jefferson 1976).

They also drift on and offline in a similar way to Matza's (1964) concept of drifting in and out of deviant behaviour. This concept helped to overcome the determinism inherent in previous 'positivistic' accounts. One exchange that we followed began with what seemed to be a purely online existence: a case of a carder being spammed by email from another trader. The restrictions placed on that seller's business by having to wade through the spam email to get to the real emails left him angry as his business began to suffer. As we followed the exchange we realised that the threats to 'take the man down' were more than just an online threat which warranted an online response in retaliation. We realised that we were viewing a hit being taken out, either in threat or with actual intent. Since these are forums that were already taken down by law enforcement agencies, it is difficult to determine what actually happened, especially since the secretive world of the carder forums utilised many techniques to render individuals anonymous. In what follows we illustrate the dynamism and diversity of the carding world, the messy humanity that is lost to the structural gaze of the security industry and computer science.

The carders: folk devils or delinquent boys?

They hide behind their computers and they steal credit cards from people around the world. That is as much as the average individual in our society knows about the carders. Our main perception of them comes from their portrayal in the media and our imagination. Using carding forums, we are presented with a unique opportunity to finally understand them from their perspectives and get to know their attitudes. Why did they choose to become a carder? Do they have plans for the future? Do they have boundaries? Are they serious organised criminals or akin to Cohen's delinquent boys (Cohen 1955)? From a conversation under the topic 'Do you have any regrets' on ShadowCrew (Glenny 2011), we find answers to these questions:[7]

Some parts of it I love. I'm a total loaner outsider, some by choice and some by the fact I've never been the type of guy that gets the girls or anything. Doing what I'm doing kind of makes me feel like I'm doing something ... something a little risky ... then when I do something, I still sometimes feel guilty about the people I'm doing it too. I hate that part of it. I'm never going to have a normal life even if I try, so this life, as shadowcrew says, 'For those who wish to play in the shadows[8]' I love the shadows. I love doing things in the shadows. That's where I'm comfortable.

(By *TheDevil*)

I agree, it gets addictive. There is always that feeling of trying to be the best between your shady friends but appear as the second (because the number one always get caught). As for the friends, in my own experience, many times those 'good guy' friends simply get away when you have some problem and the people who is there, with you, is the shady one. Anyway we are free to choose our lifestyle for a while, and most of us are here because we like what we do or what we get from it. That's my opinion.

(By *_cracker_*)

In a lot of ways I regret where I am at today. When I was younger I didn't realise the consequences of the shit I was doing – easy money was great. But once you get a record and your chances of a good legit life slip further away the less choice you have in the matter. Now that I am older I wish I had done things differently, but this is the life I chose & as long as I have to live it – I am going to try to take it as far as I can. I am hooked on the rush – there have been times when I could have resumed normal living with a 9–5 job, but I could never bring myself to do it. I need the excitement & the fast cash. The stress is just something I have to live with – that and the isolation from everyone else. With the amount of time that I put into my 'job' there is hardly any time to enjoy life – but it's addicting.

(By *Rupuze79*)

I agree with Rupuze79: once you get older and get a record, legitimate jobs become that much harder to obtain, thereby making this life that much more attractive. I've concluded that the only way I can make a decent living legit is to own my own business. Since the banks won't give me a loan I have to 'give' myself one. My only regret in this life is doing time. As for it being addictive; everyone needs an exit strategy. Even the Kennedys eventually went legit. Also don't forget where the real money is and where the real crooks are, is in legit businesses.

(By *Dr. Persistence*)

I try to have the fewest regrets possible. There is nothing you can do to change the past. What's happened has happened. My biggest regret? Not putting in the effort in High School and college. Looking back I wish I had done well enough in High School to go to an ivy league school. From there I could have made contacts and moved into the legit business world much quicker. Once you get a taste of the easy money it's hard to let it go.

(By *JediMasterC*)

From this dialogue, we can see a number of key issues in the motivation of these carders:

- the desire for higher social status
- the lack of legitimate ways to achieve higher social status, due to previous wrongdoing
- peer recognition
- disconnection from society
- addiction to the lifestyle of the underground economy.

In his thesis on social structure and anomie, Merton (1938) argues that certain social structures exert a definite pressure which triggers impulses to break social controls. Two elements are particularly relevant, culturally defined goals and the acceptable processes to achieving those goals. Since the cultural goals in our society are heavily associated with economic terms and that cybercrime, as already mentioned in the previous section, is often portrayed as a lucrative crime, it is then reasonable to hypothesise that cybercrime would appear as an attractive route for those seeking to achieve higher status in our society. However, as Cloward and Ohlin (1960) argue, there is differential access to the illegitimate routes to achieving culturally accepted goals. With regards to cybercrime, people with technical knowledge may become hackers or spammers, while others with the opportunities, connections and knowledge of carding would become carders. While hackers and spammers can achieve success alone due to the ability to author automated scripts to attack victims, carding requires many different types of skills and materials. To physically steal credit card data, also known as skimming, one would need modified point-of-sale (POS) machines or hacked ATM machines. Furthermore, one would need an encoder to encode stolen data onto replicated credit cards. The list goes on, as depicted in Figure 12.1. Therefore, networking is essential for carding and the availability of the Internet means carders from around the world can easily find each other. This is why carding forums such as ShadowCrew appeared. However, carding forums do not just serve as marketplaces but rather more akin to subcultures of underground activities. First introduced by Sutherland (1939) and advanced by Akers (1977), the differential association theory argues that criminal behaviour is learned by being associated with other criminals. Indeed how-to tutorials are commonly available on the carding forums but this is not the most crucial thing that is learned. As Sykes and Matza (1957) argue, juveniles become delinquents only after they have learned

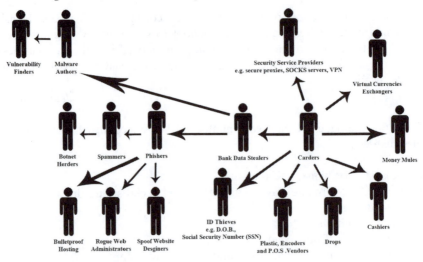

Figure 12.1 Flow of demand in the carding underworld

the techniques of neutralisation, that is, justifying their deviant actions. This is evident from replies to a topic about scamming college students:

> I agree, scamming college children is plain and simply wrong ... thats their real hard earned money and there's no way for them to get it back ... Credit Card fraud, the victim gets all his money back ... it's a victimless crime, but this is just plain wrong ... I'm not flaming you, I'm just saying, I'd feel better if you see my point of view and please not do that again. Sorry to put you on the spot like that, but it's just my opinion.
>
> (By *Fear*)

> Yeah just cuz the world is immoral doesn't mean we have to feed that fire I personally like to get credit card companies who get the young generation people getting dooped (duped) into school loans and credit cards and then not having a way to pay it back when its time to work and make a living they come for the money and make your life a living hell. so screw them Robin Hood style.
>
> (By *Campee*)

From the above replies, we can see that the carder named Fear attempts to 'deny the injury' (Sykes and Matza 1957: 667) by claiming that credit card fraud is a victimless crime as the victims always get their money back, while Campee attempts to 'deny the victim' but believing that credit card companies deserve his deviant action as they cause young people to be in debt. This dialogue also supports Sykes and Matza's argument that delinquents are at least partially committed to the more widely accepted norms and that their values are far less deviant than commonly portrayed. Lastly, it should be noted that online carding forums also facilitate carders' need for positive reinforcement for their actions. As evident from the above discussion, members of the forums are able to read each other's justifications and this has the effect of reinforcing their own beliefs.

Conclusion

The Internet has given rise to online carding forums on which online criminals communicate and trade with one another, with their dialogues recorded over the entire lifespan of the forum. This represents a unique methodological tool, a genuine insight into those who engage in criminal enterprises, the discussions they have, their frailties, triumphs and the challenges of the everyday. In the limited space available here we have outlined the roles, responsibilities and methods of overcoming a lack of trust in the business of carding. However, we have also shown the human side. Rather than being some kind of techno-genius or super-criminal, they are instead engaging in the same kinds of discussions that many of us who are not carders may have. Worry over their choice of 'career', the ethics of what they do, and how to do the job better all appear in forum posts. We also see a sense of political anarchy in the discussions and in the pseudonyms they used. For some carders, this activity was a way to cheat the system, to get one over on the banks, government and other corporations. Carding is perceived, like so much else on the Internet, as a victimless crime. Rather than the offence being against an individual like you, it is against the banks who will, in any event, compensate the victim. In the post-credit crunch world, where worldwide measures of austerity are weighing most heavily on those least able to bear the strain, it should be expected that hackers will take on the role of anarchic, anti-establishment anti-heroes. Hacking always was the prime example of innovation in the face of the seeming blocks to cherished goals, be they free telephone calls, copyright-protected games, innovative software or money from banks without the need to work too hard for it. In carding, we see Merton's innovator, retreatist and rebel combined – a unique combination that demonstrates that this cannot just be explained as another moral panic. Many of these carders take the line that they are enriching themselves in the face of a system designed to keep everyone down; they see themselves as fighting this system and winning. Of course, we all actually pay for these crimes. The sense of rebellion is misplaced, and the thought that the banks are really losing out misguided. But, none the less, we will end with the words of one carder *Campee;* as misguided as they are, these primitive rebels are expressing sentiments echoed around the world: 'screw them Robin Hood style'.

Notes

1 Where quotations are made from forums we present it as originally posted, spelling errors and shortcuts included.
2 This combination has been referred to as Web Science (see e.g. http://webscience. org/home.html)

3 http://www.bbc.co.uk/news/technology-13256817
4 http://en.wikipedia.org/wiki/Zeus_%28Trojan_horse%29
5 http://krebsonsecurity.com/2011/04/spyeye-targets-opera-google-chrome-users/
6 http://en.wikipedia.org/wiki/ShadowCrew
7 Forum discussions are based on an instant messaging system that tends to involve slang and typos. This can make it difficult to follow, where possible we have kept to the original message and only altered the layout. Consequently, there will be errors of syntax, grammar and spelling.
8 This is the forum's motto and appears at the top of the website page.

References

Aas, K.F. (2006) 'Beyond "The Desert of the Real": crime control in a virtual(ised) reality', in Y. Jewkes (ed.) *Crime Online,* Cullompton: Willan

——(2007) 'Analysing a world in motion: global flows meet "criminology of the other" ', *Theoretical Criminology,* 11 (2): 283–303

Akers, R.L. (1977) *Deviant Behavior*, Belmont, CA: Wadsworth

Bakhtin, M. (1984) *Rabelais and His World*, Bloomington: Indiana University Press

Baudrillard, J. (1994) *Simulacra and Simulation*, Ann Arbor: University of Michigan Press

Burgess, E. (1925) 'The growth of the city', R.E. Park and E. Burgess (eds) *The City,* Chicago, IL: University of Chicago Press

Castells, M. (1997) 'Introduction to the Information Age', *City,* 2 (7): 6–16

——(2000) *The Information Age: Economy, Society and Culture. Volume 1*, Oxford: Blackwell

Cloward, R. and Ohlin, L. (1960) *Delinquency and Opportunity*, London: Collier-Macmillan

Cohen, A. (1955) *Delinquent Boys*, New York: Free Press

Cohen, S. (2002) *Folk Devils and Moral Panics*, London: McGibbon and Kee

Dhamija, R., Tygar, J.D. and Hearst, M. (2006) 'Why phishing works', *Proceedings of the SIGCHI Conference on Human Factors in Computing Systems – CHI 2006* (November 2005)

Ferrell, J., Hayward, K. and Young, J. (2008) *Cultural Criminology: An Invitation*, London: Sage

Franklin, J., Paxson, V., Perrig, A. and Savage, S. (2007) 'An inquiry into the nature and causes of the wealth of internet miscreants', *Proceedings of the 14th ACM Conference on Computer and Communications Security,* New York: ACM

Glenny, M. (2011) *Darkmarket*, London: Bodley Head

Hall, S. and Jefferson, T. (eds) (1976) *Resistance through Ritual*, London: Unwin Hyman

Hall, S., Winlow, S. and Ancrum, C. (2008) *Criminal Identities and Consumer Culture*, Cullompton: Willan

Hayward, K. (2004) *City Limits*, London: Glasshouse

Hine, C. (2000) *Virtual Ethnography*, London: Sage

Jordan, T. and Taylor, P. (2004) *Hacktivism and Cyberwars*, London: Routledge

King, S.A. (1996) 'Researching internet communities: proposed ethical guidelines for the reporting of results', *Information Society*, 12: 119–27

Matza, D. (1964) *Delinquency and Drift*, New York: Wiley

Matza, D. and Sykes, G. (1961) 'Juvenile delinquency and subterranean values', *American Sociological Review,* 26: 712–19

Merton, R.K. (1938) 'Social structure and anomie', *American Sociological Review* 3 (5): 672–82

Negroponte, N. (1996) *Being Digital*, New York: Vintage Books

Peretti, K. (2008) Data Breaches: What the Underground World of 'Carding' Reveals, US Department of Justice. Available from: http://www.chtlj.org/sites/default/files/media/articles/v025/v025.i2.Peretti.pdf

Presdee, M. (2000) *Cultural Criminology and the Carnival of Crime*, London: Routledge

Raban, J. (1974), *Soft City*, London: Hamilton

Ritzer, G. (2001) *Explorations in the Sociology of Consumption*, London: Sage

Shaw, C.R. and McKay, H.D. (1942) *Juvenile Delinquency and Urban Areas*, Chicago, IL: Chicago University Press

Sutherland, E.H. (1939) *Principles of Criminology*, Philadelphia, PA: J.B. Lippincott

Sykes, G. and Matza, D. (1957) 'Techniques of neutralization: a theory of delinquency', *American Sociological Review*, 22: 664–70

Taylor, P.A. (2005) 'From hackers to hacktivists: speed bumps on the global superhighway?' *New Media and Society*, 7 (5): 625–46

The Stationery Office (2010) *A Strong Britain in an Age of Uncertainty: The National Security Strategy*, London: The Cabinet Office

Thomas, R. and Martin, J. (2006) 'The underground economy: priceless', *The USENIX Magazine*, 31 (6): 7–16

Uzzi, B. (1997) 'Social structure and competition in interfirm networks: the paradox of embeddedness', *Administrative Science Quarterly*, 42 (1): 35–67

von Lampe, K. and Johansen, P.O. (2004) 'Organized crime and trust: on the conceptualization and empirical relevance of trust in the context of criminal networks', *Global Crime*, 6 (2): 159–84

Wall, D.S. (2007) *Cybercrime*, London: Polity Press

——(2008) 'Cybercrime and the culture of fear: social science fiction(s) and the production of knowledge about cybercrime', *Information, Communication & Society*, 11: 861–84

Webber, C. (2007) 'Revaluating relative deprivation theory', *Theoretical Criminology*, 11 (1): 97–120

——(2010) *Psychology and Crime*, London: Sage

Yar, M. (2006) *Cybercrime and Society*, London: Sage

Yip, M. (2011) 'An investigation into Chinese cybercrime and the applicability of social network analysis', *Proceedings of ACM Web Science Conference*, 14–17 June, Koblenz, Germany

Young, J. (2011) *The Criminological Imagination*, Cambridge: Polity Press

13 Thinking critically about rural crime

Toward the development of a new left realist perspective

Walter S. DeKeseredy and Joseph F. Donnermeyer

Like all criminological schools of thought, left realism emerged within a particular political economic context. Its life began in the 1980s during the Thatcher years, and as Hayward (2010: 264) observes, the writings of British progressives Jock Young, John Lea, and Roger Matthews sent 'shock waves through radical criminology, opening up personal disputes and ideological cleavages that endure to this day'. These tensions are not limited to the United Kingdom. For example, left-wing attacks on the Canadian realist project range from being accused of 'an exercise in dubious politics and the cult of personality' (O'Reilly-Fleming 1995: 5) to fostering 'a form of intellectual colonization where junior Canadian critical criminologists can be more familiar with developments overseas than with what has happened in their own country' (Doyle and Moore 2011: 7). Such criticism is evidence that left realism has made its mark on progressive ways of thinking about crime and will continue to do so long into the future.

Until the publication of Lea and Young's (1984) *What Is to Be Done about Law and Order?* and Elliott Currie's (1985) *Confronting Crime: An American Challenge*, critical criminology was mainly concerned with 'crimes of the powerful' (Pearce 1976), such as white-collar and corporate crime. Undoubtedly, more people die in the workplace than on the streets because employers violate occupational health and safety standards (Reiman and Leighton 2010). However, as left realists point out, failing to take seriously muggings, robberies, and the like allows right-wing politicians in several countries to manufacture ideological support for 'law and order' policies that are detrimental to the powerless and preclude the development of more equal societies (DeKeseredy 2011a). Moreover, what conservative theorist James Q. Wilson (1985) stated over 25 years ago still holds true today to the extent that people do not bar and nail their windows shut during heat waves, avoid public parks, stay in at night, harbor deep suspicions of strangers, and in general watch the social fabric of society ripped apart because of unsafe working conditions or massive consumer fraud.

Left realists developed a sophisticated critical understanding of predatory street crime and violence behind closed doors and proposed progressive short-term ways of curbing these problems (DeKeseredy and Schwartz 2012). Although some argue left realism has seen its heyday, to be sure, it is still very much alive and has been 'rediscovered' (Matthews 2009). Consider that at the end of the last decade an international group of scholars, including John Lea (2010) and Roger Matthews (2010), published left realist articles in a special issue of *Crime, Law and Social Change* (see Vol. 54, 2010). Further, since the mid to late 1980s, Walter DeKeseredy, Martin Schwartz, and Elliott Currie routinely publish left realist work. For Currie (2010: 112–13):

> Left Realism ... is not only an essential perspective on the problems of crime and justice in the early 21st century, but ... it is the perspective that offers the best hope of providing the intellectual underpinning for a genuinely progressive approach to crime around the world.

Left realism may be reshaped in various theoretical, political, and empirical ways, but it has yet to take 'departures from criminological and sociological urbanism' (Hogg and Carrington 2006: 1). Of course, this can be said about criminology in general. Nevertheless, left realism's selective inattention to rural crime is problematic for several reasons. First, contrary to popular belief, rural communities are not less criminogenic than urban areas. In fact, rural rates may be higher than urban rates at particular types of rural places and for specific kinds of crimes, such as violence against women (DeKeseredy and Schwartz 2009; Donnermeyer and DeKeseredy 2008). Second, there are large inequities across the urban and rural geographies of many societies, with higher rates of rural poverty, unemployment and under-employment, lack of government investments in rural schools, health care facilities and other forms of institutional infrastructure, and exploitative economic relations, especially in rural communities whose economies depend on natural resource extraction industries and tourism (Lichter and Brown 2011). These are the very social forces that critical criminologists point to as the structural features of crime, and which if not understood means that ameliorative policies and actions cannot be formulated and undertaken (Currie 1985). Finally, the problem with ignoring rural crime is that discourse on this issue continues to be dominated by conservative 'get tough on crime' rhetoric while there is also strong rural support for abolishing progressive laws designed to help reduce violence, such as the Canadian federal government's long-gun registry as part of the *Firearms Act* (Lindell 2011).

The purpose of this chapter, then, is to mark the development of a new left realist perspective on rural crime and societal reactions to it. First, though, it is necessary to define the term 'rural' and then briefly review critical criminological work on crime and social control in rural communities. We follow this with a left realist discourse on agricultural crime, considering agriculturalists as both victims and offenders.

Definition of rural

Not all rural communities are alike and as noted by Websdale (1998), still, following DeKeseredy *et al.* (2007), rather than overloading a definition of 'rural' to reflect social and cultural features that promote idyllic images and suppress the rural realities of crime, we offer a nominal conceptualization of 'rural'. Here, rural communities are places with small population sizes and/or densities that exhibit variable levels of what Sampson *et al.* (1998: 1) refer to as collective efficacy, which is 'mutual trust among neighbors combined with a willingness to act on behalf of the common good, specifically to supervise children and maintain public order'. Still, we make no assumptions about collective efficacy in rural areas because it may facilitate the commission of some types of crime even as it constrains other forms of offending (Barclay, *et al.* 2004; Jobes *et al.* 2005; Donnermeyer 2007b; Donnermeyer and DeKeseredy 2008). For example, DeKeseredy and Schwartz (2009) found that many rural Ohio men can rely on their male friends and neighbors, including those who are police officers, to support a violent patriarchal status quo even while they can count on these same individuals to help prevent public crimes (e.g. vandalism, burglary, etc.), which to them is acting on 'behalf of the common good'. Additionally, in rural sections of Ohio and other states such as Kentucky, there is widespread acceptance of woman abuse and community norms prohibiting victims from publicly talking about their experiences and from seeking social support (DeKeseredy and Schwartz 2008; Websdale 1998).

Although not discussed in the extant rural criminology literature, the above definition of 'rural' is consistent with an early left realist definition of 'community'. As stated by MacLean (1992: 353–4):

> The realist conception of community is a variable not a constant. The nature of 'the community' varies from time to time, place to place, and culture to culture. The aim of realist research is to begin to map out the characteristics of the particular community being investigated, not to impose a particular ideal conception of how that community should appear.

Rural crime and critical criminology

Gagne's (1992, 1996) feminist work on rural woman abuse played an important role in sparking contemporary critical interpretations of crime and social control.[1] Shortly after came Websdale's (1998) *Rural Woman Battering and the Justice System: An Ethnography*. Nonetheless, the flames did not emerge until the latter part of last decade, with the publication of a spate of scholarly books, journal articles, and chapters (Chakraborti and Garland 2004; Coventry and Palmer 2008; DeKeseredy *et al.* 2007; DeKeseredy *et al.* 2006; DeKeseredy and Schwartz 2009; Donnermeyer *et al.* 2006; Donnermeyer 2007a; Grant 2008; Donnermeyer and DeKeseredy 2008), many of which continued along the feminist path broken by Gagne and Websdale. Still, there is plenty of room for additional ways of thinking critically about rural crime, one of which is the left realist perspective advanced here. Our goal in this chapter is to offer a broader rural left perspective, one that focuses on empirical and policy issues, as well as major theoretical concerns.

Setting the rural left realist agenda

The call for a rural left realism is not new and dates back to a paper written by U.S. criminologist Darryl Wood (1990: 14). He asserted that:

> Not only can left realism provide aid to the study of rural crime, but the study of rural crime can also support the foundations of left realism. That rural areas can also be impacted by working class crime provides much to the left realist argument that the study of such behavior must go beyond the perspectives which have been fed to scholars for a long time now. And when we consider that the political economic situations of both inner city citizens and rural citizens are similar, left realism is provided with further justification for trying to provide a socialist response to working class criminality.

Only two scholars answered Wood's call (Donnermeyer and DeKeseredy 2008), and described the relevance of the left realist 'square of crime' or what Lea (2010) calls the 'social relations of crime control' to an understanding of rural crime and social control. Still to this day, the most popular theoretical frameworks used to understand crime are place-based perspectives, such as social disorganization theory (Donnermeyer 2007b). Furthermore, the ever-expanding corpus of rural criminology is largely atheoretical and is mostly composed of either quantitative, statistical works or in-depth qualitative studies, but either way, even mainstream criminological theory is infrequently evoked by those who turn their attention to the non-urban expressions of crime and societal reactions to it (Donnermeyer 2012).

Shortly after the release of Wood's paper, DeKeseredy (1992) recommended that realist local victimization surveys be administered in rural, isolated, and Aboriginal communities. His call remains unanswered. Yet, DeKeseredy and Schwartz's (2009) qualitative study of separation/divorce sexual assault in rural Ohio incorporated a realist method defined as a 'preparatory component of qualitative investigation' which 'documents the specificities of the communities it studies' (Maclean 1992). DeKeseredy and Schwartz's approach involved several meetings, e-mail exchanges, and in-depth telephone conversations with leading researchers in the field, local battered women's shelter staff, sexual assault survivor advocates, police officers, mental health workers, and others with a vested interest in curbing the pain and suffering uncovered by their research. These people sensitized DeKeseredy and Schwartz's research team to key issues not addressed in the social scientific literature on separation/divorce sexual assault, such as the influence of broader Ohio state politics. What is more, they made several major contributions to the development of highly useful screening questions and a semi-structured interview schedule. Activists and practitioners are experts on woman abuse and 'can help researchers formulate sophisticated and intellectually rich questions' (Schechter 1988: 311).

Woman abuse and other crimes are major problems in rural communities. While theoretical and empirical work carried out within a left realist framework can provide a better sociological understanding of such harms than mainstream research, several key issues must be addressed in future work. It is to these concerns that we now turn.

Moving beyond quantitative data

In their call for the creation of an Australian rural critical criminology Coventry and Palmer (2008: 307) warn us 'about the possible drift towards a *criminology-by-numbers*, a kind of technical administrative criminology that is keen to find new fields of the "dark figure" of crime to generate research and policy action'. Needless to say, left realism is the antithesis of administrative criminology. Administrative criminologists conduct research to help governments, often to administer highly punitive criminal justice systems, while the goal of left realist local victimization surveys is to generate data aimed at helping disenfranchised people and informing progressive ways of curbing crime in streets, 'suites', and behind closed doors. Indeed, British research shows that realist survey technology can provide a defensible, alternative source of information which can effectively be used in political struggles against right-wing law and order campaigns (DeKeseredy 1992). All the same, the question still remains: to what extent might a similar strategy be useful within a rural context? The only way left realist research designs can be useful in rural areas is if criminologists develop similar strategies and advance them within practical local political forums. Certainly, all left realists would agree with Coventry and Palmer's (2008: 309) claim that 'localized projects are of the utmost importance'.

However, quantitative methods alone cannot adequately describe the complexities of rural crime and community responses to it (DeKeseredy and Schwartz 2008). Thus, it is essential that left realists go beyond using only local victimization survey data to examine violence against women, property crimes against farms, environmental crime, alcohol and drug use and youth crime. One suggestion is to specifically design qualitative projects that focus on topics of central concern to rural people and that use in-depth interviews and participant observations of community relations. Websdale's (1998) research is a good example of such a study. He rode with police officers, watched woman abuse cases in court, talked to battered women, interviewed agents of social control, and lived in eastern Kentucky, the region of his study.

We are, by no means, calling for abandoning local victimization surveys and replacing them with purely qualitative methods. It is just that there is a dearth of qualitative left realist research. This major research gap should be filled because qualitative methods produce information that cannot be obtained by other methods. For example, participant observation research is an effective way of answering questions about why rural people join and stay in subcultures that engage in lawbreaking activities, from male support systems for violence against women (DeKeseredy *et al.* 2006) to organized drug production and trafficking (Weisheit and Fuller 2004; Garriott 2011).

Any method discussed here and in scores of textbooks can provide a rich vein of information on rural crime and the criminal justice system's response to it, but the tendency is to rely on only one research technique (usually a quantitative method), even though this fosters 'methodological parochialness' (Sugarman and Hotaling 1989). Of course, research designs are often determined by time and funding limitations. Ideally, though, left realists, like all criminologists, should be open-minded and attempt to use a variety of methods, in what is often called triangulation: using a variety of 'sightings' (like a civil engineer) from different angles or viewpoints makes it more likely that researchers will correctly survey the terrain (DeKeseredy and Schwartz 1996; Kraska and Neuman 2008).

Crimes of the powerful

One of the sharpest attacks on left realism is that it ignores crimes of the powerful (Henry 1999), a criticism that is both inaccurate and accurate. An important tenet from the beginning of left realist theory is that working-class people are victimized from above and below at the same time – harmed by corporations and the state from above and by street criminals from below (Lea and Young 1984). Although the central impetus and focus of left realism was to correct the imbalance of progressive criminologists who only examined harms caused by 'trusted criminals' (Friedrichs 2010), the field began to include empirical work on variants of what Pearce (1992) defines as 'commercial crime':[2] workplace hazards, unlawful trading practices, and the victimization of housing tenants. Unfortunately, such work was mainly urban in scope, with only one left realist study of corporate crime in the rural context, which was in the form of a study of violence against farm labour (Basran *et al.* 1995).

A case in point: a left realist discourse on agricultural crime

The criticisms of left realism and the response of its advocates point to its very strengths. A case in point is agricultural crime, perhaps the 'quintessential' example of rural crime. Part of the rural idyll, which is a benign view of rural places as crime-free and peaceful (Cloke 2006), is a variant known as 'agrarian fundamentalism' (Danbom 1992). Even in advanced capitalist societies, agrarian fundamentalism has a powerful hold on the public imagination and the popular press. It frames peaceful scenes of verdant pastures, neighbourliness, and 'down-to-earth' ranchers and farmers who in early days tamed wild lands formerly inhabited by indigenous peoples (with the implication they were less worthy to keep the land because they did not build it up and exploit its natural resources), and who in later days hold stewardship over cultivated lands, efficiently providing inexpensive food for the large share of a society's population that could not otherwise live comfortably in complex urban environments.

These images belie a more complex picture in which agriculturalists are potentially not only the targets of crime, but also join that class of offenders we know by the phrase 'crimes of the powerful'. Consider first agricultural crime from the victim point of view. A number of victimization studies have been conducted in Australia, England, Scotland and the United States over the past 30 years. Using mid-range figures from a recent review of agricultural crime studies (Donnermeyer *et al.* 2011), we estimate that each year, machinery and equipment theft occurs to about 18 percent of farm operations, and a similar proportion are affected by incidents of vandalism that are costly, both in terms of replacement of property and disruption of daily operations to repair damaged property. About 8 percent of food producers suffer the theft of some type of livestock and, perhaps most telling of all, approximately 9 percent experience the breaking and entering of a farm building, a rate that far exceeds most rates of burglary for urban neighbourhoods in countries like Canada and the United States (Barclay and Donnermeyer 2011). Illegal trespassing can also be high and damage caused by hunters or those who use large ranch and farmlands for illegal marijuana, methamphetamine and other forms of drug production is also prevalent in some rural regions (Weisheit and Fuller 2004; Barclay and Donnermeyer 2011; Garriott 2011).

These rates of victimization and criminal activity should not be surprising when viewed from a left realist position, and the changing ecology of farm crime is vital to making this link. For example, the location of a break and enter varies by the geographic size of the operation, which impacts the ability of the agricultural operators to watch over buildings and property distant from the homestead where expensive machinery, equipment, and supplies are kept. Agricultural operations located near public roads are also more accessible and more likely to experience various forms of theft, illegal dumping, vandalism, and trespassing (Barclay and Donnermeyer 2011). Plus, many agricultural areas are subject to forms of urbanization brought about by the consumption of rural landscapes by tourists and recreationalists (Lichter and Brown 2011), suburban and industrial developments, and a host of other economic and cultural factors that increasingly tie together the rural and urban sectors of many societies. Farms and ranches are no longer and have really never been as isolated – physically, culturally, and socially – as portrayed by agrarian fundamentalism.

The intersection of offenders and victims is thus as applicable to understanding agricultural crime as it would be for crime in the city. In the strands of mainstream criminology known as CPTED (crime prevention through environmental design) and situational crime prevention, factors impacting visibility or surveillance are known as a form of 'guardianship' (Donnermeyer 2007a). However, the ecological patterns discovered through studies of farm victimization point to an essential feature of agricultural crime that is best interpreted from a left realist approach. Traditional interpretations of Marxist theory argue that farming would eventually follow an industrial model, with the eventual proletarianization of farm labour under the control of a small class of owners (Mann and Dickinson 1978). However, a complete transformation did not occur (Mooney 1988; Lobao and Meyer 2001). Instead, family forms of agricultural production persist in advanced capitalist societies, creating a large number of independent producers, even as the majority of food producers from former times sold out or were pushed out by these same economic forces, leaving for non-farm jobs often located in nearby urban centres. The family basis of contemporary agriculture is one reason why the ideology of agrarian fundamentalism persists today. The reality, however, is that much of farming in advanced capitalist societies today has adopted a Fordist or industrialized mode of production in order to survive (Lobao and Meyer 2001). Hence, a left realist approach views farmers and ranchers not merely as simple producers of food commodities who are occasionally victimized by a theft, burglar or trespasser. They are industrialists who produce food through capital intensive production methods, embedded within a globalized market system. These structural transformations to agriculture create a greater likelihood of farm victimization which is both frequent and expensive. Consider, for example, that in one nine-county area of California, millions of dollars in theft illustrate not only the high cost of agricultural crime, but its industrialized features (Donnermeyer *et al.* 2011). Items stolen included barbed wire fencing, saddles and other tack associated with both recreational and work horses, irrigation pipe, water pumps, welders, diesel and other kinds of fuel, various livestock, fertilizer, pesticides and herbicides, and ripened fruit from groves of trees and bushes.

Five years ago, DeKeseredy and Schwartz (2006: 312) stated, 'Of course, we don't know what left realists would say about terrorist attacks'. Gibbs (2010) now has something to say. She asserts that left realist theory is useful in explaining why it is that economically disenfranchised men and women engage in terrorist acts. Additionally, for Gibbs, the influence of terrorist-leaning subcultures helps us understand why terrorism is no better fought with 'get tough' policies than is street crime. From a left realist perspective, Gibbs's insights mark the start of work on agro-terrorism, which is a major threat to many farms around the world. Increasingly, farms are targets for politically motivated attempts to instil fear and to sabotage food production from both domestic and international groups (Moats 2007). Many agriculturalists and the industrialized forms of farming they operate are symbols of a ruling class and of the hegemonic nature of capitalist production that puts many rural localities at an economic and political disadvantage.

A left realist approach sees agriculturalists themselves as situated in complex webs of economic, political, and social class relations that blur the distinction between victim and offender. For example, a combined quantitative–qualitative study in Australia discovered a pattern that indicated a surprising degree of neighbour-to-neighbour victimization that was enabled precisely by the type of *gemeinschaft* relations that many mainstream criminologists presume to be expressions of collective efficacy and that supposedly describe neighbourhoods with relatively little crime (Barclay 2003; Donnermeyer 2007a). Victims considered the impact of reporting a crime, especially stock theft, allegedly committed by a farmer-neighbour in small agricultural communities where norms may create forms of ostracization against those who 'dob in' or snitch to the police. In turn, the police practised considerable discretion about responding to reports of stock theft based on the relative social standings of both the victim and the suspected offender within the community (Barclay *et al.* 2004). These place-based dynamics are not unlike those documented by DeKeseredy and associates in their examination of intimate partner violence, even though the type is rather different (DeKeseredy *et al.* 2006; DeKeseredy and Schwartz 2008; DeKeseredy 2011b).

Not only are agriculturalists subject to forms of street (or shall we say 'country lane') crime, but a left realist approach would give equal attention to agricultural crime as illustrative of crimes of the powerful. The phrase 'food regimes' was created by sociologists who study agriculture to describe the place of food producers within internationalized forms of complex commodity production that extend beyond the means of the state to regulate in terms of environmental policies, labour laws, and the price/distribution of food (Friedmann 1993). It can also be used to relocate agriculturalists within the square of crime, but this time as offenders, not victims.

There are two potential forms of offending among agriculturalists. First, agriculturalists can be simultaneously engaged in both legitimate and illegal activities. This form of pluriactivity (Smith 2004) refers to farmers and ranchers who grow crops and raise livestock for the marketplace, but are likewise engaged in various types of criminal activities. Some of these involve theft by farmers against other farmers, such as described in the work by Barclay (2003). Another set of activities include agriculturalists' use of their land and resources for drug production (Donnermeyer and Tunnell 2007). Still other activities encompass violations of regulations related to both flora and fauna. Previously, these might have been described as a type of 'folk crime' (Gibbons 1972), that is, as localized expressions of oppositional behaviours by agriculturalists in response to state-imposed gaming and other laws, reflecting their rootedness in forms of private property rights and control over the land they own (Weisheit *et al.* 2006). In actual fact, many food producers who engage in these activities are integrated into complex networks engaged in various forms of transnational crimes. A left realist approach sees pluriactivity as a rationalized form (Mooney 1988) of exploitative behaviour, and would seek to link the specific or micro-expressions of crime committed by agriculturalists to broader, structural characteristics of societies, which is where ultimate solutions and policy recommendations must occur.

Further, most farmers are not simply autonomous producers of food who act on their own to make a living for their family, as an agrarian fundamentalist frame would describe it, but are members of a privileged capitalist class who approach profit and efficiency in much the same way as any other business firm would (Lobao and Meyer 2001). Often, they are the local elites who react to economic, social, and political pressures that extend well beyond their home communities (McMichael 2008; Lichter and Brown 2011). Hence, for the agriculturalist as offender, behaviour is not situated within local norms, but in worldwide markets for goods and services, and associated state-sponsored regulatory features of these systems. The work of Walters (2006) points to how a left realist approach to the study of farm crime can situate certain agricultural operations as specific places where forms of corporate crime related to the control of genetically modified organisms (GMOs) and the monopolization of seeds are carried out. Walters has stressed the geo-political forces that threaten family-based farming systems in many countries, and the resultant growth of international corporations that are able to monopolize systems of raising crops and animals. Within these battles over the control of seed and living organisms, and concerns over the biological and environmental impacts of GMOs, are family-based food producers themselves, and how they fare. Taking the side of firms that seek monopolization of food production places some agriculturalists squarely as the local agents in corporate forms of biological crime, that is, crimes of the powerful.

Another variant of crimes of the powerful within the agricultural realm is the exploitation and victimization of farm labour. For example, consider Basran *et al.*'s (1995) Canadian local survey of corporate violence against Punjabi farm workers and their children. This influenced Kwantlen Polytechnic University and the British Columbia government to provide suitable and affordable childcare for Punjabi farm workers. As well, studies in other countries note the exploitative characteristics of owner–farm worker relations, especially with migrant labour (Rothenberg 1998). Yet, as Weisheit *et al.* (2006) observed, studies of rural crime have largely ignored the victimization of farm workers.

Hence, a left realist approach reminds us that not all agriculturalists look alike, and challenges various agrarian fundamentalist notions of farming as a benign enterprise and farmers as caretakers of the land. In many countries, agriculture is a high-tech, capital-intensive, multi-billion dollar industry. The vested interest of farm operators (and agricultural industries) to achieve efficiency and profit through various practices – from the use (and overuse) of farm chemicals and genetically modified organisms (Walters 2006) to the pollution of water or wetlands with effluent from dairies, irrigated pastures or grazing livestock – become part of a critical discourse on agricultural crime (Donnermeyer *et al.* 2011).

Theoretical concerns

Developing left realist theories of various types of rural-located does not require ditching concepts included in explanations of crime within urban contexts. The same applies to any other critical criminological school of thought.

For example, although DeKeseredy *et al.*'s (2007) rural masculinity crisis/ male peer support model of rural separation/divorce sexual assault is heavily influenced by feminist and male peer support theories of woman abuse in urban areas (DeKeseredy *et al.* 2004; DeKeseredy and Schwartz 2002), yet it addresses key 'rural realities',[3] such as the disappearance of work and the loss of family farms. Still, regardless of which perspectives they borrow, any new left realist theory of rural crime should answer Taylor, Walton, and Young's (1973: 270) call for situating criminal acts, regardless of whether they are committed by corporations or individuals, 'in terms of its wider structural origins'. In other words, rural left realism needs to ask, 'What are the broader social, political, and economic contexts in which crime is operating in rural communities?' (Donnermeyer and DeKeseredy 2008).

If urban left realism explains how structural transitions are 'interpreted, reacted against, or used ... at different levels in the social structure, in such a way that an essentially deviant choice is made' (Taylor *et al.* 1973: 271), so can a rural left realist approach. For instance, although not a left realist offering, DeKeseredy *et al.*'s (2007) theory of rural woman abuse responds to Taylor *et al.*'s concern and is heavily influenced by left realists' application of the concepts of strain and subculture to an understanding of crime.

Left realism is accused of failing to 'take the state seriously' and was heavily criticized in the past for not offering 'a coherent theory of the state' (Coleman *et al.* 2009: 7; Menzies 1992: 145). To a certain extent, the 'square of crime' addresses the role of the state, but not in much detail. Additionally, Matthews's (2009: 346) refashioned left realism prioritizes the state and views it as one of three 'fundamental organizing concepts that provide the conceptual frameworks through which we make sense of the social world'. Even so, theoretical work on the relationship between crime, social control, and the state in rural communities is welcomed and left realists are not the only critical criminologists who should respond to this call.

Left realist perspectives will be a refreshing change from social disorganization perspectives, which are the offerings most frequently adopted by rural criminologists (Donnermeyer 2007b). As the work of several scholars reveals (Barclay *et al.* 2004; DeKeseredy *et al.* 2007; DeKeseredy and Schwartz 2009), and for reasons described earlier in this chapter, what may appear to orthodox or mainstream criminologists as social disorganization is often 'simply a different form of social organization if one takes the trouble to look closely' (Venkatesh 2000; Wacquant, 1997: 346).

Policy issues

There is a widespread misperception that left realism simply reduces its applications to specific actions that can be initiated at the local level by citizens, law enforcement, and various criminal justice agencies (Donnermeyer and DeKeseredy 2008). Perhaps this is a function of reading only the writings of British left realists (e.g. Kinsey *et al.* 1986). To be sure, British left realism has been mainly concerned with criminal justice reform, and received particular notice for ideas on democratic control of policing with an aim toward minimal policing, or law enforcement only in those areas where the community wanted a police presence (DeKeseredy and Schwartz 2012; Schwartz and DeKeseredy 2010). Where the local community saw the police as an army of occupation or an enemy in place to hassle them, the overall effect, as noted by Kinsey *et al.* (1986) and DeKeseredy *et al.* (2003), has been to inhibit law enforcement in areas where there is more consensus, such as murder, sexual assault and aggravated assault.

Focusing on progressive criminal justice reforms earns much criticism from the left, from scholars who assert that law enforcement reforms only serve to strengthen the existing power structure (Gilroy and Sim 1987; Jamieson and Yates 2009). Such a claim is problematic on several grounds. For instance, every society requires a mixture of formal and informal means of social control and thus leaving criminal justice reforms solely in the hands of administrative criminologists and right-wing policy makers only serves to make the status quo even more punitive and inequitable. Of course, too, British left realists believe that such reforms must be part of a major system of societal change, and not just a piecemeal reform out of context (Schwartz and DeKeseredy 2010).

Another point to keep in mind is that many people strongly believe that steps to reform the police, courts, and the like are necessary. Forty-three battered and sexually abused rural Ohio women interviewed by DeKeseredy and Schwartz (2009) are prime examples. Most interviewees were dissatisfied with the criminal justice system's response to their victimization, and they had many suggestions for improvement, including hiring more female police officers and breaking up the 'good ol' boy' network of police officers that protected offenders.

All of society is a system and too often the criminal justice system is left to clean up the mess left by massive unemployment, cuts in welfare benefits, inadequate schools, and a lack of adequate housing (Currie 1985). North American realists devote much attention to these problems and some of them suggest policies specifically designed to address the broader social forces that motivate men to assault women and that preclude women from safely escaping abusive relationships in rural areas. For example, DeKeseredy and Schwartz (2009) suggest state subsidization of cars, insurance, and gasoline because public transportation is not an option in rural communities. Increasing funding for rural service providers is another one of their suggestions. That rural battered women face many barriers to service is due in large part to the lower levels of funding in rural communities compared to urban areas and to the greater efficiency required of rural service providers in using the limited government funds they receive. DeKeseredy and Schwartz (2009) propose several other left realist solutions, including building a more diverse rural economy and building community capacity, which are initiatives that not only help reduce woman abuse, but also lower rates of such as residential burglary and illegal drug dealing (Bull 2007).

Regardless of what progressive short-term solutions are developed and suggested for rural crime, from intimate partner violence to agricultural crime and everything in between, they must always be highly sensitive to the local context of the specific communities in which they are designed. Above all, left realist solutions to rural crime and ineffective means of social control must 'be translated into meaningful social action' (Currie 2010: 122). This means developing academic partnerships with progressive community-based organizations, engaging in proactive forms of 'newsmaking criminology' such as holding press conferences and disseminating information on Facebook, Twitter, etc. (DeKeseredy 2011b), and using other ways of reaching the general public.

Conclusion

The idea that crime is a predominantly urban phenomenon is pervasive in left realism, as it is in other progressive schools of thought. The paucity of critical analysis buttresses the popular belief that rural areas are much more peaceful than urban areas and indirectly contributes to the monopolization of right-wing 'law and order' discourse in rural communities. Certainly, in some countries such as Canada, rural communities are more conservative than are metropolitan areas, but they are not necessarily less criminogenic. For example, the most recent comparison of urban and rural homicide rates done by Statistics Canada (2007) shows that the rate of murder in rural communities (2.5 per 100,000) is higher than the rate for large urban areas (2.0) and the rate for small urban communities (1.7). And, this pattern held constant for over a decade. Moreover, 1992–2005 US National Crime Victimization Survey data analysed by Rennison *et al.* (in press) show that rural divorced and separated females are intimately victimized at rates exceeding their urban counterparts. As Donnermeyer *et al.* (2006: 205) put it, 'rurality does not imply the sociological equivalent of immunity from crime'.

Once again, we call for critical criminologists to apply a left realist perspective, and other critical points of view as well, to the study of rural crime (Donnermeyer and DeKeseredy 2008). But, we emphasize that a left realist perspective is advantageous because it can combine quantitative approaches, such as the victimization survey, with more qualitative data collection strategies. As well, a left realist perspective can aid in the interpretation of the substantial volume of rural crime scholarship which has developed over the past two decades, but unfortunately, as an impressive empirical body of research that has little theoretical focus of any kind, critical or not. Further, as Wood (1990: 14) notes, the study of rural crime will 'support the foundations of left realism', as well as challenge the tenets of established criminological perspectives on rural crime, such as social disorganization theory.

Contrary to what Doyle and Moore (2011) suggest, left realism is not strictly tied to British Labour Party politics during the Thatcher years. For critical criminologists seeking a richer understanding of rural social problems, there are some important lessons to be learned from left realist work done in the past and to be done in the future on both sides of the Atlantic. This is not to say that we are claiming that left realism is the best critical approach to examining and curbing rural crime. Hopefully, other perspectives will also emerge. An intense critical dialogue about rural crime, law and social control is a healthy way to develop a set of alternative explanations and policy implications to mainstream or orthodox versions of criminology.

Notes

1 To the best of our knowledge, Chambliss (1964) was the first critical criminologist to conduct rural research.
2 Pearce uses Snider's (1988: 232) definition of commercial crime. She states that this concept refers to 'a violation of law committed by a person or group of persons of an otherwise respected and legitimate occupation or financial activity'.
3 This is the title of a quarterly publication of information about trends, issues, and policy alternatives published by the Rural Sociological Society.

References

Barclay, E. (2003) 'Crime with rural communities: the dark side of *gemeinschaft.*', PhD dissertation. Armidale, New South Wales, University of New England
Barclay, E. and Donnermeyer, J. (2011) 'Crime and security on agricultural operations', *Security Journal,* 24: 1–18
Barclay, E., Donnermeyer, J. and Jobes, P. (2004) 'The dark side of *Gemeinschaft*', *Crime Prevention and Community Safety,* 6: 7–22
Basran, G., Gill, C. and MacLean, B. (1995) *Farmworkers and Their Children*, Vancouver: Collective Press
Bull, M. (2007) 'Crime prevention and rural communities', in E. Barclay, J.F. Donnermeyer, J. Scott and R. Hogg (eds) *Crime in Rural Australia*, Sydney: Federation Press
Chakraborti, N. and Garland, J. (eds) (2004) *Rural Racism*, Portland, OR: Willan
Chambliss, W.J. (1964) 'A sociological analysis of the law of vagrancy', *Social Problems,* 12: 67–77
Cloke, P. (2006) 'Conceptualising rurality', in P. Cloke (ed.) *Handbook of Rural Studies,* London: Sage
Coleman, R., Sim, J., Tombs, S. and Whyte, D. (2009) 'Introduction: state, power, crime', in R. Coleman, J. Sim, S. Tombs and D. Whyte (eds) *State, Power, Crime*, London: Sage
Coventry, G. and Palmer, D. (2008) 'Toward constituting a critical criminology for rural Australia', in T. Anthony and C. Cuneen (eds) *The Critical Criminology Companion*, Sydney: Federation Press
Currie, E. (1985) *Confronting Crime*, New York: Pantheon
——(2010) 'Plain left realism: an appreciation and some thoughts for the future', *Crime, Law and Social Change,* 54: 111–24
Danbom, D. (1992) 'Romantic agrarianism in twentieth-century America', *Agricultural History,* 65: 1–12
DeKeseredy, W.S. (1992) 'Confronting woman abuse in Canada: a left-realist approach', in J. Lowman and B.D. MacLean (eds) *Realist Criminology*, Toronto: University of Toronto Press
——(2011a) *Contemporary Critical Criminology*, London: Routledge
——(2011b) *Violence Against Women*, Toronto: University of Toronto Press

DeKeseredy, W.S. and Schwartz, M.D. (1996) *Contemporary Criminology*, Belmont, CA: Wadsworth

——(2002) 'Theorizing public housing woman abuse as a function of economic exclusion and male peer support', *Women's Health and Urban Life*, 1: 26–45

——(2006) 'Left realist theory', in S. Henry and M.M. Lanier (eds) *The Essential Criminology Reader*, Cambridge, MA: Westview

——(2008) 'Separation/divorce sexual assault in rural Ohio: survivors' perceptions', *Journal of Preventions and Interventions in the Community*, 36: 105–19

——(2009) *Dangerous Exits*, New Brunswick, NJ: Rutgers University Press

——(2012), 'Left realism', in W.S. DeKeseredy and M. Dragiewicz (eds) *Routledge Handbook of Critical Criminology*, London: Routledge

DeKeseredy, W.S., Alvi, S., Schwartz, M.D. and Tomaszewski, E.A. (2003) *Under Siege*, Lanham, MD: Lexington

DeKeseredy, W.S., Donnermeyer, J.F., Schwartz, M.D., Tunnell, K.D. and Hall, M. (2007) 'Thinking critically about rural gender relations: toward a rural masculinity crisis/male peer support model of separation/divorce sexual assault', *Critical Criminology*, 15: 295–311

DeKeseredy, W.S., Rogness, M. and Schwartz, M.D. (2004) 'Separation/divorce sexual assault: the current state of social scientific knowledge', *Aggression and Violent Behavior*, 9: 675–91

DeKeseredy, W.S., Schwartz, M.D., Fagen, D. and Hall, M. (2006) 'Separation/divorce sexual assault: the contribution of male support', *Feminist Criminology*, 1: 228–50

Donnermeyer, J.F. (2007a) 'Locating rural crime: the role of theory', in E. Barclay, J.F. Donnermeyer, J. Scott and R. Hogg (eds) *Crime in Rural Australia*, Annandale: Federation Press

——(2007b) 'Rural crime: roots and restoration', *International Journal of Rural Crime*, 1: 2–20

——(2012) 'Rural crime and critical criminology', in W.S. DeKeseredy and M. Dragiewicz (eds) *Handbook of Critical Criminology*, London: Routledge

Donnermeyer, J.F. and DeKeseredy, W.S. (2008) 'Toward a rural critical criminology', *Southern Rural Sociology*, 23: 4–28

Donnermeyer, J.F. and Tunnell, K. (2007) 'In our own backyard: metamphetamine manufacturing, trafficking and abuse in rural America', *Rural Realities Series,* 2, 2. Columbia, MO: Rural Sociological Society

Donnermeyer, J.F., Barclay, E. and Mears, D.P. (2011) 'Policing agricultural crime', in R. Mawby and R. Yarwood (eds) *Rural Policing and Policing the Rural,* Surrey: Ashgate

Donnermeyer, J.F., Jobes, P. and Barclay, E. (2006) 'Rural crime, poverty, and community', in W.S. DeKeseredy and B. Perry (eds) *Advancing Critical Criminology*, Lanham, MD: Lexington

Doyle, A. and Moore, D. (2011) 'Introduction', in A. Doyle and D. Moore (eds) *Critical Criminology in Canada*, Vancouver: University of British Columbia Press

Friedmann, H. (1993) 'The political economy of food: a global crisis', *New Left Review,* 197: 29–57

Friedrichs, D.O. (2010) *Trusted Criminals*, Belmont, CA: Wadsworth

Gagne, P.L. (1992) 'Appalachian women: violence and social control', *Journal of Contemporary Ethnography*, 20, 387–415

——(1996) 'Identity, strategy, and identity politics: clemency for battered women who kill', *Social Problems*, 43: 77–93

Garriott, W. (2011) *Policing Methamphetamine*, New York: New York University Press

Gibbons, D.C. (1972) 'Crime in the hinterlands', *Criminology*, 10: 177–91

Gibbs, J.C. (2010) 'Looking at terrorism through left realist lenses', *Crime, Law and Social Change*, 54: 171–85

Gilroy, P. and Sim, J. (1987) 'Law, order and the state of the left', in P. Scraton (ed.) *Law, Order and the Authoritarian State*, Philadelphia, PA: Open University Press.

Grant, J. (2008) *Charting Women's Journeys*, Lanham, MD: Lexington

Hayward, K.J. (2010) 'Jock Young (1942–)', in K.J. Hayward, S. Maruna and J. Mooney (eds) *Fifty Key Thinkers in Criminology*, London: Routledge

Henry, S. (1999) 'Is left realism a useful theory for addressing the problems of crime? No', in J.R. Fuller and E.W. Hickey (eds) *Controversial Issues in Criminology*, Boston, MA: Allyn and Bacon

Hogg, R. and Carrington, K. (2006) *Policing the Rural Crisis*, Sydney: Federation Press

Jamieson, J. and Yates, J. (2009) 'Young people, youth justice and the state', in R. Coleman, J. Sim, S. Tombs and D. Whyte (eds) *State, Power, Crime*, London: Sage

Jobes, P.C., Donnermeyer, J.F. and Barclay, E. (2005) 'A tale of two towns: social structure, integration, and crime in rural New South Wales', *Sociologia Ruralis*, 45: 224–44

Kinsey, R., Lea, J. and Young, J. (1986) *Losing the Fight Against Crime*, Oxford: Blackwell

Kraska, P.B. and Neuman, W.L. (2008) *Criminal Justice and Criminology Research Methods*, Boston, MA: Allyn and Bacon

Lea, J. (2010) 'Left realism, community and state building', *Crime, Law and Social Change*, 54: 141–58

Lea, J. and Young, J. (1984) *What Is to Be Done about Law and Order?* New York: Penguin

Lichter, D.T. and Brown, D.L. (2011) 'Rural America in an urban society: changing spatial and social boundaries', *Annual Review of Sociology*, 37: 1–28

Lindell, R. (2011) 'Is this gun registry map the key to swaying votes of gun owners in key ridings?' Retrieved May 5, 2011 from: http://www.globalnews.ca/decisioncanada/story.html?id=4643819

Lobao, L.M. and Meyer, K. (2001) 'The great agricultural transition: crisis, change, and social consequences of twentieth century US farming', *Annual Review of Sociology*, 27: 103–24

MacLean, B.D. (1992) 'A program of local crime survey research for Canada', in J. Lowman and B.D. MacLean (eds) *Realist Criminology*, Toronto: University of Toronto Press

McMichael, P. (2008) *Development and Social Change*, Los Angeles, CA: Pine Forge Press

Mann, S.A. and Dickinson, J.M. (1978) 'Obstacles to the development of a capitalist agriculture', *Journal of Peasant Studies*, 5: 466–81

Matthews, R. (2009) 'Beyond "so what?" criminology', *Theoretical Criminology*, 13: 341–62

——(2010) 'The construction of "so what?" Criminology: a realist analysis', *Crime, Law and Social Change*, 54: 125–40

Menzies, R. (1992) 'Beyond realist criminology', in J. Lowman and B.D. MacLean (eds) *Realist Criminology*, Toronto: University of Toronto Press

Moats, J.B. (2007) *Agroterrorism*, College Station: Texas A&M University

Mooney, P.H. (1988) *My Own Boss?* Boulder, CO: Westview Press

O'Reilly-Fleming, T. (1995) 'Left realism as theoretical retreatism or paradigm shift: toward post-critical criminology', in T. O'Reilly-Fleming (ed.) *Post-critical Criminology*, Scarborough, Ont.: Prentice Hall

Pearce, F. (1976) *Crimes of the Powerful*, London: Pluto Press

——(1992) 'The contribution of "left realism" to the study of commercial crime', in J. Lowman and B.D. MacLean (eds) *Realist Criminology*, Toronto: University of Toronto Press

Reiman, J. and Leighton, P. (2010) *The Rich Get Richer and the Poor Get Prison*, Boston, MA: Allyn and Bacon

Rennison, C.M., DeKeseredy, W.S. and Dragiewiz, M. (in press) 'Intimate relationship status variations in violence against women: urban, suburban, and rural differences', *Violence Against Women*

Rothenberg, D. (1998) *With These Hands*, New York: Harcourt, Brace

Sampson, R.J., Raudenbush, S.W. and Earls, F. (1998) *Neighborhood Collective Efficacy*, Washington, DC: US Department of Justice

Schechter, S. (1988) 'Building bridges between activists, professionals, and researchers', in K. Yllo and M. Bograd (eds) *Feminist Perspectives on Wife Abuse*, Beverly Hills, CA: Sage

Schwartz, M.D. and DeKeseredy, W.S. (2010) 'The current health of left realist theory', *Crime, Law and Social Change*, 54: 107–10

Smith, R. (2004) 'Rural rogues: a case study on the "smokies" trade', *International Journal of Entrepreneurial Behaviour and Research*, 10: 277–94

Snider, L. (1988) 'Commercial crime', in V.F. Sacco (ed.) *Deviance*, Scarborough, Ont.: Prentice Hall

Statistics Canada (2007) *A Comparison of Urban and Rural Crime Rates*, Ottawa: Author

Sugarman, D. and Hotaling, G. (1989) 'Dating violence: prevalence, context, and risk markers', in M. Pirog-Good and J. Stets (eds) *Dating Violence*, New York: Praeger

Taylor, I., Walton, P. and Young, J. (1973) *The New Criminology*, London: Routledge & Kegan Paul

Venkatesh, S.A. (2000) *American Project*, Cambridge, MA: Harvard University Press

Wacquant, L. (1997) 'Three pernicious premises in the study of the American ghetto', *International Journal of Urban and Regional Research*, July, 341–53

Walters, R. (2006) 'Crime, agriculture and the exploitation of hunger', *British Journal of Criminology*, 46: 26–45

Websdale, N. (1998) *Rural Woman Battering and the Justice System*, Thousand Oaks, CA: Sage

Weisheit, R.A. and Fuller, J. (2004) 'Methamphetamines in the heartland: a review and initial exploration', *Journal of Crime and Justice*, 27: 131–51

Weisheit, R.A., Falcone, D.N. and Wells, L.E. (2006) *Crime and Policing in Rural and Small-Town America*, Long Grove, IL: Waveland Press

Wilson, J.Q. (1985) *Thinking about Crime*, New York: Vintage

Wood, D. (1990) 'A critique of the urban focus in criminology: the need for a realist view of rural working class crime', Burnaby, BC: School of Criminology, Simon Fraser University

14 Return of the repressed?

A retrospective on policing and disorder in England, 1981 to 2011

Colin Webster

The periodic recurrence of public disorder on the streets of England has repeatedly occasioned the cry of 'sheer criminality' as an explanatory framework to capture our worst fears about an unruly, unpredictable, violent and uncontrollable inner and outer city and its young people. Each occurrence is feigned as a unique, spontaneous event triggered by an arrest or altercation, contagious by rumour, mobilised and escalated by young people living in 'anti-social "underclass" neighbourhoods where law and order and virtually all notions of civility had broken down and crime, violence and disorder had become endemic' (McLaughlin 2007: 125). On those occasions when agency is conceded – i.e. that rioters might have known what they were doing and why – this is posed either as social and political protest found in academic analysis (Bagguley and Hussain 2008) or as a 'criminal conspiracy' to loot by 'gangs' found in populist perception. There is scant evidence that either is the case (Bujra and Pearce 2011).

This chapter recalls the findings of the inquiries into the August 2011 riots before going on to present two in-depth contrasting case studies of earlier disorders in Liverpool in 1981 and Bradford 2001. In asking what was different and what were the common themes found in these disorders the chapter seeks to also ask what has changed in the areas affected in part as a consequence of the conditions and events in those places that gave rise to public disorder. A common thread running through this chapter is – according to retrospective accounts of participants and witnesses to the disorders – the culpability of the police in the way they deal with urban, working-class and young men in areas of meagre resources, yet fully confronted by a highly developed consumer culture. These historical and contemporary accounts and narratives are then subjected to a theoretical reading.

Reading the August 2011 riots?

Preliminary analysis of the causes of the English riots in August 2011 involving hundreds of interviews with participants revealed deep-seated and sometimes visceral distrust and antipathy towards the police while at the same time expressing a sense of economic and social injustice and mistreatment

('Reading the Riots' 2011). Participants cited the opportunity to acquire goods without apparent sanction while simultaneously declaring their actions to be anti-police, citing long-standing harassment through the police's power to stop and search them. Significantly, the profile of the rioters was that many were unemployed and just under half were students. Popular explanations rested on poor parenting and criminality whereas many participants dis-avowed these easy explanations instead pointing to the paucity of legitimate employment opportunities despite educational success – and in any case edu-cational opportunies were now being withdrawn for many. Many added that they were motivated by sheer acquisitive desire and the excitement and euphoria of consumerism uninhibited by the constraints of the money econ-omy (ibid.). The relationship between supposed 'sheer criminality' and 'sheer acquisitive desire' in the case of the August 2011 riots will be addressed in the conclusion to this chapter so suffice to say here that this relationship of criminality and the culture of consumerism does not lend itself easily to simplistic economic or psychological readings.

A recent quasi official inquiry into the August 2011 riots, *After the Riots* (Riots, Communities and Victims Panel 2012) placed doubt on any significant connection between poor parenting and participation because there was not a significant overlap between troubled families and rioter families. Other aspects of the report showed that within the neighbourhoods affected, youth unemployment was seen as a major problem as too was the lure of product branding, marketing and consumerism. Again, high levels of social and eco-nomic inequality were found compounded by negative and hostile contact between the police and young people, especially around stop and search, particularly in respect of black young men. Both *Reading the Riots* and *After the Riots* found broadly similar causes, the latter laced with policy 'solutions' and recommendations, most of which already appear likely to be ignored. On a different, deeper tack, the analysis by the LSE, Joseph Rowntree Founda-tion and *The Guardian* asked whether the English riots in 2011 were 'a new kind of riot?' According to the *Reading the Riots* study rioting across the capital and parts of Birmingham, Liverpool and Manchester were in many ways similar to the riots that began in Brixton in 1981 and spread to these other cities then too. Both took place while a Conservative prime minister grappled with the effects – particularly on young people – of 'global economic downturn and rising unemployment' (Newburn *et al.* 2011). The overriding theme that runs like a thread through most of the riots in post-war Britain is the fractious relationship between ethnic identity and the police. In contrast, the riots that took place in August 2011 were said by participants and close observers not to be about race but were rather about an excluded and 'grow-ing underclass in our inner cities that feels excluded, isolated and locked out of mainstream society'. Newburn *et al.* (2011: 3) argue that,

> To understand the 2011 riots one needs to look back not just to Brixton, Handsworth and Toxteth in the 1980s, but also to the outbreaks that

occurred in the early 1990s in places like Oxford, Cardiff and Tyneside. There the arson, looting and attacks on the police primarily involved white youth in suburban, working-class estates.

All of the estates involved had dramatically high levels of youth unemployment just as the August rioters shared an experience of economic deprivation – 59 per cent of working-age August rioters not in education were unemployed and came from the most deprived 20 per cent of areas in the UK. What is new according to Newburn *et al.* (2011) is the emergence of a pervasive new culture of consumption wherein status is acquired, or lost. What is clear is that when inquiries into the disorders – from Scarman in 1981 to the Riots, Communities and Victim Panel under the chairmanship of Darrah Singh in 2012 – have taken place to search for causes they have criticised both the police and the conditions of racial disadvantage found in the areas affected. It is to the question of whether the August 2011 riots represent 'a new kind of riot?' or a continuation and recurrence of the causes and conditions of past disorders in the 1981 to 2011 period that the rest of the chapter now turns. The answer to these questions will begin with two recently published contrasting and detailed retrospectives on the disorders involving mostly black young people in Liverpool in 1981 and mostly Asian young people in Bradford in 2001. These historical readings and case studies ask 'what, if anything, has changed in the places of these disorders and what can we infer from change and continuity in respect of public disorder?'

Case studies: reading the past to understand the present

Case Study One: Liverpool '81

Published on the thirtieth anniversary of the Liverpool riots in the summer of 1981, this retrospective sets out to trace the impacts on the people and places most directly affected and their wider implications and consequences (see Frost and Phillips 2011). It does this by drawing together the stories and memories of the riots from the perspective of those affected and the local and national impacts of these events. Using various published and unpublished sources, eye-witness accounts and oral histories across a range of participants, community activists, officials and former police officers, including 14 in-depth interviews with key informants, the study builds a retrospective context and the aftermath focusing on the area affected (Toxteth, Liverpool 8[1]) as well as the wider connections to the contemporaneous riots in Bristol and London in 1980 and 1981.

These riots 'destroyed at a stroke the myth of police invincibility', and they drew attention to wider social and economic tensions that could no longer be ignored (Frost and Phillips 2011: 3). If the riots had raised questions about racist policing and the militarisation of the police response – the central issue for most people – then one predominant perspective on the rioting was that it was all about criminal gangs and outside hooligans, and the other perspective was that it was all about unemployment. The key though, then as now, was the nature of neighbourhood policing as an antecedent and consequence of the riots based in conflict in the ways young urban men were policed.

Many of the personal accounts repeatedly use a metaphor of a 'war situation' between the police and rioters that had resulted from a strong sense of irritation and frustration growing into anger:

> Part of their [black boy's] anger was that they were never allowed to feel at home. Whereas a very strong feeling amongst [the youth] was this was their territory, their home, and, as there would be in any kind of inner-city area, these are/were their streets and the police are invading them.
>
> (Local Methodist minister, cited in Frost and Phillips 2011)

Then, as now, the trigger that began the build up to the riot was the stopping and detention of a young black man by the police followed by the arrest of another local black man who had frequently been the subject of police attention in the past. Full-scale rioting and fighting against the police was not initially accompanied by looting. Black young people were later joined by white young men from surrounding or outside areas whereupon looting began to take place.

In Liverpool, as elsewhere, policing is the single most important thread running through narratives and reflections of the riots, although the government had tried to shift the focus of debate towards socio-economic issues and market solutions. But most observers agreed that biased policing towards black and white working-class young men over a long time, rather than unemployment, was the main cause that sparked the riots. This history of police harassment, intimidation and brutality inflicted on particular neighbourhoods and groups set in train intensely negative feelings towards the police, and this extended to some young women. Then, as now, police stop and search powers were being abused, so that a disproportionately large number of black residents were being targeted and charged. Quite simply, the culture of policing and the operational and tactical autonomy of officers were used in highly antagonistic, provocative and unaccountable ways.

The Scarman Inquiry into the Brixton disorders, although emphasising racial disadvantage and deprivation, framed explanations that saw the disorders as a spontaneous outburst of built-up resentment against the police sparked by particular incidents. Much later Lord Gifford's inquiry into race relations in Liverpool in 1988 concluded that there was still 'racism in the police' in Liverpool and that the situation in Liverpool was 'unique' in the systematic and comprehensive racial discrimination found in labour markets and public space. Changes in police relations since 1981 through police reform and changes in the law, particularly those following the Macpherson Inquiry, have not altered the growing and continuing hugely disproportionate use of stop and search against black people. This has particularly been the case on Merseyside and in Toxteth. Meanwhile the official nomenclature that portrays the inner city and explains the riots with reference to social and economic problems experienced by inner cities rather than the ways they are policed – the latter more favoured by participants and close observers of riot areas – continues to remain the dominant explanation, apart from tautological explanations about 'sheer criminality'.

From both suburban and media perspectives the *inner city* has long been seen as an alien, separate and isolated place; its 'riots' irrational, hate-filled, violent and pecuniary. From these perspectives the police are always believed to be neutral, lacking in proper equipment, needing to suspend their normal civility to contain and control abnormal and exceptional circumstances. It is not just rioting that is abnormal but the inner city itself in all circumstances. Squalor, dereliction and desolation join with poor schooling and poor parenting to suggest *both* physical *and* mental decay and decline – all somehow self-inflicted. All ripe for post-riot intervention, control and reform, as if economic, physical and social decline were some sort of locally generated pathology to be treated and cured by national government or entrepreneurial/market 'solutions'.

The talisman surrounding all debates about the disorders is the supposed benefits to young people if they were better served by education. Repeated over and over again, education is spoken about as if having magical properties to lift young people from despondency, poverty and alienation. Stories of the riots, told by people who were very young at the time, coalesced into stories of police harassment, but the broader picture they present of life in Liverpool 8 is of being let down by poor schools and excluded from the advantages of a good formal education. This sort of retrospective, although ubiquitous in accounts, borders on expressing a kind of regret. At the time young people often rejected schooling just as schooling rejected them as it was by no means clear what the benefits of schooling were in a collapsed local youth labour market. There were consistent comments about the poor quality of the local schooling on offer. At the time this was reinforced by Lord Swann's Inquiry into the Education of Children from Ethnic Minority Groups which concluded that black children were one of the most excluded and lowest attaining groups within the UK's education system, even in places like Liverpool where the black community were very long established and often of mixed parentage. Of course, apart from low teacher expectations of them, black young people were expected to, and did enter, low-waged, poor quality jobs, when they were lucky enough to find any job at all. These sorts of employment destinations did not require formal qualifications or school success. The very assimilation of black people in Liverpool only made intense and widespread racial disadvantage in schooling and the labour market even more disturbing. And yet, since 1981 educational attainment among subsequent generations of black children has been an area of genuine and significant improvement, although this educational improvement does not guarantee or translate into success in the labour market, even for those going to university.

The long-term impacts of the riots and subsequent developments are difficult to disentangle from wider social and economic changes in the places
where they took place. Clearly attempted urban regeneration, among other
initiatives, has had its place although evaluation is highly problematic and
multifaceted (Atkinson and Helms 2007). In Liverpool, as elsewhere, urban
and economic regeneration has focused mainly on the city centre and any
benefits to places like Liverpool 8 are at best unclear (Minton 2009). Changing
perceptions of Toxteth and Liverpool 8 and indeed the wider city since 1981
and its immediate aftermath, notably its City of Culture 2008 designation,
towards more positive, favourable images and impressions have been important.
The city however remains shaped by social and political problems dating
from the 1980s.

Although the overwhelming theme of the retrospective accounts given to
the *Liverpool '81* study still focused on the antagonistic police–community
relations said to have been so prominent at the time, interviewees also
explained that tension was further fuelled by a combination of deprivation
and discrimination. This is consistent with the findings of contemporaneous
and subsequent media representations, high-profile research and various parliamentary select committees, which all portrayed the severe consequences
of disadvantage and discrimination for Liverpool-born black people. The
government's response, then as now, was to seek 'market solutions to social
problems' of unemployment and discrimination (Frost and Phillips 2011: 108).

The Conservative government's Merseyside Task Force (MTF) led by then
Minister Michael Heseltine set about tackling Liverpool's social and economic problems in the belief that rather modest economic incentives and the
refurbishment of its physical environment could forge regeneration of the city.
This task had already begun prior to the riots. Murden (2006) in Belchem's
monumental collection about the history of the city, *Liverpool 800*, argued the
approach was a 'strongly market-orientated and property-led approach to
urban regeneration' in the hope that a restored environment would lure private sector business and investment back to the city. Murden's argument is
that although the MTF created some jobs and certainly impressive city centre
refurbishment around the docks, the reliance on improving Liverpool's 'image'
through a focus on tourism, leisure, housing and tertiary employment – repeated
across all the northern cities – vaguely resting on the continental 'model' of
successful urbanism, ignored the fundamentally different and older pro-urban
cultural traditions found there; the results were mixed and uneven. Indeed,
development in the centre often encouraged further decline in the surrounding
inner city and places like Liverpool 8. Have these regeneration projects and
injections of cash brought change in Liverpool since 1981? Frost and Phillip's
(2011) interviewees have mixed feelings. Their oral histories reported continued and worsening urban decay and poverty, the dispersal of black people
from Liverpool 8 to other parts of the city and most of all the continued
blight of youth unemployment. Changes and benefits to inner-city areas are at
best cosmetic and the underlying structural problems of poverty and

overcrowding remain relatively untouched. The most obvious improvements have been to the quality of available housing amidst the continuation of boarded-up buildings and unrealised regeneration and refurbishment projects leaving a patchwork of improvement and decline.

Overall the main criticism of this environmental and economic strategy in Liverpool is its deflection from issues of inequality, policing and racism, which the riots had brought to the surface. Locals point to the unequal distribution of the benefits of investment and its lack of focus and targeting so as to create local employment training and opportunities. That is not to say that the Capital of Culture motif didn't bring very significant benefits and a rise in morale to a de-industrialised city in a parlous state. Liverpool 8 now sees the highest youth unemployment since 1992, with half of young black men available for work unemployed (Milmo *et al.* 2012).

Case Study Two: Bradford '01

From the Bradford riot of July 2001 to the very differently handled disturbances in 2010 when the English Defence League arrived in Bradford, the city's British Muslim young people have staunchly used the leitmotif of 'self-defence' as a perception and justification of their ad hoc mobilisations to ensure public order and security, sometimes through engendering periodic public disorder. The 2001 riot was as much a culmination of rising tensions between young Asian Muslims and the police – presaged in the Bradford disorders of 1995 – as it was from rumours of far right British National Party and/or National Front incursions/marches into Asian areas. A history of politically self-conscious organised resistance and protest against racism based on 'self-defence' by groups such as the Asian Youth Movement and their allies in Bradford had culminated in a politically unorganised, unaware and wholly disproportionate riot against a perceived 'fascist' threat. This threat had existed and periodically found expression from the 1970s onwards in the context of visceral racism against black and Asian people (Webster 1997, 2003, 2007). Its emergence in 2001 among a third generation of Asian Muslim young people ostensibly defending their areas from far right nationalist and racist public presence, and most recently against anti-Muslim nationalism, marks the shift from conflict around racism to conflict around religious and cultural identity – the latter in a context of the 'War on Terror'.

Bujra and Pearce's (2011) retrospective on the 2001 Bradford riots, based on contemporary media accounts and police records, interviews with participants and observers both in 2003 and 2010, asks how much or how little has changed since 2001. They note in particular how the aftermath of the 2001 disorders began to see a shift away from ethnic to religious identity as points of reference and nomenclature – from 'Asian' to 'Muslim'. Again, the trigger was a single incident of an attack on a young Asian man by a group of white men in the city centre. What followed was a series of skirmishes between white and Asian groups of young men but the core of the escalation to riot was mostly the gathering of young Asian men in various parts of the inner city confronted by police officers and their strategy of 'contain and disperse'. It quickly became clear that – contrary to some contemporary accounts – this was no 'race riot', but an anti-police riot. Then as now (in respect of the riots of August 2011) the local MP (Marsha Singh) stated that the riot 'was nothing to do with deprivation, this was sheer criminality' (cited by Bujra and Pearce 2011: 27).

In the interviews the rioters themselves confirmed there were no political demands or rationales, their profiles were that they were often single, poorly qualified, usually unemployed, mostly 'Asian Muslim', having fathers formerly textile manual workers now unemployed, often living in poverty, and lacking any devout religious practice or affiliation. Around 60 per cent had convictions for petty criminal behaviour and a few for violent offences, the majority used alcohol and two-thirds had significant social relations with white people. This sort of profile seems to belie stereotypes of segregated, religiously motivated young Muslims bent on asserting and defending cultural rather than territorial identity. The metaphor 'War Zone' runs through accounts as participants excused their own violence as self-defence – not so much against the far right as against the police as the rioting escalated and spread. As the riot built up, arson and some looting took place. The key dynamic though was widespread hostility towards and hatred of the police, even though rationalisations hinged on defending their families, communities and preserving Bradford as a 'multicultural' city from the specific racism of the far right. Their parents' very real experiences of racism in the 1970s and 1980s (Webster 2007) had provided a repertoire upon which they had built a sense of historic wrongs. Finally, their accounts strongly evoked liminal strands of the sheer excitement of participating in the riot. The police became the target of the rioters' anger because they were perceived to have allowed the National Front to enter the city, then to have protected them, and to have provoked and taken part in brutality against the rioters. Further, the police are seen by many as continually harassing people like them, but most of all, they had taken the police as proxy for the absence of far right combatants to attack. The police themselves, as well as simply losing control of the situation and being ill-prepared, felt abandoned by their senior officers, facing what they perceived to be sheer thuggery and criminality, having little sympathy or even understanding for the sense of threat that rioters felt when faced with the possibility of far right thugs and their violent racism in Bradford.

By the early 1990s inner-city areas and outlying white estates had become enclaves of the poor within a wider trajectory of northern urban economic decline. A lack of investment in machinery and the workforce over many decades had created Bradford as a low-waged city in which immigration was used to supplement and complement this lack of investment and a shortage of labour. The textile industry had been in terminal decline since the 1960s. In the 1970s deep recession hit the entire manufacturing sector in Bradford and the 1980s saw a catastrophic shedding of skilled labour. The rise of part-time and service sector work favoured women and most of the increase in unemployment was amongst the male population. Bujra and Pearce (2011) marshal evidence to show that the South Asian population was particularly hard hit by the collapse of the textile industry and their inability to transfer skills to other sectors. This parlous situation was compounded by Muslim women in Bradford being unable to take advantage of increased participation of women in service employment because of cultural strictures. Although responses including self-employment within the Asian community grew this did not compensate for major losses in manufacturing.

The profiles of the rioters as mostly employed in low status, low-waged work, with few qualifications, matched the more general profile of Bradford young Asian people. Among a predominantly young population by the early to mid-1990s half of Pakistani and Bangladeshi households contained no one in full-time employment and unemployment amongst young Asian men reached 45 per cent. As has been noted elsewhere too, 'a creeping culture of consumerism was creating its own pressures on young people and their parents' (ibid.: 106). Intergenerational unemployment saw an increase of serious drug crime and other sorts of adaptation to economic hardship, but key was the fact that inner-city young people who reached their teenage years in the 1990s were the hardest hit by the impact of the 1980s recession on families. These – the young adults of 2001 – saw the consequences of economic security unravel upon their families, while perhaps experiencing some of the solidarities of ethnic minority neighbourhood life.

Much was made at the time of the 2001 riot and in the aftermath of the concentration of the Asian Muslim population in the most deprived areas of the city (Webster 2003). Rather than this being explained in terms of local housing markets and racial discrimination, official reports framed the problem in terms of people choosing to segregate themselves on the basis of ethnicity, despite much evidence to the contrary. There was, nevertheless, very significant out-migration among whites from Bradford's inner-city wards during the 1990s while at the same time visible minorities needed social support in the areas where they reside. As human geographers like Dorling and Thomas (2004) have attempted to show, people cluster residentially as much on the basis of economic position as they do by ethnicity. Others have pointed to the significance or relevance of cultural identity to the upbringing of rioters. Still others to deprivation mediated by learned cultural norms found in Islam that provided a structure to time that replaced the industrial discipline of the mills (Kalra 2000), the most important of which are the mosque as a centre of activity and the 'biradari' network (caste based on 'honour' and cousin marriage) of mutual material and emotional help and social solidarity. The problem with this formulation is the implication and juxtaposition with the unravelling of white working-class family structures and loss of identity previously provided by a shared working-class culture. Phillip Lewis (2007) goes further, arguing that the biradari system has been responsible for trapping Muslim young people in a parochial and dysfunctional form of social capital that traps people in poverty and is inimical to educational success and the sort of bridging capital that offers networks and opportunities found in wider society. Further, that it concentrates power among religious male leaders supplanting political and social innovation among younger people. Finally, and para-doxically, that gendered role expectations created by biraderi limited young men more than young women as the weight of codes of honour and shame fell upon young men, both limiting their chances in the labour market while rejecting the humiliation of low-paid jobs.

Bujra and Pearce's (2011) thesis, garnered from their interviews with rioters, suggests that expectations about being a man, 'which included a readiness to fight on the streets', played a key indirect role in the rioting. This paradoxical 'protest masculinity' has at least in part resulted from a certain sort of 'emasculation' predicated on racism and police harassment, but also the growing public and educational success of young Asian Muslim women, who were beginning to supplant young men's status and power (Webster 2007). They conclude (Bujra and Pearce 2011: 126):

> Deprivation alone does not explain the riot. However, our generation of rioters reached adolescence under the shadow of deindustrialisation ... We have traced the effects on a cohort of young men growing up in a specific time and place, and in communities which had struggled to rebuild working lives, drawing on cultures of solidarity. Depressed, like young men from all communities without the stable job prospects of previous generations, they also knew that their fathers and grandfathers had experienced everyday disrespect and organised racism. Streetwise and angry, many seized the moment in 2001 to send a message. As one put it: 'What the message was? We're not taking no shit off no council, no NF and no police service. They've walked over us for long enough. They've walked over us for generations, but not this generation, man.'

Bradford and its Asian community and their allies had suffered far right provocations for decades. In earlier times organised responses had been politi-cally conscious and secular based on alliances of the Asian Youth Movement (AYM), the white left and the trade union movement. A series of events, including the 'Rushdie Affair' and the Gulf War of 1991, had shifted the ground of political and public discourse from concerns with racism, 'integra-tion' and 'multiculturalism' to those of Islamic and religious identity, eclipsing the more secular, non-sectarian political leadership linked to old labour and left politics, particularly amongst young people. Local politics and history had little purchase on young people at the time of the 2001 riots.

The aftermath over the decade that followed the 2001 riots can be read from the reflections of those most directly affected – the rioters themselves. Ten years on a few were interviewed in 2010–11, some of whom had been to prison for their part in the disorders. Perpetrators were treated severely and there was widespread cross-party political support at the time, which overshadowed any deeper attempt to understand the underlying 'causes'. Local politicians rallied to condemn the rioters as criminals, and by 2004, some 256 people had been charged, 178 with riot. A total of 170 of these were convicted, 110 imprisoned for which the average sentence was over four years (Bujra and Pearce 2011). Many rediscovered religion in prison and due to intensive rehabilitation efforts 70 per cent of the rioters were in employment after release. Local officials complained that as a consequence of the 2001 riot Bradford had missed out on the benefits of national economic growth and stability in the subsequent period to the crisis of 2008, although Bradford city continued to be a predominantly low-waged, low-skilled local economy.

Meanwhile, the shift from culture to religion, and the insertion of the city into a wider set of global issues and context around Islam and the West entered public consciousness in ways believed to be detrimental to the city's development and prosperity. Muslims were said to have been put on the defensive and were withdrawing into their own communities, and religion, not culture, was now the defining boundary of belonging and not belonging. On 28 August 2010, Bradford faced another threat from the far right. The English Defence League came to Bradford to protest and specifically target Muslims. This time the provocation did not work and the contrast with 2001 could not be starker. Bujra and Pearce (2011) carefully showed that the coordinated response across many agencies in the city, political leadership and popular public responses, and a radical change in police tactics and approach, all contributed to a pre-emption of probable disorder. Over the same period, city centre regeneration had been constantly delayed as investors withdrew, only recently finding fruition in the imaginative and spectacular transformation of the centre into an attractive public space (Wainwright 2012). As elsewhere, manufacturing jobs continued to decline over the decade – a fall of 35 per cent between 1998 and 2008. The district remained low-waged and low-skilled. A third of the district's working-age population remained out of work in 2010 and the recession of 2008 saw a further growth in youth unemployment. The gap between the most and the least deprived areas in Bradford was the largest in the country in 2010 and Bradford had the highest infant mortality rate in England in 2010. Compared to 2001, this socio-economic profile does not show much improvement or progress, with the single exception of very significantly improved educational achievement, especially among Asian Muslims, and especially among girls (Bujra and Pearce 2011). This general picture is of much improved public order policing in Bradford against a backdrop of greatly improved educational success, while the local economy remains extremely fragile. The key question is whether the promised benefits of educational success will be realised in the labour market across all ethnicities.

Policing disorder: harassment, provocation and the policing of surplus youth populations

There has not been significant change in the pattern of police stop and search of urban young working-class men over the 30-year period from 1981 to 2011.

This pattern has had a particularly alienating and disaffecting impact on black, mixed race and Asian young men. In the recent period mixed race and Asians have newly emerged and grown as over-represented groups. There was a striking growth in stop and searches of black, Asian *and* white young people between 2004 and 2009 (Ministry of Justice 2010). Waddington *et al.*'s (2004) study of stop and search in Reading and Slough found that white urban lower class men who were available to be stopped suffered disproportionate stop and search regardless of visible ethnicity. The police disproportionately target young males whose profile tends to be of lower class background, living in lone parent families, that have often been in care, lack education and/or are unemployed, who live in urban areas of high crime and social deprivation, who have an active street life and who consequently form a core component of the population available for policing. Once having come to the attention of the police young people are sucked into a spiral of amplified contact and conflict. Although more likely to be present among British Mixed White/ Caribbean and British Caribbean compared to the general white British population and other visible minorities, these risks are also present within marginalised white groups (see Webster 2012).

Places like London, Birmingham and Manchester in some respects seem quite different to many provincial cities in respect of the policing of minority and marginalised groups. Different forms of discrimination by the police are closely tied with variation in the social class and ethnic make-up within and between neighbourhoods and jurisdictions. The police routinely target neigh-bourhoods according to the make-up of their local populations. This varia-tion of justice by geography and class in respect of stop and search and arrest rates is related to areas of residence, disadvantage and deprivation, street availability of certain populations, the transience of the white population and housing tenure, all of which are known to be associated with ethnic and class origin (Bowling and Phillips 2007). Whites living in 'blacker' areas have a higher stop and search arrest rate than blacks and blacks living in 'whiter' areas have higher rates than whites. 'Being out of place' seems more impor-tant in Leeds than in London. The policing of working-class areas can be disproportionate to local crime levels, particularly in London. Since the police tended to deal with people of lower social class, and black people also tend to be of lower social class, it is to be expected that black and Asian young people are treated differently in multi-ethnic urban metropolitan areas. Those stopped and searched are most likely to be drawn from the population of young people not in education, employment or training, to which we shall return in the final section.

As we saw from the case studies above, the common thread running through the accounts of rioters has been unchanging complaints and distrust about how they have been policed on the streets whether in the sense of the police's inability or refusal to protect them or the routine ways the police harass them. Police powers to stop and search continue to be a major source of dis-crimination, disaffection and distrust that this tactic engenders. Police powers of stop and search have been greatly increased through the 'back door' of the Terrorism Acts (EHRC 2010). Policing and justice by geography has created a patchwork of inconsistent treatment in which the likelihood of discrimination on grounds of ethnicity, race and class is greater in some places than others. In respect of reforming stop and search as a tactic the police have continued to resist reforms and there has been no improvement, particularly in places like London and, to a lesser extent, Greater Manchester and the West Midlands, which are out of step with most of the rest of the country (Miller 2010). This treatment of urban working-class young men amounts to unusual harassment and provocation, the purpose of which is to police those who have been, continue to be, and are likely to increasingly become surplus populations within the global market economy.

Theorising urban policing and disorder over the last 30 years

According to Soja (2000) late twentieth-century urbanisation processes represent continuity and change of past trends and established forms, new developments and seemingly dramatic change. Contemporary cities in England can be characterised as focusing on consumer- and culture-oriented economies shaped by deindustrialisation, new communication systems and a new international division of labour. Attempts to radically restructure the traditional urban form in places like London, Liverpool and Bradford in an endless cycle of regeneration and pockets of decline are responses to new global trends and cultural shifts of multi-ethnicity and multi-social urban contact and interaction. As McLaughlin (2007: 116) states 'the primary objective of contemporary urban governance is to fashion a "cultural city" by restructuring the economy towards the arts, design and "high end" consumption.' He goes on to argue (ibid.: 116–17),

> Attempts to govern such volatile cityscapes are dramatically re-shaping the spatial patterning and policing of the heart and environs of many cities ... the regulation of the contemporary city has also required the public police to develop and deploy base-line disciplinary and civilizational strategies that network with the new configurations of spatial securitization and regulation.

This presents new challenges to public order policing. Over the period from 1981 to 2011 public policing of urban working-class young men has intensified and grown just as their perception of being 'out of place' in the 'new' city has grown as their marginality is accentuated. Under growing conditions of 'advanced urban marginality', their policing and its fall-out in incivility and public disorder, these surplus populations will present increasingly difficult challenges to urban peace and order (Wacquant 2008). In particular, the micro-conditions that underpin and guarantee civilised social interaction and the possibilities of 'cooperation' and urban 'community' will be sorely tested given increasingly precarious prospects for young people in Britain and across Europe.

This time around within a cycle of youth unemployment and under-employment last visited upon England at the beginning of our period in 1981, when for example 60 per cent of 16–20-year-old black young people available for work were without a job, the situation is structurally deeper and geo-graphically wider in the groups affected and the rate and rapidity at which joblessness has increased. There are grounds to suspect that this time we are seeing a more intractable creation of a surplus youth population impermeable to countermeasures of education, training and future economic recovery. The last time youth unemployment in the UK, at 18 per cent today, was this high was 1993, although not at the level seen in the mid-1980s (Briscoe 2011). Now, as then, the rate varies geographically, ethnically and socially with concentrated pockets in the inner city and peripheral estates. Today, in one of our case studies – Toxteth – youth unemployment is approaching levels last seen in the 1980s (Milmo *et al.* 2012). In the other case study figures from the Office for National Statistics (ONS) show that Bradford West has seen one of the biggest increases in unemployment in Britain of over 30 per cent over the last year.

What then is happening? In a study showing how youth transitions to the labour market have changed and stayed the same over the past 30 years, MacDonald (2011) argues that although there are loud echoes of the 1980s in current worries about 'a lost generation', a key difference is that this 'lost generation' now has a wider social membership. The extension of joblessness and underemployment to middle-class graduates from the less elite universities has led Paul Mason (2012) to describe the zeitgeist as one of 'from austerity to breakdown' encapsulated in one phrase – 'the graduate without a job'. Young people now constitute a core membership of the new precariat. Poor employment protection, casual work and low wages have been said to have increased work insecurity across a number of advanced industrialised countries since the 1980s. As a consequence, the precariat embodies both a distinctive *class* and *status* position. It has minimal 'trust' relationships with employers or the welfare state as the bargain of security in exchange for sub-ordination is removed, and its status is 'truncated' in the sense of being temporary and socially invisible. The precariat are both the working poor and the insecurely employed but, most importantly, they lack a secure work-based *identity* normally associated with building a 'career' and belonging to an occupational community. This lack of control over work at a basic level combines with a lack of work security in the forms of income-earning opportunities; employment and job security giving employment protection and work progression; protection against accidents and illness at work; reduced opportunity to gain skills; assurance of an adequate stable income; collective voice in the labour market. This social group, economically trapped, is likely to form an increasingly visible surplus population of the permanently unemployed or underemployed, policed and suspected, dis-ciplined and distrusted – a new 'suspect population' sharing those character-istics most likely to bring them to the attention of the police as urban young men without a future.

Conclusion

The period 1981 to 2011 has seen periodic public disorder directed or displaced towards the police, often as a means of 'revenge' against the routine harassment by them of urban young men with a range of grievances, many of which coalesce around a sense of intergenerational exclusion from mainstream consumer culture and decent employment. Even the promises of gaining a good education as a route to success and stability are no longer guaranteed. As young people view their inheritance and its limited scope they withdraw into enclaves that are fiercely protected against incursions by the police who are distrusted and are perceived to act with uncivil impunity against their interests. Occasional forays into wider consumer public space are met with police harassment and provocation, which under certain conditions escalate to riot, looting and arson. Abandoned and relegated to places of poverty, they break out and roam the streets, appropriating places and goods liminally rather than politically. The underlying conditions of their woes are however that they constitute a surplus population economically, socially and historically. The brief interregnum of Labour's 13-year strategy of a high-welfare, low-wage and low-industry economy paid for by a finance and housing bubble, is finished.

Note

1 This area in Liverpool was never really called Toxteth by the local people. It was always referred to as Liverpool 8.

References

Atkinson, R. and Helms, G. (2007) *Securing an Urban Renaissance*, Bristol: Policy Press

Bagguley, P. and Hussain, Y. (2008) *Riotous Citizens*, Aldershot: Ashgate

Bowling, B. and Phillips, C. (2007) 'Disproportionate and discriminatory: reviewing the evidence on police stop and search', *Modern Law Review*, 70 (6): 936–61

Briscoe, S. (2011) 'Youth unemployment: how bad is it really?' *The Guardian Data Blog*, available: http://www.guardian.co.uk/news/datablog/2011/feb/14/youth-unemployment-statistics?INTCMP=SRCH

Bujra, J. and Pearce, J. (2011) *Saturday Night and Sunday Morning*, Skipton: Vertical Editions

Dorling, D. and Thomas, B. (2004) *People and Places*, Bristol: Policy Press

Equality and Human Rights Commission (EHRC) (2010) *Stop and Think*, London: EHRC

Frost, D. and Phillips, R. (eds) (2011) *Liverpool '81: Remembering the Riots*, Liverpool: Liverpool University Press

Kalra, V.S. (2000) *From Textile Mills to Taxi Ranks*, Aldershot: Ashgate

Lewis, P. (2007) *Young, British and Muslim*, London: Continuum

MacDonald, R. (2011) 'Youth transitions, unemployment and underemployment – plus ça change, plus c'est la même chose?' *Journal of Sociology*, 47 (4): 427–44

McLaughlin, E. (2007) *The New Policing*, London: Sage

Mason, P. (2012) *Why It's Kicking Off Everywhere*, London: Verso

Miller, J. (2010) 'Stop and search in England: a reformed tactic or business as usual?' *British Journal of Criminology*, 50: 954–74

Milmo, D., Ferguson, B. and Taylor, M. (2012) ' "We're just stuck here": Toxteth's black youth on joblessness', *The Guardian*, 9 March

Ministry of Justice (2010) *Statistics on Race and the Criminal Justice System 2008/09*, London: Ministry of Justice

Minton, A. (2009) *Ground Control*, London: Penguin

Murden, J. (2006) 'City of change and challenge: Liverpool since 1945', in Belchem, J. (ed.) *Liverpool 800: Culture, Character, History*, Liverpool: Liverpool University Press

Newburn, T., Lewis, P. and Metcalf, J. (2011) 'A new kind of riot? From Brixton 1981 to Tottenham 2011', available: http://www.guardian.co.uk/uk/2011/dec/09/riots-1981-2011-differences

'Reading the Riots' (2011) 'Investigating England's summer of disorder', *The Guardian* with the LSE, available: http://www.guardian.co.uk/uk/series/reading-the-riots

Riots, Communities and Victims Panel (2012) *After the Riots: Final report of the riots, communities and victims panel*, available: http://riotspanel.independent.gov.uk/wp-content/uploads/2012/03/Riots-Panel-Final-Report1.pdf

Soja, E. (2000) *Postmetropolis*, Oxford: Blackwell

Wacquant, L. (2008) *Urban Outcasts*, Cambridge: Polity

Waddington, P.A.J., Stenson, K. and Don, D. (2004) 'In proportion: race, and police stop and search', *British Journal of Criminology*, 44: 1–26

Wainwright, M. (2012) 'Bradford's new "puddle in the park" reflects burst of Yorkshire pride', *The Guardian*, 19 February

Webster, C. (1997) 'The construction of British "Asian" criminality', *International Journal of the Sociology of Law*, 25: 65–86

——(2003) 'Race, space and fear: imagined geographies of racism, crime, violence and disorder in Northern England', *Capital & Class*, May, 80: 95–122,

——(2007) *Understanding Race and Crime*, Maidenhead: Open University Press

——(2012) 'Different forms of discrimination in the CJS', in Sveinsson, K. (ed.) *Criminal Justice v Racial Justice*, London: The Runnymede Trust

15 Accommodating harm

The domestic home in criminology

Rowland Atkinson

Introduction

> The suburbs dream of violence. Asleep in their drowsy villas ...
>
> (J. G. Ballard, *Kingdom Come*)

Each year in the USA and Australia around a third of all violent crimes occur in or near the private home while the British Crime Survey (BCS) of 2008 suggests that around 13 per cent of women and 9 per cent of men have been subject to domestic violence (abuse, threats or force), sexual victimisation or stalking in the past 12 months. We might well begin by viewing the private home as a key mediating point for the production (a place of regular violence), reproduction (the predominant site of our socialisation) and possible amelioration of such harms (the role of policies and policing to intervene within the home or to reduce the stresses of household members). Yet the home itself is not a standardised product, nor does it provide a uniform series of social experiences. As Shanafelt and Pino (Chapter 16) and others in this volume attest, a concern with where we come from and the range of private experience is critical in understanding the development of propensities to transgress social rules and much of this personal history is bound up with home and family life.

The inequality that has grown so dramatically in Western societies over the past four decades has not only driven many of the harms that criminologists are attentive to (Currie 2009; Young 2007), such polarisation has also led to varied social outcomes in and outside the home. How we treat our children, the quality and assuredness of family and kin supports, the availability of communal and state provision, and the broader economic circumstances that allow us, or not, to 'make' a home are phenomena that are central to our understanding of the forces that shape criminal and harmful acts. The home itself is also central to critical understandings of crime and law because it has been a particular space over which the state has wavered in its commitment to, or interest in, intervention and its historically muted response to a space and social relations that were conveniently and paternalistically seen to be beyond the range of public law (see DeKeseredy and Donnermeyer, Chapter 13; Dragiewicz, Chapter 11, in this volume).

Perhaps the home is also evidently important because, as social scientists are increasingly aware, space matters (Tickamyer 2000). The patterning of people and groups in urban and rural space and the design of our built environments are important in shaping opportunities and constraints for deviant conduct and predatory behaviour. Neighbourhoods, estates and blocks also speak to us symbolically, of the inequities and problems of our societies and also of social boundaries and borders of multiple kinds that offer buffers to harm in some locations, while inviting such damage to others. Whether we own our own home or not is also one of the crudest and most effective indicators of wealth, of safety from intrusion, of the deployment of domestic security systems, of reduced worry about crime and, by extension, lives lived in rented housing tend to highlight the converse. Consider burglary, a phenomenon that generates anxiety, fear and also considerable anger where and when it occurs. The experience of burglary is not in fact a general problem across social space. The risk of victimisation varies considerably according to key household and area characteristics. Households in areas where physical disorder was assessed as high in the BCS were more likely to be victims of burglary (5.1 per cent) than those in areas where the assessed level was not high (2.2 per cent). Similarly more affluent households and those who actually own their own home have both the resources and incentives to secure their homes which is found much less often among poorer owners and private renters.

Thus a spatial patchwork of risks, insecurities and harms can be opened up when we intersect society with the private home and in relation to the socio-spatial contexts in which individual homes are located. In these various considerations the home matters and how we fund, manage, regulate, defend and police this space is therefore critical to the ambitions of criminology, and it is to this connection that this brief, exploratory chapter is devoted.

Housing studies and studies of crime

Despite easily recognisable impressions of the primary locus of much crime, criminology has not tended to see the domestic home as a site of particular interest in its own right. But what prospects might a more overt emphasis on this environment open to criminologists? There are multiple ways of asserting the value of the home in discussions of social harm. Many of them are explicit in existing criminological thinking, such as domestic violence. Others are yet to be adequately explored, such as the rise of the fortress home (Atkinson and Blandy 2007) or the role of housing policy in producing concentrated desolation and the further harm of the vulnerable (Flint and Nixon 2006). In elucidating the home as a site of social control, as a defence mechanism against harm and as a space nested within other spatial, social and political contexts I seek to outline here the possible terrain of a criminology of the domestic sphere.

In a little-known early article Robert Merton (1948), long known for his oblique contribution to criminology via his work on social goals and deviance, suggested that sociological and psychological studies of housing tended at that time to be concerned with charting the links between poor housing and a range of social morbidities. Bad housing, Merton argued, was linked to 'illiteracy, crime, juvenile delinquency, high mortality rates, poverty, public relief cases, illegitimacy, venerial disease' (ibid.: 163). Despite the barely latent moralising implicit in his suggestion of the terrain of a socio-logically informed housing studies, it is already clear, from this statement of the range of that field, that harms and deviations could be considered its key constituents. For Merton a good student of society would want to be able to comment on the bad behaviour of the inhabitants of homes and to examine the social and structural influences and pressures generated by particular forms of housing, notably the US public housing system. But what might be the identifiable link between housing, crime and deviance more generally?

More than any other space we all circulate between homes that are more or less orderly, variably containing social actors that may either sustain or damage us emotionally, are more or less materially well off and, as physical dwellings, are unevenly capable of providing physical shelter from certain risks. To try and add some conceptual clarity to what is undoubtedly a con-fusing area for analysis I have partitioned a criminological concern with the home into three components, or meanings – as a site within a number of key contexts, as a physical dwelling, or object, that has particular construction and architectural qualities and, finally, as a site of crime, harm and fear (see Figure 15.1).

The first concern, the context of the home, is clearly important. This refers to the various social, political and economic contexts that lie essentially out-side the home but which act upon its constitution or the variability of out-comes within it. The key actor here is the state, varying macro-economic policies that generate homes of particular qualities and standards (consider the impact, for example, of the deregulation of sound insulation standards on levels of aggression and claims of anti-social behaviour in many new-build 'executive' flats today). The housing system is also a key sphere within which inequalities are born and reproduced. Winners and losers emerge from a pri-vate market in housing, while a socially residualised and largely privatised public housing system caters for the worst-off (I return to this particular context later). But we also know that, in Britain, the state and its myriad offshoots also operate to regulate spaces and citizens via housing associations and other semi-public providers, new players in an array of policing measures that have emerged in the past 20 years and that also contribute to attempts to control anti-social and disorderly populations in areas left behind in the move to a new economy.

What happens in these broad socio-political and economic contexts outside the home also shapes experiences inside – watchful owners shelter from dis-order and dangers generated by systemic inequalities; culturally attitudes

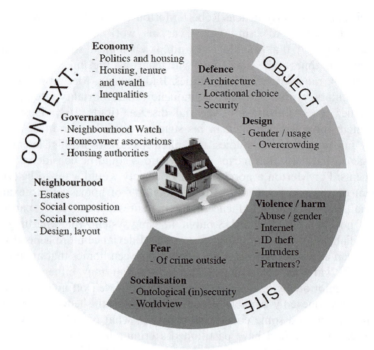

Figure 15.1 Three key meanings of the home for criminology

around gender roles shape private experiences of abuse; economic systems and politically driven resource allocations generate unequal access to safe housing. These various forces and factors, linking the micro-society of domestic space to the social forces and spatial contexts outside the front door, bedroom window or internet terminal are critical to a domestic criminology. Among other areas, debates about fear of crime implicitly locate the social subject indoors, looking out upon possible risks or worrisome events. More deeply still a political economy that directs allocations to affluent homeowners generates a set of economic winners and losers that meshes with class systems and affects our exposure to particular kinds of risk and our capacity to avoid harms. Among such patterns is, not least, the use of home search strategies that are used as elaborate avoidance strategies and which critically result in both the concentration of those *with* resources in spaces, set against and as far as possible away from those *without*.

The second aspect of home lies in its core physical constitution and socio-technical links to the household inside. Dwellings are highly varied in their design, defensive capacities and spatial configuration. This is well evidenced in concerns about target-hardening, in which home as an object is seen as being amenable to adaptation in order to reduce the risk from those who might view it as a target for vandalism or entry. Newman's (1973) early work in this field, perhaps subject to over-critique today, was, if nothing else, a bold attempt to protect public housing tenants he identified as vulnerable and living in embattled conditions during the long rise in violent crime in the 1960s and 1970s. As work on burglary and target-hardening has shown, simple adaptations make huge differences, and yet the interplay between housing tenure, design and household resources and inequalities have conspired to leave many vulnerable, particularly those in private renting, students and vulnerable households, who often see repeat victimisation. In short, it is hard to advance human security where households are not capable of resourcing such basic defences.

Finally there is the home as a scene or site in its own right, the theatre of social relations in which actors are more or less violent, aggressive, traumatising and unruly toward their neighbours, their kin or those others they might share a home with. The home as a place of socialisation is where we begin as social entities, generate the scripts that enable us to make sense of societies outside the front door and are also the points at which childhood traumas and injuries dent us or make us more prone to conduct that is more or less in line with prevailing social conventions. This complex interplay of factors and psychic demands no doubt lies at the heart of an increasing range of criminological interests (Gadd and Jefferson 2007). Private households can generate twisted social codes, private names and solipsistic forms of personal reference; evident in examples of privately observed sexual violence via the internet, the periodic discovery of dungeons and domestic slaves and private domains of serial killers and damaged childhoods.

The private home can also be seen as a container within which subjects look out, either onto a fear-inspiring world or one which is made to seem fearful via those sources that mediate the structure of that world to us – via the portals of door, window, internet connection or television. Yet the home is often neglected as a place where harm occurs because of the unease that any direct acknowledgement of such violence generates. The scale of domestic abuse, of petty injuries and banal, daily incidences of gendered and intra-household aggression are critical here and in this sense the homes we live in are almost as likely to be places of rage, conflict and dispute as they are of sustenance, nurturing and safety. I now take each of these dimensions of the home to reflect on appropriate examples to bring this framework to life in more detail.

Contexts: homes and area effects

Social units, households and families, are nested and organised within the physical unit of the home and our physical dwellings are themselves located within neighbourhoods of varying social compositions, amenities and dangers. Homes offer varying experiences to their subjects: of uneven patternings of resource, life-chances and norms that are themselves distributed across urban systems co-located within societies of more or less opportunity and inequality. These factors, ostensibly of the home, are also key ingredients to the theoretical lexicon of criminology. To talk of crime and its social rootedness is implicitly to discuss questions of segregation, neighbourhood social control, the design and resilience of homes, blocks and other building types, tenure and profound social inequality.

Homes exist in broadly constituted neighbourhoods, places with recognised names, social histories and identities that are embraced, or sometimes contested by their residents where such associations bring stigma and shame (Wacquant 2008). Of course the social composition of areas has long been of interest to criminologists precisely because these factors enable us to comment on who we might be in contact with and how local social, physical and economic conditions and networks might influence choices around criminal conduct or exposure to such actions. Since the Chicago School, these themes have been regularly picked up in sociological and criminological theory. Within housing studies interest in policies devoted to dispersing or breaking up these poor communities, or to importing marginally more affluent residents to them, has been in vogue for some time.

This is important because such programmes directly take up the suggestion that to be poor in a poor area leads to substantially worse social outcomes for the individual (what is known as the neighbourhood effects thesis), and that such violations of household potential and social exclusion should be challenged by creating more diverse areas of housing type and tenure. In this sense one might argue that wider levels of inequality are largely ignored by the actions of arms of the state concerned with housing policy insofar as these are directed at dealing with the re-engineering of social composition of neighbourhoods in order to reduce these neighbourhood effects. Here we find the state acknowledging the latent violence that emerges in its concentrated provision of public housing for the worst-off in society, while simultaneously denying the systemic violence that lies in the inequality that produces the need for such forms of provision in the first place.

There is now widespread acknowledgement among European urban policy specialists that deprived neighbourhoods are not just the receptacles of the victims of a divided and polarised society, but that living in such neighbourhoods contributes to the reproduction of inequalities and is thereby a further source of social exclusion. Yet this kind of social harm has not yet been a mainstay of criminological theorising, though the roots of such theses are apparent in work on segregation and high-risk neighbourhoods. But the question is deeper than one of basic criminality since it invokes a call to understand the threads of the operation of housing and political systems in allocating resources and attempting to ameliorate the harm that these generate. If where we live affects our potential in life then housing and urban policies become, in lieu of massive advances toward a more progressive taxation and redistribution programme, important means of thinking about how such human harm might be faced down.

However all of this is not without difficulties, as many studies have indicated that although there is evidence to suggest that living in a poor area has a detrimental effect on the life opportunities of residents (Friedrichs *et al.* 2012) these impacts are surprisingly difficult to measure in practice as net additional impacts that exceed the contribution of compositional factors at the neighbourhood level. Yet the very toxicity and socially cannibalistic quality of some of the most deprived spaces is not hard to discern, and not hard to locate in the discourse of middle-class households in their dinner party pontificating over which people, schools and neighbourhoods to avoid. No doubt it was these very same sentiments that drove the exit of black middle-class households from increasingly dangerous neighbourhoods later to be marked up as ghettos by researchers like Wilson (1996).

These points fit well with broader observations advanced by observers like Currie (2009) who have suggested that child development in poor areas points the way to social exclusion, personal stress, contact with violence and abuse more generally. More importantly Currie, Wacquant and various others have contended that the production of large agglomerations of the excluded, housed in monolithic housing estates is both a form of violence in that it creates massive detrimental impacts on human potential, while also being generative of more violent actors – either damaged by the stressed and violent household contexts they emerge from, or responding to the imperatives of organised criminal activity that operates in lieu of a sufficient formal economy.

Object: the invasion of domestic space

Domestic burglary is by no means an insignificant crime, either in material or emotional terms. In 2008 the FBI reported that victims of burglary lost an estimated $4.6 billion in property (FBI figures for 2008). Of course, a reflection on this cost and material loss belies a much more important element of the occurrence of burglary: its profound and enduring emotional impact on victims, but also the fear of its occurrence in those who may not have been touched by the crime. From the accounts of many burglars in systematic research internationally we now know that what tends to drive this problem is a need for resources, money to pay for bills, to pay for drugs and little in the way of some calculating disregard for others of whom the burglar often knows very little, either of their personal lives or the impact of their acts.

While we tend to think of the UK as a low crime society, analysis of the available international data on burglary victimisation shows that the UK experiences one of the highest levels of burglary victimisation of all the Western nations, albeit one that has declined markedly since the mid-1990s. The annual rates of burglary for the USA, Australia and the UK show rates of 73 burglaries per 10,000 people in the USA (FBI 2008), 117 in Australia (Australian Bureau of Statistics 2005) and 121 per 10,000 in the UK (in 2007/08, Home Office 2009). Using the same sources we find that this translated into 1.3 million domestic burglaries in the USA, 729,000 burglaries in the UK and 259,000 in Australia.

These bald statistics reveal little about the way that housing tenure, wealth and neighbourhood location shape the risks for households. Knowing more about these factors also contributes to a more useful, critical position that highlights how social inequalities and inequalities that are made concrete in the built environment around us influence household risks of invasion and theft. The research on burglary shows that this form of crime is highly susceptible to variabilities in particular home targets and that the defence of the home is dramatically linked to broader social inequalities – the risks of burglary are more profoundly focused on those with few resources or incentives to defend their home using basic techniques, such as effective locks. Burglary is significant not only because of the loss of possessions; more often it is the unsettling prospect of its occurrence and its psychological impact that remain the core of many people's concerns and also because these possessions reflect key elements of our private and public identities (Goldsack 1999).

In the UK, USA and Australia the geography, tenure and type of house most at risk of burglary are comparable. In each case it is homes in poorer areas, flats and rented accommodation that figure highest in terms of risk. Risk is also increased by living in a household with a single adult and children, where a head of household is young or where occupants are from a minority ethnic group (British Crime Survey data 2008). In Australia rented homes have a significantly higher break-in victimisation rate (4.7 per cent) than homes that are owned (2.9 per cent) which closely follows the British pattern (Australian Bureau of Statistics data 2005).

National-level data on burglary patterns mask wide variations in the patterns of victimisation between urban and rural areas, house types and social geographies. For example, the International Crime and Victimisation Survey in 2004/05 indicates that London had a rate of 4.5 per cent (nearly one in 20 households) which was second out of 17 national capitals, second only to Istanbul with 4.6 per cent of households. Stereotypes about the natural incidence of such crimes are also out of sync with reality. In particular this shows that the rate reported for New York was only 1.9 per cent, close to Sydney's rate of 2.2 per cent (Van Dijk *et al.* 2007). In the UK, London also did not have the highest statistical risk of burglary at 130 per 10,000 households; the highest was Nottingham at 180 per 10,000 (West Yorkshire and Manchester, both heavily urbanised and, in general, poorer areas, also feature highly).

Work on the activities of burglars and their targeting of particular kinds of properties bears out some of the key theoretical treatments of the increase of crime in the post-war period dealt with by routine activity theory (Cohen and Felson 1979). This posited that much crime was predicated on the confluence of three key factors: motivated offenders, suitable targets and absence of capable guardians. These generated or hindered the availability of targets, though perhaps said little about why offenders should be motivated to act in this way. Analysts like Tim Hope (2000) have argued that a number of factors explain the post-war pattern of property crime. The increasing pattern of women at work meant that homes were left 'unguarded' in ways that were previously uncommon. Thus a major tenet of routine activity theory, the absence of a capable guardian, became an increasingly common feature of the residential landscape. Hope has also argued that rising affluence and the growth of valuable and potentially mobile consumer products meant that more homes became worthwhile targets. This point has changed quite dramatically in recent years with the reduction in the relative re-sale value of many of these products and their increased portability. More recently it would seem that many potential burglars have turned to street robberies or other avenues that are more profitable as a result of these technological changes and also the increased fortification of homes.

Overall the BCS shows that households with no home security measures were more than ten times more likely to have been victims of burglary than those where there were security measures like deadlocks on doors (25.0 per cent compared with 2.3 per cent). According to the 2007/08 BCS there were 502 burglaries per 10,000 households in the 20 per cent most deprived areas, while there were 215 burglaries per 10,000 households in the 20 per cent least deprived areas. Thus, as Hope (2000) argues, the rich and poor have what he terms different risk positions in relation to this kind of crime which are embedded in the broader inequalities of capitalist economies.

It is also worth bearing in mind that critical criminological viewpoints that stress real declines in rates of burglary also need to acknowledge the real impacts on victims and the fact that, though burglary rates are now much lower than in the mid-1990s, the general rate of risk to burglary in the last 30 years is significantly higher than at any other time in the twentieth century. Similarly we need to be aware that, for certain groups and locations, the risks of both victimisation and repeated forms of intrusion remain very important concerns and that these are highly dependent on low levels of household resource. Further, it is critical to recognise that the bulk of fortification practices, insurance options and other defensive practices tend to accrue to those with most resources. Certainly the predation on those with little by those with little has not seemed to reduce anxieties about home invasion among higher income groups who remain motivated to exit social space in order to inhabit gated communities and fortress homes as marks of distinction and outward hostility to general social contact.

Site: abuse and violence inside the home

The final dimension, or meaning, of home discussed here relates to that of the domestic dwelling as a site of harm. In surveys from around the world, 10–69 per cent of women report being physically assaulted by an intimate male partner at some point in their lives. Very young children are at greatest risk: homicide rates among children aged 0–4 years are more than twice those among children aged 5–14 years (5.2 per 100,000 compared with 2.1 per 100,000). About 20 per cent of women and 5–10 per cent of men have suffered sexual abuse as children (WHO 2002). In the UK it is estimated that there were 12.9 million incidents of domestic violence in the preceding year and that more than a third (36 per cent) of people, predominantly women, experience domestic violence during their lifetime. Similarly more than half (54 per cent) of rapes in the UK are committed by a woman's current or former partner (Walby and Allen 2004). Perhaps the most chilling figure of these is that an average of two women a week are killed by a male partner or former partner: this constitutes around one-third of all female homicide victims in the UK.

These appalling data highlight the simple fact that such violence and abuse take place primarily in the domestic home, a space that is largely, and sometimes wholly, outside the conventional spaces of policing or community surveillance. As Rykwert (1991: 54) observed, early work on domestic violence and abuse:

> rendered problematic the notion of the home as a safe haven. Research into rape in marriage, domestic violence and sexual harassment unhinged the view that women need not fear men that they know: work colleagues, boyfriends, partners and relatives. The recognition of the familiar and the familial as no more trustworthy than the stranger put a very different complexion on who is and who is not to be trusted and, by implication, what places, times and people were risky.

If the home has been opened to angst about diffuse threats from outside, official data confirm that in fact it is more often the locus of peril. Many of our most significant terrors are reserved for the mundane routines of household life: intra-familial harassment, physical and sexual abuse and violence. It has become a social truism and statistical fact that most accidents happen in the home, but of course most homicides and cases of violence and abuse also occur here, not least perhaps because of the invisibility and possible prevention of detection. Domestic abuse is played out in what we habitually think of as 'the privacy of our own homes'. This has led researchers like Stanko (1990) to suggest that distinctions in relation to violence can be made between the generally private, domestic clustering of primarily female victimisation and the generally more public forms of male victimisation. The implication of this is that what goes on behind closed doors is partially beyond the regulatory mechanisms of society including surveillance, policing, judicial and communal sanctions. When we are at home our actions are generally invisible to such controls and makes the home feel like a space of relative emancipation, but this quality also creates a space in which the fiercest aspects of human nature are able to operate without hindrance or prevention.

The balance between the privacy of the home and the right of the state to intrude to prevent harm is a contentious issue. Not least because while freedom from any form of such intrusion is seen as a cornerstone of liberal democracies the revelation of family violence or child abuse, precisely because of a lack of such intervention, raises continued questions about approaches to 'private' problems such as these. The idea that the home was a private and morally incorruptible space was deeply entrenched until the late twentieth century when the 'problem' of domestic abuse was more clearly acknowledged.

Related matters

The preceding discussions set out the three key dimensions of home in relation to aspects of theorisation and empirical measurement of crime and harm, yet there are numerous other topics that are worthy of mention in such deliberations. To take one such area, it is clear that the rise of new information and communication technologies has repositioned the home in relation to a series of possible vulnerabilities that pass beyond or between the physical defences of the home. For example, the use of the internet, mobile phones and social networking sites have largely supplanted concerns with problems like nuisance phone callers or door-to-door salespeople. New concerns are now focused on problems like identity theft whereby criminal activity is generated through the adoption of other's identities to access credit or pay for goods and services. In the UK the 2006/7 British Crime Survey recorded the number of plastic card ID thefts in 2006 was around 48,000 account takeovers and 59,000 fraudulent applications, though, while recording large increases, ID theft remains only a small part of such crimes now totalling £34m in losses associated with this form of theft (2007). In the USA, the US Bureau of Justice Statistics for 2005 showed that 6.7 per cent of households experienced some form of identity theft, yet only 1.1 million households discovered misuse of personal information (such as a social security number), just less than 1 per cent of households.

Another key worry has become the safety of children while using the internet. This highlights further areas for the relative safety and security of young members of the household who may not be adequately supervised by parents, who misunderstand the nature of particular kinds of predation or whose parents may not be sufficiently aware of these risks themselves. For example, in the USA in 2006, 62,480,584 reports were made to the CyberTipline relating to the possession, manufacture and distribution of child pornography as well as 6,384 reports of the online enticement of children for sexual acts.

Conclusion

What added value comes from charting the relationship between the home and questions of crime and social harm? The most pertinent response to this question is to understand how the domestic home is the site upon which some of the most globally significant forms of crime and social harm are enacted every day. In considering the need for an effective criminology of the modern, domestic home we are necessarily reminded of the general public and political emphasis that is made on risks that are external to the home itself. This emphasis appears disproportionate and misaligned with the extent and profound damage of domestic abuse and violence. Research in this area has highlighted that the familial and household environment is regularly toxic in relation to its members and primarily this burden of victimhood falls on women and children who suffer acute psychic damage and developmental hindrance. This undermines how we should understand the family and the home, as sources of protection within our contemporary culture; a place that is widely linked to notions of self-reliance and protection and yet also a confined space within which our worst nightmares are most likely to be realised. Yet these deep contradictions of the home are barely recognised in the habits of discourse that we find surrounding domestic life, perhaps indeed precisely because the reality of such horrors is easier repressed than acknowledged.

While perhaps most of us feel safe at home, the place of the private realm is frequently revealed to us, through news and film media, as a façade behind which regular forms of abuse and violence are enacted. At the same time as the private home is the stage upon which such harms take place the private home is a critical point of mediation by which we learn about and prepare for the risks associated with the world outside and come to hear about such danger through news and other information conduits that are received in the home.

Technological change has also opened the way for new forms of potential harm that is sexually predatory in nature. The fears we have when we are in our homes might be based on prior experiences, or may be 'imported' into our consciousness through contact with crime dramas and alarming news items in newspapers and the internet. Even while we may feel that the source of possible attack might come in the form of burglary or unwanted visitors the kind of physical defences that we put in place to allay our fear of these occurrences – alarms, locks and fisheye viewers – do little to assuage the anxieties generated by news media and information flows which are permitted entry to our homeworld, via television, computer and mobile phone screens.

If the home is our castle then, pursuing this metaphor further, the social relationships within it can be opened up and seen as so many mini-fiefdoms in which sexual power and the extraction of duty and allegiance are played-out each day. While we live in societies in which the meaning of home is laden with the suggestion of civility, civilisation, independence, escape and freedom, it is as much the case that our homes may become at times the very reverse of these qualities.

References

Atkinson, R. and Blandy, S. (2007) 'Panic rooms: the rise of defensive homeownership', *Housing Studies*, 22 (4): 443–58

Cohen, L. and Felson, M. (1979) 'Social change and crime rate trends: a routine activity approach', *American Sociological Review*, 44 (4): 588–608

Currie, E. (2009) *The Roots of Violence*, Toronto: Prentice Hall

Flint, J. and Nixon, J. (2006) 'Governing neighbours: anti-social behaviour orders and new forms of regulating conduct in the UK', *Urban Studies,* 43: 939–55

Friedrichs, J., Galster, G. and Musterd, S. (2012) 'Neighbourhood effects on social opportunities: the European and American research and policy context', *Housing Studies*, 18 (6): 797–806

Gadd, D. and Jefferson, T. (2007) *Psychosocial Criminology*, London: Sage

Goldsack, A. (1999) 'A haven in a heartless world? Women and domestic violence', in A. Goldsack (ed.) *Ideal Homes? Social Change and Domestic Life*, London: Routledge

Hope, T. (2000) 'Inequality and the clubbing of private security', in T. Hope and R. Sparks (eds) *Crime, Risk and Insecurity*, London: Routledge

Merton, R.K. (1948) 'The social psychology of housing', *Sociometry*, pp. 163–217

Newman, O. (1973) *Defensible Space: Crime Prevention through Urban Design*, London: Macmillan.

Rykwert, J. (1991) 'House and home', *Social Research*; 58 (1): 51–62

Stanko, E. (1990) *Everyday Violence*, London: Harper Collins

Tickamyer, A. (2000) 'Space matters! Spatial inequality in future sociology', *Contemporary Sociology*, 29 (6): 805–13

Van Dijk, J., Van Kesteren, J. and Smit, P. (2007) *Criminal Victimisation in International Perspective: Key Findings from the 2004–2005 ICVS and EU ICS*, The Hague: Ministry of Justice/UNODC

Wacquant, L. (2008) *Urban Outcasts*, Cambridge: Polity

Walby, S. and Allen, J. (2004) *Domestic Violence, Sexual Assault and Stalking: Findings from the British Crime Survey*, London: Home Office

Wilson, W.J. (1996) *When Work Disappears*, New York: Knopf

Young, J. (2007) *The Vertigo of Late Modernity*, London: Sage

16 Evil and the common life

Towards a wider perspective on serial killing and atrocities

Robert Shanafelt and Nathan W. Pino

Evil and the common life: towards a wider perspective on serial killing

There is a plethora of ways to explain the motives and methods of serial killers, but individual analysts tend to focus on their favorites. To get a sense of this, a sampling of the literature is instructive. Here we can find a pulp journalist who emphasizes the killers' enjoyment of horror, a Freudian psychiatrist who emphasizes obsession with the mother, a forensic specialist who emphasizes brain injury and drug abuse, a learning theorist who emphasizes conditioning, an FBI agent who emphasizes criminal profiling, a literary critic who emphasizes the role of the imagination, a critical sociologist who emphasizes social causality, an anthropologist who emphasizes cultural frameworks, and an evolutionary psychologist who emphasizes men's violent propensities (Mitchell 2003; Abrahamsen 1975; Norris 1988; Buss 2005). This wide variety of emphases, and there are of course others, has also led to a special literature just to interpret the interpretations (Mitchell 1997).

In this chapter, our aim is not to discredit other researchers or their perspectives. While we consider a number of ways of characterizing and describing serial killers, this is not meant to be a standard literature review (for those, see Fox and Levin 2005; Holmes and Holmes 2010; Vronsky 2004). Neither is it meant to be a critique of theoretical or methodological lapses (for these, see Canter 1994; Hickey 2002; Sears 1991). Rather, our aim is to develop a synthesis of a variety of perspectives, one that can be greater than the sum of its parts. We also want to make the case that it is important to consider serial homicide in terms of more general concerns about what ultimately motivates our actions.

Some very big questions stand out particularly when it comes to explaining serial killing. Philosophers wonder about such things as the role of the will and the extent to which the killer is a free moral agent. They also may wonder if the actions of serial killers reveal something fundamental about the nature of evil (Waller 2010). Of course, one can be more specific. How much is the serial killer a victim of child abuse? Might he have some kind of chemically based addiction? Is he a cold-blooded killer without remorse? Clearly, while everyone wants to lay out the precise variables that make a serial killer, no one wants to do so with the implication that serial killers are not free moral agents who are responsible for their own actions.

Recently, the case of Richard 'The Iceman' Kuklinski (1935–2006) has received considerable attention. Kuklinksi was a professional hit man who seemed to be totally without emotional response to the suffering of others. He apparently killed transients simply for practice, and once shot a random passerby in the head with a crossbow just to see how effective it would be as a killing tool. In support of a biological model, one can point out that Kuklinski's brother was also a convicted murderer, as well as a child molester. Yet, Kuklinski was also the son of an alcoholic who had witnessed and personally suffered through innumerable beatings as a child. Even such a callous murderer may be as much made as born. Clearly, then, there are no simple answers as to what makes a serial murderer, making micro–macro analyses of 'webs of violence' essential (Turpin and Kurtz 1997) and popular tactics such as profiling and creating typologies of different types of killers inadvisable (Pino 2005).

We do want, however, to stress the usefulness of seeing serial killing in terms of the 'normal aberrations' of depersonalization, violence, and fragmented identity that can occur both in times of peace and war. In this regard, we believe the serial killing literature is not just of relevance to criminologists or specialists in homicide; it should be a central part of a more general analysis of all killing. This is because the serial killer often functions in terms of widely shared cultural and psychological processes, processes that may become particularly manifest during conditions of warfare or political terror. As we will discuss, killing in war involves some of the same learned behavioral patterns we find with serial offending (Castle and Hensley 2002). This is a radical suggestion in that its acceptance would break the taken-for-granted divide between serial killing as individual crime and the serial murders and genocides of professional and military forces. Such a divide is evident in the FBI-derived typologies of serial killers that exclude hit men and soldiers from consideration.

Another item on our agenda is the advocacy of the life-course history method. We favor this method especially because it is very conducive to consideration of issues of determinism, individual will, social learning, and choice in the development of a violent criminal persona. While findings from a few detailed life histories may not always be generalizable to a population at large, the life-course history method helps one get a deeper sense of how a person understands his or her identity and place in the world. Here we will use the life-course history method in describing two convicted serial killers. We are interested in comparing and contrasting these two individual accounts because they seem to represent a particular type of serial killer – one who is highly intelligent, articulate, and able to lead an effective double-life – yet who are very distinctive as individuals. Examination of the very different personalities and self-presentations of the killers also requires us to consider ways in which their self-discourse functioned to distance themselves from their own violent agency. Indeed, while their self-presentation and rationalizations are quite distinctive, their ability to express themselves well on paper does seem to be a shared characteristic that appears to be rare among serial killers.

Life course, will, and self-presentation: two case studies

The first case we will discuss is that of a serial rapist and killer described by Pino (2005) whom we call here 'R.R.' The second case is that of the notorious British 'Moors Murderer,' Ian Brady. Both of these serial killers appear to be self-reflective and articulate, but their self-descriptions are also masks. Brady rationalizes his behavior in terms of nihilistic philosophy, but has been reticent to discuss the more obscure sources of his pedophilic and sadistic sexual appetites. R.R. rationalizes his behavior as a 'sex addiction,' but manifestly made choices to continue on the course he had set for himself. Both Brady and R.R. were successful in leading double lives in which they hid their killing persona and blended in with conventional society. R.R. was more successful at this but was also more bothered by guilt. In contrast, Brady does not manifest guilt or remorse; rather, he claims that his killing persona was a conscious creation of his own will. This latter contrast is also what draws us to the comparison of these two cases. While R.R. thinks he is the victim of compulsions outside of his conscious control, Brady thinks of himself as a Nietzschian *überman* who deliberately made himself 'beyond good and evil' by conscious acts of choice. While we will make some critical observations as we go along, we hold off most of them until after the cases have been fully described.

R.R.

R.R. was born in Spain in 1963, but spent several of his early years in the United States, in the environs of Washington, DC.[1] After his second grade school year, the family moved to Puerto Rico, where the parents were originally from. Here, up until the age of 16, R.R. lived near the coast, first in Fajardo, then in a nearby beach resort town. In high school, he reports that he was popular and a standout in wrestling. In the fall of 1981, after a lackadaisical first semester at the University of Puerto Rico mostly spent partying, he dropped out and joined the Navy. In his 14 years in the Navy he enjoyed some success, obtaining as his highest position a Pentagon job as an aide to the Joint Chiefs of Staff. In addition, his Navy job saw him stationed in various locations in the United States, including San Diego; Columbia, South Carolina; and Pensacola, Florida. As one would expect, his Navy life also took him to exotic ports such as Singapore.

While still in the Navy, R.R. completed a university degree in South Carolina. In 1993, he married a woman he had met at school who also was of Puerto Rican heritage. In the next few years, they would have two children. After his college graduation, the Navy gave R.R. the further opportunity to attend a pre-flight training school in Florida. However, he performed poorly there, and never completed his course, as he was forced to resign in disgrace in 1995 due to his arrest for solicitation of a minor. From this period until his final arrest in 2000, he worked several jobs in car sales. When he was arrested for murder he was working in a manufacturing plant back in South Carolina.

R.R.'s life in crime reportedly begins in 1986 with the rape of a street-walking prostitute in San Diego. It ends in 1999 and 2000 in a frenzy of four serial murders and an attempted murder in South Carolina and Georgia. His victims were working class young women, aged 17 to 21, whom he especially targeted because they seemed vulnerable and easy to manipulate. From the mid-1980s until his final arrest and conviction, he admits to having committed several hundred rapes, mostly against prostitutes and escorts, but also against what he calls 'normal girls.' According to his account, this focus changed in the late 1990s when he started looking for young women by driving around in parking lots. R.R. claimed that he was a very persuasive talker, and that by posing as a professional photographer or escort service manager he was able to convince young and naive girls to admit him to their residence, where they would pose at least partially nude. He reports that he was quite successful in using his powers of persuasion to gradually get young women to engage in conversations that involved sexual topics. Sometimes he would fondle himself as he continued to talk. He claims that many of the women he targeted accepted or ignored his deviant behavior because they were young and naive and took it as a sign of their own personal and sexual maturity to be tolerant.

R.R. argues vehemently that he never fantasized about violence, only about the psychological and sexual control of young and attractive women. His ideal was to have complete control over a totally compliant girl with whom he could act out fantasies of anal sex, fantasies that he had cultivated over the years through heavy consumption of pornography. He has repeatedly claimed that he found no pleasure in killing, but needed to kill for the pragmatic reason of eliminating the witness (Hodson 2004).

Except for his rapes and murders, R.R. paints a very positive picture of himself. He describes his childhood as unhappy, but his own response as resilient. Although he claims his parents frequently argued, there was no physical abuse. He did not suffer from physical want either, as his father was a doctor. Still, he felt a lack of general affection, and indicates that he coped with this as a youngster by 'making himself invisible' or a 'ghost' in the house and by spending most of his time at the beach or out on the streets. While his father was emotionally distant from the rest of the family, and had a serious gambling problem, he says he was his father's favorite, and that this situation made his brother and sister jealous. Rather than being the 'black sheep' of the family at this time, he recalls, his good behavior made him more like the 'white sheep.' In any case, he believes that he was 'the affectionate one' in the family and that throughout his life he has been a very 'hugging-type' person with friends and loved ones.

Perhaps more significant than the interpersonal relations in his family was the fact that R.R. started using drugs heavily at quite a young age. He recalls starting to smoke marijuana at age 13. Within the next two years he had considerable experience with many drugs, including alcohol, Quaaludes, hallucinogenic mushrooms, LSD, and, to a lesser extent, cocaine. He became addicted to Quaaludes at age 14, although with little explanation he says he managed to quit them 'cold turkey' when he was 15. Later on, when he was in the Navy, R.R. says he would regularly use methamphetamine to stay awake, sometimes for days at a time. He believes that his personality is particularly prone to compulsive acts. An uncontrollable addiction, he thinks, is the major explanation of his later sexual behavior and serial killing.

R.R. believes that he has an 'authentic' self that is manifest when he is not acting under the compulsion of his addiction. Here he is a gentleman, helpful and friendly to colleagues and coworkers, a person who loves his wife and children and who is fully capable of loving and respecting women in general. His autobiographical recollections are peppered with statements such as 'I'm a very moral person,' 'I look at the positive things in people,' and 'I'm always so positive and upbeat.' Even after his arrest for multiple murder, he still can see himself in this positive way. While he expresses guilt and 'hates' the things he has done, he does not see the acts he has committed as fundamentally altering his essential good nature. The idea of sex addiction has helped him construct a sense of himself in which he is not a free moral agent. Rather, he believes he is being driven by compulsions over which he has no control.

R.R. also created active fantasies and social identifications that reinforced his sense of being controlled from without. One of these was his identification with vampires, particularly of the type portrayed in Rice's *Interview with a Vampire*. He identified in particular with the character Louis who is turned into a vampire against his will. Like Louis, R.R. thinks of himself as a deeply moral person who is compelled by forces beyond his control. Later, there is guilt. As R.R. put it, he is also like Louis because he feels great guilt, cries, 'has a conscience … has humanity; [and] it hurts him and he hates what he is doing.'

At about the same time that R.R. discovered drugs, he also discovered sex. Sex for him was associated with personal gratification rather than with affectionate consideration of another. Also of relevance may be a cultural frame about machismo and women, begun in Puerto Rico but easily carried on in the American military, a framework that suggests a fundamental divide between women perceived as sweet sexual objects and those perceived in terms of their individuality and humanity. Although R.R. recalls many sexual encounters with prostitutes, with girls on the beach and, later, in bars and clubs, there is not one substantial romantic relationship among them. In fact, other than his marital relationship, R.R. indicates that he never had any relationship that lasted more than a couple of months. Rather, he emphasizes, from high school age he most enjoyed having 'the ability to control or seduce or manipulate women,' his greatest pleasure coming 'at the point where

I've convinced them. Where I've disarmed them.' Later, in his rapes, he would particularly enjoy forcing his victims to pretend they were willing. Or, after they were bound, he would deliberately say something life-threatening to scare them even more than they were already, only so that he then could enjoy the feeling of appeasing them.

Although R.R. does not like to talk about his violence, he relishes discussions of the details of his fantasy life and sexual past. He claims to have started masturbating as a pre-teen, and that 'since I've known about it I've masturbated on average two to three times a day, [sometimes] for several hours straight.' R.R. emphasizes how his sexual practices became even more compulsive during his time in the Navy, especially during the time he was stationed in San Diego. Here R.R. experienced heightened pleasure in sexualized places, locales that become more and more associated with the deepest sexual images. In particular, he became involved in a swingers club, had numerous interactions with street prostitutes, and developed an obsessive fantasy life that revolved around pornography and masturbation. He especially reveled in the sexual pleasure zones created for the sailors. 'My whole life revolved around trying to get into strip joints,' he says; and when he went to the peep shows there, 'that was like in heaven.' In his second year at the base, he discovered Thad's, a nudist sex club that he says featured a dance floor with a huge bed in the middle, a weight room, a spa, a do-it-yourself bar, and numerous side bedrooms. At Thad's, he recalls:

> I'm in heaven. I'm in pure heaven. I'd go up there Thursday, Friday, and Saturday if I had the money. And I'd be there from 9 [or] 10 at night until sunrise. Until 6 [or] 7 in the morning ... I could talk about Thad's forever.

During this time he also started to visit prostitutes in San Diego and neighboring Tijuana. However, he soon developed an antipathy for street walkers, both because they seemed always ready to rob him, and because he was not able to create the illusion that he could control them. Rather, it was the woman who controlled him, reacting to him mechanically, or telling him to hurry up with the sex and get it over with. Now in his early twenties, he became obsessed with rape fantasies of retaliation that soon became the only sexual fantasies he could sustain.

R.R.'s first assaults on prostitutes occurred in San Diego. However, it was in Washington, DC, that R.R. says he came to perfect his techniques as a rapist. Here, in a four and a half year period beginning in 1987, he claims to have raped at least 150 prostitutes by threatening them with a knife and using handcuffs to quickly force them into submission. Later, in South Carolina and Georgia where street walkers were not so easily available, he employed the same rape techniques on women that he hired from escort services.

R.R. describes his life during these periods as a cycle of compulsion and guilt. For the moral part of himself, his inability to refrain from rape and rape fantasies became an irresolvable source of shame. Yet since it was a compulsion he would not give up, he rationalized it in other ways. Although by his own admission he had a devoted wife and children whom he loved, he blamed part of his sexual compulsion on his wife for being cold and distant. He also reveled in the heights of pleasure he achieved only in fantasy. Even after the murders, whatever pangs of conscience he felt could not overcome his visceral feelings of pleasure at the memory of the sex he obtained from the victims. From prison while awaiting trial, he admitted that 'I [still] fantasize about the girls that I killed, not the strangling or stabbing, I fantasize about the sex itself' and that 'I fantasize about things that I could have done, new positions, different things that I told myself before that I would do.' When it comes to discussing the actual murders, R.R. is most distant from his own actions and choices. In between the killings and the rapes, he would tell himself that he could stay at the less dangerous level, but then he would find himself at the next one anyway, 'caught' as he put it, 'completely into it again.'

R.R.'s fantasies of rape also involved forms of persuasive talk that he had first experienced pleasure in as a young 'pick-up artist' at the beach and bar, and that he found useful in his ordinary life as a sailor and as a car salesman as well. Here it is difficult to tell R.R.'s fantasy world from reality, but it is not unreasonable to believe him when he says that he was often able to coax women to trust him with stories about being an established photographer or the owner of an escort service who wanted to take their pictures. However, when he could not achieve his fantasy, or when it broke down, it is also not unreasonable to assume that he could distance himself intellectually from any acts of stalking, stealth, kidnapping, and forced entry that he undoubtedly committed in order to obtain his goal of complete control over an idealized victim.

Ian Brady

The case of Ian Brady and his girlfriend Myra Hindley is famous in Britain and still attracts media attention more than 40 years after the fact.[2] What shocks the British public is not only the brutal nature of their attacks, adolescent boys and girls raped, strangled, and stabbed, but also that two young, physically attractive people, seemingly reasonable and 'normal', could engage in such violence and murder with such obvious indifference. Especially shocking is the idea that a woman can be as brutal and sadistic as a man.

It is clear that Brady was the driving force behind the killings. It was he who guided Myra and converted her to his worldview. She was four and a half years his junior, impressionable and unhappy with life. While by Myra's accounts she was the subject of Brady's very effective brainwashing, in Brady's view she was a willing accomplice who relished sadistic pleasures of her own.

There are some features of Ian Brady's early life story that are peculiar, but nothing that would have led anyone at the time to predict that he would become a ruthless serial killer. He was born in 1938 to an unwed mother in one of the poorest sections of Glasgow, but that environment was at most predictive of conventional crime and poverty, not serial killing. And, this could have been offset by the natural gifts of intelligence and good looks that most everyone agreed Brady possessed. More predictive, perhaps, was the extreme physical and emotional deprivation he experienced as a young infant. This occurred not because his mother was emotionally callous, but because her class situation required her to keep a job as a waitress, and she was not always able to afford a babysitter. Young, alone, inexperienced, and lacking social support, she on some days went to work while leaving her baby home alone. Knowing how serious a problem this was, she soon decided to place an advertisement in the newspaper for someone to take little Ian from her and raise him in their home.

As a result of the advertisement, Ian was unofficially adopted into the home of Mary and John Sloane. In exchange for receipt of Ian's welfare support, the couple agreed to raise Ian along with their four own children. Ian's mother, Peggy, in the persona of an aunt, visited most Sundays until Ian was about 12, when she married and moved away from Glasgow with her new husband, Patrick Brady, to the English industrial city of Manchester. The Sloanes remember Ian as unresponsive to affection, and that he often threw fits of temper. Looking back on his life as a 50-year-old man, Brady blamed none of his problems on bad childhood experiences. In fact, in an open letter to the British Broadcasting Corporation from his place of incarceration Brady included the comment, 'It is fashionable nowadays to blame one's faults and crimes on abuse as a child. [However,] I had a happy childhood' (BBC, August 27, 1998).

Around the time that his birth mother disappeared so precipitously from his life, Brady missed an important opportunity for educational and class advancement. Although high test scores had gained him admission to the prestigious Shawlands Academy at age 11, he became thereafter an indifferent student. Instead, he came to prefer the company of a rough crowd, and took on the demeanor of a street tough who could smoke and lead a gang. In his book, *Gates of Janus*, Brady claims that despite the popular depictions of him as socially isolated, he was in fact a gang leader. It was probably also in the context of youthful gang activity that he developed what became for him the supreme value of loyalty, but a loyalty restricted 'only to relatives and close friends.'

Within a year after his birth mother left town, young Brady was in trouble with the law for theft. In the next few years, by the time he was 16, he had already been arrested for burglary three times. After the last occasion, in 1954, he was given back over to the custody of his mother and her husband in Manchester. Shortly after this he took on the surname Brady, that of his stepfather.

Ian's stepfather Patrick Brady tried to reform Ian through work. However, this was not very effective, and Ian continued to steal. At 17, he was arrested for stealing from his workplace. For this crime he was sentenced to two years at an institution for young offenders, but because there was no space available he had to spend the first three months of it at an adult prison. He was finally admitted to the juvenile facility, but soon got into trouble for gambling and drinking. Despite this, while incarcerated Brady received training in book-keeping. After his release this helped him get a job – the job through which he would meet and develop a relationship with Myra. These prison experi-ences, in both adult and juvenile contexts, undoubtedly also gave Brady direct experience of sadistic pleasure and various forms of prison homosexuality.

Many have made much of the fact that Brady had a youthful fascination with World War II and the Nazis. For someone of his generation this was far from unusual; what was unusual is that he identified strongly with the Nazis, insisting on taking their part in games with his friends. Although he was not a diligent student in the classroom, he did follow up his personal passions with extensive reading. As time passed he became an ardent admirer of the writ-ings of Dostoevsky and Nietzsche, finding in them inspiration for personal amorality and sadism. Among materials collected at his residence after his arrest for murder, for example, was a notebook with a number of mis-anthropic statements written in Brady's hand. These included a quote from the Marquis de Sade's *Justine* that 'murder is a hobby and a supreme plea-sure.' Another of Brady's favorite adages at the time was: 'You are your own master. You live for one thing, supreme pleasure in everything you do. Sadism is the supreme pleasure!!!' (quoted in Fenton and Bunyon 2005).

The years Brady has spent in a high security mental hospital since 1966 have not led to much revision in this sadistic philosophy. In fact, Brady argues in his 2001 book that imprisonment has only 'therianthropically preserved' it on ice. According to him, those who do not act on Dostoevsky's adage that 'if there is no God then all things are possible' are mere conformists. They are 'just spiritless minions of the underclass.' Typical serial killers, on the other hand, are social rebels who have declared a personal war on society, even coming to 'regard society in much the same way as professional soldiers do an enemy state' (Brady 2001: 53). Countering the usual image of the killer as a monster, he introduces a new and ironic image: serial killers operate according to 'reverse Buddhist principles.' Rather than seek to eliminate desire from their being through ascetic denial, they seek on the contrary to 'purge each desire by [unfettered] gratification.'

In keeping with the self-analysis of R.R., *The Gates of Janus* concludes that for the typical serial killer, killing itself is not pleasurable, but a 'necessary conclusion to an exercise of power and will' and a 'wearisome cleaning up after the feast' (Brady 2001: 45, 89). Yet there is a particularly strong contrast here with R.R.'s philosophy. R.R. sees himself as a moral man who through no real choice of his own finds himself doing evil deeds. Brady, on the other hand, sees killing as a choice of the intellectually strong, a rational and con-scious path taken in pursuit of pleasure and power in a meaningless and sociologically skewed world. Furthermore, while both R.R. and Brady talk of pleasure, R.R.'s comments are explicit and graphic, Brady's abstract and removed from sexual specifics. If R.R. loves his fantasies of desire but suppresses the reality of his aggression, Brady loves to spin philosophical rationalizations that make of his murders something cold and calculated; his sexual fantasies he keeps to himself.

The claims Brady makes in a letter published in February 2005 seem particularly to reveal his peculiar philosophy to be a rather stretched form of intellectualization, one that especially stands out for ignoring the ugly and violent fact that all the youthful victims he and Hindley killed and buried on Saddleworth Moor, outside Manchester, were brutally raped:

> Contrary to popular perception, the so-called Moors Murders were merely an existential exercise for just over a year, which was concluded in December 1964. The exercise originated from frustration with 'reliables' who were continually being arrested for embroilments in trivial crimes and causing delay in our mercenary objectives. So the final 10 months of our freedom in 1965 were entirely preoccupied with return to mercenary priorities, to re-organizing and eradicating liabilities. All these facts testify that the Moors Murders ended in December 1964, and that throughout 1965 we were hurrying to make up for wasted time, cutting reliance on others down to the bone, with Myra doubling as driver and sole reliable backup. All we required was a 'mule' to pick up and carry during [our] robberies.
>
> (Quoted in Fenton and Bunyon 2005)

This interpretation so many years after the fact rather makes Brady and Hindley sound like social bandits, ready to do battle against the powers that be, a would-be Bonnie and Clyde. However, Brady did not simply seek to coldly gain some practical experience in killing to develop the steel will and hard-heartedness of the Gestapo; he was luring vulnerable youths to the slaughter for sexual pleasure. This was not for an abstract philosophy, but for repressed physical passion, consummation of which Brady manipulated Hindley to accept. Consider the nature of the killings. First, in July 1963, a 16-year-old girl was lured by Hindley to Saddleworth Moor, where she was raped and murdered by Brady. Four months later Hindley lured a 12-year-old boy to the same area, where Brady also raped and killed him. Seven months later a young boy is again a victim. The last two known victims from 1965 were also young and naive. One was a 10-year-old girl, the other a 17-year-old boy. For them the murder scene was Hindley and Brady's house, where they had to endure more extended forms of torture.

A key segment of Brady's book suggests an insightful way to look at the chronology of these killings. Here he describes a first killing as a kind of rite of passage, then goes on to talk about the importance of the second killing as the real fulfillment of fantasy. It is with the second killing, he argues, that the killer feels confidence and has an 'expanding sense of omnipotence,' one that allows him to exert his fantasies as an 'aesthetic experience' (Brady 2001: 87). The nature of Brady's own second killing then is particularly important. The evidence from this murder shows that a key to Brady's own fantasy life was his desire for anal intercourse and his desire for the pre-pubescent body. Most accounts also say that Brady picked up his last young victim in either a pub or in a gay bar, even though he has always denied this. Furthermore, forensic evidence suggests that the victim was nude in Hindley's house that night, prior to the time he was murdered (Hawkins 2004). Myra Hindley also described Brady's homosexual fantasy life (ibid.). Yet, as Hawkins writes (ibid.) 'Brady always denied any homosexuality on his part.' This taboo desire helps explain Brady's passion for intellectual rationalization.

One final thing important to note here is Brady's description of his killing persona. Not surprisingly, given his emphasis on the conscious will, he suggests that he consciously created his killing self. One can learn to control ones subconscious, and to create a second, or even multiple, personality, he writes, thus giving oneself the power to 'act like a chameleon.' This can be done through techniques he calls self-programming by acute hypnosis or 'auto-hypnotic techniques.' In this way one can overcome one's own physical and spiritual weaknesses, committing the most amoral acts without qualm. According to Brady, if only Dostoevsky's character Raskolnikov in *Crime and Punishment* had learned to do this, he would never have been such a pathetic murderer (Brady 2001: 39, 72, 101). Myra Hindley too seems active in such processes. With Brady's prodding, but also certainly with some internal decision to become other than she had been, she refashioned her external appearance from that of a wholesome-looking school girl to the fashion in dress and hairstyle of the noted Nazi women Ilse Hess, wife of Rudolf Hess, and Irma Grese, a notorious Nazi prison camp guard (Hawkins 2004).

Models and theories

In his analysis of Jeffrey Dahmer, Richard Tithecott (1997) describes a number of popular understandings of the serial killer and their influence on the way that even the 'experts' think about them. One especially relevant component of this is the depiction of serial killers as sane but wicked monsters, from which it follows that they must be the embodiment of evil. One consequence of this can be that there is a tacit rejection of further explanation or sympathy. Rather than explanation, what is anticipated is a countervailing force. While in myth this takes the form of the heroic monster slayer, in popular culture one gets a mythologized police, like Clarice Starling in the *Silence of the Lambs*, who are conceived of as modern-day demon hunters, champions doing battle with evil on both the physical and psychological planes. Moreover, this repetitive fiction represents an archetypal story of good and evil, one that has been told for generations around the world (Gilmore 2003).

There are several consequences of this narrative form that require analysis. First, elements of it have crept into the criminological literature, with words like 'evil' and 'monster' becoming commonplace. When these types of words and their implications slip in unnoticed, they can lead one to think of serial killers as acting almost as mechanically as ravenous monsters, mysteriously impelled by impulse, instinctual compulsion, drive, or addiction – phenomena all assumed to be explanatory in and of themselves. Second, an evocation of the monstrous can foster a romanticizing of killers. The focus on the serial killer as a powerful being without limits can also serve to promote a cult of celebrity, with 'fans' happy to marry the perpetrators, produce their trading cards, develop their websites, and flock to TV shows and movies which never seem to tire of dramatizing one version or another of their stories (Fox and Levin 2005; Buss 2005). Third, the popular narratives of demon and monster are often incorporated into the model of identity that serial killers construct of themselves. While R.R. speaks of himself in this way with a sense of despair; Brady gloats that it is a helpful way to turn oneself 'cold' to killing.

There are several other examples, including: (1) Ted Bundy, who referred to his murderous impulses variously as 'the entity,' the 'malignant being,' or the 'Hunchback;' (2) 'Son of Sam' murderer David Berkowitz who talked of the 'demon' living inside him; (3) British killer Dennis Nilsen who spoke of his evil 'dragon;' (4) Dennis Rader, who called himself a monster as well as 'Bind, Torture, Kill (BTK);' and (5) Jeffrey Dahmer who spoke in the language of ritual demons when he attempted to create 'zombies' of his victims (Tithecott 1997: 50–1; CNN 2005).

Less remarked upon in the literature, the conception of the serial killer as an evil monster obscures the fact that there are serial killers who become so during conditions of war and political repression. Given conditions of state-sanctioned and monitored terror, it seems a significant percentage of ordinary and everyday soldiers, paramilitaries, and internal security police, of widely differing national and cultural backgrounds, are rather too easily transformed into indifferent killers and torturers – and a certain much smaller percentage of them come to take great pleasure in conditions of terror. This last conception may be another version of the 'potential monster-in-us' view or it may be a rejection of the 'monster versus us' dichotomy all together. Either way, it suggests the need to consider serial killing in a larger context than is typically the case.

Recent work on the Holocaust and the numerous other genocides and mass killings of living memory are making this increasingly evident (Waller 2002). Clearly, understanding the human propensity for genocide is not just a matter of understanding some crazed or deviant monsters. As Nazi concentration camp survivor Primo Levi pointed out, the extreme sadists in the camps were 'too few in number to be truly dangerous' while it was the common men who were more dangerous (quoted in Todorov 1997: 123). As with many serial killers, Nazi officers thoroughly enjoyed their killings, kept trophies of their victims, and ridiculed and tortured their victims before killing them (Goldhagen 1998). Some officers even brought their wives along, and genocidal assignments were put on police bulletin boards in plain view. Officers who did not want to participate asked for transfers and were almost always granted them, and most officers would return to duty to participate in more killings after a holiday (Goldhagen 1998). This suggests that, as Goldhagen's (1998) book title indicates, these were 'willing executioners' and not officers forced to perform their duties under penalty of death.

Similar enjoyment of killing or torture has been so widespread that it is difficult to track. It has been reported with many examples from Central America, the former Yugoslavia, various countries in Africa, and, of course, in Iraq. The US population also is not immune, as exemplified by the case of US soldiers and private contractors at Abu Ghraib who took photos of their torture activities and appeared to enjoy what they were doing. Numerous other examples of US soldiers and private contractors committing atrocities in Iraq and Afghanistan have been discovered, including the notorious kill teams in Afghanistan uncovered by Mark Boal (2011) of *Rolling Stone* magazine. Men from Bravo Company's third platoon, stationed in Kandahar, discussed killing Afghan civilians ('savages') over a number of weeks. One day in a farming village two soldiers threw a grenade and shot at a 15-year-old boy, killing him. Soldiers later stripped the boy half-naked and took celebratory pictures with the body, lifting the boy's head as if he were a hunting trophy. One soldier that killed the boy also got one of his fingers as a trophy and wanted to keep it in a bag until it dried out so he could keep it forever; soldiers passed pictures and videos of their activities around to other soldiers as if they were trading movie DVDs; and peer pressure was used to keep soldiers involved, and the dehumanization of the Afghan people made the killings that much easier. Other fingers were later taken as trophies from other victims. The soldiers were not punished even though they operated in front of others in the company who were not involved and higher brass tried to justify the killings instead of investigating them. Villagers demanded an investigation, but this fell on deaf ears, and over the next few months the same group of soldiers felt empowered to kill numerous other harmless civilians by staging ambushes (Boal 2011). Later on, only the lower level soldiers directly involved were indicted even though higher level brass knew of the killings initially and did nothing, and some leaders even told the soldiers that they should be prepared to attack not only Taliban members but also civilians who support the Taliban (Boal 2011). It was later revealed that these soldiers were also using drugs heavily, particularly hashish.

Although the rape, torture, and mutilation of civilians have long been used strategically by elite power holders with the deliberate and reasoned intent of destroying any political opposition (Vikman 2005), the question remains how it is possible for 'common men' to become rapists when they are practically knee-deep in bloody corpses. To put it bluntly, how is it possible for them to perform sexually under such conditions? Any theory purporting to explain serial killing in terms of biological abnormality or severe childhood trauma must also be able to explain how 'typical men' can become sexually excited in the wretched Nazi concentration camps, in the horror created by the Japanese military at Nanjin in 1937 (when 20,000–80,000 women were said to have been raped then stabbed and thousands of men were beheaded, among other brutalities), in the ditches of My Lai of 1968, and in the burned-out villages and hamlets of El Salvador and Guatemala in the 1980s. Although simplistic, soldier and military historian Dave Grossman's (1996: 302) argument that violence among 'normal' individuals is enabled by the basic psychological mechanisms of classical conditioning (pairing normal pleasures with violence), operant conditioning (rewarding increasingly violent acts), and imitation (copying the violent acts of prestigious others), cannot be easily dismissed. We must also not dismiss structured and gendered inequalities that promote violence against women. Neither can the view coming from evolutionary psychology that men harbor potentials to rape and murder because such behaviors in the heritage of our species have been reproductively functional (Buss 2005). Yet, these mechanistic views need to be tempered with more in-depth psycho-cultural analysis of particular cases; especially in that such studies can show both how sexual violence is normalized in wartime situations, and how some initially reluctant men can be verbally shamed and coerced by fellow combatants into participating (Vikman 2005).

However this may be, what Hamm (2004) has called mainstream criminology's tendency to 'define genocidal killings as outside the scope of the criminological enterprise' looks rather odd. It is certainly peculiar that criminologists have come to compartmentalize killing in such a way as to separate their studies so cleanly away from the many acts of terrifying political violence conducted by the ordinary soldiers, state functionaries, and terrorists of our era, acts that somehow keep reappearing in new and different guises around the world. Fortunately, Hagan and Rymond-Richmond (2009) have attempted to increase mainstream criminology's acceptance of genocide and other atrocities as an important area of inquiry, especially since little work had been conducted on genocide by criminologists since Glueck's work on Nazi war crimes.

While it is obviously important to restrict the serial murderer category so as to facilitate the apprehension of perpetrators, it is also important to consider serial murder in larger questions about what psychologist James Waller (2002) describes as 'becoming evil.' Furthermore, warfare and civilian murder might not be as unrelated as a conventional criminological view might suggest, as there is some indication that levels of serial killing and mass murder increase following periods of state-sanctioned military violence, a situation Hamamoto (2002) has labeled 'civilian blowback.'

There is another simple but often overlooked anomaly about serial killing: most murders involve the killing of a friend or of a family member, a familiar person with whom one has some sort of falling out. On the other hand, except for the victims of 'hedonist comfort killers,' those who kill kin or close associates for material gain (Vronsky 2004: 163), the victims of serial killers are overwhelmingly strangers or casual acquaintances. Not only does this fact make serial killings similar to those typical of warfare and of an authoritarian state, it also makes them similar to the sacrificial killings of archaic societies. Here the leaders of ancient states regularly took the blood of enemies as a royal prerogative. Primitive human sacrifice, though, is even more similar to the case of the serial killer in that the kings or the high priests often reveled in their dominance and in their freedom from restraint. In this power, they are more like the warrior who stands above his vanquished enemy in bloodlust after battle than they are like an everyday soldier who waits in trepidation for the time when he must face an equally equipped opponent.

One particularly acute analyst of early complex societies, the historian and social critic Eli Sagan, has observed both that an 'almost psychotic sexual behavior' was tolerated among ancient kings while at the same time 'nothing was forbidden' to them to the extent that they could 'kill at will.' In such societies acts of human sacrifice and even cannibalism were thought to be empowering; indeed, such death was often conceived as providing a spiritual force necessary to energize the world as a whole. The epitome of this view was probably represented by the Aztec sacrifice of enemy warriors to the sun god; but its most eroticized aspects occurred during the annual sacrifice made of a young woman to the mother goddess. At the culmination of this event, a specially chosen maiden was deflowered by the king and then killed in a highly ritualized manner. Her heart was removed and her body was skillfully flayed so as to make a costume of her skin. The skin was then taken and worn by two strong males who immediately took on the personae of the gods, racing through the streets in a frantic procession, with one masquerading as the living mother goddess herself. A further association between pleasurable spectacle and murder occurred the next day when the goddess impersonator cut open the chests of four male captives and extracted their hearts in a public ceremony (Carrasco 1999).

Is it not revealing of common human rational–emotional processes (rather than purely monstrous ones) to find, then, that some serial killers of our times have independently developed similar logics of sexually charged personal empowerment through murder? Jeffrey Dahmer and his shrine of skulls comes immediately to mind here, as does Ed Gein and the fantasy versions of his human taxidermy given in the films *The Texas Chainsaw Massacre* and *The Silence of the Lambs*. The sentiment of killing as empowering and mystical is also explicitly expressed by Ian Brady, who suggests that a serial killer's first kill is a rite of passage akin to that of religious initiation. With the first killing, Brady says, the perpetrator is ritually reborn and a 'new persona' emerges who experiences an 'expanding sense of omnipotence.' Indeed, he describes serial killers as 'metaphorically gods in their own kingdom, whimsically sampling everything that was once forbidden' (2001: 87, 102).

Double lives, choice, and the complexities of the self

Recently publicized evidence about Dennis Rader and his life as the killer known as 'BTK' shows him to be an example of one of the most puzzling types in the taxonomy of serial killers – the type who successfully hides behind the mask of a bland middle-class 'regular guy.' This type is also one whose situation seems to resonate with popular imagery about opposing forces of good and evil residing within the same skin. Cases like Rader's are most disturbing in that they upset our expectations that what is bad should be clearly visible. Even for these 'normal guy' serial killers, in hindsight, it is always possible to find some simple explanation. In the case of Tacoma-raised college-student killer Ted Bundy, it has been taken to be his adoption and his subsequent obsession with status (although prior to his execution Bundy himself famously blamed it all on an obsession with pornography that unleashed an immoral 'entity' within). For the 'Rostov Ripper,' Andre Chikatilo, the explanation has been said to lie with his early childhood experiences of Stalinism and the hunger and terror he experienced during World War II. For Chicago's 'Killer Clown' John Wayne Gacy it was that he was molested as a child or that he received a blow to the head that caused a blood clot in his brain. On the other hand, one can give up trying to explain; it was some unknown factor that somehow prodded these individuals. From whatever explanatory perspective, one needs to leave some room for contingency, accident, and choice in the discussion of an individual's life story. Peculiar features of a life pathway are both determined and made by what one does and, as chaos theorists have emphasized, the small choices made in everyday life could send one ultimately down paths neither anticipated nor entirely predictable.

In being convicted of murder, R.R. found a final resolution between the internal contradictions of his 'rape–murder self' and his 'authentic self,' between the competing forces of secret sexual compulsion and the guilt dominating his moral life. During the sentencing phase of his trial in Georgia, he would tell the jury that 'by God, the right decision for you to make is to give me the death penalty' (Associated Press 2004). In order to drive home the point of his irredeemable wickedness, he revealed to us that 'I still fantasize about hurting the same girls that I killed.' While R.R. retained a moral consciousness in cycling between his rapist and his legitimate persona, he was not finally able to rationalize his murders. Here more useful to him was the idea of a drug-like compulsion. It was this that allowed him to have a sense of a unified self, but with the immoral part existing outside of his agency and control. From consideration of the particular details of Brady's murders, as well as from consideration of the role played by his lover Myra, it seems more likely that all of Brady's talk of nihilism and the non-existence of god is a rather elaborate rationalization for some strong emotions and physical desires that are not always under his conscious control. He was not in such great intellectual control of himself as he would like to believe.

The life courses of serial killers like R.R. and Brady show that one cannot simply reckon the self to be a rational, calculating machine that spins out choices of good or evil from infancy. The self, even a serial killer's self, is a complex combination of processes that idiosyncratically incorporate emotions, feelings, memories, intentions, fantasies, cultural schema, and plans into a multifaceted whole. At bottom, there is a core of only partly conscious feelings and desires. Above this there are our fleeting perceptions, with self-consciousness and awareness continuously attending to different situations.

Only after the fact can we put together a coherent autobiographical narrative of our actions. For the best realized of us, our thoughts and memories are more like a symphony than a cacophony, but even the self of a serial killer is usually not the jumbled chaos of a schizophrenic. On the contrary, many give every indication of being 'normal' in judgment, moral reasoning, inner awareness, and sense of self.

The literature on serial killing has touched closest to the complexities of self-interpretation when referencing psychologist Robert Jay Lifton's concept of 'doubling' (Fox and Levin 2005: 66–8). Taking a cue from the idea of a double or the evil shadow self that so fascinated writers of an earlier era such as Edgar Allen Poe, Henry Melville, Fyodor Dostoevsky, and Robert Louis Stevenson, as well as the prominent early modern psychologists William James and Carl Jung (Rank 1971; McNamara 1994; Lifton 1986), Lifton developed the concept of doubling to help explain how doctors sworn to heal could participate in the murders and gruesome experiments sanctioned in the Nazi camp at Auschwitz and elsewhere. Essentially Lifton argued that an otherwise normal doctor made himself capable of atrocity by actively engaging in a process that partially succeeded in walling off a part of himself, his 'killing self' or 'Auschwitz self,' that allowed the original self to maintain a semblance of normal morality. It is important to emphasize process here, because unlike the static image of a 'double,' Lifton sees doubling as an active product, a conscious and ongoing interaction between the mind, one's behavior, and the social and environmental circumstances. However, unlike the disassociation of multiple personality, the division of the self is only partial; the splitting that occurred among the Nazi doctors was the result of an active process of willing *not* to be concerned about daily conditions of mass murder. For the doctors, the ordinary self was experienced as in a continuous dialectical relationship with the killing self as double. This splitting of self-consciousness facilitated active participation in the killing in several ways. First, it served as a defense mechanism that protected against the guilt associated with routinely committing murder. Second, it allowed the doctors to experience their actions at a removed emotional distance. Third, it offered some protection against the doctors' personal fears of being killed themselves. Finally, with respect to the individual will, Lifton suggests that the activation of a doubled personality also represented a kind of moral choice, a 'Faustian bargain' useful in facilitating accommodations to the general conditions of evil or to individual acts that one 'found oneself doing' without an inner awareness of conscious intent.

This last point about choice raises further questions about the role of individual agency. Here Lifton's work is open to different interpretations. For example, Waller (2002) finds Lifton's concept of doubling as too simplistic an explanation for why seemingly normal people commit genocide and other atrocities. Waller (2002) criticized the concept of doubling, first by contending that doubling is a defense mechanism for avoiding guilt rather than a solid explanation for how people commit evil acts. In other words, doubling is a consequence of the deviant act rather than a cause of it. Second, doubling is a better short-term mechanism for dissociating acts from conceptions of self than a long-term mechanism, owing to the fact that 'the psychological desire for integration and wholeness' is so strong (Waller 2002: 118). Lifton mentioned that the residual selves of the Nazis remained with them many years after they engaged in atrocities, which makes it highly likely that in similar circumstances the individuals would engage in atrocities again. Third, doubling may be only one of many ways that people work to divorce their acts from their supposed ordinary selves. For example, while the Nazis depicted in Lifton's book did return home to their families and live normal lives, they also engaged in alcohol abuse.

Waller (2002) argues persuasively that in the end there is a unitary self rather than a set of multiple selves within us. There is no credible reason to believe that we temporarily become different people; divided-self theories reduce individual responsibility for behaviors, and the potential to commit evil is in all of us. Indeed, Waller's model explains how seemingly normal people can commit horrible acts when they are socialized to commit atrocities in a given social context. All individuals have the potential for ethnocentrism, xenophobia, and a desire for social dominance, and our identities are rooted in cultural belief systems, moral disengagement, and rational self-interest. In order for human beings to commit atrocities, however, there must be a social context that facilitates it. This social context that encourages atrocities professionally socializes people within a 'culture of cruelty' (Waller 2002: 203) that rewards cruel behavior. The group is bound together by a diffusion of responsibility, an inability to distinguish individuals within the group, and conformity to peer pressure. Eventually, through such socialization the role one plays as an evildoer becomes a part of the individual's identity. Victims are dehumanized and blamed for their own victimization based on us vs. them thinking. As Waller (2002: 135) posits, 'an ordinary person becomes something different; a new self takes shape, and the extraordinarily evil acts become part of that self.'

The question of doubling's precise role in the psychology of serial killers, however, still remains. Lifton's perspective is obviously of relevance for helping to explain why many serial killers talk of their killing self as a separate entity, often as a demon or a monster. If this type of analysis is correct, then the demon or monster is the killer's 'doubled' self, not a mere fabrication of a delusional mind or even a cynical imitation of popular perceptions. Rather, and in line with what serial killer Brady has written about the first murder as initiation, the double is something that comes into active being in the very process of killing. As with the Nazi doctors, doubling seems most likely in killers like John Wayne Gacy, Ted Bundy, and Dennis Rader who manage to function effectively in middle-class and professional roles. However, Waller's critique of Lifton leads us to question whether the capacity to separate oneself into a 'nice-guy self' and a 'sex-crazed murdering self' is itself a cause or a consequence of the bloody experience of murder. Doubling could occur either because the killer is trying to deal with feelings of guilt after a murder or, contrarily, because the killer must maintain periods of normality between the times of killing and sexual release that they really relish. In his critique of Lifton, Waller suggests that in the long term, the self seeks integration, and that therefore doubling cannot be an effective long-term strategy. Yet, for serial killers such as Brady and Dennis Rader, this might not be quite the case. Decades after his crimes, Brady still admitted that 'I have to keep mental blocks tightly shut to keep control' (Brady 2001: 18). Whatever one's opinion of Lifton's theory of doubling, it is clear that he was on to something in recognizing the existence of a complex psychology of rationalizations and ideologies emergent in a murdering individual, even those typically said to be 'monsters' without conscience. Given that as a species we operate within a context of others, and are endowed with social brains geared toward monitoring them and as we ourselves are monitored, we exist in a world of ongoing posing and deception – including the poses and deceptions we build into ourselves.

Concluding comments

Consideration of the life-course pathway of any individual who becomes a serial killer reveals both the strength and weaknesses of social scientific perspectives. On the one hand, the individual is always enmeshed in social structures and networks that shape the choices that it is possible to make. On the other hand, the individual is more than a robot responding to measurable internal cues and environmental triggers. In between the two extremes somewhere is a 'true reality,' one in which the complexity of multiply interacting variables is often too complex for us to completely understand. Yet, as philosopher Daniel Dennett (2003) has put it, although we are not absolutely free, we do retain sufficient freedom of choice in the domains of morality that matter most to us. In this freedom, however, one can overemphasize the power of the conscious will. The will is not an undetermined homunculus floating freely in our brains; and it is not free from the shaping influences of our deepest physical impulses. Rather, the will is a commentator, facilitating or inhibiting a network of processes occurring below the level of consciousness. The greatest choices we make, then, are not abstractions like 'I will refrain from indulging in such fantasies' or 'I shall reward myself with uninhibited physical pleasure,' but the more specific and ongoing decisions one makes whether or not to place oneself in environments where our unconscious desires will be least restrained. These specific and ongoing decisions may be indicators of an offender's agency in developing his own 'monster'.

R.R. and Ian Brady represent two distinct pathways to serial murder, one through a life course positioned in terms of unrestrained sexuality and egocentric passion, the other in terms of repressed pedophilic desire and intellectual rationalization. Yet, neither was predetermined to become a serial killer. Not only were different choices possible, but even small changes in their background experiences could have had tremendous effects.

Consideration of the details of the life courses of Brady and R.R. shows the inherent problem of emphasizing their monstrousness in lieu of the very ordinariness of their human natures. While their separate paths to serial killing were certainly paved with aberrancies, they were also paved with banal processes. These processes are ones familiar to all who care to look; they are but extreme versions of what makes possible our everyday callousness to suffering in times of peace and our indifference to the deaths of enemies in times of strife. As Todorov (1997) has shown in his analysis of concentration camps, psychological fragmentation, depersonalization of strangers, and the enjoyment of power are not bizarre aberrancies of the mind confined to demagogues and deviants. Rather, they are 'ordinary vices' shared widely across the human spectrum. Although in the rarer cases of complete amoral sociopathology we surely do need a special psychology, here we do not need anything new to understand Brady or R.R. What we need to understand is the special way they employed ordinary vices in the creation of their killing selves.

We see examples of doubling in Nazi executions, death squads, ritualistic sacrifice, and serial killing, but in different ways and for different reasons, due to differences in group norms and other facets of the social contexts in which people are embedded. While the same behaviors may occur among military officials and serial killers, they each become what they are in different ways because of the social context of their behaviors. The serial killer must do his (or, in rare cases, her) activity in secret in order not to get caught. The larger society condemns the behavior of the person to the extent that the behavior is rare and often linked to addictive pathways developed over time throughout the life course. The Nazi who openly kills and tortures Jews and the US soldier who tortures detainees in plain view of other soldiers does not have to engage in these activities in secret because they are sanctioned, normalized activities that require training over an extended period. Nazis did not have to fantasize as much about their behaviors because they could do them openly and more often.

Doubling takes on a different form in the case of the individual who is not punished for his deeds. The person with official status to kill is following orders and serving God and Country, and is therefore absolved from responsibility. Others in his immediate group reward him for this behavior, which acts as positive reinforcement to repeat the behavior. At home he is a respectable family man who loves his wife and children, and his home life is removed from what he does at his job, as if his self involves two completely different persons. He knows that the larger society may frown on what he does, but in his group it is OK. On the other hand, the serial killer may see himself sick, afflicted with an addiction or disease he cannot control. He is a monster, or there are demons that reside within him. He cannot dislocate responsibility by saying he took orders as part of an official duty. There is more guilt to reckon with in the case of the serial killer.

Larger society treats the official killer differently from the serial killer. The official, when detected, is usually not considered mentally ill, and is not considered to be afflicted with a biological abnormality. Sometimes the offending person with a recognized status is treated in the popular media based in the officer's home country as an unsophisticated lower class miscreant, not a monster. Some may even justify the behavior of the official killer because we praise the killer's commitment to duty and country. In the case of the serial killer, we instead look for evidence of mental illness and instability, we probe for biological abnormalities, and we ask questions about the offender's parents and childhood.

What should this mean for the future of homicide studies? Examining the life-course histories of offenders and their behaviors utilizing the criminal events perspective can shed light on the issues we have raised. While there is plenty of room for multiple pathways of study, and for the continued use of particular specializations, we also call for a field of study that is less bounded by disciplinary walls, more devoted to the study of the nuances of life courses that lead to serial murder and atrocities, and more aware of the full range of human proclivities to kill.

We find that behaviors identified with serial offenders are found in all types of societies in different social contexts. It is human behavior occurring in a social context, not that of an inhuman monster that overtook a human being. In the social sciences we overly categorize these behaviors based on how we perceive them, forgetting the similarities among the behaviors we categorize differently. The behaviors of cannibals, religious sacrificial leaders, Nazi officers, death squads, soldiers in war and genocide, and some street gangs, are studied separately and in some cases even ignored by certain social science disciplines. We will have a better understanding of all of these behaviors if we take the best research and theorizing from these different disciplines. We must also be sensitive enough to avoid the overgeneralizations and sensationalism found in academic published works on these subjects. To not avoid this practice means that we would continue to limit our understanding by our own language.

Notes

1 Unless otherwise stated, information about R.R.'s life and his self-descriptions come from two sources: Pino's taped interviews and R.R.'s handwritten autobiography, a copy of which is in the authors' possession.

2 Unless otherwise referenced, the information given here about Brady's early life is taken from Fiona Steel's 'Murder on the Moors: The Ian Brady and Myra Hindley Story,' available at: http://www.crimelibrary.com. The fullest account of Brady and Hindley and their murders is that given by the prosecutor at their trial (see Williams 1968).

References

Abrahamsen, D. (1975) *The Murdering Mind*, New York: Harper and Row

Associated Press (2004) 'Man convicted of murder asks for death penalty', http://www.sun herald.com

Boal, M. (2011) 'The kill team: how U.S. soldiers murdered innocent civilians in Afghanistan', *Rolling Stone*, 27 March: http://www.rollingstone.com/politics/news/the-kill-team-20110327

Brady, I. (2001) *The Gates of Janus*, Los Angeles, CA: Feral House

Buss, D. (2005) *The Killer Next Door*, New York: Penguin

Canter, D. (1994), *Criminal Shadows*, London: Harper Collins

Carrasco, D. (1999) *City of Sacrifice*, Boston, MA: Beacon Press

Castle, T. and Hensley, C. (2002) 'Serial killers with military experience: applying learning theory to serial murder', *International Journal of Offender Therapy and Comparative Criminology*, 46 (4): 453–65

CNN (2005) 'Investigator: BTK killer called himself a "monster"', http://www.cnn.com

Dennett, D. (2003) *Freedom Evolves*, New York: Penguin

Fenton, B. and Bunyon, N. (2005) 'Revealed: the schoolgirl who escaped the clutches of the Moors Murderers', *The Telegraph*, 30 December

Fox, J. and Levin, J. (2005) *Extreme Killing*, Thousand Oaks, CA: Sage

Gilmore, D. (2003) *Monsters*, Philadelphia: University of Pennsylvania Press

Goldhagen, D. (1998). *Hitler's Willing Executioners*, New York: Alfred A. Knopf

Grossman, D. (1996) *On Killing*, Boston, MA: Little Brown

Hagan, J. and Rymond-Richmond, W. (2009) *Darfur and the Crime of Genocide*, New York: Cambridge University Press

Hamamoto, D. (2002) 'Empire of death: militarized society and the rise of serial killing and mass murder', *New Political Scientist*, 24 (1): 105–20

Hamm, M. (2004) 'Apocalyptic violence: the seduction of terrorist subcultures', *Theoretical Criminology*, 8 (3): 323–29

Hawkins, C. (2004) 'The monster body of Myra Hindley', *Scan Journal* 1 (3). Retrieved online at: http://scan.net.au

Hickey, E. (2002) *Serial Killers and Their Victims*, Belmont, CA: Wadsworth

Hodson, S. (2004) '[R.R.] trial', *Augusta Chronicle*, 23 January. Retrieved online from LexisNexis Academic

Holmes, R. and Holmes, S. (2010) *Serial Murders*, Thousand Oaks, CA: Sage

Lifton, R. (1986) *The Nazi Doctors*, New York: Basic Books

McNamara, P. (1994) 'Memory, double, shadow, and evil', *Journal of Analytical Psychology* 39: 233–51

Mitchell, C. (2003) *Dead and Buried*, New York: Pinnacle Books

Mitchell, E. (1997) 'The aetiology of serial murder: towards an integrated model', unpublished thesis, Cambridge: University of Cambridge

Norris, J. (1988) *Serial Killers*, New York: Doubleday

Pino, N. (2005) 'Serial offending and the criminal events perspective', *Homicide Studies*, 9 (2): 109–48

Rank, O. (1971) *The Double: A Psychoanalytic Study*, Chapel Hill: University of North Carolina Press

Sears, D. (1991) *To Kill Again*, Wilmington, DE: Scholarly Resources

Tithecott, R. (1997) *Of Men and Monsters*, Madison: University of Wisconsin Press

Todorov, T. (1997) *Facing the Extreme*, New York: Henry Holt

Turpin, J. and Kurtz, L. (1997) *The Web of Violence*, Urbana, IL: University of Chicago Press

Vikman, E. (2005) 'Ancient origins: sexual violence in warfare, part I. Modern combat: sexual violence in warfare, part II', *Anthropology and Medicine*, 12 (1): 21–46

Vronsky, P. (2004) *Serial Killers*, New York: Berkley Books

Waller, J. (2002) *Becoming Evil*, Oxford: Oxford University Press

Waller, S. (ed.) (2010), *Serial Killers*, Chichester: Wiley-Blackwell

Williams, E. (1968) *Beyond Belief*, New York: Macmillan

Name index

Subject index

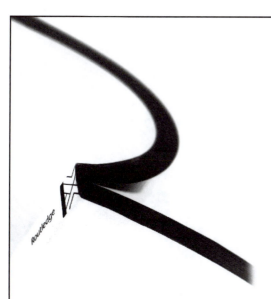